"What an extraordinary study! Abraham Kuruvilla has applied himself with resolution and enthusiasm to all 150 psalms, and here he shares the results with us. He thus takes us through the entire Psalter with careful and suggestive outlines of the Psalms for preachers, and with judicious comments on their theological significance. It will be wonderful if pastors make them a resource for preaching. Indeed, any student of the Psalms will learn from them."

—**John Goldingay**, senior professor of Old Testament, Fuller Theological Seminary

"What a delightful surprise this series of commentaries on the Psalms is. Working with proper regard for the newest academic insights, Abraham Kuruvilla makes an innovative synthesis of the meaning of each psalm, building a bridge between its theological essence and practical application of the text in various situations. This series will be extremely useful for anyone who preaches, teaches, or studies the Bible seriously."

—**Philippus (Phil) J. Botha**, professor emeritus of ancient and modern languages and cultures, University of Pretoria, Pretoria, South Africa

"Whenever my friend and former colleague Abe Kuruvilla speaks about preaching, I'm all ears. If you've read his books on preaching or listened to his sermons, you understand why. His hermeneutical approach is carefully crafted, producing penetrating insights and proposals worthy of consideration. This commentary is wonderful and, crafted in the crucible of Abe's personal suffering, will be immensely helpful to those who love the Psalms and the God who inspired ancient authors to compose them."

—**Robert B. Chisholm Jr.**, chair and senior professor of Old Testament studies, Dallas Theological Seminary

"Why is it that we don't hear more excellent sermons on the Psalms that engage the text in deep and serious ways? Abe Kuruvilla has written a monumental three-volume work to help address this shortcoming. He recognizes that the Psalms, as captivating as they may be, are not necessarily easy to interpret and many of their contexts and occasions remain in the shadows. Nevertheless, through close attention to each psalm, Kuruvilla shows that their theology can result in preaching that engages both the heart and the mind."

—**Stanley E. Porter**, president, dean, and professor of New Testament, McMaster Divinity College

"Although preaching from the Psalter was a regular practice in the early church, nowadays Christians might sing and pray the Psalms, but rarely listen to a sermon on one of them. Abraham Kuruvilla's commentary skillfully reverses this trend. He takes seriously each psalm in its poetic Hebrew medium, then applies its theological message, however difficult, to Christian discipleship today. No minister now has an excuse for avoiding preaching from the book of Psalms."

—**Susan Gillingham**, professor emeritus of Hebrew Bible, University of Oxford

"This three-volume series on preaching the Psalms is a masterful work, combining exegesis, hermeneutics, biblical theology, and homiletics. Abraham Kuruvilla astutely guides the preacher through the most difficult step of sermon development in the Psalms. In my opinion, this is the best work on preaching the Psalms that is available today, and it should be on the shelf of all preachers who aspire to proclaim the wonderful message of the Psalms to their congregations."

—**J. Daniel Hays**, senior professor of Old Testament, Southwestern Baptist Theological Seminary

"Abraham Kuruvilla has provided the kind of theological exegesis preachers need to engage in sermon preparation. His thorough exploration draws on his own attention to the literary complexities of the text and his engagement with the best of scholarship. A literal translation, structural analysis, theological focus statement, discerning commentary, and sermon map for each psalm efficiently guide the preacher through the essential steps of sermon development. This will be my go-to commentary on the Psalms."

—**Timothy S. Warren**, senior professor emeritus of pastoral ministries, Dallas Theological Seminary

"In his commentary, Abe Kuruvilla approaches the Psalms with the eye and the heart of a preacher/pastor. He draws deeply from the scholarly literature, but he focuses on the needs of the expositor. His primary emphasis is upon how Christians are to align their lives to what God reveals in the various songs in the Psalter, and how the Psalms guide the people of God in their spiritual transformation toward Christlikeness. What he has written will both stretch the mind and warm the heart of the reader. I highly recommend it!"

—**Daniel Estes**, distinguished professor of Old Testament, Cedarville University

"Abraham Kuruvilla has produced another helpful commentary to guide faithful preaching of God's word. Although best known as a leading scholar in homiletics, he proves himself to be a competent Hebrew exegete as well. His Christiconic hermeneutic allows the Psalms to fully speak their multidimensional message for spiritual formation today."

—**John W. Hilber**, professor of Old Testament, McMaster Divinity College

"This is a valuable addition to Abraham Kuruvilla's existing work on Christian preaching of Scripture. He knows the issues, provides a fresh translation of the Hebrew text to ponder, and offers theologically robust content. Though it is oriented to those who would preach the Psalms, it also has value for those who pray them."

—**Walter Moberly**, professor emeritus of theology and biblical interpretation, Durham University

"Abraham Kuruvilla's commentary set on the Psalter is unique and helpful. He clearly explains the text of each Psalm, laying out its meaning as well as aspects of divine demand, calling its readers to Christlikeness. I thank him for his faithful ministry in helping students bring and use God's word to push believers toward Christlikeness."

—**Michael A. Grisanti**, distinguished research professor of Old Testament, The Master's Seminary

"With keen appreciation for literary and rhetorical features of each psalm, Kuruvilla keeps his finger on the text. He resists a 'homiletical hermeneutic' that is driven by what one wants to preach *out of the text* rather than what the psalmists tried to communicate *with the text*. Although he is an authority on preaching, Kuruvilla does not prescribe how to preach individual psalms, but teachers of Scripture will be inspired by his commentary and find the 'sermon maps' that conclude the commentary on each psalm helpful."

—**Daniel I. Block**, professor emeritus of Old Testament, Wheaton College

Psalms 1–44

PSALMS 1–44

A Theological Commentary for Preachers

Abraham Kuruvilla

CASCADE *Books* • Eugene, Oregon

PSALMS 1–44
A Theological Commentary for Preachers

Copyright © 2024 Abraham Kuruvilla. All rights reserved. Except for brief quotations in critical publications or reviews, no part of this book may be reproduced in any manner without prior written permission from the publisher. Write: Permissions, Wipf and Stock Publishers, 199 W. 8th Ave., Suite 3, Eugene, OR 97401.

Cascade Books
An Imprint of Wipf and Stock Publishers
199 W. 8th Ave., Suite 3
Eugene, OR 97401

www.wipfandstock.com

PAPERBACK ISBN: 978-1-6667-5167-3
HARDCOVER ISBN: 978-1-6667-5168-0
EBOOK ISBN: 978-1-6667-5169-7

Cataloguing-in-Publication data:

Names: Kuruvilla, Abraham, author.
Title: Psalms 1–44 : a theological commentary for preachers / Abraham Kuruvilla.
Description: Eugene, OR: Cascade Books, 2024. | Includes bibliographical references and index.
Identifiers: ISBN 978-1-6667-5167-3 (paperback). | ISBN 978-1-6667-5168-0 (hardcover). | ISBN 978-1-6667-5169-7 (ebook).
Subjects: LCSH: Bible.—Psalms I–XLIV—Commentaries. | Preaching.
Classification: BS1430.3 K87 2024 (print). | BS1430.3 (epub).

VERSION NUMBER 05/09/24

IN MEMORIAM

A. K. Kuruvilla
(1927–2020)

Mariamma Kuruvilla
(1933–1984)

For everything
. . . and also for the love of song!

Contents

Preface | ix
List of Abbreviations | xi

Introduction | 1

Psalm 1:1–6	*Delighting in the Word*	30
Psalm 2:1–12	*Respecting the King*	37
Psalm 3:1–8	*Bane of Enemies*	45
Psalm 4:1–8	*Correcting False Friends*	52
Psalm 5:1–12	*Access to God in Prayer*	57
Psalm 6:1–10	*Supplication for Serious Physical Affliction*	64
Psalm 7:1–17	*Vindication from Accusation*	71
Psalm 8:1–9	*Humanity's Delegated Dominion*	77
Psalm 9:1–20	*Divine Judgment and Order*	82
Psalm 10:1–18	*God's Kingship Defeats the Wicked's Disorder*	90
Psalm 11:1–7	*Resisting the Temptation to Defect*	96
Psalm 12:1–8	*Words of God vs. Words of the Wicked*	100
Psalm 13:1–6	*How Long?*	105
Psalm 14:1–7	*Refutation of the Fool*	109
Psalm 15:1–5	*Criteria for Fellowship with God*	114
Psalm 16:1–11	*Devotion to God*	119
Psalm 17:1–15	*Defending Self and Seeking Protection*	125
Psalm 18:1–50	*God's Awesome Protection of the Righteous*	132
Psalm 19:1–14	*The Sun and the Servant*	142
Psalm 20:1–9	*Intercession for Success*	150
Psalm 21:1–13	*Success of God's People*	156
Psalm 22:1–31	*Divine Presence in Deadly Persecution*	161
Psalm 23:1–6	*Guided by the Shepherd; Going to the King*	171
Psalm 24:1–10	*Order Consummated over Chaos*	177
Psalm 25:1–22	*Hope from Hopelessness*	184
Psalm 26:1–12	*Plea of the Committed*	192

CONTENTS

Psalm 27:1–14	*Hoping in the Divine Presence*	199
Psalm 28:1–9	*The Shepherd Hears*	205
Psalm 29:1–11	*The Voice of the Victor*	211
Psalm 30:1–12	*Lamenting to Rejoicing*	219
Psalm 31:1–24	*Falling upon God's Hand*	225
Psalm 32:1–11	*The Blessed Confessor*	233
Psalm 33:1–22	*Singing of the Sovereign*	239
Psalm 34:1–22	*God-Fearers Praising God*	246
Psalm 35:1–28	*God Fighting for His People, Against Their Enemies*	254
Psalm 36:1–12	*The Overthrow of the Wicked*	262
Psalm 37:1–40	*Hope of the Righteous Against the Wicked*	268
Psalm 38:1–22	*Sin and Suffering*	279
Psalm 39:1–13	*God's Discipline and the Brevity of Life*	285
Psalm 40:1–17	*Distress, Duty, and Deliverance*	291
Psalm 41:1–13	*Caring for Others; Cared for by God*	298
Psalms 42:1—43:5	*Depression to Deliverance*	303
Psalm 44:1–26	*Hanging on to Lovingkindness*	310

Bibliography | 317
Index of Authors | 325
Index of Scripture | 327

Preface

I lift my eyes towards the mountains.
From where comes my help?
My help [comes] from Yahweh,
the One who made the heavens and the earth.

Psalm 121:1–2

IN THE SPRING OF 2020, as I was teaching a class on preaching the Psalter, I recognized that my homiletics students needed help of a kind hard to find in standard commentaries on the Psalms. Thus began my project of producing a tome geared to help preachers tackle these psalms in the pulpit. I thought I was choosing the Psalms . . .

Then came the pandemic that shut most things down. And the death of a beloved parent whom I had been caring for during the second half of that year, and much of my heart was shut down. But I kept on trucking through the Psalter. In the laments. And what a truck it was.

Soon came a major move to a new city, leaving family, friends, and familiar surroundings (not to mention academic institution and dermatology practice). The Psalms kept me going.

I finished the work after Thanksgiving 2022 and proceeded to commence my first round of editing. That Christmas, while I was traveling abroad, a major North American freeze resulted in a busted pipe that destroyed almost 70 percent of the interior of my house (as of this writing, it is still being reconstructed). And guess where I had arrived at, once again, in the Psalter? Yes, in the laments. (I did hope then that I wouldn't have to do another round of editing. Who knew what calamity another rehearsal of the laments might bring!)

But looking back at these last three years, all I can say is, "If it weren't for the psalms . . ."

Yes, I thought I had chosen the Psalms, but I was wrong. The Psalms had chosen me. And changed and molded me in the midst of all the suffering without and within. And so I offer this work with the prayer:

> May He not give your foot to tottering;
> > may He not slumber—the One who keeps you.
> Behold, He will not slumber and He will not sleep—
> > the One who keeps Israel.
> Yahweh [is] the One who keeps you;
> > Yahweh [is] your shade on your right hand.

PREFACE

> By day, the sun, it will not strike you,
>   or the moon by night.
> Yahweh, He will keep you from all evil;
>   He will keep your soul.
> Yahweh, He will keep your going and your coming
>   from now unto forever.
> *Psalm 121:3–8*

He will. He has. He is.

Abraham Kuruvilla
Louisville, Kentucky
Ascension Sunday 2023

Abbreviations

ANET   *Ancient Near Eastern Texts Relating to the Old Testament*, edited by James B. Pritchard

ANF   *Ante-Nicene Fathers*, edited by Alexander Roberts and James Donaldson

b. Ber   *Babylonian Talmud, Berakot*

KTU   *Die keilalphabetischen Texte aus Ugarit*, translated by N. Wyatt in *Religious Texts from Ugarit*

LXX   Septuagint

MT   Masoretic Text

NASB   New American Standard Bible

NPNF1   *Nicene and Post-Nicene Fathers*, Series 1, edited by Alexander Roberts and James Donaldson

NT   New Testament

OT   Old Testament

TLG   *Thesaurus Linguae Graecae*

Introduction

*Who would even dare assert that anyone had completely
understood one single psalm?*

Martin Luther[1]

THE GOAL OF PREACHING is to bring to bear divine guidelines for life from the biblical text upon the situations of the congregation, to align the community of God to the will of God for the glory of God. In other words, the ancient text is to be applied to the modern (Christian) audience.[2] This is the preacher's burden—the translation from the *then* of the text to the *now* of listeners, with authority and relevance. This commentary is part of a larger endeavor to help the preacher make this move from text to praxis.[3]

Particularly pertinent is how this translation from text to praxis may be conducted with respect to the bite-sized portion of scriptural text (pericope) that is employed weekly in preaching at the corporate worship gathering of the body of Christ.[4] The pericope is the basic textual unit of Scripture handled in such assemblies, the foundational element of the weekly address from the word of God, and the primary way in which the people of God encounter their Scriptures. What exactly is the author of the text communicating in a given pericope that needs to be heeded by the listeners of the sermon?[5]

Prolegomenon

Theology

Elsewhere it was proposed that the critical component of the ancient text to be borne into the lives of the modern audience was the *theology of the pericope*, or what the author is *doing* with

---

1. Luther, "Psalms 1 and 2," 285.

2. For more on this concept of preaching, see my *Privilege the Text!* and *Vision for Preaching*, as well as *Manual for Preaching*. Much of the first part of this introduction is taken from Kuruvilla, *1–2 Timothy, Titus*, 1–5.

3. The other commentaries currently available in this series are those on Genesis, Judges, Mark, Ephesians, 1–2 Timothy, and Titus.

4. "Pericope" is employed here to demarcate a segment of Scripture, irrespective of genre or length, that forms the textual basis for an individual sermon and that has a discrete theological thrust that is sermonically and applicationally distinguishable from the thrusts of the pericopes preceding and following.

5. For the purposes of the commentaries in this series no particular distinction is made between the divine and human authors of the biblical text.

what he is saying in a particular slice of the biblical text that is chosen for the sermon. This is the engine that drives the people of God towards valid application, for pericopal theology is the literary and ideological vehicle through which the divine precepts, priorities, and practices of God's ideal world are propounded by the Holy Spirit for appropriation by readers.[6] A biblical pericope is therefore a literary instrument inviting God's people to organize their lives in congruence with the theology of that pericope. The goal of any homiletical transaction, thus, is the gradual alignment of the people of God, week by week, to the theology of the biblical pericopes preached. Pericope by pericope, the various aspects of Christian life, individual as well as corporate, are progressively brought into accord with God's design for his creation. This is the goal of preaching: faith nourished, hope animated, confidence made steadfast, good habits confirmed, dispositions created, character molded, Christlikeness established.[7]

All such discrete units of pericopal theology together compose a holistic understanding of God and his relationship to his people, and each individual quantum of pericopal theology forms the weekly ground of life transformation by calling for alignment to the demands of God, resulting in the assimilation of Christlikeness. I, therefore, call this a *christiconic* hermeneutic.[8] In brief, if each pericope depicts a facet of God's ideal world, then each pericope projects an aspect of divine demand, how that world (and its citizens) is to function, as called for in that particular pericope. Since the only one to comprehensively and perfectly fulfill the requirement of every pericope in Scripture is the Lord Jesus Christ, the perfect Man, every pericope is, in essence, projecting what it means to be more like Christ, i.e., depicting a facet of Christlikeness, a pixel of the *Christicon*, with the whole canon portraying the plenary image of Christ.[9] Indeed, it is God's ultimate design to conform his children into the "image" (εἰκών, *eikōn*) of his Son, Christ (Rom 8:29). This week-by-week and sermon-by-sermon alignment to the divine demand in each pericope is an imitation of Christ,[10] a purposeful movement by those who are already the children of God towards increasing alignment with the humanity of the Son of God, i.e., towards Christlikeness. This is at the core of the theological interpretation followed in this commentary series: a hermeneutic specifically geared for preachers and their noble task—a *christiconic* hermeneutic.[11] Because children of God are called to conform to the image of Christ, preachers everywhere are, in turn, to discern the theology of the pericope—i.e., the pixel of the image of Christ depicted therein—and

---

6. See Kuruvilla, *Text to Praxis*, 142–90; Kuruvilla, *Vision for Preaching*, 91–109; and Kuruvilla, "Pericopal Theology," 3–17.

7. Modified from Tertullian, *Apology* 39 (*ANF* 3:46). Needless to say, I view preaching as an activity directed to those already in relationship to God, through Christ, and by the Spirit; after all, only such are able to worship God and respond to his word.

8. See Kuruvilla, *Privilege the Text!*, 238–68; Kuruvilla, *Vision for Preaching*, 111–48; Kuruvilla, "Christiconic Interpretation," 131–46; and Kuruvilla, "Christiconic View," 43–70.

9. This, of course, is not to deny the fullness of the deity of Jesus Christ. But it must be remembered that it is into the likeness of his perfect humanity that God's people are being transformed.

10. Or a fearing of God: Pss 2:11; 5:7; 15:4; 19:9; 22:23, 25; 25:12, 14; 31:19; 33:8, 18; 34:7, 9–11; 40:3; 47:2; 55:19; 60:4; 61:5; 64:9; 66:16; 67:7; 72:5; 76:7–8, 11–12; 85:9; 86:11; 90:11; 96:4; 102:15; 103:11, 13, 17; 111:5, 10; 112:1, 7–8; 115:11, 13; 118:4; 119:38, 63, 74, 79; 128:1, 4; 130:4; 135:20; 145:19; 147:11. Another synonymous notion for this alignment with God and his will is walking with God in his ways: 5:8; 10:5; 16:11; 17:5; 18:21, 30, 32; 25:4, 8–10; 27:11; 32:8; 37:23, 34; 44:18; 50:23; 51:13; 67:1–2; 77:13, 19; 81:13; 85:13; 86:11; 95:10; 101:2, 6; 103:7; 119:1, 3, 5, 14–15, 27, 29, 30, 32, 33, 35, 37; 128:1; 138:5; 139:24; 143:8.

11. For a comparative review of hermeneutics for preaching from a mostly evangelical point of view, that includes my contributions, see Gibson and Kim, *Homiletics and Hermeneutics*. While all the proponents therein appear to agree that Scripture is christological, the debate is on *how* it is christological.

apply it to the widely diverse situations of believers across the globe, across millennia, and across cultures, to enable them to emulate the perfect Man, their Lord Jesus Christ. In other words, while pericopal theology tells us *what* Christ looks like, application in sermons directs us to *how* we can look more like him, in our own particular circumstances, thus becoming "capable, fully equipped for every good work" (2 Tim 3:17).[12]

Such a conception of preaching should not cause one to construe divine demand for holiness as merely a litany of dos and don'ts that a capricious God burdens his people with. Rather, God's call to be aligned with his requirements and standards is a gracious invitation to mankind (those in Christ, that is) to inhabit his ideal world by the power of the Spirit, to enjoy its fullness of blessing, in the presence of the divine. So it is the biblical canon, preached by the leader of the people of God in the context of their worship of God, that portrays what this world of God (the kingdom of God) looks like, how it functions, and how the community is to inhabit it. Pericope by pericope, a theological picture of God's ideal world is unveiled. This is the world God would have; and that is the kind of people God would have us be.

Indeed, of the Psalter, Mays declares that the notion of the divine kingdom[13] is "the centre of the Psalms," particularly, that this fulcrum is found in the sentence יְהוָה מָלָךְ, *yhwh malak*, "Yahweh, He reigns" (10:16; 29:10 [×2]; 96:10; 97:1; 99:1).[14] Dealing primarily with Psalms 93–98, Mays notes that יְהוָה מָלָךְ connotes: the universal sphere of his dominion (over gods, over created matter, over nations and peoples, and over Zion); the particular institutions that are the instruments and expressions of his reign (throne and the denizens around it; the royal house where his presence is available to humanity); and those unique actions stemming from his sovereignty (including his cosmic dominion and the sustaining thereof, the reliability of his decree, and the manifestations of his transcendence and holiness).[15] "The instrument of this ordering is named his law, decrees, statutes, precepts, commandments, ordinances, covenant, and word. By these various forms of the will of the LORD his people learn and are directed into his ways and paths."[16] God rules. His kingdom comes. His will is done. And to that end, the Holy Spirit works, preachers exhort, and Christians strive, in the power of the Author of Scripture.

Goals

I come to the Psalms, and indeed to all of Scripture, with a reading bias that is Protestant and evangelical. I take it that a biblical author writes purposefully, creating a text with intention, each part of it contributing to the overall theological agenda of the individual book. This commentary also assumes that every pericope in the canonical Scriptures may be employed gainfully for application by the church universal.[17] Thus, no psalm in the Psalter may be disregarded for

---

12. All translations of Scripture in this work are my own. Please note that the translations of the Psalms within the body of this work are intended to aid study; they are not necessarily rendered in felicitous English for devotional reading—that would prevent the reader from appreciating the literary nuances and emphases of the original.

13. A notion synonymous with "God's ideal world."

14. God as king is also noted in Pss 5:2; 24:7–10; 44:4; 47:2, 6, 7; 58:2; 68:24; 74:12; 84:13; 93:1; 95:3; 98:6; 145:1; 149:2.

15. See Mays, "Centre of the Psalms," 232–36.

16. Mays, "Centre of the Psalms," 242. This is, of course, true of every book and pericope of Scripture.

17. See Kuruvilla, *Privilege the Text!*, 65–86, for a set of "Rules for Reading" that respects the special

the purposes of sermons. And the employment of the Bible as the foundation of the existence, beliefs, and activities of the church assumes that its interpretation *will* result in a response of application—life change in Christ, by the power of the Spirit, for the glory of God.

Most Bible scholars and theologians have unfortunately not been coming to the text of Scripture with the eyes and hearts of preachers. Therefore, the pericope is generally neglected as a textual unit of theological value, and the goal of life transformation—a pastoral concern—has tended to be subjugated to other academic interests. The aim of this commentary series, part of a long-term endeavor to rectify this misdirection, is to develop the theology of every pericope in every book of the Bible so that preachers may be able to proceed from this crucial intermediary to a sermon that offers valid application, authoritative and relevant. There is, thus, a twofold aspect to the homiletical transaction: the discernment of the theology of the pericope, and the derivation of application, how the theology may be actualized in real life.

The first move, from text to (pericopal) theology, draws meaning *from* the biblical text with authority, the second, from theology to application, directs meaning *to* the situations of listeners with relevance. The advantage of employing pericopal theology as the intermediary between text and praxis is that its specificity for the chosen text makes possible a weekly movement from pericope to pericope with a clear progression and development of distinct but connected theological thrusts as one preaches through a book. In sum, the theology of the pericope functions as the bridge between text and application, between the circumstances of the text and those of the reading community, enabling the move from the *then* to the *now*.[18] The resulting transformation of lives reflects a gradual and increasing alignment to the values of God's kingdom (or a gradual and increasing approximation of Christlikeness) as pericopes are sequentially preached. Thus, a pericope, as a quantum of the biblical text, is more than *informing*; it is *transforming*, for as the people of God adopt its theological values, they are becoming rightly oriented to God's will, inhabiting God's ideal world as its citizens, and becoming more like Christ.

This series of commentaries does not lead preachers all the way to a fully developed sermon on each pericope (i.e., each psalm, in this work). Rather, it seeks to take them through first move from text to (pericopal) theology: the *hermeneutical* aspect of sermon preparation. Though that is the primary focus, each commentary provides suggestions for Sermon

---

nature and hermeneutics of the biblical text.

18. A crystallization of pericopal theology is labeled "Theological Focus" in this commentary. These theological foci are *not* the communicational goals of the sermon (à la the "Big Idea" modus operandi of traditional homiletics). These are merely reductions or distillations of pericopal theologies, created to help the sermon preparer to map the sermon, to remain focused on the goal while fleshing out that map, and to derive application. The goal of the preacher is not to create a masterpiece (that explains, validates, and applies the Big Idea/Theological Focus); rather the aim is to curate the Master's piece, the text in toto, such that it may be experienced as its A/author intended. See Kuruvilla, *Manual for Preaching*, and Kuruvilla, "Time to Kill the Big Idea?" This latter essay, and a few rounds of responses (from others) and rejoinders (from me) are available on my website, at http://homiletix.com/kill-the-big-idea/.

INTRODUCTION

Maps, to advance preachers a few more steps closer to a sermon.[19] However, preachers are left to work out this second move from theology to sermon/application (the *rhetorical* aspect of sermon preparation) on their own, providing appropriate moves-to-relevance, specific application, illustrations, etc., all of which can be done only by the shepherd who knows the flock well.[20] Beyond a few general guidelines, it is impossible for a third party to determine what exactly specific application might look like for a particular audience. That task is between the preacher, the Holy Spirit, and the congregation. Therefore, this is not a "preaching" commentary in the usual sense. Rather it is a "theology-for-preaching" commentary, a work that seeks to undertake an extremely focused interpretation of the text, one that moves the preacher from text to theology, *en route* to a sermon. Thus, these productions are *theological* commentaries, with theology defined as pericopal theology.

The commentary on the Psalms is primarily geared for those interested in preaching from this collection (in any context of the people of God, including corporate gatherings, Bible studies, age- or gender-segregated groups, etc.[21]) and seeks to aid their preparation for such expositions by isolating the theology of each psalm (pericope), i.e., the pixel of the *Christicon* depicted by each psalm, which each child of God must adopt into his or her own life.

Commentaries were described by Ernest Best as "the backbone of all serious studies of scripture."[22] Therefore, it is hoped that not only preachers, but all interested laypersons, Sunday School teachers, and others who teach Scripture for application will find this commentary—a small vertebra in that spinal column—helpful. For that matter, if applicational response is the goal of Bible study of any kind and at any level, a work such as this promises to be useful even for those making their way through the Psalter on their own.[23]

Needless to say, in all sermonic enterprises, quality and depth and intensity of preaching go only so far towards accomplishing the spiritual formation of listeners. Augustine noted wisely: "But whatever may be the majesty of the style [of the preaching], the life of the speaker will count for more in securing the hearer's compliance," not to mention the divine work of the Spirit in the hearts of listeners.[24] Therefore, this commentary, along with the others in this series, is submitted with the prayer that preachers, the leaders of God's people, will pay attention to their own lives first and foremost, as they work through the Psalms, seeking to

---

19. I have chosen to call these "maps," rather than "outlines." An *outline* has some self-imposed constraints: its points are constructed as full sentences (usually propositions with subjects and complements), with main points subsuming subsidiary points, and so on, all of which pedantries are unnecessary for a *map* that aids the sermonic curation of "text+theology" (I see the pericope and its theology as a unified and inseparable entity). That does not deny that a sermonic undertaking deals with ideas, and even arguments, but simply points an accusatory finger at the dominant metaphor of the traditional approach and its complicit nomenclature that, in my opinion, have stultified the way we think about preaching, especially in light of our fast-advancing understanding of how language works, and how the brain works to comprehend texts and speech. See Kuruvilla, "'What Is the Author *Doing* with What He Is *Saying*?,'" 557–80 (also available, with a colleague's response and my rejoinder, at https://homiletix.com/kuruvillajets2017).

20. For more on these and other aspects of preaching, see Kuruvilla, *Manual for Preaching*.

21. Though the primary context for such application-oriented sermons is the weekly gathering of the people of God for the worship of God, where the shepherd, the pastor, expounds the word of God.

22. Best, "Reading and Writing of Commentaries," 358.

23. Which brings me to another point: while a working knowledge of Hebrew will be very handy for the reader of this work, Hebrew terms and phrases (and the rare Greek ones), wherever referred to in the commentary, have been both transliterated and translated, in order to enable those not as facile with the original language to use this work fruitfully.

24. Augustine, *On Christian Doctrine* 4.27.59 (NPNF1 2:595).

5

align themselves to God's demand in each pericope/psalm of the Psalter, thus becoming, in the power of the Spirit, more Christlike.

Analysis of the Psalms

Alter confesses that "poetry, working through a complex system of linkages of sound, image, word, rhythm, syntax, theme, ideas, is an instrument for conveying densely patterned meanings . . . that are not readily conveyable through other kinds of discourse," and therefore they are the "most demanding" of literary systems to interpret:

> Within the formal limits of a poem the poet can take advantage of the emphatic repetitions dictated by the particular prosodic system, the symmetries and antitheses and internal echoes intensified by a closed verbal structure, the fine intertwinings of sound and image and reported act, the modulated shifts in grammatical voice and object of address, to give coherence and authority to his perceptions of the world. The psalmist's delight in the suppleness and serendipities of poetic form is not a distraction from the spiritual seriousness of the poems but his chief means of realizing his spiritual vision, and it is one source of the power these poems continue to have not only to excite our imaginations but also to engage our lives.[25]

In this work, my analysis of the psalms begins with a structuring of the text, an undertaking I have found particularly helpful for the interpretation of hymnody. After all, as Berlin declared, "to understand how a poem is constructed is to begin to understand what it expresses."[26] That being said, the interpreter should not forget that such transactions are only the beginning of the interpretive journey. Arriving at the destination—the discerning of the pericopal theology of any given psalm for the purposes of deriving valid application—is complicated by the fact that historical context, for the most part, is lacking in these compositions. After all, a poem, British-American poet Denise Levertov claimed, is "not an examination of what happens but an immersion in what happens."[27] And in the case of the psalms, the reader is directly plunged into the exigencies of the particular situation of the supplicant, God, and the world (with a collection of enemies sprinkled in). Without the benefit of much background, the interpreter has to mine the text of the psalm itself, till it yields its riches—its thrust, its theology—without much recourse to its literary surroundings, precincts, and environments. "What has been written with imagination must be read with imagination, provided the individual has imagination and it is in working order."[28] Stimulating this hermeneutical and homiletical imagination of the preacher-theologian is the goal of the entire series of my commentaries.

But the lack of context, no doubt, is deliberate, giving the Psalter a "paradigmatic openness," facilitating its employment in situations far in space and time from those of its provenance, rendering them apt "vehicles for praise and prayer throughout the story of God's

---

25. Alter, *Art of Biblical Poetry*, 140, 170.
26. Berlin, "Rhetoric of Psalm 145," 18. Elsewhere she declares that the "psalms are mini-dramas" (Berlin, "Speakers and Scenarios," 343). To catch the plot of these thespian poems, paying close attention to the text, to both what it is saying and how it is said (which generates what the author is *doing* with what he is saying—pericopal theology), is critical. However, in my experience, such structural analyses of pericopes in other genres have not been equally fruitful.
27. Levertov, *Poet in the World*, 239.
28. Alonso Schökel, *Manual of Hebrew Poetics*, 104.

people."²⁹ There is no doubt that this book was intended for all of God's children of all time. There are a number of reasons to take this for granted (beyond the canonicity of the Psalter): the universally relevant nature of its contents, the ambiguity of historical references, the indistinction of background events, the non-identification of antagonists, the imprecision of afflictions and distress, and the gaps in narrativity due to poetic terseness—all render the Psalms suitable for appropriation and application by all of God's people in all ages. Besides there are the numerous first-person references in the poems, encouraging the readers and the community to identify with the psalmist and supplicant. There is also the generality of pronounced blessings and banes, and the abundant employment of "all" (and "every[one]") that encompasses the devout (or the wicked) of all history.³⁰

Categorization of the Psalms

As a general scheme of categorization, I have followed Brueggemann's typology, seeing three thematic sets of psalms: those of orientation, those of disorientation, and those of reorientation. When things are going as they should (*all is right*) it is the psalms of orientation that are uttered, reflecting blessings experienced, and the attendant joy, goodness, and delight that stabilize life in God's creation, under God's law, with God's presence. There is no tension, no obvious plot, no resolution sought. "The mind-set and world-view of those who enjoy a serene location of their lives is a sense of the orderliness, goodness and reliability of life."³¹

Then there are the "anguished seasons of hurt, alienation, suffering, and death (*all is wrong*). These evoke rage, resentment, self-pity, and hatred" in those psalms of disorientation that include the laments. A resolution is necessary, and Yahweh is called upon to provide that restoration.³² Often these contain thanksgiving, and declarative statements of deliverance, possibly anticipated though recounted as if they had already occurred.³³

And when God does answer, there is the surprise of being overwhelmed by God's grace, and despair gives way to delight, resulting in psalms of reorientation (*all is/will be better*). "These psalms affirm a sovereign God who puts humankind in a new situation."³⁴ Indeed the

---

29. Miller, *Interpreting the Psalms*, 8; Goldingay, *Psalms*, 1:25.

30. See Pss 2:12; 3:7; 5:5, 11; 6:7–8; 7:1; 9:17; 14:3; 18:30; 21:8; 22:23, 27; 25:3; 29:9; 31:11, 23–24; 32:6, 11; 33:8, 13–14; 39:5, 11; 40:16; 41:7; 47:1–2; 49:1; 53:3; 59:5, 8; 62:8; 63:11; 64:8–10; 65:2, 5; 66:1, 4, 16; 67:3, 5, 7; 70:4; 71:18; 72:11, 17; 73:27; 75:8; 76:9, 11; 82:8; 86:5, 9; 92:7; 94:4, 15; 96:1, 3, 9; 97:5–7; 98:3–4; 99:2; 100:1; 101:8; 102:15; 103:6; 106:48; 111:2, 10; 113:4; 115:8; 116:18; 119:63, 118–119; 128:1; 129:5; 134:1; 135:18; 136:25; 138:4; 143:2, 12; 145:9, 14–15, 18–21; 148:11, 14; 149:9; 150:6.

31. Brueggemann, "Psalms and the Life of Faith," 6. These psalms are characterized by statements such as: "God has done/does . . ."; "God is . . ."; "God is to be praised/served"; "I/we praise/serve God"; "The enemy does not praise/serve God"; "God loves/blesses me/us"; "God hates/rejects the enemy"; "I/we am/are happy/prosperous"; "The enemy is not happy/prosperous." See Collins, "Decoding the Psalms," 41–60.

32. Brueggemann, *Message of the Psalms*, 19.

33. These psalms are characterized by statements such as: "The enemy is happy/prosperous"; "I/we am/are not happy/prosperous"; "The enemy attacks/oppresses me/us"; "I/we claim innocence (with regard to the enemy)"; "I/we confess sin." See Collins, "Decoding the Psalms," 41–60.

34. Brueggemann, *Message of the Psalms*, 19. Originally Brueggemann designated the second category that of "dislocation"; later he called it "disorientation." His third category, "new orientation," I chose to label "reorientation."

reorientation so achieved may even be a heightened experience and way of life beyond the original mode of orientation.³⁵

Essentially then, the psalms describe life as it is lived in roughly five forms (including the two transitions between the three forms): in orientation; in the move from orientation to disorientation; in disorientation; in the move from disorientation to reorientation; and in reorientation. Of course, these stations are not static, nor are the moves unidirectional. Life is—and human beings are—far too complex for such a simplistic arrangement. In any case, the "psalm forms correspond to seasons of human life and bring those seasons to speech."³⁶ To keep matters simple, I have lumped the psalms representing "moving parts" into the categories of their respective destinations (the ones dealing with the move from orientation to disorientation fall into the psalms of disorientation; the ones dealing with the move from disorientation to reorientation are kept in the category of psalms of reorientation).

Perhaps not incidentally, the opening pair of psalms, Psalms 1–2, and the closing one of universal praise, Psalm 150, make no mention of divine lovingkindness (חֶסֶד, *chesed*); at these glorious boundaries of the Psalter there is no affliction that humankind faces to make God's חֶסֶד obviously necessary.³⁷ These boundaries of the Psalter thus demonstrate a movement from a summons to obedience unto God (Psalm 1) to a summons to render praise unto God (Psalm 150).

> Like the Psalter, life derived from and ceded back to Yahweh begins in obedience and ends in praise.... The entire Psalter lives between the pious, trusting, confident boundaries of obedience and praise. Not only are these Psalms the two boundaries of faithful living, but the sequence cannot be reversed. Faith is always obedience towards praise, and not praise toward obedience.... Obedience is the unavoidable initiating point of praise, and praise is the appropriate culmination of obedience.³⁸

Indeed, one might go so far as to aver that only the obedient (in the fashion of Psalm 1) can praise God (in the fashion of Psalm 150): the qualifying criterion for voicing praise to God is the rendition of obedience to God: "Only those who willingly begin in Psalm 1 can honestly and gladly end in Psalm 150."³⁹ As one walks with God in obedience, one abandons oneself to total praise, enthusiastic and exuberant, ecstatic and euphoric. In a sense, then, the gravity of duty has been overridden by the gaiety of doxology!⁴⁰

Obedience which is, of course, never to be abandoned, is simply assumed in Psalm 150. "Obedience is a base for Israel's life with God, but those who enter into this glad communion with Yahweh are so in tune, so delighted in covenant, so in love, so eager to make response to Yahweh's sovereignty, that no explicit requirement is any longer present."⁴¹ Thus, life is lived between the first and last psalm, so to speak—a life mingled with lament and joy, suffering and relief, doubt and trust, anger and calmness, desperation and peace. And as does the

---

35. These psalms are characterized by statements such as: "God can/will assist me/us"; "God can/will oppose the enemy"; "I/we turn to God"; "I/we praise/serve God"; "I/we testify to others"; "Others witness and respond to God." See Collins, "Decoding the Psalms," 41–60.
36. Brueggemann, *Message of the Psalms*, 19; see 20–21.
37. Though, of course, God's lovingkindness is *always* necessary, even in eternity.
38. Brueggemann, "Bounded by Obedience," 68.
39. Brueggemann, "Bounded by Obedience," 69.
40. See Brueggemann, "Bounded by Obedience," 69–70.
41. Brueggemann, "Bounded by Obedience," 70.

text, so also life moves from responsible duty to rapturous delight. Both poles are essential, required, and valid. But there is a sense that when obedience is integrated into life, praise will follow, and indeed become prominent, though not without agonizing passages "through many dangers, toils, and snares."[42] For "the Psalter is not a book of easy religion in which the settled practices of obedience and praise characterize Israel's life, but a literature which looks unflinchingly into the face of reality."[43]

Excursuses

Laments and Enemies

Perhaps it is not surprising that after the beatific introduction to the Psalter in Psalm 1 (invoking a blessing upon the *Torah*-driven person) and the triumphal psalm that follows, Psalm 2 (proclaiming the victory of God's Messiah-King), we are shoved headlong into a jarring sequence of laments in Psalms 3–7 that seemingly undercut the positivity of the first two psalms. Therein is portrayed the real (and messy) life of real (and broken) people in a real (post-fall and pre-eschaton) world.[44] "Harsh, lived reality is unavoidable for Israel, as soon as Israel leaves the safe boundary of Psalm 1 and enters into the midst of the abrasion and the candor of the Psalter."[45] Those excoriations of life are expressed in fifty-eight laments (both individual and corporate), making up more than a third of the Psalter.[46] And those vocalized sufferings appeal to the only one capable of extricating his people from those agonies. However, these laments do not evince a lack of faith; on the contrary, it is faith that enables the child of God to express those outcries of grief to the Father. Author, Holocaust survivor, and Nobel Peace Prize laureate Elie Wiesel (1928–2016), noting that he had been named as one who lost his faith, declared that nothing could be further from the truth: "I have never renounced my faith in God. I have risen against His justice, protested His silence and sometimes His absence, but my anger rises up within faith not outside of it."[47]

Without a doubt, laments are an integral part of the relationship of the people of God with their deity, reflecting the reality, on this side of eternity, of suffering intermingled with joy.

---

42. From "Amazing Grace," by John Newton (1772).
43. Brueggemann, "Bounded by Obedience," 89.
44. Brueggemann and Bellinger, *Psalms*, 37.
45. Brueggemann, "Bounded by Obedience," 78.
46. From a medical professional's standpoint, I wondered why there was not a comparable number of psalms dealing with the ravages of diseases (for psalms mentioning physical debilitation, see Psalms 6; 31; 38; 41; 103; 109; etc.). Perhaps the smaller spans of life and relatively less sophisticated medical care available in those days precluded chronic illnesses and long-drawn-out sufferings? From investigations at Givʻat ha-Mivtar, a cemetery near the walls of Jerusalem, whose burials date to the second and first centuries BCE, it appears that 94 percent of deaths occurred before the age of 60 (see Mays, *Lord Reigns*, 53).
47. Wiesel, *All Rivers*, 84. He adds: "I admit that this is hardly an original position. It is part of Jewish tradition. But in these matters I have never sought originality" (*All Rivers*, 84). N. T. Wright distinguishes between complaint and lament thus: "a complaint is an accusation against God that maligns His character, but a lament is an appeal to God based on confidence in His character" (emphases removed; "Five Things to Know," §4). Thus it is proof of a relationship between supplicant and deity. For those vicariously praying the laments, it is also a participation in the sufferings of others.

> It is an illusion to suppose or to postulate that there could be a relationship with God in which there was only praise and never lamentation. Just as joy and sorrow in alternation are a part of the finitude of human existence . . . , so praise and lamentation are a part of man's relationship to God. Hence, something must be amiss if praise of God has a place in Christian worship but lamentation does not. Praise can retain its authenticity and naturalness only in polarity with lamentation.[48]

Which is probably why writer Anne Lamott quipped: "Here are the two best prayers I know: 'Help me, help me, help me,' and 'Thank you, thank you, thank you.'"[49]

To enter into the Psalter is for God's people to undertake a "dangerous, dynamic life," which is, I hasten to add, also a delightful and divinely directed course of earthly existence.[50] Nonetheless, it is only with the resolution of lament that valid praise can be expressed. "In a sense, doxology and praise are best understood only in response to God's salvific intervention which in turn is evoked by the lament."[51] Just the acknowledgment that all is not right with us in the world (at least not yet) is worth making, especially in a culture that espouses suffering-denying and bliss-seeking therapeutic models of religion and spirituality. Rather, bad things *do* happen to good people, God's people!

It is, therefore, unfortunate that within a Christian worship service, laments are often neglected both in the public reading and in the preaching of Scripture, giving the impression that praise alone is the appropriate component of such gatherings, not the ejaculations and exclamations of depression, distress, and desperation. "Consequently, the language of laments, particularly resentment and anger, is often muted both within private and public Christian piety."[52] May that mute be removed, as God's people vigorously pray the laments and God's leaders enthusiastically preach them.

"The God of Israel's Psalter does not live safely at the two boundaries of obedience and praise. This God is situated in the heart of the Psalter, in the midst of Israel's suffering and Israel's hope." And through the course of the Psalter, his people are held by the right hand of God, as the psalmist declares: "I am continually with You; You hold my hand, [on] the right" (Ps 73:23).[53] And so, all throughout this journey—"a staggering drama" calling for "a daily work of faith"[54]—the people of God are barricaded from evil, borne into safety, and blessed by God's everlasting חֶסֶד ("lovingkindness")! Psalm 150, it certainly will be, one day soon and very soon, and that day will last forever and ever! Amen!

It is those eternal days that are adumbrated in the praise of the Psalter. Brueggemann brings out several ramifications of uttering the psalms of praise. Such an act is one "of imagination, not description. It sees the world through the lens of faith and dares to line out a world engaged in dialogical transactions between creator and creation." Indeed, such hymns, "with political and polemical overtones," engage in "'world making.'" God's new world (or ideal world) is envisioned and imagined, and into this world, the devout are invited. Thus "hymns of praise are acts of defiance of the [real] world that is in front of us. The work of doxology is to engage and enter another [ideal] world," a world in which Yahweh is the protagonist,

---

48. Westermann, "Role of Lament," 27.
49. Lamott, *Traveling Mercies*, 82.
50. Brueggemann, "Bounded by Obedience," 88.
51. Brueggemann, "Costly Loss of Lament," 58.
52. Harris, "Psalm 88," 44–45.
53. Brueggemann, "Bounded by Obedience," 91.
54. Brueggemann, "Bounded by Obedience," 88.

INTRODUCTION

Creator and Sustainer, and Deliverer and Protector, the Champion of his people. And in such an engagement of praise, "doxology is the exuberant abandonment of self over to God. In singing praise, all claims for the self are given up as the self is ceded over to God," a total subjection relinquishment of one's being to deity.[55]

Assaults on the people of God come from a number of quarters, usually described in the Psalter with stereotypical, clichéd language.[56] "This situation, however, . . . has its positive consequence. It leaves an openness for understanding who these enemies are in a way that pinning them down to one particular category, group, or type of person within the community would not. That is, the enemies are in fact whoever the enemies are for the singers of the psalms. . . . The language of the psalms is *open* and *metaphorical*."[57] Both the psalmist and his devout cohort, and the enemies and their evil company, are labeled with a variety of names. In this work, while respecting the disparate labels, for the sake of simplicity and clarity, I will generally refer to them as the righteous (the pro-God faction, members of the community of God, under the protection of God, and enjoying divine approval[58]) and the wicked (the anti-God faction, outside the divine community, under the judgment of God, and incurring divine wrath). These wicked ones include those labeled "enemies," a term that can refer to both Israelites unfaithful to Yahweh, and foreigners unconcerned about him. The foes may be individuals or a small group of people (as in 127:5), or national, and composed of entire armies (44:9–11).

And, of course, one's own self can be the enemy. In that regard, the church has traditionally recognized seven Penitential Psalms in the Psalter (Pss 6; 32; 38; 51; 102; 130; 143). While there is no doubt that the book operates on the assumptions of human fallibility, the numerous claims of innocence and of righteousness voiced by the psalmist will come as a surprise to modern readers coached in Pauline theology.

> The Psalms themselves recognize that everyone is a sinner, but they focus more on the importance of the general orientation of one's life as involving commitment to God than on the peccadilloes that mar this. They assume that the people of God are basically committed to Yhwh. That is part of the basis for an appeal to Yhwh. If they are not so committed, then they had better not be praying at all but putting this right. Then they can praise and pray.[59]

In this connection, mark the distinct parallels voiced in Psalm 125 between "the ones trusting in Yahweh" (125:1), "His people" (125:2), "the righteous" (125:3 [×2]), "those good" (125:4),

---

55. Brueggemann, *From Whom No Secrets Are Hid*, 46–47. Perceptively, Brueggemann offers this trenchant critique of current worship music: "Contemporary praise songs, in comparison to the hymns of praise in the Psalter, seem more often than not tepid and timid, lacking narratives that are either large or particular, void of political polemic or the taking of sides, and too often end in narcissistic reductions. Such singing constitutes not a *ceding of self*, but a *preoccupation with self* and a private religious expression that lacks depth or breadth. Such songs amount to an accommodation to an economic, political, and psychological status quo, without running any risks of being disruptive for the sake of another world" (*From Whom No Secrets Are Hid*, 48 [italics original]). I would add that such "tepid and timid" offerings also include many hymns that are entirely focused on what God has done for "me" or "us," without much attention to God's grand plan to consummate all things in Christ (Eph 1:10). This assessment is, unfortunately, true of sermons as well!

56. The word "wicked" and its cognates occur over ninety times in the Psalter, more than in any other OT book (see Tate, *Psalms 51–100*, 85–86).

57. Miller, *Interpreting the Psalms*, 50–51 (italics original).

58. This group includes the עֲנִיִּים, *'aniyyim* ("afflicted"), צַדִּיקִם, *tsaddiqim* ("righteous"), and חֲסִידִים, *chasidim* ("devout").

59. Goldingay, *Psalms*, 1:64–65.

and "the upright in heart" (125:4).[60] Indeed, twenty-five of the thirty-two instances of "devout" (חָסִיד, *chasid*) in the OT occur in the Psalms. These are the ones committed to God, walking with God, serving God. In similar vein, the "righteous" (צַדִּיק, *tsaddiq*) show up over fifty times in the Psalms. They and the devout are the blessed, the ones who belong to the congregation of God's people: Yahweh knows their ways (1:6) and Yahweh loves them (146:8).[61]

Imprecations

An imprecatory psalm is one "that contains an imprecation, a speech act that calls for, demands, requests, or expresses a wish for divine judgment and vengeance to befall an enemy, whether an individual or a corporate entity."[62] Essentially any "invocation of judgment, calamity, or curse uttered against one's enemies or the enemies of God" falls into the category of imprecation.[63]

Imprecations do not arise *de novo* in Scripture. Althann shows that law codices, treaties, and statements of property ownership in the ancient Near East often invoke a series of curses from deity upon any who dare infringe the arrangements agreed upon by the parties in question.[64] These imprecations involve the eradication of offspring and descendants,[65] all kinds of violence inflicted upon enemies,[66] causing their terror,[67] and their perishing.[68] Clearly the God we deal with, whose eyes are too pure to behold evil (Hab 1:13), and with whom no evil dwells (Ps 5:4), is one who is intensely angry with such predations of goodness.[69] A deity unconcerned about sin is not the God of the Bible. "Wrath is the holy revulsion of God's being

---

60. One might add "Israel" in 125:5.

61. Needless to say, they are, of course, in relationship to God, accomplished by deity's gracious and sovereign choice, and are represented in this dispensation by those who constitute the universal Church, those in relationship to God through Jesus Christ by the Spirit.

62. Laurence, *Cursing with God*, 10. While imprecatory poems in the Psalter commonly include Pss 7; 35; 58; 59; 69; 83; 109; 137; and 139, invocations against foes are found elsewhere: 3:7; 5:10; 6:10; 7:6; 9:5–6, 12, 15–20; 10:12, 15–18; 11:6; 12:3–4; 17:13–14; 28:4; 31:17–18; 34:16; 35:1–6, 8, 19, 23–26; 37:9–10, 15, 17, 20; 40:14–15; 41:10; 45:5; 52:5; 54:5; 55:9, 15, 23; 56:7; 58:6–9; 59:5, 11–13; 64:7–8; 66:3; 68:1–2, 21–23, 30; 69:22–25, 27–28; 70:2–3; 71:13; 72:4, 9; 74:11, 22–23; 75:10; 79:6, 10, 12; 80:16; 81:14–15; 82:7–8; 83:9–18; 86:7; 89:10; 92:9; 94:1–2; 104:35; 105:36; 109:6–15, 19–20, 29; 110:1, 5–6; 119:78; 125:5; 129:5–8; 132:18; 137:7–9; 139:19; 140:8–11; 141:10; 143:12; 144:6 (modified from Laurence, *Cursing with God*, 10n24). Not all are imprecations; some are prophetic utterances, others look back at divine retribution; nonetheless, all deal with the debacles of the evil and wicked. According to Ross, 65 of the 370 verses in the Psalms have imprecations in them, almost 18 percent of the Psalter (*Psalms*, 1:115). Prophecies directed against various nations, though not specifically imprecations, resound frequently in the OT. As well, such utterances are at times directed even against God's own people when they have backslidden and done evil: Isa 1; 22; 29–31; Hos 8–10; Joel 2:1–17; 3:1–17; Amos 2:4—9:15; Mic 3; Zeph 1:2–18; 3:1–7. All of these are consistent with the imprecations of the Psalms.

63. Laney, "Fresh Look," 35.

64. Althann, "Psalms of Vengeance," 2–3.

65. As in Pss 21:10; 37:28, 38; 105:36; 136:10; 137:9; etc.

66. As in Pss 3:7; 10:15; 18:14; 21:12; 35:1–8; 37:12–15; 45:5; 52:1–5; 58:6–9; 64:7; etc.

67. As in Pss 6:10; 9:20; 11:6; 14:5; 48:4–6; 53:5; 73:19; 83:15; etc.

68. As in Pss 7:9; 17:14; 37:36, 38; 52:5; 54:5; 55:23; 59:13; 63:9; 68:2; 73:27; 82:7; 83:17; 92:7; 94:23; 106:17–18; 110:6; 119:118; 135:10–11; 136:17–20; 139:19; 141:6; in some cases, even eternally: 9:5–6; 69:28; 81:15.

69. See Pss 2:12; 21:9; 75:8; 76:5–9; 79:6; 94:1.

against that which is the contradiction of his holiness."[70] And if God's people are to reflect God's holiness, then anger against sin and evil must be an integral attribute of God's devout:

> The OT implies that anger along with (e.g.) hatred is a proper aspect of being a person. It has a place in the full-orbed character of God and thus in that of the human person made in God's image.... Both divine and human anger are important to the fulfillment of God's purpose in the world. In the context of the Psalms, this means that anger has an essential place in prayer, often expressed as an urgent plea for terrible trouble to come on one's attackers.... [Ps 69:22–25] In light of Christ's command to love our enemies, this might seem a prayer no Christian could pray.... Yet Peter and Paul both quote it (Acts 1:16, 20; Rom 11:9–10).... It seems that the NT accepts the notion of praying against one's enemies as well as the notion of praying for them.[71]

Essentially biblical imprecations wish for the manifestations of Satan, his agents, and their nefarious activities to be "crushed ... under your feet" (Rom 16:20). Likewise, Eph 1:21–23 describes God's placement of all supernatural anti-God entities, "every rule and authority and power and dominion," under the feet of the exalted Lord Jesus Christ. But God has also given Christ as the body of the church, and that makes all of those inimical actors (who are under Christ's feet) simultaneously under the feet of God's people (who constitute the body of Christ). Of course, the final disposition of all these traffickers of evil arrayed against God and his kingdom is yet to happen, but it will (see Rev 20:10). Imprecations further this subduing of evil by the body of Christ, the church.

In the Psalter, enemies curse (Pss 10:3, 7; 59:12; 109:28). On the other hand, the people of God, afflicted and oppressed by evil, do not return these curses, but instead "abandon [themselves]" upon God (10:14; also see 109:4).[72] David, the author of many of the psalms, is explicitly recorded as demurring at suggestions to avenge himself even when it was in his power to do so (see his treatment of Saul in 1 Sam 24:11–12; and of Shimei who cursed David, in 2 Sam 19:21–23). After all, "vengeance is Mine," declares the God who repays evil (Deut 32:35; Rom 12:19; Heb 10:30; also see 2 Thess 1:6).[73] Perhaps that is substantiated by the fact that the first one to utter an imprecation in the Bible was God himself, after the fall (Gen 3:14, 17 has curses upon the serpent and the ground, respectively; see also 4:11, upon Cain; and 12:3, upon those who cursed Abraham).[74] "Perhaps there is a division of labor here to be celebrated: Israel

---

70. Murray, *Epistle to the Romans*, 35. Ours is a holy God who takes sin extremely seriously; after all, he sent his Son to die for that cause!

71. Goldingay, *Psalms*, 1:66. See below for a potential resolution of the seeming antithesis between love of enemies and hatred for them. On the imprecations of Psalm 137, see in that chapter, where I argue that the "dashing of babies against a rock" had likely become a stereotypical depiction of wartime violence—designed to express outrage against cruelty directed towards non-combatants. It may not necessarily be historical, though one cannot rule out its actual occurrence either, a standard action by enemies against victims, much as rape and pillage carried out by ravaging armies in modern times.

72. Laurence, *Cursing with God*, 151.

73. Obviously, several of the petitions for harm to be inflicted on evildoers are addressed directly to the sovereign deity: 5:10; 28:4–5; 31:17–18; 79:10–12. Imprecations that explicitly surrender vengeance to God are found in Jer 11:20; 18:19–23. God's vengeance noted in the NT is also linked to Psalms. See, for instance: "fire and brimstone" and "cup" shared by Rev 14:10 and LXX Ps 11:6 (also see Rev 19:20 that also has "fire" and "brimstone"); "vengeance" and "blood" and "servants" employed by both Rev 19:2 and LXX Ps 79:10.

74. Noah was the first human in the Bible to utter a curse (Gen 9:25). God's imprecation is also mentioned in Ps 37:22. Deuteronomy 28:15–68 details deity's covenant curses directed against those in Israel who would break the law. The numerous references in the Psalter to "covenant" (Pss 25:10, 14; 44:17; 50:5,

hopes; Yahweh avenges as he chooses."[75] Indeed, "it is an act of profound faith to entrust one's most precious hatreds to God, knowing they will be taken seriously."[76] It is this relinquishing of desperation, anger, and the desire for justice into God's hands that actually gives the suffering people of God reason for hope, an anticipation of a future when all will be better.

Utility of Imprecatory Prayers

P. D. James, in her mystery *Original Sin*, has one of its characters, detective inspector Kate, say to her Jewish colleague on the police force, Daniel: "'I don't go in for all this emphasis on sin, suffering and judgement. If I had a God, I'd like him to be intelligent, cheerful and amusing.'" Daniel replies: "'I doubt whether you'd find him much of a comfort when they herded you into the gas chambers. You might prefer a god of vengeance.'"[77] Much of modern culture's disdain for the imprecatory psalms stems from a lack of experience, direct or indirect, of abysmal evil, such as that which occurred in the Holocaust (for a modern-day example). For those undergoing these harrowing and agonizing persecutions, praying to God for the retribution, or even the destruction, of their evil oppressors is quite appropriate. But even for others at a distance from these infernal adversities, there are ancillary benefits of praying the imprecatory psalms. Such prayers force those praying (and those reading and studying those prayers, as well as those hearing those prayers being preached) to identify with the oppressed and disenfranchised—a vicarious suffering of sorts.

> The psalms which deal with enemies invite those of us who read and hear them to enter into them on *behalf of others*, if not for ourselves. The language of these psalms evokes in us an awareness of the terrible wickedness that is in the world. They may not be our prayers, at the moment at least, but they are the prayers of our sisters and brothers who are trampled down by persons and powers beyond their control.[78]

Clearly all of Scripture is "God-breathed and profitable for teaching, for reproof, for correction, for training in righteousness so that the person of God may be capable, fully equipped for every good work" (2 Tim 3:16–17). That renders even imprecatory texts valuable for preaching, i.e., the exposition of the thrust (pericopal theology) of these passages for application by God's people in every space and in every time.

But how about *praying* these psalms? It will not do to say that we only *preach* the imprecatory psalms. The pastor-preacher will have to make a determination as to whether these psalms can also be prayed.

> The psalms make certain claims upon us . . . [They] are *sui generis* to the extent that they put words in our mouths, calling for our tacit affirmation and implicating us

---

16; 55:20; 74:20; 78:10, 37; 89:3, 28, 34, 39; 103:18; 105:8–10; 106:45; 111:5, 9; 132:12) render many of the curses in the Psalms relatable to such covenant violations.

75. Brueggemann, *Message of the Psalms*, 77.

76. Brueggemann, *Message of the Psalms*, 77. See the expressions of God's trustworthiness in the context of opposition and distress in Pss 4:5; 9:10; 13:5; 21:7–13; 22:4–5, 9; 25:2; 26:2; 28:7; 31:5–6, 14; 32:10–11; 33:21; 37:3, 5; 40:3–4; 52:8; 55:23; 56:3–4, 11; 62:8; 65:5; 71:5; 84:12; 86:2; 91:2; 112:7; 115:9–12; 118:8; 119:42; 125:1; 143:8.

77. James, *Original Sin*, 232.

78. Tate, *Psalms 51–100*, 88.

INTRODUCTION

in their prayers. With their liturgical indicators and first-person pronouns, the psalms reach from the past into the present and invite us to make the petitions our own. Demanding to be taken up and prayed, the psalms implicate us in their affirmations and denials, their loves and longings, and these implicatory [sic] imprecatory prayers thus pose distinct challenges for any Christian who dares wander into the Psalter.[79]

The fact that the people of God live in a wayward world is reason enough for the employment of imprecatory psalms in the life of the church. Evils abound: wars, genocides, abuse of civilians and refugees during these crises, mass shootings, threats of nuclear war, persecution of Christians, abortion, non-war-related abuse of individuals, including domestic violence, and even "proliferation of public misinformation and outright lies [creating] epistemic chaos" that "stretches the social fabric to its breaking point."[80] This waxing of wickedness necessitates an earnestness among the people of God to do all they can, in the power of God, to work against these powers and these iniquities. Imprecatory prayer is part of that responsible work.

According to Genesis 1–11, God's creation is to be viewed as the cosmic Temple of God.[81] And humans were created to care for this Temple, with the Garden of Eden as the chamber of divine residence. This locus served as the place where man engaged in "cultivation" (from עבד, *'vd*; Gen 2:5, 15). The verb is commonly used of agricultural tasks;[82] it later acquired strong liturgical connotations and came to be employed regularly for the service of God and his worship.[83] Likewise, the verb "keep," the role of humanity with relation to the Garden (from שמר, *shmr*; 2:15), is employed in a non-sacral sense (also in 3:24; 4:9; etc.), as well as for the fulfilling covenantal responsibilities towards God.[84] But it, too, connotes the priestly duties with regard to the sanctuary and its cultic activities.[85] All of this hints at the kind of activity Adam had symbolically been engaged in, in that primeval agricultural paradise that served as the cosmic Temple's center of operations. It is no coincidence, then, that the δοῦλοι, *douloi*, "servants," of the Lamb, in the restored garden that is the heavenly city, will also be "serving" (Rev 22:3; from λατρεύω, *latreuō*, also used frequently of worship as, for example, in Heb 10:2; 13:10; Rev 7:15; etc.). In sum, man was created to serve God in his Temple, in his perfectly ordered creation, fulfilling covenantal responsibilities—"caring for sacred space."[86]

Of course, this Temple, once pristine, was invaded by sin and brokenness at the fall: any and every facet of evil is a blotch upon the holiness of the Creator and the goodness of his creation. And any activity by word or by hand undertaken by the people of God against these sinister satanic stains is a partnering with God in the sanctifying of his sacred space—an integral role of humanity, as it "cultivates" and "keeps" the Garden—a priestly responsibility (Exod 19:5–6; Rev 1:6; 5:10). Those enemies of the divine Temple, God's kingdom, are destined for

---

79. Laurence, *Cursing with God*, 2.
80. Laurence, *Cursing with God*, 4.
81. Walton, *Genesis 1*, 185, 187; Levenson, "Temple," 288.
82. See also Gen 3:23; 4:2, 12; 9:25, 26, 27; etc.
83. As in Exod 3:12; Num 3:7–8; 4:23, 24, 26; 8:25–26; 18:5–6; Deut 4:19; etc. The noun form of the verb, עֲבֹדָה, *'avodah*, "service," also describes Levitical duties in the tabernacle and temple (Exod 4:23; 38:21; Num 3:7–8, 10, 26; 18:6–7; 1 Chr 23:32; 24:3, 19; 2 Chr 8:14).
84. See Gen 17:9–10; 18:19; 26:5; Lev 18:5; Deut 4:6; 7:12; 29:9.
85. See Num 1:53; 3:7, 8, 10, 28, 32, 38; 18:3–5; 28:2; Ezek 44:14; etc.
86. Walton, *Genesis 1*, 173. Most of the discussion of the cosmic Temple and humankind's role therein was modified from Kuruvilla, *Genesis*, 58.

destruction as Scripture unequivocally affirms (see Ps 79:1, 6, 10; 1 Cor 3:17; 5:13). Thus, praying the imprecatory psalms is a critical aspect of the divinely ordained role of the people of God, as agents of the justice of a holy God with whom "no evil dwells" (Ps 5:4).

Besides being a failure on the part of God's people to discharge their responsibility, the neglect of imprecatory psalms, both in preaching and in prayer, leads to another critical loss:

> Too many Christians find themselves bereft of meaningful, biblical language to name the terrors that saturate the world, to proclaim God's commitment to righting violent wrongs, to cry out for God's justice against the slaughter of so many innocents, to channel and express the pain-filled fury of personal victimization.... The community that does not learn together through Scripture's psalmic script how to bring its wounds and the wounds of the world before God, cultivate a rightly ordered anger, and plead in prayer for the justice of divine judgment[,] will be uncertain whether their longings for justice belong in the presence of God at all and will risk inadvertently shaping its members to nurse wounds, vent anger, and pursue justice after the pattern of the world—contributing to, rather than confronting and challenging, the seemingly perpetual cycles of violence.[87]

Laurence, therefore, argues that "prayerful performance of the imprecatory psalms is an ethically permissible—even obligatory—means by which the Christian church faithfully enacts her God-given calling as a royal priesthood in the world."[88] It is a form of the widow's prayer for justice that Jesus himself applauded (Luke 18:1-8). "A Psalter without imprecation—while perhaps more palatable for many modern readers—would represent a gross dereliction of duty, a sinful rejection of God's call."[89] I concur.

Violence in Imprecatory Prayers

What about all the violence in the Psalter, especially in the imprecations thereof? "God's violence, whether in judgment or salvation, is never an end in itself, but is always exercised in the service of God's more comprehensive salvific purposes for creation":[90] the liberation of his people;[91] the rescue of the righteous from the wicked;[92] the deliverance of the needy and afflicted from their oppressors;[93] and salvation of the devout from their enemies.[94]

> There is a clear marker that distinguishes the violence that takes hold of God's kingdom from that which wreaks destruction in our world—a difference between the saints' violence, always conjoined with God's high praise, and the unholy violence that rings as shrill mockery in God's ears.... Every kind of godless violence

---

87. Laurence, *Cursing with God*, 5-6.
88. Laurence, *Cursing with God*, 14.
89. Laurence, *Cursing with God*, 181.
90. Fretheim, "God and Violence," 25.
91. See Pss 18:19; 25:15, 17; 31:5; 60:11-12; 68:7-8, 22; 78:53-54; 80:8-11; 105:37; 107:14.
92. See Pss 5:10-12; 7:6-11; 11:4-7; 32:10-11; 34:15-22; 37:12-17; 55:22-23; 58:10-11; 64:5-10; 68:1-3; 69:26-28; 75:10; 92:9-15.
93. See Pss 9:12; 10:12-18; 12:5-8; 35:8-10; 37:9-17; 40:14-17; 69:28-33; 70:1-5; 76:6-9; 82:4-8; 109:22-31; 132:15-18; 140:1-13.
94. See Pss 3:7-8; 6:9-10; 9:1-6; 17:8-15; 18:35-48; 21:8-13; 31:15-18; 35:19-28; 37:18-20; 45:5; 59:1-5; 66:3; 68:1-2, 21, 23; 69:18-28; 81:13-16; 83:1-18; 89:10; 92:9-10; 110:1, 5-6; 132:17-18; 138:7-8; 143:9-12.

is directed at getting something or holding on to it—power, oil, satisfaction, vengeance, personal or national security. But the battle of the saint is always fundamentally directed toward giving praise to God.[95]

In fact, "godly" violence, that exercised by God or his agents under his auspices and for his glory, is best labeled "*counter*violence," which, as Brueggemann points out, "functions primarily as a critical principle in order to undermine and destabilize other [ungodly] violence," whether of human or non-human origin.[96] Needless to say, violence is not to be exercised thoughtlessly even if directed against evil. Jesus forcibly cleansed the temple, the account of which is found in all the Gospels (Matt 21:12–17; Mark 11:15–19; Luke 19:45–48; John 2:13–16), but he also rebuked his disciples for desiring to smite the recalcitrant Samaritans with fire from heaven (Luke 9:51–55), and later he admonished Peter to refrain from swinging swords even against enemies (Matt 26:52–53).

Imprecatory Prayers and Love?

But there is no doubt that the imprecatory psalms make the Christian uncomfortable. How does the hatred so blatant in those petitions, even to the point of rejoicing in the punishment of fellow humans (Ps 58:7–12), comport with the biblical call to love neighbors and even enemies (Lev 19:17–18; Matt 5:44; Rom 12:14; 1 Thess 5:15; 1 Pet 3:9)?[97]

There is a strong tendency (perhaps an inadvertent one) in Christendom to sever the OT from the NT by considering the former as picturing God's stern justice and the latter God's gracious mercy. That is an unbiblical prejudice that must be strongly deprecated.[98] After all, the command to "love one's neighbor as oneself" came from the OT (Lev 19:17–18), as also did Jesus's command to give enemies food and drink (Prov 25:21–22). "A fundamental reason that we see tension between the call to love enemies in the Sermon on the Mount and the imprecatory psalms is that we assume love and judgment are incompatible. At stake here is more than an ethic of which to prefer: the Sermon on the Mount or the Psalms. What is really at stake is our doctrine of God."[99] A deity who is only loving and never angry, and only forgiving and never just, is not the God of the Bible. He, needless to say, is immutable across biblical history, and so are the demands he makes of his people to reflect him in holiness, whether in their love of all that is good and godly or in their hatred of all that is evil and ungodly!

Aquinas's sage observations on "charity" are helpful in the consideration of love for one's enemies. He notes that as far as the *nature* of the sinner is concerned, that person is to be loved: "we ought to love sinners, out of charity, in respect of their nature." But there is also their *guilt*. "Their guilt is opposed to God, and is an obstacle to happiness. Wherefore, in respect of their guilt whereby they are opposed to God, all sinners are to be hated, even one's father or mother or kindred . . . [Luke 12:26]. For it is our duty to hate, in the sinner, his being a sinner, and to love in him, his being a [person] capable of bliss; and this is to love him truly, out of charity, for God's sake."[100]

---

95. Davis, "Self-Inflicted Violence," 296.
96. Brueggemann, *Theology of the Old Testament*, 244.
97. Also see Exod 23:4–5; Pss 35:12–14; 109:4–5; Prov 24:17–18; 25:21–22.
98. It is almost a functional Marcionism!
99. Nehrbass, *Praying Curses*, 90.
100. *Summa Theologiæ* II-II, 25, 6.

He continues:

> Love is due to our neighbor in respect of what he holds from God, i.e. in respect of nature and grace, but not in respect of what he has of himself and from the devil, i.e. in respect of sin and lack of justice.... It is part of our love for our brother that we hate the fault and the lack of good in him, since desire for another's good is equivalent to hatred of his evil.[101]

The Dominican Doctor declares that because God himself hates the sin of the sinner, and not his nature, God's people also can hate sinners, without themselves sinning.[102] Vos's words are wise:

> There may exist cases in which the glory God and the welfare of man conflict, and in such cases it is wrong to seek the welfare of the particular persons involved. This presupposition, that the welfare of man is the chief end of man, is essentially humanistic, is contrary to theism, and overlooks the fact that man is not self-existent but a created being who is therefore dependent on God and who does not exist for himself but for God's glory.... If it is right for God to destroy evil and evil men in his universe, or to command his servants to effect that destruction, then it was also right for him to inspire the Psalmists to pray for that same work of destruction, and it was moreover right for the Psalmists to offer such prayers.[103]

No prayer asking God to take action in a manner that is harmonious with God's nature, attributes, and promises can be wrong. And for God's will to be done and for his kingdom to come, evil has to be eradicated, sin has to be abrogated. "The total destruction of evil, including the judicial destruction of evil men, is the prerogative of the sovereign God, and it is right not only to pray for the accomplishment of this destruction, but even to assist in effecting it when commanded to do so by God himself."[104]

In any case, it is evident that a fully orbed theological exposition that harmonizes love for another with zeal for the justice of God is not—and cannot be—provided with each imprecatory prayer in the Psalms. Kidner, explaining such a potential imbalance in the forces of various assertions in Scripture (for e.g.: Proverbs—prosperity for the righteous; Job—adversity for the righteous; Ecclesiastes—the incomprehensibility of why prosperity or adversity happens to the righteous) observes:

> It is worth pointing out that this single-minded pursuit of their respective interests is typical of the Old Testament's way of doing things. It tends to give itself wholly to one thing at a time, saying it with maximum force and leaving any resulting imbalance to be corrected in due course by an equally massive counterweight. In this way more justice can be done to a many-sided subject than by steering a middle course between its extremes.[105]

This explanation is valid for biblical imprecations as well, that are easily misconstrued as unbalanced. After all, there is more to the treatment of others than simply anger at their

---

101. *Summa Theologiæ* II-II, 34, 3.
102. *Summa Theologiæ* II-II, 34, 3.
103. Vos, "Ethical Problem," 131, 134.
104. Vos, "Ethical Problem," 135.
105. Kidner, *Wisdom of Proverbs*, 123–24.

perpetration of evil; there are other aspects to Christians' treatment of enemies that are not considered in imprecatory prayers uttered in the heat of persecution and in the face of utter evil.

In a broader sense also, calling upon God to halt the wickedness being perpetrated by an individual is consistent with love, in that it keeps that sinner from sinning further and incurring greater guilt.

> From this perspective, the imprecator's prayers may be read as petitions to spare the enemy the disintegrating and agonizing moral, spiritual, and psychological effects of further violence by neutralizing his capacity to reap destruction ([Ps] 58:6–7), refusing to give him the distorted desires of his heart (35:4, 25), challenging his self-exaltation (9:20; 59:12–13; 140:8), and disappointing his murderous schemes (40:14–15)—in short, by interrupting his violence in judgment.[106]

This is true even with a wish for death (Pss 54:5; 55:15; 58:7–8; 69:28; 104:35; 109:8–9). "The divine withdrawal of life may be understood as a merciful last resort, a sovereignly administered preventative that restrains the enemy from adding to his iniquity, bearing responsibility for yet more horrific injustice, sinking even further into inhumanity."[107] Perhaps if there are degrees of punishment in eternal separation from God, death may spare the evildoer from more intense retribution than would have been the case had the wicked one been allowed to live longer and engage in greater sin. "One must love rightly in order to hate rightly, but there are times when one must hate truly in order to love fully."[108]

The fact remains that God hates evildoers (Pss 5:5–6; 11:5); if that is not a contradiction with his holy nature—his being a "holy hatred"—then the people of God may also, under certain circumstances, hate such nefarious personnel (5:4–5; 11:5; 15:4; 26:5; 31:6; 45:7; 97:10; 101:3–4, 7; 119:104, 113, 128, 158, 163; 139:1–4, 21–22[109]). Needless to add, even the NT gives evidence of imprecation of people and institutions inimical to God and his agenda.[110] Jesus himself engaged in such activities (Matt 11:20–24; 12:34; 23:13–39; 25:41; 26:24; Mark 11:12–14, 20–21; 14:21).

Praying Imprecations

The inspiration and profitability of Scripture makes the preaching of the imprecatory psalms an imperative. As to praying those imprecatory psalms, taking into account all that has been discussed thus far, I submit that careful praying of imprecatory prayers in the contemporary

---

106. Laurence, *Cursing with God*, 168.

107. Laurence, *Cursing with God*, 169.

108. Laurence, *Cursing with God*, 171.

109. Also see Lev 20:23; 26:30, 44; Deut 7:25–26; 12:31; 16:22; Prov 8:13; Hos 9:15; Amos 5:15, 21; Zech 8:17; Mal 2:16. Neither is the NT silent about such matters: Jude 23; Rev 2:6. Since the ones raising the issue of retribution in Rev 6:9–10 are ostensibly perfected saints who are in the presence of God, such an imprecatory attitude cannot be ruled *tout court* as wrong, sinful, or evil.

110. See Acts 23:1–6; 1 Cor 16:22; Gal 1:8–9; 5:12; 1 Tim 1:19–20; 2 Tim 4:14; Jas 5:1–6; 2 Pet 2:14; Jude 11–13; Rev 6:9–10; 18:6–8. The imprecatory psalms cited or alluded to in the NT include Ps 35:8 (in 1 Thess 5:3); Ps 69:23 (in Rom 11:7–10); Ps 69:25 (in Matt 23:38; Luke 13:35—both by Jesus; Acts 1:20); Ps 109:8 (in Acts 1:20); as well, Ps 31:5 (in Luke 23:46; Acts 7:59); and Ps 110:1 (in Matt 22:44; 26:64; Mark 12:36; Luke 20:42–43; Acts 2:34–35; 1 Cor 15:25; Eph 1:20, 22; Col 3:1; Heb 1:13; 8:1; 10:12; 12:2). Perhaps most striking is how Jesus's words in Luke 19:44 and Ps 137:9 sound quite similar.

church, whether by praying the particular psalms or by creating similar invocations, is acceptable, and perhaps to be recommended.

As with all prayers, such petitions, too, are susceptible to being abused and misused: "The illicit exercise of licit prayers can reinforce affections and reify ways of being and relating to God that bend, distort, and malform disciples in vice rather than shaping them in virtue."[111] As feeble and fallible creatures possessing our own foibles, recycling the biblical imprecations should be accompanied by a grave sense of humility, and a keen appreciation of Eccl 5:2: "Do not be hasty with your mouth or with your heart be precipitate to bring forth a matter [דָּבָר, *davar*] before God, for God is in the heavens and you upon the earth; therefore let your words [דְּבָרִ] be few." Yet, for the right reasons, in the right way, at the right time, and with the right guidance from the right leadership, such prayers may be—nay, *should be*—prayed by the people of God. "God is both sovereign and righteous; he possesses the unquestionable right to destroy all evil in his universe; if it is right for God to plan and effect this destruction, then it is also right for the saints to pray for the same."[112] So then, if imprecatory prayers should be utilized by the body of Christ, how shall we go about employing them?

It is helpful to be guided on this issue with four questions: Why must we imprecate (the *reason* for imprecation)? Who may imprecate (the *agent* of imprecation)? Who may be imprecated against (the *objects* of imprecation)? and What may be the imprecation (the *content* of imprecation)?[113]

Why Imprecate? The reason for imprecation has been developed above, but it is worth reiterating that the goal of such prayers (and of any other kind of prayer) is the glory of God and love for him and his interests. This is evident in the frequent recourse to the "name" of Yahweh by the psalmist as he calls for divine help against virulent oppressors,[114] the praise that redounds to God post-deliverance that glorifies God,[115] and the constant focus upon the weal of Jerusalem and the welfare of its citizens.[116]

Who May Imprecate? That the psalmist or the people of God are agents of divine punishment is clear in the Psalter.[117] One notices that in Jesus' story of the widow calling upon the judge for justice (Luke 18:1–8), no particular state of righteousness of the supplicant is assumed. Yet, in the Psalter, even though the psalmist does not hesitate to confess sinfulness, he maintains his innocence frequently, even calling upon God to examine him for the veracity of that claim.[118] Of course, that assertion is not one of perfect sinlessness, but of righteousness in the sense

---

111. Laurence, *Cursing with God*, 256. This is true of preaching these texts, as well: with shepherdly love for the flock, the preacher must exercise care and discretion in what texts/books are chosen to be preached from and when. Not every psalm is appropriate for every occasion, much as not every song in a hymnbook is suitable for every occasion of worship.

112. Vos, "Ethical Problems," 136.

113. Modified from Laurence, *Cursing with God*, 260–64.

114. See Pss 31:3; 44:8; 54:1, 5; 57:5; 74:7, 10, 18; 79:6, 9; 83:16–18; 86:9; 109:21; 135:13; 142:7; 143:11.

115. See Pss 35:20; 74:3–10; 69:9, 35–36; 72:4, 12–14; 74:20; 79:1–7; 82:3–4; 102:13–14; 137:5–7.

116. See Pss 5:11; 7:17; 9:2, 14; 18:46; 21:13; 28:7; 30:1; 35:9–10, 18, 27–28; 40:16; 46:10; 57:5; 58:10–11; 68:3–4; 70:4; 92:8; 109:30; 149:5–6. And no doubt, God is also glorified if his enemies repent (see below).

117. See Pss 18:34, 37–40, 42–45, 47; 41:10–11; 44:5–7; 60:12; 101:5, 8; 110:5; 118:10–12; 137:8–9; 149:5–9.

118. See Pss 6:1; 7:3–5; 18:20–26; 25:18–19; 26:9–11; 40:12; 69:4–7; 78:8, 10–11, 17–19, 22, 32–33, 36–37, 40–42, 56–57; 79:8; 130:3–4; 139:1–4, 23–24; 143:2.

INTRODUCTION

that, overall, he and his cohort have walked with God as integral members of the divine community (7:3–5, 8–12; 9:4; 17:1–5; 18:19–26; 26:3–8, 11–12; 139:23–24).[119]

Who May Be Imprecated Against? The enemies of God and of his kingdom are both spiritual[120] and human (including systemic and institutional entities): all may be (*are* to be) imprecated against by the guardians of the cosmic Temple of God, the people of God. This means that even *self*-imprecations may be in order, for believers are not exempt from the danger of themselves being the polluters of the sanctity of God's cosmos-Temple. Even as children of God, there is the dangerous possibility of their flesh gaining control over them, and the Spirit losing control (so to speak), such that they sin (Rom 7:15–23; 2 Cor 7:1; Gal 5:17; Eph 5:1–4; etc.). The fact that believers in this dispensation are the temple(s) of the Spirit (1 Cor 3:16; 6:19; 2 Cor 6:16; Eph 2:19–22) should stand as a warning to those who would desecrate and denigrate the abode of God. Thus every agent or organized body that, in unrepentant and rebellious fashion, seeks to do evil may be an appropriate object of imprecation.

What May Be the Imprecation? Obviously, the petition is that God may intervene and disrupt the performance and progress of evil that is desecrating his cosmic-Temple,[121] bringing disrepute to his name, and destroying his people—any and every event that disrupts the performance and progress of all that is good and is a barrier to the glorification of God. It is essentially a prayer that "Thy kingdom come," as the community of God participates in the divine agenda for his creation.[122] But while judgment, both temporal[123] and eternal,[124] are being sought, the repentance and conversion of the oppressor and the enemy are not forgotten.[125] In sum, the people of God pray that deity will take whatever action is necessary to halt the advance of evil, and that perhaps in his grace, he will see fit that those engaging in evil, who also bear the *imago Dei*, come to salvation in Christ, in the marvelous sovereign grace of God, and by the inscrutable workings of his Spirit. There is no contradiction between justice-seeking prayers for an entity's downfall and punishment, and mercy-seeking prayers for their repentance and salvation.

In any case, imprecatory prayers must never be viewed as standing alone apart from all the other activities of the people of God, including doing good to enemies, loving them for their nature and the image of God in them, performing good works for the benefit of God's

---

119. That the attacks on the people of God are entirely unjustified (Pss 35:7, 12, 19–21; 69:4; 109:3–5; 119:69, 161) also substantiates this affirmation of righteousness.

120. See Eph 1:20–22; 6:11–12; Col 2:15; 1 Pet 5:8; Rev 12:9, 13–17.

121. See Pss 7:11–13; 9:16–17; 28:4–5; 35:22–26; 37:28; 52:5; 58:10–11; 75:2–3; 79:5–6, 10–12; 94:1–2; 129:4; 137:7. Often it is a *lex talionis*, commensurate, form of recompense upon the wicked that is petitioned.

122. This includes an ardent desire on the part of God's people for the reputation of God (Pss 9:1–2; 57:5–11; 59:16–17; 76:4–12), their yearning for the divine kingdom (5:1–12; 9:4–8; 10:15–16; 37:22; 46:8–11; 48:1–8; 101:1–8; 132:18), their solicitude for his capital city (102:12–14; 137:5), and their own adoption of deity's concerns for the poor, afflicted, fatherless, foreigner, disenfranchised, and subjugated (9:9, 12–13, 18; 10:12, 17; 12:5; 22:24; 31:7; 34:6, 18; 35:10; 40:17; 68:5–6, 10; 69:29, 32–33; 70:5; 72:2, 4, 12–13; 76:8–9; 82:3–4; 86:1; 107:41; 109:31; 113:7; 132:15; 140:12; 147:6; 149:4).

123. See Pss 7:9; 10:15; 17:14; 28:4; 34:16, 21; 35:4, 26; 37:20, 28; 40:14; 52:5; 55:9, 15, 23; 58:6–9; 92:9; 94:2; 104:35; 109:8–9; 110:5–6; 129:5.

124. See Pss 9:5–6; 69:28; 81:15.

125. I.e., the redemption either of the perpetrators of evil (who also bear the *imago Dei*) or of others who observe their downfall (as well as the edification of the community of God, as their faith is strengthened). See Pss 2:12; 6:10; 7:12; 40:3–4; 46:8–10; 59:13; 64:9; 68:28–31; 71:13; 83:17–18; 109:26–29; 138:4–5.

cosmos-Temple and its citizens, etc. Imprecations form only a part of what it means to be a member of the body of Christ in a fallen world; an undue focus on this issue (or on any other facet of the Christian life) can become unhealthy if not balanced by the alignment of our lives to all the other necessary calls of God upon us to become Christlike.

In sum, in situations of dreadful wickedness—that inspire God's people to resolve that they will never be unfaithful to God, instead "remembering" (and never "forgetting") God and his locus and focus of operations (137:5a, 6b)—it is proper for Christians to call upon their deity also to "remember" (137:7a), and even to expect that he may unleash dreadful consequences upon the nefarious. This is the "counterviolence" of a God of perfect and holy wrath, in the service of his perfect and holy justice, to demonstrate his perfect and holy mercy to his people, the objects of his perfect and holy love.[126]

Translation

My translation of the Masoretic text of the Psalter attempts to be as literal and word-for-word as possible, not for the sake of slavish correspondence, but to aid the preacher in catching the text's literary clues to its thrust: wordplays, unique word choices, chiasms, sequences, organizations, alliterations, puns, repetitions—the many filigrees of structure and nuances of language—all of which enable one to catch the *how* of the text (that significantly affects the *what* of the text), and most of which are hardly discernible in standard translations. "For a reader to attend to these elements of literary art is not merely an exercise in 'appreciation' but a discipline of understanding: the literary vehicle is so much the necessary medium through which the Hebrew writers realize their meanings[,] that we will grasp the meanings at best imperfectly if we ignore their fine articulations as literature. This general principle applies as much to biblical poetry as to prose."[127] But that Italian adage *traduttore, traditore* ("translator [is a] traitor") gets it right. No translation can fully convey the intricacies of the original text. Of necessity then, my English rendition of the Hebrew will be somewhat wooden, but the goal is to retain the textual evidences to the thrust of the psalm, and not to plow these clues under to serve felicity of syntax and euphony of language.

Subsections (colas) within verses of the Psalter are disputed, and line breaks contested; my translation is somewhat idiosyncratic in that respect, though my attempts are indebted to Goldingay's translation and to the NASB (1995). Overall, I have striven to keep emendation of the text to a minimum and have tried to make (and have hopefully succeeded in making) sense of the MT as it is. The conjunction ו, *w*, I have sought to keep nondescript for the most part, leaving it to the reader to decide how it functions, as an "and," or a "so," or a "then," or a "therefore," etc. But the greatest challenge to a translator of biblical Hebrew poetry is the rendition of verbs into English.

> It is evident that there can be no simple rule of thumb with respect to the appropriate English tense which may be indicated by the forms of the Hebrew verb. In practice, the context is the principle guide to determining the most appropriate

---

126. Brueggemann, *Theology of the Old Testament*, 244.

127. Alter, "Introduction," 21. So much so, I have even retained the word order in many cases to make (for example) the chiastic structures visible in English. Verse numbering in the English versions is followed, both in the translations and the references thereto, when there is a discrepancy between these translations and the MT.

translation, but difficulties arise precisely because context, in nonhistorical poetic texts (which is the case with respect to the majority of the psalms), may leave room for considerable ambiguity and uncertainty.[128]

The jury is still out on how exactly the verb forms in Hebrew poetry are to be rendered in English. Adding to the complication is the question of how the aspect of the verbs (perfective or imperfective) interact with their *Aktionsart* (whether they are fientive, describing an action, or stative, describing a state of being).[129] These temporal problems of verbs in Hebrew poetry have afflicted many a scholar with literary *phthisis*.[130] The good news for us preachers is that, since we are in the business of drawing somewhat more general conclusions as to the application of pericopal theology, the fine nuances descried by grammarians may not make much difference for homileticians. For instance, take the following forms of an English proverb:

Curiosity had killed the cat.
Curiosity killed the cat.
Curiosity kills the cat.
Curiosity is killing the cat.
Curiosity will kill the cat.

For preaching purposes any of those will generate a reasonable application: *Don't be curious, lest something awful befall you!* Nonetheless, I confess that the task of a translator of Hebrew poetry remains arduous. The ambiguity and unclarity of verb translation is further compounded by other features of Hebrew poetry, such as "terseness, contrast, juxtaposition, phonetic considerations, and the like. The paratactic character of the cola [clauses without words to clarify coordination or subordination] and the caesura [line interruptions/pauses] break the sequential mode of connection characteristic of narrative.... An effort to give a full and logical accounting of verb tense and word order in some texts (i.e., poetic) still escapes us and perhaps always will."[131]

In my translation I render divine pronouns capitalized for the sake of clarity; they refer to deity without the need for glossing. But I also agree with Moberly that "capitalization implicitly presupposes and gestures towards the classic theological understanding that God is beyond gender as we understand it and that the biblical writers' own gendered usage is to be understood in a qualified way when the Bible is read as Scripture."[132] I have also maintained "Yahweh" as the translation of יהוה, *yhwh*; I hold that the term indicates the Trinitarian Godhead.[133]

"Selah" occurs about seventy-one times in thirty-nine Psalms.[134] In the Psalter it occurs, for the most part, in those psalms that have titles, usually those associated with David and/

---

128. Craigie, *Psalms 1–50*, 111.

129. For the most part, for these distinctions I have followed Zwighuizen, "Time Reference of Verbs," particularly her three appendices, 139–97.

130. I.e., φθίσις, "consumption," likely tuberculosis, as used by Hippocrates of Cos (fifth century BCE) (*Aphorisms* 7.16 [*Nature of Man*, 196–97]).

131. Miller, "Theological Significance," 221–22. He notes that prophetic poetry is often more predictable and tends towards standardized Hebrew prose syntax, unlike psalmic poetry (222n30).

132. Moberly, *God of the Old Testament*, 12.

133. See Eldhose, "Trinitarian Interpretation."

134. And thrice in Habakkuk: 3:3, 9, 13.

or the "Music Director" (see below for my take on superscriptions). This suggests that it has some musical connotation, either for vocalists or for instrumentalists.[135] It might be derived from the root "to raise, lift up," and thus could be an indication to singers of the volume of sound to be produced. The LXX translates "Selah" as διάψαλμα, *diapsalma*, "apart from the psalm," perhaps meaning "pause/interlude." Targumic tradition has לעלמין, *l'lmyn*, "forever," for סֶלָה, *selah*; the Vulgate omits it altogether. But I think Goldingay's take on the meaning of "Selah" is the most attractive explanation of them all: "I understand that David Allan Hubbard advocated the theory that it was what David said when he broke a string, which is the most illuminating theory because there is no logic about when you break a string, and there is no logic about the occurrence of *selâ*."[136] To that I say, "Selah!"

Superscriptions of the Psalter

As for superscriptions, they are present in 116 of the 150 psalms in the MT, while 148 of the 150 psalms in the LXX possess them (the ones lacking them in the LXX are Psalms 1–2). Though the evidence is not consistent between the various Qumran scrolls, generally David is given credit for four more psalms in the Dead Sea Psalter than in the MT (Psalms 33; 91; 104; 123). On the other hand, in those documents David does not get the credit for Psalm 144 (as he does in the MT and LXX). Clearly there was an ongoing fine-tuning of the superscriptions of those texts. This variation suggests that superscriptions were an evolved addendum to the text rather than an integral portion thereof.

In particular, attribution of Davidic authorship to many of the psalms appears to have been a notion that took hold later than the time of the text's composition.[137] Middleton, after surveying "Davidic" superscriptions in the MT, LXX, and the Qumran Psalter, suggests that "psalms superscriptions were still in a state of flux even into the early first century of the Common Era (when the Qumran Psalms scroll from Cave 11 is dated). This would indicate that the superscriptions are later than the psalms themselves, and cannot be taken as definitive historical evidence for Davidic authorship."[138] The associated events in David's life noted in the various superscriptions do not show up in them in any chronological order of incidents that we know of, and they are scattered among the different books of the Psalms, again suggesting their later addition.

In any case, the denotation of the phrase לדוד, *ldwd*, is rather ambiguous. The preposition לְ, *l*, could indicate "*to/of/for* David," "*sponsored by* David,"[139] "*on behalf of* David," or

---

135. Craigie, *Psalms 1–50*, 76.

136. Goldingay, *Psalms*, 3:643. Hubbard was Fuller Seminary's president for thirty years; Goldingay occupied the David Allan Hubbard Chair in Old Testament at that institution for two decades, until his retirement in 2018. In the Psalter, *Selah* occurs at the end of four psalms (Pss 3; 9; 24; and 46) and in the middle of two verses (55:19; 57:3). It does not show up at all in Book IV. These oddities confound any rationalization. There are what appear to be other musical directions both within (in Pss 6; 7; 9; 32; 46; 53) and without (9:16) the superscriptions; these have not been rendered here in English either.

137. See Kugel, "David the Prophet," 45–55 (especially 49–55). Also see Mroczek, "Hegemony," 2–35.

138. See Middleton, "Psalm against David?," 30.

139. David's patronage of psalm hymnody is attested in 1 Chr 15:16–24. The general admission of the Psalms as being Davidic is supported by the Psalter's association with music and David described as the "pleasant singer of Israel" (2 Sam 23:1), an inventor of musical instruments (Amos 6:5), one who appointed musicians for temple worship (1 Chr 15:16–24; 16:7), who left directions for performance of praise (Ezra 3:10; Neh 12:24), and with whom generally biblical history has associated the Psalms (in the OT: 2 Sam 22 =

perhaps even indicating "*belonging to* the Davidic collection." Besides, there is also the possibility "David" can mean the "Davidide," a subsequent Davidic king, perhaps messianic (as in Jer 30:9; Ezek 34:23–24; 37:24–25; Hos 3:5). Indeed, this imprecision of the meaning of ל is indicated by the employment of that preposition in superscriptions of psalms that have both למנצח, *lmntstsch* (relating to "The Music Director") *and* לדוד—Psalms 11–14. There is no particular reason why they should be considered differently—"*for* the Music Director" and "*by* David," respectively.[140] Albert Pietersma has shown that the predominant equivalent of לדוד in the LXX is τῷ Δαυίδ [*tō Dauid*]. Some Greek manuscripts, however, read τοῦ Δαυίδ [*tou Dauid*]: the genitive seems to have been introduced secondarily, because of the widespread understanding of the difference in the two terms, with the latter more precisely indicating Davidic authorship.[141] For instance, Didymus the Blind in the fourth century explained that the two phrases meant different things: "τοῦ Δαυίδ it says w[he]n he himself composed or sang it; 'to him' [i.e., τῷ Δαυίδ] it says when it refers to him."[142]

The NT does link Davidic authorship with certain psalms (Psalm 2 in Acts 4:24–28; Psalm 16 in Acts 2:25–32; Psalm 32 in Rom 4:6–8; Psalms 69 and 109 in Acts 1:15–20; Rom 11:9–10; Psalm 95 in Heb 4:7; and Psalm 110 in Mark 12:35–37; Acts 2:33–35). However, that may simply indicate the accepted convention by the time of the Christian era of the Psalter as being, in general, the production of David.[143] For instance, Acts 4 acknowledges Psalm 2 as Davidic though neither the MT nor the LXX has a superscription for Psalm 2. And only the LXX attributes Psalm 95 to David with τῷ Δαυίδ (Psalm 95 does not have a superscription in the MT).

It appears then that these superscriptions "are frequently of more importance for understanding the role of particular psalms in the context of the Psalter and in the historical context of Israel's worship than they are for understanding the original meaning and context of the individual psalms."[144] Perhaps they intend to point the reader in the general direction of application. In any case, I concur with Ross that, "in the final analysis, the message of the psalm will come from the exegesis of the psalm itself, without the need for a reference to a

---

Ps 18:2–50; 1 Chr 16:8–36 = Ps 105:1–15; etc.; and in the NT: Mark 12:35–37; Acts 2:29–35; 13:35–37; etc.). A non-poetic epilogue to 11QPs[a] also describes David's literary activity—a total of 4,050 songs, making him more prolific than Solomon, who composed only 4,005 (that is, proverbs + songs; 1 Kgs 4:32).

140. The only instance of an unambiguous use of ל to ascribe authorship is in Hab 3:1: תְּפִלָּה לַחֲבַקּוּק, *tphillah lachavaqquq*, "a prayer *of* Habakkuk." In fact, even the two similar psalms, Psalms 14 and 53, have different superscriptions (Palms 14 has "The Music Director's. David's."; and Psalm 53 has "The Music Director's. Set to *Machalat*. Instruction. David's."). Rather than parse the preposition ל, I would rather translate those terms neutrally, as shown: "The Music Director's" and "David's" (following Goldingay in his commentaries on the Psalter, *Psalms* [3 volumes]).

141. See Pietersma, "David in the Greek Psalms," 215–17.

142. My translation from Didymus's Greek introduction to Ps 24:1 in the Tura Psalms commentary (in *TLG* online).

143. Jesus himself connects David with Ps 110, integrating Davidic authorship in his argumentation in the NT (110:1 in Matt 22:43–44; Mark 12:36; Luke 20:42–43). Of course, there is no reason to think that David had not written *that particular psalm*; Jesus's attestation renders that possibility distinct, but it does not say anything about the psalmic superscriptions as a whole. Perhaps the attributions to David in psalm headings may be likened to the common practice of calling the English Bible (and its descendants), that was first translated in 1611 under the auspices of King James VI and I (1566–1625), the "King James Version." The use of *specific* nomenclature to indicate *generalities* occurs commonly in language, for e.g., brand names like Kleenex and Huggies stand for more than those specific products manufactured by the Kimberly-Clark Corporation.

144. Craigie, *Psalms 1–51*, 31.

specific event."[145] That may well have been the deliberate intent of the Psalter: the relative absence of context renders every psalm applicable to the lives of God's people living in any era and in any place.

Preaching the Psalms

Some might question the validity of preaching from a "hymnbook" such as the Psalter. But it, too, as was noted, is an integral part of God-breathed Scripture, and as such "profitable for teaching, for reproof, for correction, for training in righteousness so that the person of God may be capable, fully equipped for every good work" (2 Tim 3:16–17). Perhaps its division into five books (Psalms 1–41, 42–72, 73–89, 90–106, and 107–150) suggests that the Psalter is intended for use as a manual for teaching, just as is the fivefold Torah.[146] Goldingay submits, however, that the division of the books of the Psalms is "random."[147] For preaching purposes at least, it is best not to make too much of intra-book or inter-book connections, or even of canonical ones at that. Pericopal theology cannot be preached in any other way but by attending to a given pericope (in this case, a given psalm).[148] In this, a psalm is no different from a pericope of prophetic, didactic, or narrative literature.[149]

I see the Psalter as a gathering of prayers, grouped together by any number of criteria: catch words, themes, sometimes clearly discernible progressions between members, etc. I do not see the book as having any specific overarching theme, as do narratives or even epistolary literature, beyond the generalities encompassed by the first and last psalm—the journey from duty to delight—with real life lived by real people depicted in between (see above). Therefore,

---

145. Ross, *Psalms*, 1:47.

146. But, with regard to "teaching," I would strongly recommend that the exposition of other theologies (systematic, biblical, canonical) not be the staple and stable diet proffered to the people of God from the pulpit at their formal weekly corporate gathering for worship. Such discourses are best carried out outside of such assemblies of the church, say in Sunday School classes, Adult Bible Fellowships, Wednesday prayer meetings, and so on. What has been sorely lacking in pulpit preaching is the exposition of pericopal theology leading to valid application.

147. Goldingay, *Psalms*, 1:23.

148. That is not a neglect of the biblical metanarrative or even categories of biblical or systematic theology; the grand story and broad trajectory of Scripture, as well as an understanding of who God is and what he is all about, undergirds, and is foundational to, the theological thrust of each pericope. The former stands as the guardrail for the latter; the latter must not contradict the former. The former, for preaching purposes, is quite general, while the latter is far more specific and narrowly directs the response of God's people to the call of that particular pericope. Of course, the sequences of pericopes in a given book, like Genesis, or Mark, or Ephesians, generates an inter-pericopal coherence that must be respected in order to discern the intra-pericopal thrust (pericopal theology) of a given passage chosen for preaching. However, that is not the case for the Psalter, the church's hymnbook/prayerbook.

149. While there are, of course, genre differences, and considerations that must be given to such differences, the discernment of pericopal theology occurs at a level more foundational to language than the distinction of genres. As an analogy, if one is analyzing the foundational elements of foods—carbohydrates, lipids, and proteins—these are found in all kinds of "genres" of foods: breakfast foods, lunch foods, and dinner foods, food from the US, food from India, and food from Kuwait, in foods from the first century, from the twenty-first, and from every other era. For an analysis of food composition, those "genres" are quite irrelevant. I am not minimizing discriminations of genres, but only claiming that the discernment of pericopal theology occurs at the fundamental level of how language functions (whether spoken or scripted). Therefore preachers should, of necessity, be focused upon discerning the foundational element of biblical texts, pericopal theology, that furthers the deriving of application. For further reading, see Kuruvilla, *Privilege the Text!* and Kuruvilla, *Text to Praxis*.

for preaching purposes, it is best to see the Psalter a library; the preacher is responsible for choosing the right psalm for the right occasion.[150] All that to say, besides Psalms 42 and 43 that I have treated as a single unit, the remaining 148 units are analyzed individually.[151]

Achtemeier is right:

> Sermons from the Psalms have the principal aim of calling forth from the covenant people of God a response appropriate to their nature as God's chosen people and a response worthy to be made to the God of the covenant. Thus, sermons from the Psalms are absolutely indispensable for growth into Christian maturity. For this reason, I think it absolutely important that we preach often from the Psalter—because that growth into Christian maturity is a goal we have lost in modern American life—growth in sanctification, the theologians call it, growth in personal and congregational goodness, or in New Testament terms, growth up into the measure of the fullness of the stature of Christ. We have largely lost that as a goal for even Christian lives. Who wants to be good anymore in our particular cultures? We want to be successful, assertive, integrated, liberated . . . but good? That is not a goal that comes often to our minds.[152]

With the goal of preaching being primarily the conveyance of the thrust of the word of God (pericopal theology) so that listeners' lives may be changed unto Christlikeness by the power of the Spirit and for the glory of God (a christiconic interpretation of the text), the force and impact of every pericope of every book of every Testament of Scripture is to be preached, including of those individual chapters in the Psalms (a pericope here is a particular psalm).[153] In fact, in the early church, the requirement for elders/bishops/overseers (those leaders in the church exercising a pastoral role) to possess a profound understanding of the Psalms was codified in Canon 2 of the Second Council of Nicaea (787 CE): "We decree that everyone who is to be advanced to the grade of bishop [ἐπισκοπή, episkopē; Latin: episcopatus; "overseer"/"elder"] should have a thorough knowledge of the psalter, in order that he may instruct all the clergy subordinate to him, to be initiated in that book."[154]

---

150. To that end, I have also attempted to categorize the psalms generally: see Topical Index of Psalms in volume 3 of this work. This is an attempt to aid the preacher in choosing a particular psalm for preaching. It might be worthwhile to scan the list of topics in that index as one tries to decide on which psalm to employ in a sermon.

151. A word on Psalm 119: I suggest that *one* (or a couple) of its alphabetical sections be preached at a time, and that this psalm not be preached in its entirety, either at a single session, or as a series of sermons in back-to-back sessions. The individual thrusts of each section are too similar to be able to derive unique sermons from each. They are, however, different enough for each section to be employed for a particular situation or *Sitz im Leben* of the congregation, as the pastor sees fit.

152. Achtemeier, "Preaching from the Psalms," 442–43. Of course, such a goal is valid for the exposition of *every* pericope of Scripture.

153. The secondary role of the preacher as the spiritual formation director, pastor, elder, parent-figure of the flock calls upon the homiletician to make the discerned pericopal theology relevant to the current and contemporary circumstances of listeners, and to derive for them valid and specific application. (For more on these notions, see Kuruvilla, *Vision for Preaching* and Kuruvilla, *Manual for Preaching*, as well as a number of journal articles: "Pericopal Theology," 3–17; "Christiconic Interpretation," 131–46; "Theological Exegesis," 259–72; and "Applicational Preaching," 387–400.) To further this end, I provide a barebones sermon map for each psalm, a scaffolding upon which the preacher may build. (Needless to add, the obsessive alliteration in those maps is something I engaged in purely for the thrill of the challenge it posed, to find appropriate words while operating within certain alphabetic or assonant constraints.)

154. Tanner, *Decrees of the Ecumenical Councils, Volume 1*, 139.

Organization of the Psalter

The origins of the psalms are not very clear. They are attributed to David (Psalms 3–32; 34–41; 51–65; 68–72; 108–110; 138–145); Asaph (Psalms 50; 73–83); Solomon (Psalms 72; 127); Moses (Psalm 90); Heman the Ezrahite (Psalm 88); Ethan the Ezrahite (Psalm 89); and the sons of Korah (Psalms 42; 44–49; 84–85; 87–88). It is likely that the Psalter became a "collection of collections":[155] from individual writings to a collation of those writings, and later to a compilation of those collections. That was perhaps followed by (if not simultaneously undergoing) the editing of this collection of collections to create the final product, the Psalter.[156]

The psalms in the Psalter are organized in "books," as shown, distinguished by the doxologies that occur at the end of each book:

BOOKS	*PSALMS*	DOXOLOGIES
Book I	Psalms 1–41	41:13
Book II	Psalms 42–72	72:18–19
Book III	Psalms 73–89	89:52
Book IV	Psalms 90–106	106:48
Book V	Psalms 107–150	150:1–6 (150:6)

These "books" (and even the whole book of Psalms) are roughly organized,[157] but not necessarily creating an order that makes it incumbent for the interpreter to proceed through sequentially for preaching. Goldingay asserts, and I agree, "that I am not enamored of this study [of] the arrangement of the psalms and the way sequences of psalms belong together and expound a theological view of their own." He explains: "It seems to me to involve too much imagination in the connecting of too few dots. I recognize that there are often links between adjacent psalms, but I remain of the view that the main focus of psalm study needs to be the individual psalm."[158] From the days of yore, interpreters clearly have struggled (unsuccessfully, in my opinion) to formulate a homiletical order for the Psalter that would necessitate a sequential psalm-by-psalm preaching of pericopal theology.

---

155. Craigie, *Psalms 1–50*, 28.

156. The obvious collections within the Psalter are the Psalms of Ascent (Psalms 120–134), the Egyptian Hallel collection (Psalms 113–118), and the Hallel Psalms (Psalms 146–150). Though Ps 72:20 indicates the end of the prayers of David, there are eighteen more psalms attributed to him, further evidence that the Psalms is a "collection of collections." Validating that notion is also the fact that the same psalm is found in different books of the Psalter (Ps 14 = Ps 53; Ps 40:13–17 = Ps 70; Ps 108 = Ps 57:7–11 + 60:5–12).

157. For instance, at least as far as superscriptions are concerned, Psalms 11–15 are both "The Music Director's [לַמְנַצֵּחַ, *lmnatstseach*]" and "David's [לְדָוִד, *ldawid*]"; and Psalms 65–68 are designated both as "Song [שִׁיר, *shir*]" and as "Psalm [מִזְמוֹר, *mizmor*]." With regard to psalm themes: Psalms 95–99 deal with kingship; Psalms 113–118 constitute the Egyptian Hallel used at Passover, the first two before the meal and the last four after; Psalms 120–134 are the Psalms of Ascents; Psalms 135–136 is the Great Hallel; and Psalms 146–150 are the Hallel Psalms. This is akin to contiguous hymns being related in theme in any hymnbook (and possibly sharing vocabulary as well).

158. Goldingay, *Psalms*, 2:11. The Midrash on the Psalms declares: "As to the exact order of David's Psalms, Scripture says elsewhere: '*Man knoweth not the order thereof* (Job 28:13).' . . . The proper order of the sections of Scripture is hidden from mortals and is known only to the Holy One, blessed be He, who said: '*Who, as I, can read and declare it, and set it in order[?]*' (Isa 44:7)." Thus "when R. Joshua ben Levi sought to arrange the Psalms in their proper order, a heavenly voice came forth and commanded: 'Do not rouse that which slumbers!'" (Braude, *Midrash on the Psalms*, 50 [italics original]).

> The arrangement of the Psalms, which seems to me to contain the secret of a mighty mystery, hath not yet been revealed unto me [on Psalm 150:1]. . . . Now in that some have believed that the Psalms are divided into five books, they have been led by the fact, that so often at the end of Psalms are the words, "so be it, so be it" ["Amen and amen"]. But when I endeavoured to make out the principle of this division, I was not able; for neither are the five parts equal one to another, neither in quantity of contents, nor yet even in number of Psalms [on Psalm 150:2].[159]

Clearly hymns in a hymnbook are not intended to be sung through sequentially from the first to the last in the order they are printed. So also, the psalms are not intended to be preached from the first to the last in the order within the Psalter. Rather, these are the ultimate texts for topical preaching—i.e., the responsible leader, understanding the people and the times, decides on a particular topic and then picks a psalm that addresses that issue.[160] All that to say, while I do not deny a canonical shaping of the Psalter (its beginning and end are validation enough), I do not necessarily see its value in the preaching an individual psalm.

The analogy between the Psalter and a standard hymnbook is not adventitious. Wesley's preface to his 1780 hymnal may well have served as a comment on the Psalter: "The hymns are not carelessly jumbled together, but carefully ranged under proper heads, according to the experience of real Christians. So that this book is, in effect, a little body of experimental and practical divinity."[161] One may well consider the Psalms a bank of preachable prayers from which to draw. May the preaching of those prayers edify the people of God by the power of the Spirit of God, extend the kingdom of the Son of God, and exalt the name of the Father God!

---

159. Augustine, *Exposition on the Psalms* (*NPNF1* 8:681).

160. Not topical in the sense of preaching multiple verses from discrete biblical pericopes, all being brought to bear upon a single topic, but rather that according to the pastoral need of the hour, a psalm is chosen for homiletical purposes, just as is a song from a hymnbook.

161. Wesley, *Collection of Hymns*, 4.

PSALM 1:1–6

Psalm of Orientation

Delighting in the Word

THE PSALTER IS A book of songs, but Psalm 1 is hardly a representative of that genre. Rather, as a psalm of orientation, it is "a poem commenting on how life works," more in line with Wisdom literature (as for e.g., Prov 2:1–15, 20–22) and, in particular, functioning as a beatitude.[1] But, along with Psalm 2 that proclaims the reign of God and his Anointed, this first psalm sets the stage for the rest of the collection with its emphasis on the way of the righteous. Aquinas called it "as it were, the title of the entire work."[2] And, Psalm 1, Jerome claimed, is "the main entrance to the mansion of the Psalter."[3]

Psalms 1 and 2

In Book 1 (Psalms 1–41) of the Psalter, there are only four psalms without superscriptions: Psalms 1 and 2, 10 (considered as continuing Psalm 9), and 33 (but it has τῷ Δαυιδ, *tō Dauid*, "David's," in the LXX).[4] This suggests that Psalms 1 and 2 may well belong together, forming a joint introduction to the Psalms.[5] Links between the first two psalms include: "blessing" in 1:1a and 2:12d;[6] "sit" in 1:1d (and scoffing) and 2:4a (and laughing and mocking); הגה, *hgh*, in 1:2b ("meditate") and 2:1b ("conspire"); "path" and the "perishing" with regard to it (1:1c,

---

1. Goldingay, *Psalms*, 1:80.

2. Aquinas, *Exposition of the Psalms of David: Psalm 1*. Indeed, the first word of this psalm begins with א, *aleph*, the last begins with ת, *taw*—from "A to Z" so to speak. So "this psalm embraces all that a happy/blessed individual needs for living life according to the Lord's precepts. An acrostic is suited to this emphasis on totality" (Petersen and Richards, *Interpreting Hebrew Poetry*, 94). Notably, in the Leningrad Codex, Psalm 1 is unnumbered.

3. *Homilies of Saint Jerome, Vol. 1*, 3.

4. On superscriptions and my take on them, please see Introduction.

5. There are references in the Talmud that assert the union of the first two psalms. According to R. Yehuda: "'Happy is the man' [Ps 1:1a] and 'Why are the nations in uproar' [Ps 2:1a] constitute a single chapter" (*b. Ber.* 9b; also see 10a) (see https://www.sefaria.org/Berakhot.9b.30). Justin Martyr (*Apology* 1.40) quoted Psalms 1–2 without a break, and Tertullian cited Ps 2:7 as coming from the "first psalm" (*Against Marcion* 4.22 [ANF 3:384]), as also does Bezae Cantabrigiensis (D^ea, a fifth-century NT codex) in Acts 13:33.

6. In fact, the final macarism of 2:12d does not seem particularly necessary to the conclusion of Psalm 2, but it creates an explicit link to 1:1.

6 and 2:12b); noun עֵץ, *'ets*, "tree," in 1:3a and adverb עַתָּה, *'attah*, "now," in 2:10a; "day" (יוֹמָם, *yomam*) in 1:2b and "today" (הַיּוֹם, *hayyom*) in 2:7c; "judgment" in 1:5a and "judges" in 2:10b; fate of the wicked/rebellious (1:4 and 2:5, 9, 12abc; and in both, this is portrayed by similes: 1:4b and 2:9b). Indeed, the righteous individual of Psalm 1 is a parallel to Yahweh's Anointed in Psalm 2: the delight of the former in Yahweh's "law" (1:2) is matched by the declaration of the latter of Yahweh's "statute" (2:7a); the one is "transplanted by canals of water" (1:3b), and the other is "installed . . . upon Zion, My holy mountain" (2:6).[7] And likewise, the "wicked" and "sinners" and "scoffers" of Psalm 1 meet their kin in "nations" and "peoples" and "kings" and "rulers" of Psalm 2; the former are scattered like chaff blown in the wind (1:4b), and the latter are shattered like pots by one wielding a rod of iron (2:9). Fruitfulness, delight, and honor are for those who disassociate themselves from the wicked (Psalm 1), and also for those who associate themselves with Yahweh's Anointed (Psalm 2).[8]

Translation

1:1 Blessing [upon] the person
    who has not walked by the advice of the wicked,
    or in the path of sinners stood,
    nor in the seat of scoffers sat.

1:2 But, instead, in the law of Yahweh [is] his delight,
    and in His law he meditates day and night.

1:3 And he is like a tree
    transplanted by canals of water,
which its fruit—it yields in its season,
    and its foliage—it does not wither;
    and [in] all he does, he succeeds.

1:4 Not so the wicked;
    instead, [they are] like chaff which is blown away [by] wind.

1:5 Therefore the wicked will not rise up in the judgment,
    nor sinners in the assembly of the righteous.

1:6 For Yahweh knows the path of the righteous,
    but the path of the wicked perishes.

---

7. If the channels of water are an allusion to the temple (Ezek 47:12), and if the "transplantation" is into the house of Yahweh (Ps 92:13), then the referents of 1:3 and 2:6 may be even more similar.

8. Botha, "Ideological Interface," 202.

Structure

The psalm appears to be carefully structured:[9]

> **The Blessing of the Righteous (1:1–3)**
> *Introduction* (1:1a; "blessing")
> **A** Description of the righteous (1:1b–2): 3 negations (לֹא, *lo'*; "path")
> **B** Agricultural simile with אֲשֶׁר ... כְּעֵץ (*k'ets ... 'asher*), 1:3abcd)
> **C** Summary: righteous (1:3e)
>
> **The Bane of the Wicked (1:4–6)**
> **C'** Summary: wicked (1:4a)
> **B'** Agricultural simile with אֲשֶׁר כַּמֹּץ (*kamotz 'asher*, 1:4b)
> **A'** Description of the wicked (1:5): 1 negation (לֹא); "path" (×2)
> *Conclusion* (1:6; "perishes")

Theological Focus

> The fertile stasis of the righteous—constant, affective intercourse with divine revelation, the outcome of which is fruitfulness—results in the blessing of divine care of their ways; but the futile kinesis of the wicked, the outcome of which is fruitlessness, results in divine judgment, the destruction of their ways.

Commentary

The Blessing of the Righteous (1:1–3)

There clearly is a "profound awareness of a deep ideological divide between two groups of people in society"—righteous vs. wicked.[10] The wicked have all kinds of schemes, stances, seats, and scoffing (1:1); the righteous are characterized by one delight—the constant meditation upon the *Torah* of Yahweh. The two are incompatible and cannot mingle, as 1:1 and 1:5 detail. Alter notes that,

> in a manner rather uncharacteristic of biblical poetic style, the psalmist takes pains to place explicit indicators of logical transition ... [כִּי אִם, *ki 'im*, "instead" (1:2); לֹא־כֵן, *lo'-ken*, "not so" (1:4a); כִּי אִם, *ki 'im* (1:4b); and עַל־כֵּן, *'al-ken*, "therefore" (1:5)]. Reality is thus made to yield an exact moral calculus: there are things the just man will not do; indeed, there is something antithetical he does instead; the

---

9. Modified from Petersen and Richards, *Interpreting Hebrew Poetry*, 96.
10. Botha, "Ideological Interface," 192. The "righteous" one is not to be mistaken for one who is sinless; in the Psalms it indicates guiltlessness and innocence in the generality of one's life, describing one who is loyal to Yahweh, an integral member of the community of God. The first word of the Psalm is "blessing," and the last, "perishes" (as was noted, they respectively begin with the first and last letters of the alphabet: אַשְׁרֵי, *'ashre*, and תֹּאבֵד, *to'ved*). The contrast is further heightened by "instead" in 1:2a, 4b.

fate of the wicked is the contrary of the fate of the just; and there is a consequential generalizing summary . . . [1:6] to be drawn from what has been asserted.[11]

There appears to be a progression in the walking, standing, and sitting that is characteristic of the wicked and those who choose their ways:[12] "Listening to people formulating plans is one thing. Acting on them is another. Spending one's life in the company of such schemers is to walk into a marsh from which one is unlikely to emerge."[13] So there is clearly work involved in the gaining of divine blessing by the righteous: "Their happy estate is not something given automatically by God, but is a direct result of their activity."[14] They are to "not . . . walk," "[not] stand," and "[not] sit" with the wicked, but they are to "delight" and "meditate" in Yahweh's *Torah*.[15] In light of the negations of 1:1, the "law of Yahweh" (1:2) is, in contrast, to be reckoned as the righteous person's "advice" to walk by, "path" to stand on, and "seat" to be established upon. This is an invitation to the joy of divine revelation for communion with the *Torah*-giver and for the conduct of one's life as a *Torah*-lover.

Broadly, תּוֹרָה, *torah*, indicates "instruction" or "teaching"; "specifically, it is the instruction which God gives to mankind as a guide for life. Thus it may include that which is technically law, but it also includes other more general parts of God's revelation," whether narrative (the Pentateuch), poetry (Prov 3:1; 7:2; 28:4, 7, 9), or prophecy (Isa 1:10; Dan 9:10).[16] Therein is guidance for life from the Creator of life, without which guidance the life of mankind is futile; but with it—by its delight to the devout and in their meditation of it, as Ps 1:3 affirms—life is fertile.

The verb הגה, *hgh*, "meditate" (1:2b) is also found in Josh 1:8, also in connection to the *Torah*. Indeed, the similarities are significant: both texts have "meditate day and night"; both have "law" and "success" (Ps 1:2–3). The linkage of the verb "meditate" with "mouth" in Josh 1:8 of course suggests reading, but it might include "recitation from memory or of rehearsing the traditional narratives [35:28; 37:30; 71:24]. Meditation might also signify the 'audible murmuring' of one whose thoughts are occupied in deep reflection upon God's words and deeds [143:5]."[17] הגה is also associated with singing: 71:23–24; and 77:12 with 77:6; the associated noun הִגָּיוֹן, *higgayon* (9:16; 92:3; untranslated), apparently a musical direction, may also link it with song. In any case, an intensive and continuous interaction with divine revelation—the outcome of a positive affect towards it—is the mark of the righteous person.

---

11. Alter, *Art of Biblical Poetry*, 144.

12. The "advice of the wicked" (1:1b) is their scheming, and "the path of sinners" (1:1c) their arrant lifestyle; "the seat of scoffers" (1:1d) is likely their derisive disposal of all matters theological.

13. Goldingay, *Psalms*, 1:83.

14. Craigie, *Psalms 1–50*, 60. On the distinction between good fortune and blessing, Goldingay (*Psalms*, 3:511) notes that "'good fortune' describes a state or an experience and does not comment on the agency that brings it about, while 'bless' refers to the personal action that generates that state or experience."

15. Seow observes that אַשְׁרֵי recalls אָשַׁר, *'ashar*, "to proceed/walk" (as in Prov 9:15); in fact, "walking" and "being blessed" are closely associated, not only in Ps 1:1 (negatively), but also in Pss 89:15; 119:1; 128:1 ("Exquisitely Poetic Introduction," 279n28).

16. Craigie, *Psalms 1–50*, 60. *Torah* is used in all these references. Janzen ("Psalm 1," 120) perspicaciously notes: "In 'Ikea' terms, *tôrāh* offers 'directions for assembling and enjoying a life.'" Indeed, I would argue that every pericope of Scripture, in both the Old and New Testaments, provides such a guide to life in its various aspects and parts, that facilitates the person of God becoming complete, inhabiting the ideal world of God, with God (i.e., becoming Christlike). Thereby, every pericope becomes a portion of the *Torah* in this broad sense.

17. Martin, "Delighting in the Torah," 722. The verb הגה is used in all these references, too.

While there is no doubt that this involves obedience to God's word, the emphasis here is upon the affections of the righteous: חפץ, *hpts*, "delight," 1:2a, can refer to romantic attraction (Gen 34:19; also see Pss 5:4; 16:3; 37:23; etc., where it refers to divine pleasure). "Delight" in the divine word is also found in 40:8; 112:1. If the focus here in 1:2 were on *Torah* as commandment to be obeyed, that could have been more precisely stated in a parallelism with another commandment-related word, as in 78:10 ("covenant"); 89:31 ("judgments"); or 105:45 ("statutes"). But the psalmist employs תּוֹרָה in both lines of the parallelism (1:2a and 1:2b). Indeed, though the term is found thirty-six times in the Psalter, only here is it found in parallel to itself. All that to say, "to delight in the Torah is an affective inclination, a passionate disposition. To delight in the Torah is to rejoice in it, to love it, to long for it, to desire it more than gold, and to enjoy it more than honey.... The emphasis of Ps 1 is not upon deeds but delight, not on duty but desire, not on obedience but on affections that are rightly oriented towards God."[18] A right attitude to the word of God is being inculcated here.

Such a one who is entranced in every way by God's word "is like a tree transplanted [שׁתל, *shtl*] by canals of water" (1:3a), ostensibly by God himself (the verb is passive), and perhaps into the very "house of Yahweh" and into "the courts of our God" (92:13; the same verb שׁתל occurs there, as well as the simile of trees that bear fruit: 92:12–14). That is to say, the righteous one, who "day and night" dwells on the divine word, dwells in the very presence of deity.

The agricultural simile proceeds to describe the fertility of the righteous person, the tree, culminating in "fruit" that "it yields in its season" (1:3c)—doing what the tree was grown for, producing what the tree was supposed to. So much so, "the state of blessedness or happiness is not a *reward*; rather it is the result of a particular type of life. Just as a tree with a constant water supply *naturally* flourishes, so too the person who avoids evil and delights in Torah *naturally* prospers, for such a person is living within the guidelines set down by the Creator. Thus the prosperity of the righteous reflects the wisdom of a life lived according to the plan of the Giver of all life."[19]

The Bane of the Wicked (1:3–6)

Interestingly enough, reading the three verbs applied to the wicked ones—walking, standing, and sitting (1:1)—we spy the nefarious person as being constantly on the move, active, lively, dynamic. On the other hand, the righteous one does not even get a verb in 1:2a. Then in 1:2b, with "meditate," this person is pictured as being relatively static, compared to the perpetually perambulating profane persons who are engaged in activities that are futile. Subsequently, in 1:3b, the verb "transplant" is employed, a participle that denotes the very opposite of active movement: this "tree" is docked and moored and anchored to a water supply. And thereby, the righteous becomes fruitful, non-withering, and successful (1:3cde)—fertile!—for this is the activity that matters: delight in Yahweh's law, meditating upon Yahweh's instruction for life (and consequently following it, of course). This is the life-trajectory of the righteous, one that extends into the future on a "path" that does not perish, for Yahweh intimately "knows" their

---

18. Martin, "Delighting in the Torah," 716 (and see 714).

19. Craigie, *Psalms 1–50*, 61 (emphases original). Though, as was noted earlier, there are responsibilities to be undertaken (1:1–2), fruit is a "natural" consequence of those activities.

way (1:6a).[20] That makes sense: if they know *him* (through their constant intercourse with his revelation), he knows *them* and their ways, too.

In contrast, we again see the wicked in perpetual motion in 1:4, but this time suffering a punitive outcome: they are unstable, scattered, and susceptible to the caprices of the wind—chaff, worthless husks, merely the feckless and sterile object of another agent that blows them away![21] "The wicked are in constant motion, restless, without direction, carried hither and thither by forces over which they exert no control."[22] They are unable to rise (1:5a),[23] and finally they perish (1:6b). In other words, "the poem is shown to run into a dead end for the wicked: walking, standing, and sitting on and along the road of the wicked spell deceleration, a coming to a standstill . . . and eventually destruction."[24] What an irony—the "evocation of impotent kinesis over against fruitful stasis."[25]

The destruction apparently happens via a divine judgment (1:5) in which the wicked are unable to "rise up" or stand successfully, unlike the righteous who come out of that divine assize to join a triumphant assembly. Notably, at the end, there is no mention of how, or at whose hands, the wicked perish.[26]

> Like chaff it is insubstantial waste and goes with the wind. While there are many biblical hints of God's judgment upon those who go such a way, in this psalm one senses that it is almost in the nature of things that the wicked way goes under. . . . This psalm suggests to us—and bids us open our eyes to look for the evidence—that in a more proximate sense wickedness often does itself in and leads to its own destruction in a world that is shaped and governed by God's moral order.[27]

That, too, holds up to scrutiny, for the contrasting picture asserts equivalently that the seemingly natural outcome of deep interaction with God's word is fruitfulness (1:2–3; see above), just as the rejection thereof attains its own seemingly natural end—perdition (1:4–5, 6b). And now, for the first time in this Psalm (and in the Psalter), in 1:6a Yahweh appears as subject of a verb. God "knows," intimately, the "path" of the righteous: he is personally involved with them. But as for the wicked, he simply lets those reprobates go their own way, on their own "path"—and they "perish"! Thus we see further contrasts: the "advice of the wicked" (בַּעֲצַת רְשָׁעִים, *ba'atsat rsha'im*; 1:1) vs. the "assembly of the righteous (בַּעֲדַת צַדִּיקִים, *ba'adat tsaddiqim*; 1:5); as well as the "path of sinners" that began the psalm (1:1c) and the "path of the righteous" and the "path of the wicked" that conclude it (1:6).

---

20. God's "knowing," from ידע, *yd'*, is an intimate acquaintance, not a distant perception.

21. "The wicked themselves are not even accorded the dignity of being a proper grammatical subject of an active verb: windblown like chaff, whatever way they go on is trackless, directionless, doomed" (Alter, *Art of Biblical Poetry*, 146). Notice the phonological contrast between the agricultural similes: כְּעֵץ, "like a tree" (1:3a) vs. כַּמֹּץ, "like chaff" (1:4b).

22. Alter, *Art of Biblical Poetry*, 145 (see 144–45).

23. I.e., they have no place, no respect, and no standing, before the divine Judge.

24. Botha, "Ideological Interface," 194.

25. Alter, *Art of Biblical Poetry*, 146.

26. For unbelievers, this destruction is eschatological, but in the Psalms and much of OT literature, with their primary focus on the here-and-now, the perishing of the wicked might be more the antithesis of the success of the righteous in this life (1:3e), the counterposed general failure of the wicked person's schemes, stances, seats, and scoffing.

27. Miller, "Beginning of the Psalter," 85.

Sermon Map

I. Futility
   Wicked in constant kinesis (1:1b–d)
   Scheming, sinning, scoffing (1:1b–d)
   Outcome: judgment and perishing of ways (1:5a, 6b)
   Move-to-relevance: How we may be like the wicked

II. Fertility
   Righteous in relative stasis (1:2–3)
   Interaction with God's word and fruit-bearing (1:2–3)
   Outcome: judgment and divine care of ways (1:5b, 6a)
   Move-to-relevance: Why we are not like the righteous

III. *Be Blessed in Righteousness!*
   Specifics on a deeper interaction with divine revelation

PSALM 2:1–12

Psalm of Orientation

Respecting the King

LIKE PSALM 1, PSALM 2 is not a typical song; it is more of a proclamation or declaration. In the first psalm, the contrast was between the righteous and wicked in moral/ethical terms; here in the second, a similar contrast is created, but in political/national terms. And references to the righteous people of God are scant in Psalm 2; they show up only in the final macarism of 2:12d. Whereas the wicked in Psalm 1 were likely to be those within the community of God's people, the nefarious ones in Psalm 2 point to foreigners: "nations" and "peoples" and "kings" and "rulers" and "judges" (2:1–2b, 8b, 10). But like those in the first psalm who reject divine revelation, the evil ones in the second psalm reject divine reign (2:3). Thus the polarity in the second psalm is mostly between rebellious kings and Yahweh's King; ultimately it is "a declaration of faith in Yahweh's global rule."[1]

For much of the psalm, the focus is on utterances: it is a war of words. Most of the criticism of the wicked in Psalm 2 is directed against their verbal thrusts. They "rebel" and "conspire" (הגה, *hgh*, 2:1; this, in contrast to the righteous in 1:2 who "meditate" [also הגה] upon God's word[2]), they "take their stand" and "take counsel together" (2:2), and they arrogantly make announcements of secession from God, liberation from the constraints of deity and his interests (2:3). Correspondingly, their heavenly opponent parries: he "laughs" and "mocks" (2:4) and speaks angrily to them (2:5), and he makes his counter-announcement in 2:6. In turn, God's Anointed makes his own declaration, couching within it what God had affirmed to him (2:7–9). Then it is the psalmist's turn to appeal to the rebellious ones (2:10–12c).

Since in the history of Israel there was no time when its reign was as widespread as the psalm presupposes, and since we know of no such rebellion as is described in 2:1–3 or of the subjugation of recalcitrant potentates by deity, it must be an eschatological divine reign that is in view here, with the "Son" of God, the Anointed, as King. It is therefore fair to characterize Psalm 2 as a psalm of orientation describing an ideal state of matters: God rules, no matter who rebels, and the latter had best submit.

---

1. Botha, "Ideological Interface," 196–97.
2. Other links with Psalm 1 were noted under that chapter. Of course, 1:1 and 2:12 commence and conclude, respectively, with beatitudes, forming bookends around the first two psalms.

Translation

2:1 Why do they agitate, the nations,
    and the peoples, [why do] they conspire in vain?
2:2 They take their stand—kings of the earth,
    and rulers take counsel together
    against Yahweh and against His Anointed:
2:3 "Let us tear away their fetters,
    and let us throw off from us their ropes."
2:4 He who sits in the heavens laughs;
    the Lord mocks them.
2:5 Then He will speak to them in His anger,
    and in His fury He will terrify them.
2:6 "But I—I have installed My King
    upon Zion, My holy mountain."
2:7 "I shall tell of the statute of Yahweh:
    He said to Me, 'You are My Son;
    today I—I have begotten You.
2:8 Ask of Me, and I will give
    the nations as Your inheritance,
    and as Your possession, the ends of the earth.
2:9 You will break them with a rod of iron,
    like a vessel of a potter You will shatter them.'"
2:10 So now, kings, be sensible;
    be warned, judges of the earth.
2:11 Serve Yahweh with fear,
    and rejoice with trembling.
2:12 Do homage to the Son, that He not be angry,
    and you perish on the [rebellious] path,
    for His anger may soon blaze.
    Blessing [upon] all who seek refuge in Him.

PSALM 2:1–12

Structure

This psalm, too, is carefully structured:

> A
>> **Rebellion (2:1–3)**
>> *Extent*: "kings of the earth" (2:2a)
>> *Deity*: "Yahweh" (2:2c)
>> *Representative*: "Anointed" (2:2c)
>
> B
>> **Reaction (2:4–6)**
>> *Extent*: "heavens" (2:4a)
>> *Deity*: "Lord" (2:4b); "I myself" (2:6a)
>> *Representative*: "My King" (2:6a)
>
> B'
>> **Response (2:7–9)**
>> *Extent*: "ends of the earth" (2:8c)
>> *Deity*: "Yahweh" (2:7a); "I myself" (2:7c)
>> *Representative*: "My Son" (2:7b)
>
> A'
>> **Recommendation (2:10–12)**
>> *Extent*: "judges of the earth" (2:10b)
>> *Deity*: "Yahweh" (2:11a)
>> *Representative*: "Son" (2:12a)

There is an intriguing distribution of the name of deity in Psalm 2 (see figure above). In each of the four sections, the divine name occurs once, and the arrangement is chiastic in terms of its placement within each section. They are found in the middle verse of the first and fourth sections (יְהוָה, *yhwh*, in 2:2c and 2:11a), and in the first verses of the second and third sections (אֲדֹנָי, *'adonai*, and יְהוָה, respectively, in 2:4b and 2:7a). Remarkably, there are also four specific references to deity's representative, once in each section: "His Anointed" (2:2c), "My King" (2:6a), "My Son" (2:7b, the Hebrew בֵּן, *ben*), and "Son" (2:12a, the Aramaic בַּר, *bar*, ensuring that all four titles are different[3]). All that to show, this psalm is about God and his regent, their sovereignty over all, particularly over those who vainly attempt to reject their unified reign over creation.

Theological Focus

> The refusal of rebelling, conspiring, or opposing rulers anywhere to submit reverentially to divine rule, the scope and extent of which has no bounds, meets with an appropriate response—dismissive, dreadful, and destructive—from God and his personally appointed Son-King with whom he is closely identified.

---

3. This noun, בַּר, is also found in Prov 31:2–3 (×3) and in the Aramaic part of Daniel (in 3:25; 5:22; and 7:13). This also gives the psalm the three characters, enemies, God, and the Son/King, all three showing up in every section of the composition.

Commentary

Rebellion (2:1–3)

With הגה in 2:1b, the psalm commences by seeming to suggest that the nations are doing what was recommended in 1:2b, "meditate" (also הגה). But that is obviously not the case—they are "conspiring" (like a lion "growling," Isa 31:4; a sorcerer "muttering," 8:19; or the wicked "plotting," Prov 24:2—all employing הגה). The multitude of synonyms used of the wicked in 2:1–2—"nations," "peoples," "kings of the earth," and "rulers"—points to this rebellion and conspiracy as being global (later in 2:10 we also have "judges"). These petty despots "of the earth" (2:2a) pit themselves against God "in the heavens" (2:4a). "Why?" (2:1a). These revolts are in vain, for these same dodgy characters become the inheritance and possession of Yahweh's Son, the King (2:8). Implicitly Psalm 2 thus presents God's ideal world in which such things do *not* occur; instead, all nations, peoples, kings, rulers, and judges (are to) recognize the sovereignty of "Yahweh and His Anointed" (2:2c).

The artistry of the chiasm (with verb and noun elements), emphasizes the incredulity of what is happening:

"Why ...		
2:1aα	"agitate" (*perfect*)	
2:1aβ	"nations"	
2:1bα	"peoples"	
2:1bβ		"conspire" (*imperfect*)
2:2aα		"take their stand" (*imperfect*)
2:2aβ	"kings"	
2:2bα	"rulers"	
2:2bβ	"take counsel" (*perfect*)	
... against Yahweh and against His Anointed"		

Thus we have in *Rebellion*, 2:1–3, a description of a potential revolution against God (2:1–2), ending with a direct quote of the dissidents (2:3[4]); the form is repeated in the second section, *Reaction*, 2:4–6, with a description of divine reaction (2:4–5), followed by a direct quote of Yahweh (2:6).

Reaction (2:4–6)

The divine *Reaction* has four elements (corresponding with the four categories of impious dissenters in 2:1–2b): he "laughs," he "mocks," he "speaks," and he "terrifies" (2:4–5).[5] Yahweh's derision leads to scorn that leads to anger that culminates in his fury (2:4–5). This is

---

4. What exactly these restraints were is unclear. Perhaps it was the statutes of God, his word, that they were rebelling against.

5. Psalm 2:5 is chiastic in structure, with the wrath of God at its center: "Then He will speak to them / in His anger, // and in His fury / He will terrify them."

no trivial pique! The gang of rebels incur an appropriate response from God; and as a result, they will be terrified (2:5b).

Notice that the entirety of this second section (2:4–6) is bracketed by "in the heavens" (deity's center of operations; 2:4a) and the earthly "Zion, My holy mountain" (wherefrom deity's earthly representative officiates; 2:6b). The entire cosmos is under the dominion of God, from its highest reaches to its lowest depths. No anti-God rebellion is going to be overlooked or disregarded.

While the "King" installed by Yahweh may well have indicated a human king on the throne of David, there is a far closer association between God and King implied in Psalm 2 than would be expected of deity and a mere human: the nearest antecedent of "He" (in the participle "He who sits," 2:4a) is "His Anointed" (2:2c), but the parallelism with "Lord" (2:4b) and the subsequent verses in this section (2:5–6) suggest that the pronoun in 2:4a might also refer to Yahweh. The ambiguity is likely deliberate, portraying a complex and intertwined identity of deity and his regent. Both Yahweh and the Anointed gain the same preposition ("against") and are linked by "and" in 2:2c; the plural pronominal suffixes in "*their* fetters" and "*their* ropes" (2:3) include God and the King, thus seemingly equating both parties.

Then there is God's determination to install "My King" (2:6a) emphasized by the redundant use of אֲנִי, *ani*, "I," in 2:6a and 2:7c: "I—I have . . ." Deity is resolved to take action once and for all against the wicked rebels, and he does it himself by installing and begetting his King/Son—an unusually direct connection between God and his regent (more on this below).

Striking also is the absence of any mention of the royal descendants in Psalm 2. Second Samuel 7, on the other hand, declared God's blessings upon the posterity of David. But here this Son/King seems to have corralled for himself—as a single individual—the position allotted to all of David's descendants. In sum, this close association (identification?) of deity and ruler evokes messianic overtones, with a potential significance that extends beyond the earthly king (David) and his earthly kingdom (Israel).

Response (2:7–9)

There is a shift of speaker in the third section, 2:7–9; it is now the King who takes the microphone, and he makes a *Response*. But, rather surprisingly, all this one does is cite Yahweh: his is simply to do the will of the One who installed him.[6] For the first time in the psalm we hear of yet another intimate link between deity and his representative: the latter is the former's "Son," "begotten" of God. Sonship under the fatherhood of Yahweh was a position granted to the Davidic king (2 Sam 7:14; Ps 89:26–27), but it is far greater in scope and substance here. The "ends of the earth" (2:8c) are given by God to the Son—yes, it is his to give!—as his "inheritance" and "possession" (2:8), and thus the "judges of the earth" (2:10c; and the "kings of the earth," 2:2) are put on notice: they don't stand a chance rebelling against deity and his "Son." This Son-King will break them and shatter them (2:9), as he appropriates his

---

6. The "statute" and its telling (2:7a) may allude to a coronation ceremony, with its formal presentation of a written document to the successor regent (2 Kgs 11:12), with the "begetting" "today" (Ps 2:7c) likely being the day of installation. For the messianic King, his coronation, so to speak, may have occurred with Christ's resurrection and ascension to the right hand of the Father (Matt 26:24; Mark 14:62; Luke 22:69; Acts 7:56; Rom 8:34; Eph 1:20; 1 Pet 3:22; Heb 1:3, 13; 8:1; 10:12; 12:2). In that case, the Anointed is speaking proleptically here in Psalm 2.

"inheritance" and "possession."[7] With a double chiasm, the psalmist literarily pictures the fate of the rebellers in the hands of the Son-King: they are his property, and he does with them as he wishes, to destroy their rebellions:

2:8bα	"the nations"	
2:8bβ		"as Your inheritance"
2:8cα		"as Your possession"
2:8cβ	"the ends of the earth"	
2:9aα	"You will break them"	
2:9aβ		"with a rod of iron"
2:9bα		"like a vessel of a potter"
2:9bβ	"You will shatter them"	

This individual is clearly no mere Davidic regent; he possesses a remarkable extent of reign and power of rule.

Recommendation (2:10–12)

In light of the Son-King's might and power, the unsubmissive ones are warned to change their ways, or else . . . .[8] A number of wordplays depict just deserts phonologically being handed out to the miscreants: while the rebels wanted to "tear away" their fetters (שׁלך, *shlk*, 2:3a), they are recommended to "be sensible" (שׂכל, *shkl*, 2:10a); or else the wicked "judge" (שׁפט, *shpht*, 2:10b) will receive the "rod" (שֵׁבֶט, *shevet*, 2:9a); and they who do not "serve" (עבד, *'vd*, 2:11a) will "perish" (אבד, *'vd*, 2:12b).

There is also the issue of whether "He" in 2:12aβ refers to the "Son" (the nearest antecedent) or to Yahweh. In light of the "anger" of Yahweh in 2:5a, and "angry" and "anger" showing up again in 2:12ab, as well as the macarism in 2:12d that is similar to others pointing to Yahweh as the refuge (see 128:1; Isa 30:18; also see Pss 5:11; 34:22), it seems likely that Yahweh is the referent of "He" in 2:12a. In any case, as was seen earlier in the psalm, this equivocality seems to be deliberately superposing deity and his regent. As well, the three commands to the wicked—"serve" (object: Yahweh); "mourn" (object: none[9]) (2:11ab); and "do homage"[10]

---

7. While this is applied to Christ in the New Testament (e.g., Rev 12:15; 19:15), it must be noted that the destruction of enemies employing the language of Ps 2:9 is also described in the Apocalypse as the work of the people of Christ (Rev 2:27).

8. And we have another chiasm in 2:10: "kings / be sensible; // be warned, / judges."

9. The verb גיל, *gyl*, usually means "to shout with joy," but that does not fit this context, where רְעָדָה, *r'adahh*, "trembling" has the connotation of utter terror (Ps 48:6; 55:5 [that uses "horror" in parallel]; 104:32; etc.). It is likely the verb has polar meanings, and that it, as in Hos 10:5, means something entirely the opposite: "to mourn." See Andersen and Freedman, *Hosea*, 556–57.

10. The verb actually means "kiss," metonymically standing for "do homage" (as in 1 Kgs 19:18; Job 31:27; Hos 13:2).

(object: Son) (2:12a)—seem to assimilate Yahweh with the Son.[11] In any case, the Son-King is indeed coming to rule, and to rule decisively![12]

When all this will happen is not explained in the psalm; the fact that such a final putdown of rebellion has not occurred in the two or three millennia since the composition of Psalm 2 indicates that its fulfillment is likely to be in the eschaton, with the actual establishment of the kingdom of God and of his Christ.[13] But there is a word for those of God's people who wait eagerly for that day, the saints of now, and that good news is expressed in a coda to the psalm (2:12d): "Blessed are those who seek refuge in Him!"[14]

Whereas for the average reader (whether ancient Israelite or modern Texan[15]) there is much that can be done to apply Psalm 1, how may one respond to Psalm 2 that deals with the transactions of a much more political nature on a far more broader stage? Here's where the macarisms, both in Psalm 1 and Psalm 2, provide clues. In the first psalm, the blessed one was the person who was intensely grounded on God's word; an applicational response is obvious. Likewise, in the second psalm, the blessed one is the person who, despite the turbulences of nation and hubris of leaders, seeks refuge in God. And here, too, the applicational response is obvious: with full confidence in the sovereignty of God and of his King, the child of God seeks a haven in the presence of the God and his Son-King and is thereby blessed!

---

11. See Eldhose, "Trinitarian Interpretation," for the incisive demonstration that "Yahweh" indicates the Trinitarian Godhead, thus explaining these ambiguities.

12. The "kingdom of God" is a major theme in Scripture. In general, in the OT days, the divine King ruled Israel as a theocracy with a human king as his representative ("son"). Of course, Christ, the Messiah/Anointed, now reigns over the cosmos at the right hand of God (Mark 12:36), though his reign is not altogether manifest on earth; Satan, sin, and sinners continue to wreak havoc in rebellion. Yet, for the people of God, the "kingdom of God has come near" (1:11–15), and they participate in it in a non-manifest sense, for into this kingdom all humanity are invited through Christ. And those who become its citizens are, in a sense, instantiating and actualizing his reign—creating a multiplicity of microcosms across the world. Until the Second Advent, the kingdom will not be in earthly existence, and for that momentous turn of events we wait (15:43)—and it will then be a macrocosm. Psalm 2 bears witness to this "already, but not yet" state of affairs.

13. The NT citations of 2:9 validate this conclusion (see Rev 2:27; 12:5; 19:15—2:27 actually applies Ps 2:9 to the believer who will co-rule with Christ!).

14. It is unlikely that the psalm was written for the rebels to read/hear; instead, it is the people of God who gain confidence from the divine disposition of the wicked powers-that-be under the hand of the Son-King.

15. This was written during my sojourn in the Lone Star State.

Sermon Map

I. Rebellion
   Extent of earthly powers: all over the earth (2:1–2b)
   Action of rebels: non-submission to God (2:2b–3)
   Move-to-relevance: suffering under anti-God rulers/leaders

II. Response and Reaction
   Extent of divine power: heavens, ends of the earth (2:4a, 8c)
   Action of God: anger, establishment of his Son's kingdom (2:4–8)
   Move-to-relevance: recognition of the overwhelming power of God

III. Recommendation
   Preventive action by rebels: submission (2:10–12a)
   Punitive action by God: subjugation (2:9, 12bc)
   Move-to-relevance: recognition of the overwhelming power of God

IV. *Be Blessed in Refuge!*
   Specifics on seeking a confident refuge in God (2:12d)

PSALM 3:1–8
Psalm of Disorientation

Bane of Enemies

TRADITIONALLY, PSALM 3 HAS been considered a prayer for the morning (see 3:5), and Psalm 4 a prayer for the evening (see 4:8). It is the first actual *prayer* in the Psalter, the first to call upon Yahweh, and the first with a superscription.[1] Psalm 3 is also the first in a series of twelve psalms (Psalms 3–14) that has two sets of five prayers (Psalms 3–7 and 9–14) plus a sixth one with each set dealing specifically with the human condition (Psalms 8 and 14[2]).

Excursus: Holy War and Life

Perhaps it is a reflection of real life that the beatitude-laden and triumphal opening psalms of the Psalter (Psalms 1–2[3]) are followed by a whole series of laments (Psalms 3–7). Life is not all good and, yes, bad things happen to good people, even to the people of God. Acknowledging the violent distresses facing the latter on this side of eternity, military terminology abounds in Psalm 3: besides "adversaries" (3:1a); "enemies" (3:7c); and "deliver/deliverance" (3:2b, 7b, 8a), there is "rising" (3:1b; see Deut 28:7); "shield" (Ps 3:3a; see Deut 33:29); "set [themselves]" (Ps 3:6b; see Isa 22:7); "arise, Yahweh" (3:7a; see Num 10:35); and the battle cry, "to Yahweh [belongs] deliverance" (Ps 3:8a; see 2 Chr 20:17). All this verbiage is likely to be an allusion to the tenets of Israel's holy war, that was undergirded by the confidence that Yahweh saves his people not with the standard panoplies and paraphernalia of warfare (Deut 20:1–9; Judges 7; 1 Samuel 17; 2 Chronicles 20; etc.). And so deity comes through (or is expected to come through) in a surprising reversal of fate, as in Ps 3:8, right after a battle cry in 3:7. "This suddenness of confidence must be related to an ideology of holy war that has its origins in a faith in divine intervention eliminating any human accomplishment and effort."[4] Also of note, the portrait of the "enemy" becomes rather stylized, an entity in opposition to both the psalmist and God. And, thereby, the military metaphor equates life (or at least the

---

1. And as far as superscriptions go, Psalm 3 is the first to be labeled "Psalm" (מִזְמוֹר, *mizmor*), the first attributed to David (לְדָוִד, *ldawid*; not translated in this work).
2. See under these psalms.
3. The Psalter is bounded at the other end by the joyous "Hallelujah" songs of Psalms 146–150.
4. Kim, "Holy War Ideology," 88 (see 86–90).

insalubrious parts thereof) to a war. That is to say, many of the notions expressed in Psalm 3 (and others like it) are quite likely to be symbolic: life is war!

> To live in this world is to be surrounded by powerful and hostile forces capable of destroying and killing. The metaphor invites a consideration of this on all levels both individual and community, both earthly and cosmic. All evil from the minor clashes with neighbors in a community, to the earthly dangers of war, to the cosmic forces which seek to engulf the universe itself are all seen as part of a single spectrum. To deal with the minor is to deal with the major. To deal with the trivial is to deal with the ultimate. Opposed to this is Yahweh who alone can be victorious at the cosmic level of good and evil and can deal with the forces which loom far beyond the possibility of human comprehension or control.[5]

Get ready for the war that is going to be waged in life!

Translation

3:1 Yahweh, how many my adversaries have become.
     Many [are] rising against me.
3:2 Many [are] saying about my soul,
     "There is no deliverance for him in God."
3:3 But You, Yahweh, [are] a shield about me;
     my glory, and the One who lifts my head.
3:4 With my voice, to Yahweh I called out,
     and He answered me from His holy mountain.
3:5 I—I lay down and I slept;
     I awoke, for Yahweh—He sustains me.
3:6 I will not be afraid of ten thousand people
     who have set [themselves] against me all around.
3:7 Arise, Yahweh;
     deliver me, my God.
     For You have smitten all my enemies on the jaw;
     the teeth of the wicked You have shattered.
3:8 To Yahweh [belongs] deliverance;
     upon Your people [is] Your blessing.

---

5. Culley, "Psalm 3," 37.

Structure

The psalm may be structured with a past-present-future sequence:[6]

> **Problem**: *Declaration of Confidence* [PRESENT]
> **3:1–2** Crisis ("Yahweh," 3:1a; "God," 3:2b)
> **3:3** Confidence ("Yahweh," 3:3a)
>
> **Protection**: *Declaration of Confidence* [PAST]
> **3:4** Response ("Yahweh," 3:4a)
> **3:5–6** Confidence ("Yahweh," 3:5b)
>
> **Power**: *Declaration of Confidence* [FUTURE]
> **3:7** Petition ("Yahweh," 3:7a; "God," 3:7b)
> **3:8** Confidence ("Yahweh," 3:8a)

The reading of the time-sequence, based on the syntax of verbs, is important for this psalm. But grammatically speaking, "poetic texts characteristically have a less tight connection of sequences and time-frames."[7] Following the standard option exercised by most English translations, I have the present (3:1–3), the past (3:4–6; perhaps a flashback to a past distress, or a remembrance of an appeal to God earlier in the current distress), and a closing anticipation of the future of deliverance and blessing (3:7–8). In any case, the lament of Psalm 3 has "Yahweh" showing up twice in each section: in the second person in the present *Problem* section, 3:1–3; in the third person in the past *Protection* section, 3:4–5; and in the second person again in the future *Power* section, 3:7–8.[8]

Theological Focus

> Almost in a holy war, God's people are often in danger of being annihilated by the myriad of their enemies, but their confidence in God is unbounded, their proximity to God unquestionable, and God's might is unchallengeable, his deliverance inevitable, and his blessing incontrovertible.

Commentary

Problem (Present: 3:1–3)

"Yahweh" begins 3:1, and "against me" ends it; thus we have the psalmist seemingly separated from God by "my adversaries" that shows up on the middle of the verse. However, 3:3 begins by counteracting this distancing with an emphatic "but You, Yahweh" juxtaposed to

---

6. Figure is modified from Smith, "Redactional Criteria," 97.
7. Botha and Weber, "'Killing Them Softly,'" 25.
8. The "present" and "future" sections also have one instance of "God" each—first uttered by enemies denying deity's deliverance (3:2b), and then by the psalmist appealing for deity's deliverance (3:7b). Though technically a lament, as is evident from 3:1–2, thereafter it becomes an affirmation of trust in God.

"about me" as a "shield." No longer is the supplicant separated from deity by enemies, for God is a protective barrier, a "shield" around him. In fact, the point is further portrayed in the structure of 3:2–3, creating a poignant contrast between the assertion of the adversaries and that of the psalmist:

3:2a	"Many are saying about my soul, [אֹמְרִים לְנַפְשִׁי, *'omrim lnaphshi*]
3:2bα	'There is no deliverance for him
3:2bβ	in God.'
3:3aα	But You, Yahweh,
3:3aβ	[are] a shield about me,
3:3b	my glory, and the One who lifts my head." [וּמֵרִים רֹאשִׁי, *umerim ro'shi*]."

In the "story" of the psalm,[9] the psalmist and his cohort are a minority, signified by the repeated use of the root רב, *rb* (רבב, *rbb*, "many," 3:1a; רַבִּים, *rabbim*, "many," 3:1b, 2a; and רְבָבָה, *rvavah*, "ten thousand," 3:6a)—reaching a crescendo with "*all* my enemies" (3:7c). They are "adversaries" who "rise up" in opposition (3:1), they are "enemies," and they are the "wicked"[10] (3:7cd), who "set [themselves] against me all around" (3:6b), and who contemptuously scorn the psalmist: "There is no deliverance for him in God" (3:2).

There may be hordes of enemies "against me" and "against me all around" (3:1b, 6b), but God's shield is "about me" (3:3a). Notice the assonance in Hebrew between אֹמְרִים לְנַפְשִׁי, "saying about my soul" (the verbal hostility of the foes, 3:2a) and וּמֵרִים רֹאשִׁי, "and the One who lifts my head" (the protective activity of God, 3:3b; see figure above[11]). Clearly the focus, even in the "present" crisis (3:1–3) is upon God, and not upon enemies or their number. "If one gazes too long upon the enemy and his might, the enemy grows in the mind's eye to gigantic proportions and his citadels reach up to the skies (Deut 1:28). The hypnotic power of the enemy is broken when one turns one's gaze toward God, who is able to fight and grant victory (Deut 1:29–30)."[12] For he who answered "*from* [מִן, *min*] His holy mountain" (Ps 3:4b) would help the psalmist not to be afraid "*of* ten thousands [מֵרִבְבוֹת, *merivvot*]" (3:6a, employing the same preposition). No wonder God is called "my glory" (3:3b): the glory of God's people lies not in genes, status, accomplishments, portfolios, or resumes, but in God the deliverer and sustainer, the King of "glory" (3:3b).

---

9. It is helpful to see every pericope (even a psalm, or even a portion of didactic literature) as "storying" something, presuming a sequence of events or progressions of thought. That enables the preacher to discern better the thrust and intended response of the text.

10. That the foes are "wicked" makes the cause of these adversaries and foes an immoral one, directed not only against God's people, but against God himself.

11. "In victory we hold our heads high," by the grace of God being translocated from despair to hope (Goldingay, *Psalms*, 1:111).

12. Craigie, *Psalms 1–50*, 73.

Protection (Past: 3:4–6)

In the past *Protection* section (3:4–6), the psalmist recounts what must have been an earlier similar situation of human call and divine answer[13] amidst trouble that enabled him to sleep in peace at night: no nightmares, no insomnia, no worries.[14] At that time, the emphatic "I—I lay down" at the beginning of 3:5 was made possible by the equally emphatic "Yahweh—He sustains me" at the end of the verse (separated in the middle by two verbs: "I slept" and "I awoke"). The declaration of 3:6 is more gnomic rather than future—"God sustains me, so I will not be/am not afraid"—based on the past (recent or distant) liberation by God. In short, the psalmist and all of God's people do nothing—they just lie down and sleep. God does everything.[15]

Protection (Future: 3:7–8)

In the *Protection* section, first, there is an appeal to Yahweh with two imperatives in 3:7a, 7b ("arise" and "deliver"). Many were "rising" against the psalmist (3:1b), so his commensurate plea to Yahweh is "arise!" (3:7a).

Then comes the report of God's response given as an already accomplished fact with two perfects in 3:7c, 7d (or it might be the sure expectation of what is going to happen, a perfected future or a prophetic perfect, so to speak). The poetic structure is precise:

3:7cα	"You have smitten
3:7cβ	all my enemies
3:7cγ	on the jaw;
3:7dα	the teeth
3:7dβ	of the wicked
3:7dγ	You have shattered."

The enemies (3:7cβ, dβ) and their body parts (3:7cγ, 7dα) are trapped inextricably between the actions of Yahweh (3:7cα, 7dγ). These adversaries don't stand a chance!

Finally, the psalm concludes by stating what is always true with two verbless clauses in 3:8a, 8b. While the enemies claimed "God" (impersonal to them) would not give "deliverance" (3:2b), the psalmist, after his plea to "*my* God" (personal to him) to "deliver" (3:7b), proclaimed that "Yahweh"—the God of the covenant—would indeed provide "deliverance" to his people (3:8a). "This inversion . . . of the taunt . . . is a literary realization of the reversal of the psalmist's fortunes."[16]

---

13. Not from the heavens (2:4), but from his "holy mountain" (2:6; 3:4a)—on earth and in proximity to his people!

14. It is also possible that the psalmist is recounting what happened at an earlier point in the current crisis, after he had appealed for divine intervention.

15. I am reminded of Luther's exertions (or lack thereof) during the controversies with the Roman church: "I simply taught, preached, and wrote God's Word; otherwise I did nothing. And while I slept [cf. Mark 4:26–29], or drank Wittenberg beer with my friends Philip [Melanchthon] and [Nicolaus von] Amsdorf, the Word so greatly weakened the papacy that no prince or emperor ever inflicted such losses upon it. I did nothing; the Word did everything. . . . I did nothing; I let the Word do its work" (Luther, "Second Sermon," 77–78).

16. Kselman, "Psalm 3," 579.

And so the story comes around full circle:

3:2bα	"'There is no *deliverance* for him
3:2bβ	in *God*.'"
3:7ab	"Arise *Yahweh*, deliver me, my *God*!"
3:8aα	"To *Yahweh*
3:8aβ	[belongs] *deliverance*."

While his "head," the psalmist hopes, will be lifted by God (3:3b), he expects that God will requite all these enemies on the head (or at least on parts thereof: jaw and teeth, 3:7cd). While the violence makes the reader flinch, it is quite likely that the focus on jaw and teeth was to show these foes' verbal impotence. They who had insulted the psalmist and his God, casting aspersions on the faith of the former and the faithfulness of the latter—"There is no deliverance for him in God" (3:2)—are now rendered speechless. With smashed mandibles and crushed teeth, not to mention mouths flooded with curdling blood, it was going to be a bit difficult for them to give an encore. "In the real world, protection and deliverance mean the defeat of enemies and this is not a pretty matter."[17] That is to say, the blessing of God's people often runs a parallel course with the bane of God's (and his people's) enemies.

The "ten thousand *people*" (3:6) are foes intent upon decimating the righteous, but the ones delivered by Yahweh are blessed by Yahweh as "Your *people*" (3:8b).

> The actions of blessing and salvation [are] the primary poles around which the activity of God revolves in the Old Testament, salvation in the sense of Yahweh's deliverance of the community and individuals from particular crises, oppressions, need of various sorts, and blessing in the sense of Yahweh's ongoing provision of the needs and possibilities for life—birth, food, general care, divine protection in the daily experiences of life, the provision for the continuities of life—work, space, food, family.[18]

This blessing is, thus, "systemic well-being," appropriately granted by a Creator who desires shalom for his creation.[19]

---

17. Goldingay, *Psalms*, 1:113.
18. Miller, "Psalms and Inscriptions," 319.
19. Brueggemann and Bellinger, *Psalms*, 38.

PSALM 3:1–8

Sermon Map

I. Problem in the Present
   Foes innumerable (3:1, 2a, 6)
   Their taunt (3:2)
   Move-to-relevance: our tenuous situation as a minority
II. Protection in the Past
   God's answer from his position of proximity (3:4)
   Response to God's sustenance: fearlessness (3:6)
   Move-to-relevance: our past experience of God's protection
III. Power in the Future
   God's power requiting enemies (3:7)
   God's deliverance and blessing upon his people (3:8)
   Move-to-relevance: our faithlessness
IV. *Remember . . . and Awake!* (or *Sleep in Heavenly Peace!*)
   Specifics on remembering the past

PSALM 4:1–8

Psalm of Disorientation

Correcting False Friends

PSALM 4 HAS BEEN considered a song for the evening (see 4:4b, 8), and Psalm 3 for the morning (see 3:5). Links with Psalm 3 include: "call" and "answer me" (4:1a and 3:4); "distress"/ "adversary" (4:1c and 3:1a; both צַר, *tsar*); "my honor/glory" (4:2a and 3:3b); "many [are] saying" (4:6a and 3:2a; also "many" in 3:1b); "abound"/"many . . . have become" (4:7b and 3:1a; both רבב, *rbb*); "lie down and sleep" (4:8a; 3:5a).

Translation

4:1   When I call, answer me,
         God of my righteousness.
      In [my] distress, relieve me;
         be gracious to me and hear my prayer.
4:2   People, until when [is] my honor [turned] to disgrace?
         Will you love what is worthless,
         seek falsehood?
4:3   But know that Yahweh has set apart the devout for Himself;
         Yahweh himself hears when I call Him.
4:4   Tremble, and do not sin;
         say in your heart upon your bed and be silent.
4:5   Sacrifice sacrifices of righteousness,
         and trust in Yahweh.
4:6   Many [are] saying, "Who will show us good?
         The light of Your face has fled from over us, Yahweh."
4:7   You have put joy in my heart
         more than when their grain and new wine abound.
4:8   In peace I will both lie down and sleep,
         for You alone [are] Yahweh;
         You make me to dwell in safety.

Structure

The psalm is best visualized with a structure of three addresses, two to Yahweh and one to enemies in between those two:

To Yahweh
- **4:1   Distress and Cry**

To Enemies
- **4:2–5   Disparagement and Counter**
  - 4:2   Question to opponents
  - 4:3   Yahweh's action
  - 4:4–5   Advice to "trust" (בָּטַח, *batach*)

To Yahweh
- **4:6–8   Declaration and Confidence**
  - 4:6   Question of opponents
  - 4:7   Yahweh's action
  - 4:8   Declaration of "safety" (בֶּטַח, *betach*)

Theological Focus

God's people in distress, when facing detractors who malign their faith, continue to trust God without wavering, seeking to redirect those carpers towards God, and looking only for the joy God provides, not for material abundance, for with that attitude of heart, they rest in peace and safety.

Commentary

Distress and Cry (4:1)

The only lines of petition are in 4:1. Chrysostom observes: "He did not say, note, 'After my calling upon him he hearkened to me,' but *On my calling upon him*."[1] Or, "when I call" (the verb has the preposition בְּ, *b*, acting in temporal fashion). Thus, God hears even as we speak. What exactly the psalmist wants God to do, beyond answering his call, being gracious to him, and listening to his prayer (three imperatives in 4:1a, 1d), is to relieve him from his distress (4:1c).[2] The psalmist is in "distress" (literally, "narrowness") and needs "relieving" (literally, "broadening"). It appears that the supplicant was successful in getting God's attention and persuading him to take action, for the psalm begins "in distress" (4:1c) but ends "in peace" and "in safety" (4:8a, 8c).

---

1. Chrysostom, *Commentary on the Psalms*, 1:45.
2. "Relieve me" translates an unusual use of the perfect form of the verb (functioning as a wish: a precative perfect), but it makes sense contextually and puts it in line with the imperatives before and after it in 4:1.

Disparagement and Counter (4:2–5)

From addressing God in 4:1, the psalmist moves to the opponents in 4:2–5. And these "people" were denigrating "my honor" (4:2a), making him a "disgrace." How they were doing so is described in 4:2bc—by loving what was "worthless" and seeking what was "falsehood." Goldingay suggests how the story of Job may explain the "story" of this psalm. That ancient patriarch, too, was in "distress" (צַר; Job 7:11; 15:24; 36:19; etc., as in Ps 4:1c), and his three advisors calumniated him for being, as they thought, guilty of some sin that had brought about his calamity. Elihu, in particular, claimed that God was not "relieving" (רחב, rchv; Job 36:16, as in Ps 4:1c) Job's "distress." And Job, like the psalmist, also saw his "honor" (כָּבוֹד, kavod; Job 19:9; 29:20, as in Ps 4:2a) exchanged for humiliation and disgrace (Job 16:10; 19:5; though not using כְּלִמָּה, klimmah, "disgrace," as in Ps 4:2a). It is quite likely, then, that these "people" of 4:2a were disparaging the distressed psalmist (4:1), with lies and untruths, empty and unfounded: "worthless" things, characterized by "falsehood" (4:2bc). No wonder the psalmist addressed deity as "God of my righteousness" (4:1b)—i.e., "God of my vindication/right," the one who justifies the cause of the pilloried psalmist. But "until when" or "how long" would this flak be directed against him (4:2a)?

Whatever may have been the primary cause of the psalmist's turmoil—and we are never told in this psalm what it was or the source thereof—these maligning "people," adding to the sufferer's perturbation, were unlikely to have been outsiders or the primary distressers of the supplicant: they were later advised by the psalmist to offer sacrifices and to trust in Yahweh (4:5). It makes sense to see them akin to the "friends" of Job, vilifying and defaming one of their own. Indeed, we see in 4:6, that "many" (the same company as the "people" of 4:2a) were even questioning God's goodness and his beneficence towards his people, in light of the psalmist's "distress." In effect, they were countering the psalmist's plea to God to "relieve" him (4:1c). No one, they claimed, would show good, certainly not Yahweh.

But the psalmist, the person of God, is not dissuaded or discouraged by these false counselors. He reciprocates by declaring that "Yahweh has set apart the devout for Himself" (4:3a). He, the sufferer, was no scandalous sinner, but still a חָסִיד (chasid, "devout" one), one who had experienced—and, no doubt, continues to anticipate—God's חֶסֶד (chesed, "lovingkindness"). This Yahweh, covenantally bound to his people, would hear when called upon. And so those defaming "people" had better "tremble"[3] and "not sin"[4] (4:4a); rather, they ought to "say in your heart"[5] and "be silent"[6] (4:4b), and "sacrifice sacrifices of righteousness"[7] and "trust in Yahweh" (4:5a, 5b): three pairs of commandments, with the elements in each pair linked by a conjunction. There appears to be an upward movement to the sequence: trembling and not sinning → reflecting and resting → sacrificing and trusting! Their falsehoods and worthless

---

3. A response of "awed submission" to Yahweh (Goldingay, *Psalms*, 1:121).

4. By loving what is worthless and seeking falsehood—their contemptuous remarks regarding the psalmist (4:2; and regarding God, 4:6).

5. A heartfelt acknowledgment of Yahweh, perhaps in meditation and reflection. What they are to "say" in their hearts is not specified—perhaps they, too, are being urged to "call" upon God, as the psalmist was doing (4:1a, 3b).

6. Taking וּדֹמּוּ, *dommu*, as a form of the verb דמה, *dmh*, "be silent." They are being asked to cease uttering those maledictions (4:2, 6) against the devout and their deity.

7. Instead of casting aspersions on God and his people, they were to worship God with his people. What was the psalmist's "righteousness" (4:1b) was now also to be the "righteousness" of the "people" who were against him (4:5a).

ideas needed to be corrected; they needed to be set right, with God and with God's people (as implied in the public action of sacrifice).

The length of this exhortation to those "people" reflects the psalmist's intent—unusual in the Psalter—to get these mistaken folks "to change their ways more for their own sake than for the suppliant's."[8] This is further validation for reading this psalm as focusing on these false friends and their wrong ideas than on the suffering and lament of the psalmist himself.

Declaration and Confidence (4:6–8)

The psalm concludes with a return to addressing Yahweh (4:6–8). The dissenting and impious voices of the "many" question if there is anyone showing them good (4:6a). Perhaps in a twist of the Aaronic blessing in Num 6:26 ("May Yahweh lift His face upon you"), they were claiming that the light of Yahweh's "face has fled from over us" (Ps 4:6b).[9] Instead, the psalmist asserts that Yahweh has "put joy in my heart" (4:7a).

This reference to the supplicant's "heart" in 4:7a suggests a contrast between the organs of the devout and those of the slanderers (the "heart" of the latter was mentioned in 4:4b): the faithful, trusting ones had hearts full of joy in God; the others were asked to develop such hearts, initiating the process by saying the right things, calling upon God, etc. (4:4–5). The psalmist, in peace, "lies down [שׁכב, *shkv*]" to sleep (4:8a) manifesting, even in total rest, a confidence in God's working on his behalf. Note that the denouncers were exhorted earlier to "say in your heart *upon your bed* [(מִשְׁכָּב, *mishkav*)]" (4:4a); i.e., they, too, were to develop the same late-night attitude of the psalmist.

The material goods of the "many" (רַבִּים, *rabbim*, 4:6a) detractors may "abound" (רבב, *rbb*, 4:7b), but as for the psalmist, this inner joy is all that he asks God for (4:7a).[10] Therefore, appropriating another word from the Aaronic blessing, the psalmist declares that he will lie down and sleep in "peace" (שָׁלוֹם, *shalom*, 4:8a; Num 6:26), as he proceeds to make an even grander asseveration: "You alone [are] Yahweh!" (Ps 4:8b)—the answer to the question raised in 4:6a, "Who will show us good?" Yahweh, and Yahweh alone, will.

The rest, as they say, is history, and the psalmist is made to dwell in "safety." The play on בטח, *btch*, "trust," in 4:5b and בֶּטַח, *betach*, "safety" in 4:8c, emphasizes that trust in God begets safety, for this is a God who cares for the welfare of his people, the "devout."

---

8. Goldingay, *Psalms*, 1:119.

9. However, the verb נסה, *nsh*, here, usually taken to be a form of נשׂא (*ns'*, "lift"), as it is in Num 6:26, may not be precisely echoing that earlier text. The consonants of נסה indicate that the root verb is נוס (*nws*, "flee"). Also, the preposition in the priestly blessing is אֵלֶיךָ, *'eleka*, "lift His face *upon you* . . . ," whereas in Ps 4:6b it is עָלֵינוּ, *'alenu*, which can have the sense of "from over us" (as in my translation). See Eaton, "Hard Sayings," 356; and Goldingay, "Psalm 4," 68. That 4:6b is part of the direct quote begun in 4:6a seems obvious: the first-person plural suffix ("us") in 4:6a recurs in 4:6b.

10. Is there a hint here that unlike the barns and cellars of those "many," the psalmist's larders and pantries are not full? Perhaps these victuals and chattels of life were the "good" the opponents were seeking in 4:6a?

Sermon Map

I. Distress and Cry[11]
    Times of difficulty and plea for help (4:1)
    Move-to-relevance: Turmoil a part of our lives

II. Disparagement and Counter
    Detractors' attack (4:2)
    Their attitude to God (4:6)
    Christian's correction (4:3–5)
    Move-to-relevance: Discouraged by others' attitudes

III. Declaration and Confidence
    Trust in God's providence (4:7)
    Safety in God (4:8)
    Move-to-relevance: Our insomnia

IV. *Remember . . . and Sleep!*
    Specifics on handling discouragement in difficulty

---

11. There is no constraint that a sermon map should follow the structure of the text, but in this case, the latter can be used gainfully to create one.

PSALM 5:1–12

Psalm of Orientation

Access to God in Prayer

THE TWO PREVIOUS PSALMS, both psalms of disorientation like this one, dealt with oppression. Psalm 5, too, has a supplicant that is in distress—he cries for help (5:1–3). But unlike those earlier compositions, this one is focused on the prayer itself, uttered in times of distress, and more precisely upon prayer-related *access to God*, a privilege enjoyed by the psalmist and his righteous cohort, and lacked by the wicked.[1]

Translation

5:1   To my utterances give ear, Yahweh,
         consider my groaning.
5:2   Attend to the sound of my cry for help,
         my King and my God,
         for to You I pray.
5:3   Yahweh, in the morning, You hear my voice;
         in the morning I lay [my petition] to You and watch.
5:4   For You are not a God who takes pleasure in wickedness;
         with You no evil dwells.
5:5   The arrogant cannot stand before Your eyes;
         You hate all doers of harm.
5:6   You destroy those who speak falsehood;
         the person of bloodshed and deceit Yahweh abhors.
5:7   But I—in Your abundant lovingkindness, I enter Your house;
         I bow down at Your holy temple in fear of You.

---

1. I label this a psalm of orientation, despite the presence of enemies arrayed against the people of God, simply because it pictures the access of the latter to their deity in prayer, no matter what external distress or internal despair they suffer.

5:8   Yahweh, lead me in Your righteousness;
         because of my watchful foes
         make Your path straight before me.
5:9   For there is no truthfulness in his mouth;
         their inward part [is] destruction.
      An open tomb their throat;
         with their tongue they flatter.
5:10 Hold them guilty, God;
         may they fall by their plans.
      In the abundance of their insurrections thrust them out,
         for they are rebellious against You.
5:11 But may all who seek refuge in You rejoice;
         forever may they shout with joy;
      and You put a cover upon them;
         may those who love Your name exult in You.
5:12 For You—You bless the righteous one, Yahweh,
         with favor like a shield You surround him.

Structure

Psalm 5 is best understood as a prayer that alternates between describing the wicked and the righteous:

5:1–3	**Prayer**	
5:4–6	**Wicked: no access to God** (God's hatred, loathing)	
	God: 3 negations (5:4a, 4b, 5a)	
	God: 3 assertions (5:5b, 6a, 6b)	
5:7–8	**Righteous: access to God** (God's lovingkindness, righteousness)	
	Righteous: 2 verbs—"enter," "bow down" (5:7a, 7b)	
	God: 2 verbs—"lead," "make ... straight" (5:8a, 8c)	
5:9–10	**Wicked: guilt, rejection**	
	God: 3 reprisals (5:10a, 10b, 10c)	
5:11–12	**Righteous: joy, blessing**	
	Righteous: 3 exultations (5:11a, 11b, 11d)	
	God: 3 blessings (5:11c, 12a, 12b)	

Strikingly, this psalm is entirely addressed to God, except for 5:6b, that has *five* words in Hebrew. "Yahweh" occurs *five* times in this song (5:1a, 3a, 6a, 8a, 12a) and, of course, this is the *fifth* psalm.[2]

---

2. Van der Lugt, *Cantos and Strophes in Biblical Hebrew Poetry: With Special Reference to the First Book of the Psalter*, 121.

PSALM 5:1–12

Theological Focus

The righteous, in a personal relationship with their God that involves reverential awe—having the assurance of access to God, of their prayers of distress being heard, and of being ultimately protected by God—rejoice in him forever as blessed ones, unlike the wicked who, with their evil words and deeds, are loathed by God, found guilty, and ultimately destroyed for their anti-God rebellion.

Commentary

Prayer (5:1–3)

Though the psalmist is in trouble of some sort, what exactly the problem is we are not told. But he groans (5:1b), he cries for help (5:2a), he prays (5:2c), he voices his pain (5:3a), he lays out his petition to God (5:3bα), and he waits (5:3bβ). His petition is audible: he wants Yahweh to "give ear" (5:1a) and "attend to the sound" of his plea (5:2a), and he knows Yahweh will "hear my voice" (5:3a).[3] Both 5:1 and 5:2 are constructed with deity in the center of each verse:

5:1aα	"To my utterances give ear,
5:1aβ	Yahweh,
5:1b	consider my groaning."
5:2a	"Attend to the sound of my cry for help,
5:2b	my King and my God,
5:2c	for to You I pray."

And that God to whom this prayer is directed is "Yahweh" (5:1a), the covenantally faithful deity, addressed as "*my* King and *my* God" (5:2b). Clearly, the psalmist (and his righteous companions) has a personal relationship with this divine being and is confident of being heard. "Declaring simply that Yhwh is king makes an objective affirmation about Yhwh's sovereignty; declaring that Yhwh is 'my king' makes an affirmation about the application of that sovereignty on my behalf."[4] Indeed, 5:3 asserts in gnomic fashion what always happens: Yahweh hears when the child of God lays out his/her petition and waits.[5] *Always!*

We also see here the notion of prayer as including waiting, with the confidence that God gives ear, considers, attends, and hears the utterances, groanings, and cries for help—the voices of his people (5:1–3). In a sense, then, with these first three verses, we are given a heading or statement of subject for the rest of the psalm: it is about access to God in prayer.

---

3. This is one of the three longest personal invocations in the Psalms (along with 22:1–2; and 88:1–2).
4. Goldingay, *Psalms*, 1:128.
5. In biblical tradition, divine and human regents administered justice in the morning (5:3a; see 2 Sam 15:2; Job 7:18; Ps 101:8; Jer 21:12; Zeph 3:5). Here the repetition of "in the morning" (Ps 5:3a, 3b) emphasizes the urgency of the psalmist's petition.

Wicked: No Access to God (5:4–6)

On the other hand, the wicked are bereft of this access to God, made clear in deity's reactions to them. There are three negations ("*not* a God who takes pleasure in wickedness," 5:4a; "with You *no* evil dwells," 5:4b; and "the arrogant *cannot* stand before Your eyes," 5:5a)—all employing לֹא, *lo'*, and three assertions ("You hate," 5:5b; "You destroy," 5:6a; and "Yahweh abhors," 5:6b). All these mark a downward progression from lack of access to God (5:4–5a) to his very loathing of the wicked (5:5b–6)—strong expressions of the exception God takes to the offenses of evil and to the offenders, the doers of evil.

And rightly so, for these opponents of the psalmist and the righteous are characterized starkly and extensively as being "arrogant," "doers of harm" (5:5), "who speak falsehood," who are persons of "bloodshed and deceit" (5:6), without "truthfulness" of speech (5:9a), who are marked inwardly by "destruction" (5:9b), with throats that trap and tongues that flatter (5:9cd), and who incite insurrections and raise rebellions against God (5:10cd). While all this implies that the transactions of these nefarious characters may have affected the supplicant personally (though how exactly we are not told; see 5:8b), the sum and substance of these allegations is that their attitudes and actions are distasteful in the extreme to God (5:4–6). "Life lived in direct contradiction to God is doomed from the beginning."[6] The wicked do not have access to God in prayer!

Righteous: Access to God (5:7–8)

"But"—5:7 begins with a strong adversative in the disjunctive clause that is emphatic. As well, with the redundant pronoun, "I," a forceful assertion is made that the psalmist enjoys privileges of access to God, unlike the depredators of the previous section. There is always access to God's presence for the righteous (5:7–8). And in contrast to God's hate and his abhorring of evil and evildoers, the righteous are the recipients of his abundant lovingkindness, his manifold grace by which they gain access to him (5:7a). Besides, their reverential awe ("fear," 5:7b) makes their entry into divine presence acceptable. This is clear in the chiastic design of 5:7.

Prepositional phrase	"in [בְּ, *b*] Your ... lovingkindness"
Verb + Noun	"I enter" + "Your house"
Verb + Noun	"I bow down" + "Your holy temple"
Prepositional phrase	"in [בְּ] fear of You"

The divine initiative of lovingkindness is reciprocated in the human response of fear, reverential awe of deity. The righteous "enter" and they "bow down" (5:7); and they seek to have God "lead" them in his righteousness, and "make [his] path straight" for them (5:8a, 8c)—i.e., they desire to walk in God's way, not in the way of the evildoers excoriated in 5:4–6. And by that very walk of righteousness, the "watchful foes," likely waiting in ambush (5:8b), would be frustrated and even defeated—"Your path," that God's people walk on, is safe (5:8c). In any case, it is the grace of God that enables them to walk righteously on God's righteous path: "lead me," the psalmist pleads to God (5:8a), on that straight, smooth,

---

6. Craigie, *Psalms 1–50*, 87. It is from the Hebrew verb תעב (*t'v*, "abhors") that we get the noun תּוֹעֵבָה (*to'evah*, "abomination"), one of the most denunciatory words for anti-God people and things in the OT.

and obstacle-free course. That God's initiative is essential for this perambulation is made clear in 5:7–8 with a number of nouns that have second-person possessive suffixes referring to Yahweh: "*Your* abundant lovingkindness," "*Your* house," "*Your* holy temple," "in fear *of You*" (or "in *Your* fear"), "*Your* righteousness," and "*Your* path." "*His* house can be accessed through *his* mercy; in the direction of *his* holy temple is where the suppliant will bow in *his* fear; *he* must lead the suppliant in *his* righteousness and *he* must straighten *his* way before the psalmist. Entrance for the suppliant to the temple is not because of [the psalmist's] own holiness but through the 'abundance' of Yahweh's 'mercy' ['lovingkindness']."[7] God's demand of his people could not be depicted more clearly. Neither could God's grace.

Wicked: Guilt, Rejection (5:9–10)

Returning to the wicked in 5:9–10, their guilt (5:9) and rejection by God (5:10) are detailed. Body parts (lightly shaded; below) and dangers therefrom (darkly shaded) form the core of 5:9, creating a double chiasm. At the center of this doublet is the doom of the wicked (shaded black):

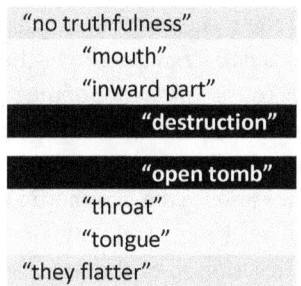

Again, showing the focus of the psalm on speech (prayer of the psalmist [5:1–3]; and falsehoods [5:6] of the unrighteous), here in 5:9 three of the body parts mentioned are involved in speech, too: "mouth," "throat," and "tongue." It is likely that the composer intends "inward part" as contributing to speech, the fount where words are formulated; in that case, the four elements participating in speech balance the four nouns describing the psalmist's petition in 5:1–3: "words," "groaning," "cry," and "voice." The actions on either end of the chiastic pairs, of course, relate to utterances: "no truthfulness" and "they flatter."

> The evil are characterized here entirely in terms of their speech in a manner which illustrates forcefully the potential evil of the tongue . . . Their words, in the absence of "truth," were without foundation or certainty, and hence altogether unreliable. The inner emotions and desires of the wicked are of such a destructive nature that their throat is like an "open grave ["tomb"]," symbolizing death, but more forcefully (in a hot climate) an abominable stench; in the pure air of morality, their words created an unbearable smell. Their tongues articulate no truth, but only the smooth words of flattery, which are lies designed cunningly to

---

7. Botha, "Psalm 5," 4.

enable the evil to achieve their ends . . . Their thought and words are not only a danger to the righteous, but an insult to God.[8]

Notice also בְּרֹב (*brov*, "in . . . abundance") in 5:7a and 5:10c; in the former it denotes the "abundance" of divine lovingkindness; in the latter the "abundance" of the insurrections of the wicked, the result of their rebellious nature (5:10cd). No wonder then, that the psalmist pleads with God to "hold them guilty!" (5:10a).

Righteous: Joy, Blessing (5:11–12)

In 5:11–12, the camera swings back to the righteous to conclude the psalm. Only two verses in this psalm, 5:11 and 5:7, commence with a וְ, *w*; both times a strong adversative is implied, translated "but." Here, in 5:11a, it reads: "*But* may all who seek refuge in You rejoice"—in contrast to the wicked whose guilt and rejection were noted in 5:9–10. With this contrary fate of the righteous, we see three synonymous expressions of gladness from God's people: they "rejoice" (5:11a), they have "joy" (5:11b), and they "exult" (5:11d); correspondingly there are three acts of God's blessing upon his people: "You put a cover upon them" (5:11c); "You—You bless the righteous one" (5:12a; emphatic), and "You surround him" (5:12b). Furthering the contrast between the wicked and the righteous are three uses of the preposition, בְּ, with the second-person masculine suffix: בָּךְ, *bak* ("against You"—the stance of the wicked; 5:10d); and בְךָ and בָךְ, *bka* (both denoting "in You"—the stance of the righteous; 5:11a, 11d, respectively). Such are the ones who pray, such are the privileges of prayer they have access to, and such are the benefits of prayer afforded them by the lovingkindness of God!

As the psalm commenced, we observed a symmetric presentation of four divine names ("Yahweh" twice [5:1a, 3a], and "my King," and "my God" [5:2b]). Appropriately enough, the psalm now concludes with a description of the righteous as "those who love your *name*" (5:11d). These latter, "shout with joy"—making a noisy celebration (also verbal) that is not just a one-time event, but one that lasts "forever" (5:11b). And not just for the psalmist, but for "all who seek refuge in You" (5:11a)—all the righteous. These are covered, sheltered by God himself (5:11c), surrounded with divine favor as a shield of protection (5:12b).

> Psalm 5 illustrates with clarity the polarity and tension which characterize certain dimensions of the life of prayer. On the one side, there is God: on the other, evil human beings. And the thought of the psalmist alternates between these two poles. He begins by asking God to hear him, but recalls that evil persons have no place in God's presence. He turns back to God again, expressing his desire to worship and his need of guidance, but then is reminded of the human evils of the tongue. Eventually, he concludes in confidence, praying for protection and blessing.[9]

Malefactors verbally abuse and suffer the consequences; the righteous verbalize prayer and enjoy the blessings. And thus, the poem that began as a lament, ends as a hymn.[10]

---

8. Craigie, *Psalms 1–50*, 88.
9. Craigie, *Psalms 1–50*, 89.
10. Prinsloo, "Psalm 5," 636.

PSALM 5:1–12

Sermon Map

I. Prayer and Access to God
   Righteous in distress pray (5:1–3)
   Righteous have access to God (5:7–8)
   Move-to-relevance: Our times of distress
II. Perfidy and Abhorrence by God
   Wicked are loathed by God (5:4–7)
   Wicked are guilty and punished (5:19–10)
   Move-to-relevance: The fate of the wicked
III. Protection and Approval from God
   Righteous are protected (5:11c, 12b)
   Righteous are blessed with divine favor (5:12)
   Righteous rejoice forever (5:11a, 11b, 11d)
   Move-to-relevance: Our desire for divine blessing
IV. *Pray and Party!*
   Specifics on frequent access to God (and waiting) in prayer

PSALM 6:1–10

Psalm of Disorientation

Supplication for Serious Physical Affliction

THE EARLY CHURCH PLACED Psalm 6 with the other Penitential Psalms (Psalms 32; 38; 51; 102; 130; and 143). But there is no explicit confession of sin or plea for forgiveness (though there is an appeal that the supplicant not be rebuked or chastened, 6:1). And, despite brief mentions towards the end of the psalm of foes (6:7b, 8a, 10a), the composition is silent about what these threats actually constituted for the psalmist or whence they came.

Translation

6:1	Yahweh, in Your anger do not rebuke me,
	nor in Your fury chasten me.
6:2	Be gracious to me, Yahweh, for I [am] frail;
	heal me, Yahweh, for my bones are terrified.
6:3	And my soul has become terrified greatly;
	but You, Yahweh—until when?
6:4	Return, Yahweh, save my soul;
	deliver me because of Your lovingkindness.
6:5	For there is no memory of You in death;
	in Sheol who will give thanks to You?
6:6	I have become weary with my groaning;
	I flood my bed every night;
	with my tears, I dissolve my couch.
6:7	My eye has wasted away with grief;
	it has grown weak because of all my adversaries.
6:8	Depart from me, all who do harm,
	for Yahweh has heard the voice of my weeping.

6:9   He has heard—Yahweh—my supplication [for grace];
      Yahweh, my prayer He accepts.
6:10 They will be ashamed and they will be terrified greatly—all my enemies;
      they will turn back, they will be ashamed suddenly.

Structure

The structure of Psalm 6 is straightforward, most of it being addressed to deity (6:1–7), the rest to the psalmist's detractors (6:8–9), and to his cohort, God's devout (6:10):

> **Frailty and Fear (6:1–3)**
>   To Deity (6:1–3)
>
> **Death and Desperation (6:4–5)**
>   To Deity (6:4–5)
>
> **Groaning and Grief (6:6–7)**
>   To Deity (6:6–7)
>
> **Reassurance and Recompense (6:8–10)**
>   To Detractors (6:8–9)
>   To Devout (6:10)

Theological Focus

> Stricken with frailty and debility, terrified by impending mortality, dissolved by grief, and assailed by opportunists and opponents, the child of God makes bold to beseech God in persistent prayer for the gracious intervention of his lovingkindness, with the confidence that God will hear and take action.

Commentary

Frailty and Fear (6:1–3)

In Psalm 6, there is evidence of divine wrath ("anger," "rebuke," "fury," and "chasten" in 6:1), of physical infirmity ("frail," "heal me," and "bones" in 6:2), and of psychological fear ("my soul" and "terrified greatly" in 6:3). One might suppose from 6:1 that there was some prior human sin of the psalmist inciting this divine anger that led to the physical and psychological afflictions. But there is no obvious indication of any moral failing on part of the supplicant. And what about the mentions of "adversaries," "all who do harm," and "all my enemies" (6:7b, 8a, 10a)?

Craigie's "storying" of the psalm seems to fit the textual data best. According to him, the psalmist's plea not to be rebuked by God in anger or chastened in divine fury relates to his hesitation in bringing the problem of his bane and burden to the Creator. "Whatever the reason for his sickness, it must have been sent or permitted by God, and it might seem presumptuous of a mere mortal, albeit a suffering mortal, to complain of the experience which God has permitted to fall on him."[1] So the supplicant commences by begging Yahweh's indulgence, so to speak, that he may be permitted to raise the matter of his stricken situation with him. May God not rebuke and chasten the psalmist for bringing this issue to his attention. The real petition then is regarding his physical debility (6:2: "I [am] frail; heal me, Yahweh, for my bones are terrified"), that God be gracious to him in this time of need. Apparently his failing health is panicking the psalmist ("my soul has become terrified greatly," 6:3a), and so he asks God to intervene without delay ("Yahweh—until when?" or "how long," 6:3b).

> He does not claim that he deserves God's grace, for by definition it cannot be deserved or earned, but he pleads for it nevertheless on the basis of his sorry estate. He needs God's grace, knows that he needs it, and in desperation asks for God's grace. But, eventually, the anguish exceeds words and overcomes the psalmist's power to articulate his agony: he can only ask "How long" [i.e., "until when"]? How much longer must he continue to suffer? How much longer will it be until he experiences the gracious action of God?[2]

Indeed, the unusual structure of the Hebrew in 6:1a and 6:1b separates the negation אַל from the verbs ("rebuke" and "chasten") by "in Your anger" and "in Your fury," respectively (in the Hebrew word order):

Yahweh,	do **not** in your anger	**rebuke** me,
יְהוָה	אַל־בְּאַפְּךָ	תּוֹכִיחֵנִי
yhwh	'al-b'apka	tokicheni
	and **not** in your fury	**chasten** me.
	וְאַל־בַּחֲמָתְךָ	תְיַסְּרֵנִי
	w'al-bachamatka	tyassreni

In other words, "Please do not get angry" is the thrust of 6:1, which fits well with Craigie's reading. The psalmist's sense of the imminence of his death and his grief in 6:4–6 also contributes to this understanding: bodily breakdown appears to be the main concern of the sufferer, at least thus far in the psalm. In sum, the two negative requests made of Yahweh in 6:1 ("do not rebuke me" and "nor ... chasten me") are the psalmist's attempt to preempt divine wrath for bringing before God his two positive requests, his actual petitions, in 6:2 ("be gracious" and "heal me"). The psalmist adds 6:3 summarizing his desperate situation, and asking in a broken sentence, an anacoluthon, "But You, Yahweh—until when?"[3]

---

1. Craigie, *Psalms 1–50*, 92.
2. Craigie, *Psalms 1–50*, 92–93.
3. "Yahweh—how long?" was, according to Spurgeon, "Calvin's favorite exclamation" (Spurgeon, *Treasury of David*, 1:57). I would be so bold as to say it is probably one of the favorite exclamations of all of God's people, perhaps second only to "Yahweh—help me!"

Death and Desperation (6:4–6)

The plea begun in 6:2 ("be gracious to me" and "heal me") is continued in 6:4: "return, Yahweh, save my soul; deliver me"—all based on God's covenantal relationship, his "lovingkindness" (6:4b) and, of course, his grace (6:2a: the verb חנן, *chnn*, "be gracious," is derived from חֵן, *chen*, "grace"[4]). It is all God's—and *only* God's—to resolve: "The entire span of sickness and health is understood in relation to the Lord. Life and death of a person are in God's hands. No other cause is contemplated, and no other relief is sought."[5]

Along the way, the psalmist also uses his dire situation and his imminent death to motivate God: there would be one fewer voice praising God if he were to go to Sheol, i.e., perish (6:5b).[6]

> Mortality is of the essence of the human condition. In a life filled with uncertainty and an unknown future, there remains always one certainty, that one day we shall die . . . Health is normal and it may result in praise, but sickness is a reminder and an anticipation of death. Life itself is no longer so good, for it is marred with pain, and the experience of imperfection in living evokes awareness of that ultimate enemy, death. In sickness, the body does not function properly; in death it ceases to function altogether. Thus it is that the psalms conceived on the sickbed are marked by a profound pathos, for though they contain the words of the living, they are haunted by the shadow of dying.[7]

And though the people of God in this current dispensation have the explicit promise of a life with God beyond the grave, we must not be too quick to read this psalm from our post-cross vantage point, for there is then the danger of trivializing earthly afflictions of sickness, infirmity, and even death. "Like the psalmist, we need a full appreciation of this life [and its deprivations and dangers] before we can look beyond it. And like the psalmist, we may have to undergo the anguish of pain and the sense of separation from God before we can emerge to the faith that rests confidently upon God."[8]

In the psalmist's state of utter helplessness, brought on by his physical debilitation, he urges God to "return" (6:4a), suggesting that he felt God had gone away from him in the midst of his agonies, and that for a long time ("Yahweh—until when?" [6:3b]).

Groaning and Grief (6:6–7)

The invalid is not only "terrified" (6:2b, 3a), but he is also grief-stricken, "weary with my groaning," drenching his bed in tears "every night," so much so his couch was dissolving (6:6)! Besides the terror confessed to in 6:2–3, the psalmist is in the death-grip of exhaustion,

---

4. Later, in 6:9, the psalmist affirms that God had heard his "supplication [for grace]": תְּחִנָּה, *tchinnah*, is also derived from חֵן.

5. Mays, *Psalms*, 60.

6. The possibility of an afterlife in God's presence is not an issue in this psalm; in any case, such a notion was not overly developed in OT days. Besides, the thrust of the psalmist's utterance in 6:5 is only that *on earth*, the givers of thanks to God would be one person short if he were to die.

7. Craigie, *Psalms 1–50*, 95.

8. Craigie, *Psalms 1–50*, 96. In sermons on this psalm, preachers today do not have to relate to the Sheol beliefs of the OT; we just need to take disease and death seriously, without minimizing its pathos and dreadfulness.

grief, insomnia, and wasting (6:4–6)—all pointing out, again, the seriousness of the psalmist's physical suffering. Mays is right:

> Physical vigor wanes, body and life are disturbed, unbalanced, groaning and grief have gone on and on, and vitality seems to leak away with the outpouring of sighs and tears. Death is an imminent probability. No specific terms for particular diseases are used; the description is not clinical in any sense. But illness in the Old Testament thought world is not comprehended in a diagnostic way; it is not sickness as an objective phenomenon that is spoken about but the experience of being sick, what a person can express in words of feeling, emotion, and meaning. Anyone who has been seriously ill senses what is finding its way to language in this anguished poetry. Often in the concentration of modern medical treatment on strictly physical causes and procedures, the need for suffering to find words and be heard is overlooked or suppressed. This and similar psalms bring that dimension of serious illness to light and give it its necessary place.[9]

But it is not only his frailty and fear of death and desperation at illness that the psalmist has to deal with. Inexplicably and unexpectedly, "adversaries" are introduced in 6:7b, as well as "all who do harm" (6:8a), and later, "all my enemies" (6:10a). They too are part of the supplicant's grief: both 6:6 and 6:7 deal with issues of the eyes—weeping in 6:6 and wasting away in 6:7. This late in the psalm, it is unlikely these new arrivals are direct or proximal causes of the psalmist's agony; rather these foes were possibly exploiting the already hapless sufferer and exacerbating his suffering. "Perhaps in the very face of the psalmist's appeal to God they have publicly and willingly given him up for dead, reckoned him deserving of his misfortune, and even intended to profit from his demise."[10] The tearful flooding of his bed and dissolving of his couch (6:6bc)—"every [בְּכָל, vkal] night" (6:6b)—were the result of the work of "all [בְּכָל, bkal] my adversaries" (6:7b). Whatever they were doing, they were only multiplying the anguish of the psalmist.

Reassurance and Recompense (6:8–10)

The remainder of the psalm, 6:8–10, deals with these seemingly secondary distress-creating entities, the enemies (they are addressed directly in 6:8). Here, in yet another sudden turn, this time towards confidence, the psalmist dispatches his enemies: "Depart from me" (6:8a) he enjoins, because Yahweh has heard "the voice of my weeping" and his "supplication [for grace]" (6:8b–9a): his prayer has been accepted (6:9b). That again leads one to think that the action of these foes were only secondary to the primary distressing factor, serious ill health and physical debilitation. In any case, in an aside to the cohort of God's devout, the supplicant testifies that the fate of these enemies has been sealed (6:10).[11]

Until now, first person suffixes had dominated (in 6:1–7): "my bones" (6:2b) and "my soul" are terrified (6:3a), "my soul" is need of rescue (6:4), "my groaning" is wearying, "my bed" is flooded with "my tears," "my couch" is liquefying (6:6), and "my eye" has wasted away because of "my adversaries" (6:7). But henceforth, in 6:8–10, the same noun forms are exclusively

---

9. Mays, *Psalms*, 59–60.

10. Mays, *Psalms*, 61. So also Goldingay, *Psalms*, 1:139.

11. That they are only "ashamed" (×2; 6:10) and not defeated or destroyed or otherwise incapacitated also hints at their secondary role in the causing the psalmist anguish (see below).

positive: "my weeping" has been noticed by God (6:8); "my supplication [for grace]" and "my prayer" have been heard by God (6:8b, 9a), and "my enemies" have been scared and chased off by God (6:10b). Whereas the name "Yahweh" had been employed for the extended petition of one in the agony of debilitation, in 6:1–7 (6:1, 2 [×2], 3, 4), hereafter in the psalm, in 6:8–10, the name of deity is used by one in assurance of deliverance (6:8, 9 [×2]).

Notice also the symmetric placement in the psalm, in 6:2 and in 6:9 (the second and the second-to-last verses, respectively, of the poem), of the root חן, *chn* ("be gracious to me," חָנֵּנִי, *channeni*, 6:2; and "my supplication [for grace]," תְּחִנָּתִי, *tchinnati*, 6:9), as well as the fact that these are the only two verses in the psalm where "Yahweh" occurs twice. The dramatic transformation of the situation of the psalmist was made possible by grace alone and that from this God alone! This confidence of prayer heard and supplication accepted is chiastically displayed in 6:9 that reads:[12]

> "[He] has heard—
> Yahweh—my supplication [for grace];
> Yahweh, my prayer
> He accepts."

All is well that ends (or is soon to end) well. Whereas earlier it was the psalmist's soul that had become "greatly terrified" at his plight and pain, and upon his physical frailty and impending demise (6:3a; and "terrified" in 6:2b), now it is the adversaries who have been discomfited, "terrified greatly" themselves—"all [כֹּל, *kol*]" of them (6:10a), echoing the use of כֹּל in 6:6b ("every") and 6:7b ("all"). And these antagonists are also "ashamed" (6:10 [×2]), perhaps at how they had taken advantage of the suffering psalmist in some way. "His healing and return to life will shame their hostility and expose their perfidy [6:10]."[13] The patterning of 6:10 is precise: on either side of "all my enemies" the syntax is identical: imperfect verb + imperfect verb + adverb:

Imperfect verb	Imperfect verb	Adverb
"They will be ashamed	and they will be terrified	greatly—
all my enemies;		
they will turn back,	they will be ashamed	suddenly."

A double shaming of enemies (6:10a, 10b) is quite appropriate after the double hearing of the psalmist's plea by Yahweh ("Yahweh has heard" in 6:8b, 9a). Right recompense for ruthless racketeers! So whereas it was Yahweh who was beseeched by the psalmist to "return" to him (שׁוּב, *shwv*, 6:4a; i.e., not abandon or neglect him), now it is those adversaries who will "turn back" (also שׁוּב, 6:10b). In fact, "return/turn back" (שׁוּב) forms an anagram with "ashamed" (בּוֹשׁ, *bwsh*)—a literal and verbal turning back! "They will be ashamed" is יֵבֹשׁוּ,

---

12. While the aspect of the perfect verbs in 6:9 indicate that God has already accepted the petition of the psalmist, that of the imperfect verbs in 6:10 show that the ousting of the enemies is still in the future. But the poet is sure that that day is coming: "The psalmist's faith, in other words, outstripped the reality of any change in his physical condition," and hence the perfects of certainty (Craigie, *Psalms 1–50*, 95).

13. Mays, *Psalms*, 61.

yevoshu; "they will turn back" is יָשֻׁבוּ, *yashuvu*. Yahweh has "returned" *towards* the psalmist; and so have the enemies, they, too, have "turned back"—but in the opposite direction, *away* from the psalmist. In other words, the calamitous circumstances have been overturned into confident comfort. With God summarily dispatching the opponents, shamed, scared, and staved off (6:10), the tide has changed, and things have been made better! And, in the end, to our surprise, we find the answer to the earlier question "until when?" (6:3b) in the final word of the psalm: it will be "suddenly" (6:10b). A brighter day is dawning and it is coming, soon and very soon—"suddenly"![14]

Sermon Map

I. Plight and Panic and Pain
    Frailty and terror of physical affliction (6:1–3)
    Impending death and extreme grief (6:5–7a)
    Trouble from opponents and exploiters (6:7b–8a)
    Move-to-relevance: Our physical burdens

II. Providence and Preservation and Peace
    Persistent prayer by the sufferer (6:1, 3b, 4–5)
    God's lovingkindness and grace (6:2a, 4b, 8b, 9)
    Opponents discomfited (6:8a, 10)
    Move-to-relevance: How God answers prayer

III. *Physical Peril? Pray!*
    Specifics on persistence in prayer

---

14. Curiously enough, whether God cured the psalmist of his physical problems we are not told; however, his enemies were discomfited. All that to say, *how* exactly God answers the prayer of his stricken people—answer them he will!—is not for us to dictate or forecast.

PSALM 7:1–17

Psalm of Disorientation

Vindication from Accusation

THIS IS THE FINAL lament of a cluster formed by Psalms 3–7. It is a prayer for vindication from false accusations of some kind; though that does not mean an absence of actual danger the psalmist is facing and from which he seeks relief: both are present in this song.

Translation

7:1	Yahweh my God, in You I have taken refuge;
	save me from all those who pursue me, and rescue me,
7:2	Lest, like a lion he rend my soul to pieces,
	dismembering [me], while there is none to rescue.
7:3	Yahweh my God, if I have done this—
	if there has been injustice on my hands,
7:4	if I have rendered evil to the one at peace with me,
	or have aided his lawless adversary—
7:5	may the enemy pursue my soul and overtake [me];
	and may he trample to the ground my life,
	and my honor in the dust may he lay.
7:6	Arise, Yahweh, in Your anger;
	lift up Yourself against the rage of my adversaries,
	and rouse [Yourself] for me
	[with the] judgment you have commanded.
7:7	Let the assembly of the peoples gather around You,
	and over it return on high [to judge].
7:8	Yahweh calls to account the peoples.
	Vindicate me, Yahweh, according to my righteousness
	and according to my integrity, Most High.

7:9	O may the evil of the wicked come to an end,
	but establish the righteous;
	for a trier of the hearts and innards
	is the righteous God
7:10	My shield [is] the Most High God,
	who delivers the upright in heart.
7:11	God is a righteous judge,
	and a God who is indignant all day.
7:12	If he [the wicked] does not repent, His sword He sharpens;
	His bow He draws and prepares it.
7:13	And for Himself He prepares weapons of death;
	His fiery arrows He makes.
7:14	Behold, he [the wicked] labors harm,
	and he conceives trouble,
	and he delivers falsehood.
7:15	A pit he has excavated, digging it [out],
	and he falls into the hole he made.
7:16	It returns—his trouble—onto his head,
	and upon his crown his violence lands.
7:17	I will give thanks to Yahweh for His righteousness,
	and will make music to the name of Yahweh Most High.

Structure

One can see from the structure of Psalm 7 that the contrast between the righteous (represented by the psalmist) and the wicked, including their fates at the hand of God, forms the bulk of the composition.

> **A** **Plea** (7:1–2): begins with "Yahweh my God" (7:1a)
>   **B** **Vindication** of righteous (7:3–5)
>   **C** **Plea** to Yahweh the Judge (7:6–8)
>   **D** **Judgment** of wicked and righteous (7:9)
>   **C'** **Declaration** about Yahweh the Judge (7:10–13)
>   **B'** **Condemnation** of wicked (7:14–16)
> **A'** **Praise** (7:17): ends with "Yahweh Most High" (7:17b)

Besides the plea to God (A, 7:1–2) and thanksgiving to God (A', 7:17b), the rest of the psalm deals with the issue of vindication of the righteous (B, 7:3–5) and the corresponding condemnation of the wicked (B', 7:14–16). As well, notice the focus on God as judge (C, D, C',

7:6–13). Deity permeates this psalm that begins and ends with a compound name for Yahweh ("Yahweh my God," 7:1a; and "Yahweh Most High," 17b).

Theological Focus

Facing false accusations, a violent hounding by enemies, the righteous trust in God, the righteous Judge and their protector and deliverer, to vindicate them and to take appropriate action against those enemies.

Commentary

Plea; Vindication (7:1–5)

The psalm commences with a plea in 7:1–2 (*A*), and a metaphorical reason for the plea is given in 7:2, the abstract nature of which enables the composition as a whole to be applicable for all God's people of all time. The plurality of pursuers in 7:1 also becomes concentrated into the singularity of one individual in 7:2, likely symbolic as well. For the reader, these adversaries may be one or many. The psalmist's foes "pursue" him (7:1b) like a "lion" capable of "rending" and "dismembering" (7:2). But what is worse, there is no help in sight (7:2b), at least not from any human source!

In 7:3–5 (*B*), the psalmist is adamant that he has done nothing to deserve this hounding by his foes. But if he is in fact guilty of injustice (7:3b), of rendering evil to "the one at peace with me" (i.e., a friend, 7:4a), or even of bestowing aid to an evil adversary of that friend (7:4b; i.e., even vicarious evildoing), he is willing to be "pursued" by the enemy, "overtaken," "trampled" to death, and to allow his honor to be sullied (7:5). The intensity of the psalmist's self-vindication is evident in the chiasm of 7:5bc, centered upon his life and his honor that he is willing to sacrifice, if found in the wrong:

> "May he trample
> to the ground
> **my life**,
> and **my honor**
> in the dust
> may he lay."

As is the case throughout the Psalter, such affirmations of innocence are not claims to sinlessness; the righteous individual, represented here by the psalmist, has lived faithfully unto God and with members of the community of God's people. Specifically, here the claim is guiltlessness with regard to the false charges laid against him. And with such righteousness, he asserts implicitly, he is on the side of God, against the wicked.[1]

---

1. Both the psalmist's community and God are described as "righteous," in 7:9b, 9d, 11a; and there is "my righteousness" in 7:8b and "His righteousness" in 7:17a. Interestingly, the phrases in 7:8b and 7:16b

The "story" of the psalm then appears to be a case of wrongful charges filed by virulent accusers of the psalmist, a particularly agonizing predicament. "The false accusation is harder to bear [than a true one], partly because it brings with it the experience of injustice, and partly because there may seem to be no escape from its consequences. We cannot repent of something we have not done, nor can we make restoration, and it is in the nature of false accusers that they do not easily depart and leave us in peace."[2]

Plea to the Judge; Judgment; Declaration about the Judge (7:6–13)

The appeal to the divine judge for a local matter concerning one individual seems to be overkill, but the child of God has the privilege of calling upon the heavenly Father for *anything*. Besides, even local matters demand "intervention from Yahweh in his cosmic role because the speaker perceives his perilous situation to reflect [ultimately] a breakdown in the world's underlying moral order—a breach of cosmic proportions which requires a cosmic remedy, the action of the world creator and sustainer . . . Only Yahweh can restore order out of chaos."[3] And what matter, however small or minute, does not impact the glory of God, the Creator of the universe? And so to Yahweh, the psalmist appeals.

The psalmist's plea to the divine Judge in 7:6–8 (C) refers to deity's "anger" against evildoing (7:6a[4]): the suppliant's hope; and his adversaries' "rage" (7:6b): the suppliant's threat. But he is confident that God will "arise," "lift up" and "rouse" himself on behalf of his people, rendering judgment (7:6) that "you have commanded," i.e., as God has rendered sentence, on behalf of the righteous and against the wicked.[5]

At the center of the psalm (D, 7:9) are the contrasting fates of the wicked (who "come to an end") and the righteous (who will be "established"). There is no pulling wool over the eyes of a "righteous God," the divine judge, for he is "a trier of the hearts and innards" (7:9c);[6] we are explicitly told in 7:11a that "God is a righteous judge." As if to emphasize the forensic nature of the psalm, both C and C' in the psalm's structure have words from the root "to judge": "judgment" (מִשְׁפָּט, *mishpat*) in 7:6d; "vindicate" (שׁפט, *shpht*) in 7:8b; and "judge" (שׁוֹפֵט, *shophet*) in 7:11a.[7] An "assembly of the peoples" of the earth are apparently gathered around this divine judge who comes to execute judgment ("over it return on high," pleads the suppliant; 7:7). For the psalmist and his cohort of the righteous, this judge, the "Most High God" is a protective "shield" that "delivers the upright in heart" (7:10). A military tone is unmistakable in the entreaty to God: "arise" (7:6a; see Num 10:35) and "rouse" (Ps 7:6c; see Jdg 5:12); and "peoples" (Ps 7:7a, 8a; see 2:1; 47:3), not to mention implements of battle ("shield," 7:10a;

---

are very similar—יְהוָה כְּצִדְקִי (*yhwh ktsidqi*, "Yahweh, according to my righteousness," 7:8b) and יְהוָה כְּצִדְקוֹ (*yhwh ktsidqo*, "Yahweh for His righteousness," 7:16b). There is also "my integrity" in 7:8c, and the self-label "upright in heart" in 7:10b.

2. Craigie, *Psalms 1–50*, 103.

3. Hubbard, "Dynamistic and Legal Processes," 273.

4. This is a God who is also "indignant" (7:11b) at the unfairness against his people.

5. God's "lifting up" (7:6b) in contrast to the suppliant's own humiliation (bringing down to the ground and laying in the dust) that he is willing to undergo if deemed guilty (7:5bc).

6. "Innards" or "kidneys."

7. In addition, there is "call to account" (דין, *dyn*) in 7:8a and "tester" (בחן, *bochen*) in 7:9c, both forensic terms.

"sword," 7:12a; "bow" and "arrows," 7:12b, 13b; "weapons of death," 7:13a; and "fiery arrows," 7:13b). All these show the divine judge also acting in his capacity as divine warrior for the benefit of his people. The war is on!

So, in a declaration about the divine magistrate (C', 7:10–13), the psalmist asserts that this judge is "indignant all day" on behalf of his people, and therefore will respond strongly to the wicked who oppress them—"sword whetted, bow taut and aimed, arrows flaming."[8] This is how God will "establish" (כון, *kwn*; 7:9b) the righteous, by unleashing the paraphernalia of war that he has "prepared" (also כון; 7:12b, 13a) against their persecutors. Interestingly enough, God is not shown to have acted yet. He is just getting prepared: there is a possibility left open that the wicked may repent and God may relent (7:12a).

Condemnation; Praise (7:14–17)

And if they do not repent, and if the opponent "labors harm," "conceives trouble," and "delivers falsehood" (7:14; referring to the opponent with a remarkable series of obstetrical analogies![9]), he will fall into the pit that he has dug out for others (7:15), his trouble will land upon his own pate (7:16). How God accomplished all this (or will surely accomplish all this, if a perfective future is the force of those verbs) is unclear, but the result is expected: as the wicked sowed, so they will reap. Indeed, 7:16 is chiastic, mirroring literally the "return" (falling back) upon the wicked all the evil he has perpetrated:

> "It returns—
>   his trouble—
>   onto his head,
>   and upon his crown
>   his violence
> lands."

"Evil eventually functions like a boomerang, bringing back upon its perpetrators the wickedness planned for others ... God was primed to act against the unrepentant sinner, but the nature of his action was simply to direct the consequences of evil away from the innocent and turn them back upon the perpetrators."[10] This is clear from the wordplay of שוב, *shwv*, in 7:12a ("repent") and 7:16a ("returns"): if the wicked does not "repent," his nefarious plots will "return" upon him. The one who "makes" holes (7:15b) had better be ready for a deity who "makes" fiery arrows for such evildoers (7:13b).

Did any of the wicked in this particular case repent? We don't know. So appropriately enough, the psalm's "story" is open-ended for the future appropriation by readers. In any case, the psalm concludes with a note of thanks and music-making to God—the righteous judge who sees, who knows, who cares, who acts on behalf of his people!

---

8. Goldingay, *Psalms*, 1:150.

9. However, the sequence of labor-conception-delivery is not medically in sequence. Besides it is a "he" that undergoes these physiological processes, and it is "harm" and "trouble" and "falsehood" that are the progeny (7:14)!

10. Craigie, *Psalms 1–50*, 103.

Sermon Map

I. Adversaries and Accusations
    Predatory adversaries (7:1–2)
    False accusations (7:3–5)
    Move-to-relevance: False accusations against us

II. Judge and Judgment
    Appeal to God to judge righteously vindicating the righteous (7:6–8)
    Appeal to God to deliver adversaries their just deserts (7:9, 11–16)
    Trust in God as protector and deliverer (7:10, 17)
    Move-to-relevance: Difficulty in trusting God

III. *Sing When Slandered!*
    Specifics on trusting God amidst false accusations

PSALM 8:1–9

Psalm of Orientation

Humanity's Delegated Dominion

THIS IS THE FIRST praise in the book of Psalms, and it is pure praise, without any invitation to others to join in, though, of course, that exhortation to participate is implicit in the text. It is also interesting that the previous psalm ended with a resolution by the psalmist to "praise Yahweh" and to "make music to the name of Yahweh" (7:17). And then we have Psalm 8, that begins (and ends) with praise to the "name" of "Yahweh."[1] Psalm 8 has the distinction of being the only psalm addressed exclusively to God.

Translation

8:1	Yahweh, our Lord, how majestic is Your name in all the earth!
	[You] who have presented Your splendor upon the heavens
8:2	from the mouth of babies and sucklings—
	You have established strength because of Your adversaries,
	to put an end to the enemy and the vindictive.
8:3	When I see Your heavens, the works of Your fingers,
	the moon and the stars, which You have appointed,
8:4	what is a human that You are mindful of him,
	and a mortal that You care for him!
8:5	But You make him lower than God by a little,
	and with glory and splendor You crown him.
8:6	You make him rule over the works of Your hands;
	all things You have set under his feet,
8:7	sheep and oxen—all—
	and also beasts of the field,

---

1. This psalm, with its mention of astronomical entities (8:3), has been described as a song for stargazers, but even more, for soul-searchers (deClaissé-Walford et al., *Book of Psalms*, 120).

8:8   birds of the heavens, and fish of the sea,
           whatever passes through the paths of the seas.

8:9   Yahweh, our Lord, how majestic is Your name in all the earth.

Structure

The psalm is carefully structured, with a number of linguistic and conceptual parallels involved (see below), and it centers upon humanity's meekness and greatness—a matter of great wonder for the psalmist (and the rest of us):[2]

					Theme
A	"Yahweh, our Lord, how majestic is Your name in all the earth! [8:1a]				Praise
	B	[You] who have presented Your splendor upon the *heavens* from the mouth of babies and sucklings— [8:1b–2a]			
		C	You have established strength because of Your adversaries, to put an end to the enemy and the vindictive. [8:2bc]		Deity's Rule
			D	When I see Your heavens, the *works of Your fingers*, the moon and the stars, which *You have appointed* [כּוֹנָנְתָּה, konanttah] [8:3]	
				E what is a *human* that You are mindful of him, and a *mortal* that You care for him? [8:4]	Humanity's Meekness
				E' But You make him lower than *God* by a little, and with glory and splendor You crown him! [8:5]	Humanity's Greatness
			D'	You make him rule over the *works of Your hands*; all things *You have set* [כֹּל שַׁתָּה, kol shattah] under his feet, [8:6]	
		C'	sheep and oxen—all— and also beasts of the field, [8:7]		Humanity's Rule
	B'	birds of the *heavens*, and fish of the sea, whatever passes through the paths of the seas. [8:8]			
A'	Yahweh, our Lord, how majestic is Your name in all the earth!" [8:9]				Praise

Theological Focus

A great God worthy of praise, who created the magnificent cosmos and all it contains, and whose dominion is boundless, demonstrates his mindfulness and care of humans by bestowing them with his glory and splendor, and delegating to them dominion over all nature.

---

2. Modified from Kraut, "Birds and the Babes," 17. Italicized elements show linguistic correspondence. This division of the psalm yields, besides the joyous exclamations of 8:1a and 8:9, eight two-line units as shown in the figure above (so also Goldingay, *Psalms*, 1:155).

PSALM 8:1–9

Commentary

Praise (8:1a); Praise (8:9)

The psalm commences and concludes with praise to Yahweh's "name" (*A*, *A'*; 8:1a, 9). "Name" indicates the person of God himself; his "majesty" (8:1a) is functionally synonymous with his "splendor" (8:1b).[3] It appears that a plurality of persons is uttering these praises ("*our* Lord," 8:1a, 9a—the first instance of this in the Psalter), but 8:3 indicates a singular party, the psalmist, discerning the work of God. In its entirety, however, this psalm is spoken to deity.

Deity's Rule (8:1b–3); Humanity's Rule (8:6–8)

The section on deity's rule (*B*, *C*, *D*; 8:1b–3) contains some interpretive difficulties that are rendered resolvable when seen in light of the corresponding elements in the section on humanity's rule (*D'*, *C'*, *B'*; 8:6–8). It is clear that *B'* (8:8) deals with the extent of *human* dominion over nature. In that case, it is likely that its counterpart *B* (8:1b–2a) deals with the extent of *divine* dominion over nature ("heavens" is repeated in both elements, in 8:1d, 8a). And God's splendor in the heavens is recounted by infants—"from the mouth of babies and sucklings" (8:2a). Kraut offers an intriguing explanation of the parallel of *B* (8:1b–2a, with its "babies" and "sucklings") and *B'* (8:8, with its "birds" and "fish"). What is characteristically mouthed by "babies" is incoherent human sounds, akin to avian chirping; and what "sucklings" do with their mouths finds its nexus with the sucking action of fish swallowing water to push through their gills. In other words, "God's mastery over the babbling and sucking humans (*B*) [who utter his praise] is compared with man's mastery over the babbling and sucking creatures of the animal kingdom (*B'*)."[4] Thus, everything—"all things bright and beautiful, all creatures great and small, all things wise and wonderful"[5]—made by the Lord God and falling under divine (direct and sovereign) dominion, are also within human (indirect and delegated) dominion.

Also raising problems is *C* (8:2bc). Here again reference to *C'* (8:7) helps. Both elements list three actors: "adversaries," "the enemy," and "the vindictive" (besides God) in *C*, and "sheep," "oxen," and "beasts of the field" in *C'*. The latter trio is part of creation that is under human dominion; the former set then must be part of creation under divine dominion. "In each element, then, the will of one actor (God in *C*, man in *C'*) is imposed upon three beings that lie within his dominion. The will of God's enemies is futile in the face of his hegemony (*C*), just as the will of animals is futile in the face of man's domination (*C'*). . . . The picture of God's dominion in the first half of the psalm finds an analogous picture of human dominion in the second half of the psalm."[6]

The parallelism between *D* (8:3) and *D'* (8:6) is obvious: in addition to "the works of Your fingers/hands" (8:3a, 6a), there is also the semantic parallel between "You have

---

3. The "name" of Yahweh and his "splendor" show up together also in 148:13.
4. Kraut, "Birds and the Babes," 20–21.
5. The title and first line of a hymn by Cecil Frances Alexander (1848).
6. Kraut, "Birds and the Babes," 22. The "establishment of strength because of . . . adversaries" is not entirely clear. The best explanation is that God exercises might against his foes; that makes sense of 8:2c. "Readers of the first eight psalms will also note that even a hymn of praise attends to enemies [8:2], following a series of lament psalms saturated with enemies" (Brueggemann and Bellinger, *Psalms*, 59). Perhaps that is to underscore the fact that though humans suffer (Psalms 1–7), and perhaps in spite of, or through, their sufferings, they are crowned with "glory and splendor."

appointed" (8:3a) and "You have set" (8:6b), as well as a sonic parallel between כּוֹנָ֫נְתָּה ("You have appointed," 8:3a) and שַׁ֣תָּה כֹ֑ל (8:6b, "all things You have set").[7] *D* continues the notion of divine dominion over the elements of the cosmos that God has appointed, and *D'* continues the notion of human dominion over nature that God has set under mankind. If the cosmos is merely part of the "works of Your fingers" (8:3a), and if creation is so extensive, so immense, and splendid, then how much more vast, boundless, and glorious must be the great God who "pushed and prodded" everything into shape with just his "divine digits"?[8] Everything else, humanity included, must be so infinitesimal! "From an objective perspective human beings are but the tiniest fragments in a giant universe; it is not conceivable that they could have significance or a central position in that universe."[9] No wonder the psalmist moves into his rhapsodic questioning in 8:4, as he marvels about mankind deputized to rule over these magnificent "works of Your hands" (8:6a).

Humanity's Meekness (8:4); Humanity's Greatness (8:5)

That *E* (8:4; humanity's meekness) and *E'* (8:5; humanity's greatness) form the center of the chiastic structure of Psalm 8 is well accepted. In the former there is "human" and "mortal" (literally "son of man"), feeble and fallible: humanity's meekness. In the latter we see mankind made only "lower than God by a little": humanity's greatness. "God is so much greater than is man and should not, therefore, be mindful of him. Yet, on the other hand, God chooses to take note of man and endow him with godlike power, to be exercised over nature and its creatures."[10] In fact, in 8:4–5, God is the subject of all the verbs: He "is mindful"; he "cares"; he "makes him lower"; and he "crowns." The four verbs also form two pairs of assonant words, thus further emphasizing it is all of God, and that all that is of God is harmonious and good: תִזְכְּרֶ֑נּוּ and תִפְקְדֶֽנּוּ (*tizkrennu* and *tiphqdennu*; 8:4); and תְּחַסְּרֵ֣הוּ and תְּעַטְּרֵֽהוּ (*tchassrehu* and *t'attrehu*; 8:5). Remarkably, the only verb in all of Psalm 8 that has the psalmist (or even any human) for a subject is "see" in 8:3a. That's all humankind does apparently—gaze in awed wonder!

And so the same exclamatory query raised earlier of God, "how . . ." (מָה, *mah*, 8:1, 9), is now raised again of humanity: "what . . . ?" (also מָה, 8:4a). Attributes normally belonging to God—"glory" and "splendor" (הָדָר, *hadar*, in 8:5a; הוֹד, *hod*, in 8:1b; also see 21:5; 29:1; 45:3; 104:1)—are now used of mankind: humanity now shares the dignity of deity! Thus the centerpiece, *E* and *E'* (8:4–5), makes the transition from humanity's meekness to humanity's greatness. Indeed, "what is a human that You are mindful of him" and "[what is] a mortal that You care for him" (8:4) are not questions to be answered, but exclamations and proclamations of wonder!

---

7. Kraut, "Birds and the Babes," 19n20.

8. Craigie, *Psalms 1–50*, 108.

9. Craigie, *Psalms 1–50*, 108. If one were to sequence the gradation of greatness noted in Psalm 8 as one moves through the composition, it might look like this, in descending order: heavens → humanity → nature, with God on either side bookending the song (8:1, 9a).

10. Kraut, "Birds and the Babes," 23. This reading also makes it clear that, since it is the dominion of God and humanity that are contrasted on either side of 8:4–5, אֱלֹהִים, *'elohim*, in 8:5a must refer to deity and not to a constellation of heavenly beings, "gods" (a possible translation of the plural word, as in 82:6).

PSALM 8:1–9

Cosmic heavens and earthly nature, both the "works of his fingers/hands" (8:3a, 6a), have been placed under the feet of mankind! The chiasm of 8:6 demonstrates the extent and scope of humanity's rule:

> "You make him rule over
> the works of Your hands;
> all things
> You have set under his feet."

The work of God's *hands* are now set under mankind's *feet*. God is over "all" (8:1, 9); and now human beings have dominion over the same "all" ("*all* things" in 8:6b; and "all" in 8:7a). Thus, it is further established that humanity, with indirect and delegated dominion over all of God's direct and sovereign dominion, is only "lower than God by a little" (8:5a). Great, therefore, is mankind's responsibility to God, under God.

It must be noted that "human disobedience did not undo God's placing the animate world under humanity's authority any more than it eliminated the divine image from humanity."[11] In fact, such human governance and superintendence of divine creation may have been rendered all the more necessary with the post-fall entrance of evil into God's perfect handiwork. In sum, "subtly our understanding of the ground for praising Yahweh has shifted from the first verse to the last. At the beginning our praise began by affirming the magnificence of the creator. At the end, we stand in awe at the unexpected grace that has elevated his human works to unimaginable heights of glory, honor, and responsibility."[12] What a God and what gracious condescension is his!

Sermon Map

I. The Dominion of God
   Majestic creator (8:1–3, 9)
   Meekness of humanity (8:4)
   Move-to-relevance: The manifestation of God's majesty
II. The Dominion of Humanity
   Delegation of humanity (8:5)
   Glorious ruler (8:6–8)
   Move-to-relevance: Our responsibility as rulers under God
III. *Rule Responsibly with The Ruler!*
   Specifics on discharging our responsibility as rulers of creation

---

11. Goldingay, *Psalms*, 1:161.
12. Wilson, *Psalms*, 1:209.

PSALM 9:1–20

Psalm of Disorientation

Divine Judgment and Order

THERE ARE SEVERAL REASONS to believe that Psalms 9 and 10 in some prior iteration formed a single psalm (as the LXX has them). Jointly, they form an acrostic or alphabetic psalm, though an incomplete one, with almost a third of the letters missing: the segments of Psalm 9 run from א to כ (*Aleph* to *Kaph*); those of Psalm 10, from ל to ת (*Lamed* to *Taw*): presumably half the Hebrew alphabet (eleven letters) in each psalm, but with gaps.[1] Other reasons to suspect the unity of Psalms 9 and 10 include: Psalm 9 closes with "Selah" (untranslated here)—it is elsewhere found only in the middle of a psalm; Psalm 10 has no superscription, while most others in this section and book have one; a number of words are shared between the two psalms;[2] the theme of God's rule is common to both (9:4, 7, 11; 10:16). However, there is more praise in Psalm 9, with God on the center stage (though enemies are present), and more lament in Psalm 10, with the wicked in the limelight (though God is victorious). Broadly, Psalm 9 deals with a more corporate prayer: nations and the kingship of Yahweh shows up early

---

1. The acrostic also demonstrates an inconsistent verse-to-letter distribution, some letters with one verse each, others with two or more. Most of the data on the acrostics in this chapter are taken from Ronald Benun's perspicuous observations in "Evil and the Disruption of Order," 2–30.

2. Including: "perish/destroy [אבד, *'vd*]" in 9:3b, 5a, 6c, 18b and 10:16b; "sit" in 9:4b, 7a, 11a and 10:8a; "judgment/judge/justice" in 9:4, 7b, 8a, 16a, 19b and 10:5b, 18a (all from the root שפט, *shpht*); "always" in 9:5b, 18b and 10:16a; "forever" in 9:5b, 7a and 10:16a; "wicked" in 9:5a, 16b, 17a and 10:2a, 3a, 4a, 13a, 15a; "nations" in 9:5a, 15a, 17b, 19b, 20b and 10:16b; "perpetuity" in 9:6a, 18a and 10:11b; "establish" in 9:7b and 10:17b; "time" in 9:9b and 10:1b, 5a; "in times of trouble" in 9:9b and 10:1b; "oppressed" in 9:9a and 10:18b; "seek/call to account [דרש, *drsh*]" in 9:10b, 12a and 10:4b, 13b, 15b; "abandon" in 9:10b and 10:14c; "forget" in 9:12b, 17b, 18a and 10:11a, 12b; "afflicted/affliction" in 9:12b, 13b, 18b and 10:2a, 9b, 9c, 12b, 17a; "see" in 9:13b and 10:11b, 14a; "that/these" (a rare relative pronoun, זו, *zu*: 11× in the Psalms) in 9:15b and 10:2b; "mortal" in 9:19a, 20b and 10:18b (at the final verse[s] of each psalm); "arise" in 9:19a and 10:12a. The righteous in both psalms are in a minority position and adopt a persecuted stance as the "oppressed" (9:9a and 10:18a), "those who know Your name" and "those who seek You" (9:10), "afflicted/affliction" (9:12b, 13b, 18b and 10:2a, 9b, 9c, 12b, 17a), "needy one" (9:18a), "unfortunate" (10:10b, 14c), "orphan" (10:14d, 18a). Also, considering Psalms 9–10 together, the categories of righteous and wicked are each labeled by or compared using *nine* different nouns or participles. The righteous: "peoples," "oppressed," "those who know Your name," "those who seek You," "afflicted," "needy one," "innocent," "unfortunate one," and "orphan. The wicked: "enemy/ies," "nations," "wicked," "those who hate," "human/person," "greedy one," "lion," "mighty ones," and "evildoer." But deity wins with *ten* discrete mentions: "Yahweh," "Most High," "refuge," "who sits [enthroned] in Zion," "who seeks blood," "who lift me," "God [אלהים, *'elohim*]," "God [אל, *'el*]," "helper," and "King."

(9:4–10; and only later in Psalm 10, and just a single verse, 10:16); there is praise, corporately engaged, in Psalm 9 (9:1–2, 11–12; it is absent in Psalm 10). It is therefore appropriate to deal with each separately, respecting the intent of the Hebrew text as we have it.

Leaving out the two instances of "Selah" in Psalm 9, we find that that psalm has 162 words, exactly the same word count as in Psalm 10. It is quite remarkable that the former, with only ten of the first eleven Hebrew letters of the alphabet, should have a word count identical to the latter, that has only five of the last eleven letters. One must conclude, therefore, that no words have been deleted in the process of redaction in the MT, and that the final "aberrations in the acrostic structure may be intentional."[3] This trail will be followed in the analysis of both psalms in this work.

There are a number of ambiguities in Psalms 9–10: the psalm uses both the plural and singular to describe both oppressors and afflicted (wicked: 9:3a and 9:6a; righteous 9:1–4 and 9:9–10; etc.).[4] Occasionally plural verbs are employed with singular subjects ("was finished," 9:6a; "fall," 10:10b). There is also the description of God's actions in the past (9:4–6, 15; 10:16–17; etc.). "[The joint psalm] then provides a wide-ranging portrayal of personal and communal attacks that individuals and communities can utilize in different situations."[5]

Translation

9:1	[א ALEPH]	I will give thanks to Yahweh with all my heart;
		I will tell of all Your wonders.
9:2		I will rejoice and exult in You;
		I will make music to Your name, Most High.
9:3	[ב BETH]	When my enemies turn back,
		they stumble and they perish before You.
9:4		For You have upheld my justice and my cause;
		You have sat on the throne judging righteously.
9:5	[ג GIMEL]	You have rebuked the nations, You have destroyed the wicked;
		their name You have blotted out forever and always.
9:6	[ה HE]	The enemy was finished—ruins for perpetuity,
		and the cities You have uprooted;
		they have perished—[even] their memory.
9:7	[ו WAW]	But Yahweh sits forever;
		He has established His throne for judgment,
9:8		And He—He judges the world in righteousness;
		He decides the cause for the peoples with equity.

---

3. Benun, "Evil and the Disruption of Order," 3. Word counts appear to be integral to the acrostic: the primary verse (the first verse associated with a given letter) of each of four successive letters in the psalm—ו (9:7), ז (9:11), ח (9:13), and ט (9:15)—have the same number of words as the numerical value of those letters (6, 7, 8, and 9, respectively) (Benun, "Evil and the Disruption of Order," 4).

4. Psalm 9 generally leans towards a corporate and national crisis, Psalm 10 towards a more individual situation.

5. Goldingay, *Psalms*, 1:169.

9:9		So Yahweh is a refuge for the oppressed,
		a refuge in times of trouble;
9:10		And those who know Your name trust in You,
		for You have not abandoned those who seek You, Yahweh.
9:11	[ז ZAYIN]	Make music to Yahweh, who sits [enthroned] in Zion;
		announce among the peoples His deeds.
9:12		For He who seeks blood, them he has remembered;
		He has not forgotten the wailing of the afflicted.
9:13	[ח CHETH]	Be gracious to me, Yahweh;
		see my affliction from those who hate me,
		You who lift me up from the gates of death,
9:14		that I may tell of all Your praises;
		in the gates of daughter Zion
		I jubilate in Your deliverance.
9:15	[ט TETH]	The nations have sunk down in the hole which they have made;
		in that net they had hidden, their foot has been caught.
9:16		Yahweh has caused Himself to be known; judgment he has worked;
		by the doing of His hands the wicked has been snared.
9:17	[י YODH]	The wicked return to Sheol,
		all the nations who forget God.
9:18	[כ KAPH]	For the needy one will not be forgotten in perpetuity,
		[nor] the hope of the afflicted perish for always.
9:19		Arise, Yahweh, do not let a mortal defy;
		may the nations be judged before Your presence.
9:20		Put them in fear, Yahweh;
		may the nations know they are mortal.

Structure

The structure of Psalm 9 is straightforward, with praise (9:1–2, 11–12) and plea (9:13–14, 19–20) sections broken up by God's portrayal as judge of both the wicked and the righteous (9:3–10), and the final disposition of each group (9:15–18).

9:1–2	**Praise** ("sing praise," 9:2b)	
9:3–6		God: Judge against the wicked
9:7–10		God: Judge for the righteous
9:11–12	**Praise** ("sing praises," 9:11a)	
9:13–14	**Plea**	
9:15–17		Fate of the wicked
9:18		Hope of the righteous
9:19–20	**Plea**	

Theological Focus

When the wicked disrupt life and shalom with their oppression and affliction, the community of the righteous trusts in their divine avenger and deliverer and his grace, the one who never forgets his people, to see and to take action, by casting down enemies and lifting up God-seekers, ultimately establishing order, thus causing celebration among them.

Commentary

Praise (9:1–2)

Psalm 9 commences with a typical declaration of intent to praise (9:1–2), making up its א *Aleph* segment. Not only does the א *Aleph* primary verse (9:1) begin with that letter, so do its second line and both lines of its associated secondary verse (9:2): i.e., 9:1a, 1b, 2a, 2b all begin with א.

The depth of gratitude to God is evident: the psalmist gives thanks "with all my heart" and intends to tell of "all Your wonders" (9:1). Not only does he "tell," he also "makes music" (9:2b).

God: Judge (9:3–10)

In the next two sections (making up 9:3–10), we see God as judge against the wicked (9:3–6), and God as judge for the righteous (9:7–10). In both, God is explicitly said to be "judging" (9:4b, 8a; the root שפט, *shpht*, also shows up in 9:4a, "justice," and in 9:7b, "judgment"[6]) "righteously/in righteousness" (9:4b, 8a), "sitting" (9:4b, 7a; also see 9:11a) on his "throne" (9:4b, 7b); in both sections, God is said to uphold the legal claim of the righteous against the wicked (דין, *din*, "cause" [noun], 9:4a; דין, *dyn*, "decide the cause" [verb], 9:8b). While, no doubt, this judgment encompasses eschatological events, that is not what is in view here.

---

6. Also see 9:16a, 19b for the repetition of the root.

"The psalmist experiences present enemies and anticipates the present reality of deliverance. His anticipation is based on the conviction that God is seated, that—despite his experience of affliction—God is still on the throne!"[7]

The general recitation of the acts of God with the perfect form of the verbs in this section (9:4–6) may indicate prior events, but this is more likely to be poetic and gnomic assertions of how God always acts (the imperfect verbs employed in 9:3b, 7a, 8a, 8b, 9a, 10a validate this reading). Drawing upon these characteristic performances of deity in this judgment section of 9:3–10, the psalmist can move to praise again (9:11–12), before launching into his plea (9:13–14), emphasizing the fate of the wicked and the hope of the righteous (9:15–18), and returning to end the psalm with a resumption of his plea (9:19–20).

Let us now examine God's judging activities separately, also paying attention to the idiosyncrasies of the acrostic.

God: Judge against the Wicked (9:3–6)

God as judge against the wicked is the focus of 9:3–6: "justice/judge/judgment" occurs in 9:4b, 7b, 8a (from the same root שׁפט); and "enemies" and "enemy" occur for the only time in the psalm in 9:3a and 9:6a, bookending this subsection. These foes "perish" before God (אבד, 'vd, 9:3a; also see 9:6c, 18b)—they were "destroyed" by God (also אבד, 9:5a). Their overthrow—"ruins for perpetuity," "cities . . . uprooted"—was metaphorically total: "[even] their memory" had perished (9:6c). This is what happens when the divine Judge is on his throne judging. The wicked is wiped out "forever" (9:5b), for God is seated on his throne, judging, "forever" (9:7a). The permanence of God's judgeship is matched by the permanence of the elimination of the wicked. Therefore the psalmist and his comrades can draw comfort.

Like the א *Aleph* segment, the ב *Beth* segment of the psalm also has a primary verse (9:3) and a secondary verse (9:4). So far, good. But then in the ג *Gimel* segment, we hear the first mention of "wicked" in its primary verse (9:5) and immediately the regularity and order established thus far is disrupted: the ג *Gimel* segment is bereft of a secondary verse, and there is no ד *Daleth* segment. Strikingly, where the ד *Daleth* segment ought to have been, the now "blank space" (so to speak) between 9:5 and 9:6 is "preceded" by the blotting out of the name of the wicked forever and eternally (9:5b) and "followed" by the perpetual ruining of the enemy (9:6a). This erasure of the wicked is thereby literally carried out in the effacement of the ד *Daleth* segment. (The following ה *He* segment, too, has no associated verse, only a primary one [9:6].) All that to say: What is textually asserted is being textually pictured![8]

God: Judge for the Righteous (9:7–10)

Whereas God was a destroying judge *against* the wicked (9:3–6), he is a vindicating judge *for* the righteous (9:7–10), "a refuge" for them "in times of trouble" (9:9). Therefore those

---

7. Craigie, *Psalms 1–50*, 119.

8. Also marking intentionality in this careful construction of the acrostic is the fact that the ה *He* segment's verse (9:6) begins and ends with ה (first word: הָאוֹיֵב, ha'oyev; last word: הֵמָּה, hemmah) and the ו *Waw* segment's primary verse (9:7) begins and ends with ו (first word: וַיהוָה, wayhwh; last word: כִּסְאוֹ, kis'o); however, the ג *Gimel* segment's verse (9:5) begins with ג (first word: גָּעַרְתָּ, ga'artta), but ends with ד (last word: וָעֶד, wa'ed)—a suspicious finger pointing to the (intentional) deletion of the ד *Daleth* segment. See Benun, "Evil and the Disruption of Order," 3.

who know God's "name" (9:10)—those who, with the psalmist, praise his "name" (9:2b)—can trust this divine judge.[9]

After the disruption of the acrostic in 9:5–6, proper order is reestablished with the ו *Waw* segment that has in its primary verse (9:7) "But Yahweh sits forever"![10] Indeed, "Yahweh" is the first word (וַיהוָה), the last word, and the middle word (the fifteenth), in the twenty-nine words of 9:7–10 (in 9:7a, 9a, 10b). Besides, this ו *Waw* segment not only has a primary and secondary verse (9:7, 8), but also a tertiary and quaternary verse (9:9, 10). A plenitude and abundance of order under Yahweh! And we see this decorum continuing to be represented in the fullness of primary and secondary verses for each of the next three letters: the ז *Zayin* segment (9:11–12), the ח *Cheth* segment (9:13–14), and the ט *Teth* segment (9:15–16).

Praise (9:11–12)

The psalmist returns to praise in 9:11–12, based on what he had just said of the judgment of God, *against* the wicked and *for* the righteous (9:3–10). The righteous, he had noted, were those who "seek" God (דרש, *drsh*, 9:10b); this God who "seeks" (דרש, 9:12a) the blood of the wicked as a divine avenger, would, in turn, remember the righteous who "seek" him, and he will not forget their wailing.[11] So the one who "makes music" in 9:2b now exhorts the entire company of the righteous to "make music" (9:11a) to the one seated (i.e., enthroned, as in 9:4b, 7) in Zion. God's enthronement in Zion (9:11) bespeaks the immanence of divine presence among his people. What a relief! No wonder the righteous can produce music.

Plea (9:13–14)

In 9:13–14 we hear, for the first time in this psalm, the plea of the righteous. Addressed to Yahweh, it seeks the grace of the one who rescues (or can/will rescue) the psalmist from the "gates" of death (9:13c), so that the liberated soul may celebrate God in the "gates" of "daughter Zion" (9:14).[12] The avenger who requires the blood of the wicked who try to kill (9:12a), is the same Deliverer who keeps the righteous from being killed.[13] And to counter the wicked who "hate" the psalmist (9:13b), the latter requests graciousness from his God (9:13a).

Curiously enough the plea to be gracious is accompanied by a rather non-specific "see my affliction" (9:13ab). For the psalmist and the righteous, that is apparently more than enough: God sees. They are confident that a seeing God is an acting God, who will engage on their behalf, for their welfare, in his grace. The psalmist is so sure of this that 9:14 has him shouting for joy, "that I may tell of all Your praises" (9:14a; a line very similar to 9:1b: "I will tell of all Your wonders"), exulting in his deliverance.

---

9. But the "name" of the wicked nations is destroyed (9:5a).

10. Likely in the heavenlies, but he also "sits" in Zion (9:11a), and in judgment (9:4b); see "throne" in 9:4b, 7b.

11. The "them" in 9:12a, the ones Yahweh remembers, are "those who know Your name" and "trust in You" (9:10a); these are equated to the "afflicted" in 9:12b.

12. "'Ms. Zion' ['daughter Zion'] occurs only here in the Psalms . . . as a personification of the city to which Yhwh is committed as father or lover" (Goldingay, *Psalms*, 1:175). Elsewhere the term is found often in the OT, for instance in 2 Kgs 19:21; Isa 1:8; 62:11; Jer 6:2; Lam 1:6; Mic 1:13; Zeph 3:14; Zech 2:10; etc.

13. Craigie, *Psalms 1–50*, 120.

Fate of the Wicked (9:15–17)

Anticipating the grace of God and the answer to his plea, the psalmist deals with the fate of the wicked (9:15–17) and the hope of the righteous (9:18).

The nations in vain "made" a hole (עשׂה, *'sh*, 9:15a) into which they have sunk. In more ways than one we are shown that what the wicked sow, they reap, for against these hole-makers (grave-diggers?) God "worked" a judgment (also עשׂה, 9:16a). It is not as though they underwent some kind of accidental entrapment—their foot getting caught in the net they had hidden (9:15b). No, it was "by the doing [עשׂה] of His hands" that the wicked was "snared" (9:16b)—his "hands" ensnared their "foot"! The "hole" they made for others becomes the destination of the wicked (9:15a), and into Sheol they are escorted (9:17a[14]), all who had forgotten God.

Hope of the Righteous (9:18)

Earlier, the psalmist had asserted that "the enemy was finished—ruins for *perpetuity*" (9:6a). But here it is declared that the righteous, the needy one, "will not be forgotten in *perpetuity*" (9:18a). One is ruined perpetually; the other is remembered perpetually. Likewise, the wicked are those who "forget" God (9:17b); but the righteous will not be "forgotten" (9:18; the passive indicating that it is God who does not forget them; also see 9:12b). And the "name"[15] of the wicked had been "blotted out . . . *forever and always*" (9:5b)—even their memory (9:6b)—but the hope of the righteous would "[not] perish *for always*" (9:18b). Whereas the wicked "perish" and are "destroyed" by God (9:3b, 5a, 6c: all employing אבד), the righteous are assured that their hope will *not* "perish [אבד]" (9:18b).

In 9:16 we have the second mention of "wicked" in this psalm, followed right away by a third mention in 9:17 (two instances back-to-back). And again, immediately there is literary disruption, a gash in the texture of the text, so to speak: the י *Yodh* segment is missing a secondary verse—it has only a primary one (9:17). But upon entry into the כ *Kaph* segment that bears the hope of the righteous (9:18), order is restored again.

Plea (9:19–20)

This resumption of order in text is marked by the כ *Kaph* segment having not the usual primary, but a secondary and a tertiary verse (9:19–20) that invoke Yahweh: "Arise, Yahweh" (9:19a) and "Put them in fear, Yahweh" (9:20a). This constitutes the resumption of the psalmist's plea (from 9:13–14). With that double invocation comes restoration of order from the disorder created by the corresponding double mention of the "wicked" in 9:16b, 17a.[16] And thus, with that duo of imperatives addressed to deity, order returns to Psalm 9, and the psalmist concludes his song of disorientation. Both verses in this section mention "mortal" (9:19a,

---

14. Now we understand that when the "enemies *turned back*" to flee (שׁוב, *shwv*, 9:3a), they were attempting to "*return* to Sheol" (also 9:17, שׁוב): they were escaping . . . into the grave! "Hole" (or "grave") as a synonym for "Sheol" or "death" is common in the Psalms (see 16:10; 30:9; 49:9; 55:23; 103:4).

15. In another contrast to the "name" of Yahweh (9:2b, 10a).

16. Benun, "Evil and the Disruption of Order," 7.

20b; and, as noted, "Yahweh" occurs twice) as if to motivate God to respond: "*Mortals* cannot defy you, *Lord*. Let the enemies realize they are only *mortal*, *Lord*!"

If we consider Psalm 10 to be part of this psalm, then 9:19—10:1a constitutes a delightful twist on your standard chiasm:

9:19aα	"Yahweh"	
9:19aβ	"human"	
9:19b		"nations"
9:20a	**"Yahweh"**	
9:20bα		"nations"
9:20bβ	"human"	
10:1a	"Yahweh"	

Yahweh is literally barricading the offenders off, both individual humans and institutional nations! And why not? The righteous judge, the avenger, the deliverer, can be trusted to protect, for he is the refuge of the righteous, the hope of the hopeless—he is at the center of it all!

Sermon Map

I. Oppression of the Community by the Wicked
   Enemies (9:3, 6), wicked (9:5, 16, 17), oppression/trouble (9:9)
   Affliction (9:12, 13, 18), hatred, near death (9:13), entrapment (9:15)
   Nations (9:15, 19, 20), in need (9:18)
   Textual disorder
   Move-to-relevance: Our oppression

II. Adjudication by the Divine
   Enthroned Judge (9:4, 7–9)
   Destruction of enemies (9:3, 5–6, 15–17, 19–20)
   Grace to the righteous (9:13, 18)
   Glorious ruler (9:6–8)
   Restoration of textual order
   Move-to-relevance: Our responsibility as rulers under God

III. Preservation of the Righteous
   Trust in the Refuge (9:10)
   Praise to the Deliverer (9:1–2, 11–12, 14)

IV. *Group Praise for Gracious Protection!*
   Specifics on communal trust in, and praise to, God for deliverance

PSALM 10:1–18

Psalm of Disorientation

God's Kingship Defeats the Wicked's Disorder

As was noted under Psalm 9, that composition and this current one were likely united in a single song at some point in their histories. However, there are reasons to treat them separately, as does the Hebrew text as we have received it. There is more praise in Psalm 9, more lament in Psalm 10 (no praise section here); God is front and center in Psalm 9, the wicked are prominent and belligerent in Psalm 10.

Translation

10:1 [ל LAMED] Why, Yahweh, do You stand far off,
    [and] hide in times of trouble?

10:2 In arrogance the wicked hounds the afflicted one;
    they are caught in these schemes they have devised.

10:3 For the wicked boasts upon his soul's desire,
    and the greedy one curses [and] reviles Yahweh.

10:4 The wicked, haughty in his countenance,
    does not seek [Him]; that there is no God
    [is the basis of] all his schemes.

10:5 His paths endure at all times.
    Your judgments are high, [away] from before him;
    all his adversaries—he snorts at them.

10:6 He says to his heart, "I will not be moved;
    [for] whom, from generation to generation, [is] no calamity."

10:7 His mouth is full of cursing and deceit and oppression;
    under his tongue is trouble and harm.

10:8 He sits in ambush [near] the villages;
    in the hiding places he slaughters the innocent;

		his eyes stealthily watch for the unfortunate one.
10:9		He lies in ambush in a hiding place as a lion in its lair;
		he lies in ambush, to catch the afflicted;
		he catches the afflicted, drawing him into his net.
10:10		Crushed, bowed down,
		and the unfortunate fall by his mighty ones.
10:11		He says to his heart, "God has forgotten;
		He has concealed His face; He will not see in perpetuity."
10:12	[ק QOPH]	Arise, Yahweh; God, lift up Your hand;
		do not forget the afflicted.
10:13		Why has the wicked reviled God?
		He says to his heart, "You will not call to account."
10:14	[ר RESH]	You have seen—trouble and provocation You Yourself behold.
		He gives [himself] into Your hand;
		upon You he abandons [himself]—the unfortunate one;
		to the orphan You Yourself have been the helper.
10:15	[ש SHIN]	Break the arm of the wicked and the evildoer;
		call him to account for his wickedness [until] You find none.
10:16		Yahweh is King forever and always;
		nations have perished from His land.
10:17	[ת TAW]	The desire of the afflicted you have heard, Yahweh;
		You establish their heart, You attend [with] Your ear
10:18		to do justice for the orphan and the oppressed;
		[that] a mortal of the land [will] no longer—ever—terrorize.

Structure

The structure of Psalm 10 may be visualized as moving from *Lament* to *Plea* to *Confidence*:[1]

10:1–11	**Lament** ["afflicted" in 10:2a, 9b, 9c; "why" in 10:1a]	
	10:1–6	Wicked: Arrogance
		Direct speech of wicked (10:6)
	10:7–11	Wicked: Antagonism
		Direct speech of wicked (10:11)
10:12–15	**Plea** ["afflicted" in 10:12; "why" in 10:13a]	
		Direct speech of wicked (10:13)
10:16–18	**Confidence** ["afflicted" in 10:17]	
	10:16	Fate of the wicked
	10:17–18	Hope of the righteous

---

1. The question "why" in the *Lament* (10:1a) and in the *Plea* (10:13a) disappears in the *Confidence*!

Theological Focus

The wicked—violent and belligerent in their arrogance and antagonism towards God and his people—oppress righteous individuals, disrupting life and shalom, but the latter are confident that God, their King forever, sees, hears, does not forget, and is their helper, rendering aid and dispensing justice.

Commentary

Lament (10:1–11)

Without any ado, the psalm plunges directly into a lament. The wicked are extensively portrayed:[2] their arrogance (10:1–6, ending with a direct quote in 10:6), and their antagonism towards others (10:7–11, ending in a direct quote in 10:11).[3] These evil ones are "arrogant" (10:2a) and "haughty" (10:4a[4]), they violently "hound" the afflicted (10:2a, 8–9[5]) with "schemes they have devised" to trap the righteous (10:2b), they "boast" (10:3a[6]), they are "greedy" (10:3b), they "curse"[7] and "revile" God (10:3b; also see 10:13a), they reject God (10:4, 5b), they prosper long-term (10:5a), they are hubristic in their security (10:6, 11), their mouths produce only evil (10:7), and they are "mighty" (10:10b). That is an incredible piling up of negative descriptions of these immoral ones.

A number of body parts of the wicked also show up in 10:1–11: nose (10:4a, translated "countenance"), "heart" (10:6a, 11a), "mouth" (10:7a), "tongue" (10:7b), and "eyes" (10:8c). All are engaged in nefarious activities, bespeaking the totality of the wicked person's depravity and anti-God outlook and actions. These are some adversaries! And the threefold direct quotes of these wicked, in the *Lament* and *Plea* portions of the psalm (in 10:6, 11, and 13), attest to the God-dismissing, morality-discarding, self-promoting nature of these predators. No wonder the afflicted, the "unfortunate" are "crushed, bowed down"—they "fall" before these formidable foes (10:10).[8] All of "these schemes they have devised" (10:2b) are grounded in their mistaken assumption that "there is no God"—the "[basis of] all his schemes" (10:4c). And what breaks the back of the righteous, the oppressed ones, is that

---

2. "Wicked/ness" shows up throughout the psalm, in 10:2a, 3a, 4a (in the *Lament*), and in 10:13a, 15a, 15b (in the *Plea*). The righteous in Psalm 10 are, variously, those in trouble (10:1b), the "afflicted" (10:2a, 9c, 12b, 17a), the "innocent" (10:8b), the "unfortunate" (10:8c, 10b, 14c), the "orphan" (10:14d, 18a), and the "oppressed" (10:18a).

3. Both these direct quotes, and the one in 10:13b, are introduced with "He says to his heart . . . ."

4. "Haughty in his countenance" is literally "according to the height of his nose"!

5. The images are striking: a brigand ambushing (10:8), a lion devouring (10:9a), and a hunter trapping (10:9c).

6. The verb "boast" is הלל, *hll*, an ironic use of a verb (and this is the first time it appears in the Psalms) that usually means "praise," most often directed to God, himself. Here the evil one is "praising" his own selfish appetites and desires. Goldingay, *Psalms*, 1:179, notes dryly: "It is an inauspicious beginning for the career of this verb in the Psalter, but it will recover."

7. The verb "curse" is ברך, *brk*, another ironic and polarized use of a verb that normally means "bless."

8. One would have thought, after Psalms 1–2, that it would be the righteous who are firm, secure, confident, and unshaken. But, alas, life . . . ! (That's why there are laments in the Psalter.)

God seems to be far away, "hiding in *times* of trouble" (10:1), while the ways of the wicked, the oppressors, "endure at all *times*" (10:5a). It is because the latter seem to be always prospering that the former think God is always far away!

With regard to the acrostic (begun in Psalm 9), the ל *Lamed* segment commences the second half of the Hebrew alphabet in 10:1, but there are a number of salvos launched against structural order: "wicked" (רָשָׁע, *rasha'*) shows up in 10:2a, 3a, 4a, and "calamity" (רַע, *ra'*) in 10:6b. With this extended focus on the wicked, their arrogance, and their antagonism in 10:1–11, everything becomes garbled (again, as in Psalm 9), and six segments go AWOL, corresponding to the letters מ, נ, ס, ע, פ, and צ (*Mem, Nun, Samekh, Ayin, Pe,* and *Tsade*).[9] And correspondingly, "Yahweh" appears only twice in 10:1–11: in 10:1a, he is suspected of being uninvolved, in 10:3b, he is cursed and reviled. Essentially, "God," as the wicked claim, is nowhere (10:4b), and even if he is somewhere, he doesn't care (10:11). And, sadly enough, the righteous appear to agree: "Yahweh" is "far off" (10:1a; corresponding to "there is no God," 10:4b), and he "hides" (10:1b; corresponding to "He has concealed His face," 10:11b). That the righteous, in essence, concur with the conclusion of the wicked makes their situation even more depressing.

> It is noteworthy that this lengthy meditation on the warped logic of the wicked falls exactly at the place where six consecutive letters are omitted. This correlation leads us to suggest that the structure of the psalm reflects its message. The alphabetic acrostic represents proper order—the way the world should be when God is present. Mention and discussion of the wicked, who represent a breakdown in appropriate divine order, come at precisely the point where there is a breakdown in the acrostic sequence.[10]

All that to say, the psalmist has eloquently and artistically portrayed, both in life and in text, the chaos that results from the dominance of the wicked. And so the righteous lament.

Plea (10:12–15)

After the detailed description of the wicked (10:1–11), the plea of the psalmist is found in 10:12–15. Whereas the wicked asserted "God has *forgotten*" (10:11a), the righteous appeal to God to "not *forget* the afflicted" (10:12b). Whereas the wicked think "He will not see" (10:11b), the righteous are confident that "You have seen" (10:14a; and "You Yourself behold")—he has looked upon the plight of his people. Whereas the wicked were sure "You will not call to account" (10:13b), the righteous beseech God to "call him [the wicked] to account" (10:15b). God was called upon to "lift up Your *hand*" (10:12a) in a declaration of divine hostility against the wicked. But into that same divine "hand" of sanctuary the "unfortunate" righteous abandon themselves (10:14bc).[11] Same God and same hand, but dealing recompense for the wicked, and serving as a refuge for the righteous. God is

---

9. Attempts to relocate these letters and their segments in 10:1–11 have not been convincing: for e.g., 10:5b begins with a מ-word; 10:8c with a ע-word. Since they do not occur at the commencement of their respective verses, they are unlikely to be part of the acrostic. Besides, as in Psalm 9, there is, in Psalm 10 also, good reason to understand those six letters as deliberately omitted, as we shall see.

10. Benun, "Evil and the Disruption of Order," 6.

11. The "unfortunate" who was nearly slaughtered by the wicked (10:8bc), the "unfortunate" who was crushed and cowed and bowed down (10:10), is the same "unfortunate" who is now sheltered in the presence of the divine (10:14bc).

emphatically asserted to be the "Helper" ("You Yourself," 10:14d). And he would "break the *arm* of the wicked and the evildoer" (10:15a). "If there is to be rescue, there has to be putting down. Literally, the plea is for Yhwh to break the arm of the faithless in order to stop his strong-arm tactics."[12] As was seen in Psalm 9, the retribution is precise: one divine "hand" (10:12a, 14b) against the puny human "arm" (10:15a).

The plea in 10:12–15 invokes Yahweh at the start, "Arise, Yahweh!" (10:12a), and with that first positive mention of deity in the psalm and the appeal that he may intervene to stop the wicked, order is immediately reestablished in the text: the acrostic gets right back on track.[13] After a series of letters gone missing in 10:1–11, regularity resumes with the ק *Qoph* (10:12–13), ר *Resh* (10:14), ש *Shin* (10:15–16), and ת *Taw* (10:17–18) segments. But "wicked" is mentioned again in the secondary verse of the ק *Qoph* segment, 10:13. That explains the anomaly of the ר *Resh* segment having only a primary verse (10:14), and not a secondary one as is the normal pattern. However, there is also "wicked" and "wickedness" in the following verse, 10:15 (the primary verse of the ש *Shin* segment), yet there is no resulting discrepancy thereafter. The reason for that stability of the text is in the content of 10:15–16: God is called to "*hold* [the wicked] *accountable* for his wickedness" (דרש; or "*seek out* his wickedness," 10:15b). God, "King forever and always" (10:16a), has indeed held the wicked and his wickedness in check, preventing any outbreak of disorderliness in the text (or in life)! Benun also observes that if we take 10:15b as being "a self-referential comment about the structure of this acrostic," we could read it as: "Call him [the wicked] to account for [the text's disarray resulting from] his wickedness, [until] you find none." And, indeed, we "find none," for disorder has, once and for all, disappeared from Psalm 10. In other words, God is in total control, and there will be no more wickedness, evil, or upheaval either of text or of life. And with that the psalm proceeds to its concluding praise without further untidiness. God has won!

> The very form of the acrostic reflects its central message. The message is that evil disrupts the natural order of the world and the ramifications of evil are far reaching. However, evil can only exist when God allows this to happen. This is poetically represented in the structure of the acrostic where any occurrence of the word רשע disrupts either the acrostic or the primary-attached verse pattern. However, an invocation of God to act . . . or a description of God in His active role as king puts the acrostic back on track.[14]

Confidence (10:15–18)

Not surprisingly, God's kingship is the content of the final section of praise in the psalm (10:16–18), with the focus on the consequent fate of the wicked—their perishing (10:16); and the hope of the righteous—their establishment in safety, because God hears and God acts (10:17–18). And this is the first time in the Psalter that Yahweh is explicitly called "King" (יְהוָה מֶלֶךְ, *yhwh melek*), the regent who rules "forever and always" (10:16a).[15]

Whereas the wicked were shouting hallelujahs to their evil "desires" (10:3a; "boast" is הלל), it will ultimately be the "desire" of the righteous afflicted that will be heard by deity

---

12. Goldingay, *Psalms*, 1:183.
13. One remembers that the same thing happened in 9:18–20 (9:19a also has "arise, Yahweh").
14. Benun, "Evil and the Disruption of Order," 7.
15. Psalms 2:6 and 5:2 only had "M/my king."

(10:17a). Whereas the "heart" of the wicked uttered brash and boastful words (10:6a, 11a, 13b—all introduced with "he says to his heart"), it will be the "heart" of the righteous that will be established (10:17b). And whereas the wicked assumed wrongly that divine "judgment" was far away from touching them (מִשְׁפָּט, *mishpat*, 10:5b), it will be on behalf of the righteous oppressed that divine "justice" is executed (שָׁפַט, *shpht*, 10:18a).

So a psalm that began with a lament of "Why, Yahweh?" (10:1a) ends with the confidence that "Yahweh is King forever and always" (10:16a), the one who would provide "justice for the orphan and oppressed" (10:18a). The wicked would "no longer—ever—terrorize" (10:18b). "No other psalm so fully joins the basic themes of the Psalter—the rule of God, the representative role of the king, the plea for help in time of trouble, the ways of the wicked and the righteous, and the justice of God on behalf of the weak and the poor."[16] Strikingly, we are not told if and when deliverance actually came for the righteous. Perhaps that is not important for the psalmist or for us—God sees (10:14a), he hears (10:17), and he and we trust in his care and his unceasing rulership. What more does one need?

Sermon Map

I. Oppression of Individuals by the Belligerent Wicked
    Intensity of oppression (10:2–11)
    Seeming distancing of God (10:1)
    Textual disorder
    Move-to-relevance: Our oppression and God's silence

II. Intervention by the Regent God
    Mighty God (10:12–14a, 15)
    Ruling God (10:16)
    Restoration of textual order
    Move-to-relevance: Our failure to see God as mighty King

III. Anticipation of the Righteous
    Refuge in the King (10:14bcd)
    Justice from the King (10:15, 17–18)

IV. *Hand It Over to the Hand of the King!*
    Specifics on individual trust in God the King for deliverance

---

16. Miller, "Ruler in Zion," 188–89 (he makes this observation of the joint song, Psalms 9–10).

PSALM 11:1–7

Psalm of Disorientation

Resisting the Temptation to Defect

PSALM 11 IS UNIQUE in this early set of psalms in that there is no obvious plea to Yahweh, except for the indirect jussive in 11:6a ("may He . . ."). It is actually addressed to those in the psalmist's company who are recommending that he (and the rest of his righteous cohort—"Your" and "upright" in 11:1c, 2c, respectively, are masculine plurals) flee the enemy—a sign of lack of faith in God. Perhaps the psalmist himself was tempted to do so, but responds to these pessimists and counters their counsel.

Translation

11:1 In Yahweh I have taken refuge;
    how can you say to my soul,
    "Flee your mountain, bird.

11:2 For, behold, the wicked draw the bow,
    they have taken aim, their arrow on the bowstring,
    to shoot in darkness at the upright of heart.

11:3 If the foundations are destroyed,
    the righteous one, what can he do?"

11:4 Yahweh in His holy temple—
    Yahweh on His heavenly throne—
His eyes see,
    His eyelids try the children of humanity.

11:5 Yahweh—He tries the righteous one and the wicked,
    and the one who loves violence His soul hates.

11:6 Upon the wicked may He rain fire and brimstone,
    and [may] a raging wind [be] the portion of their cup.

11:7 For Yahweh [is] righteous,
    righteousness He loves;
    the upright will see His face.

Structure

The psalm may be structured as follows:

Recommendation (11:1–3)	
11:1a	Psalmist's resolve
11:1b–3	Pessimists' doubt

Response (11:4–7)	
11:4–5a	Yahweh, the royal judge
11:5bc	Yahweh's hatred of the wicked
11:6	Yahweh's fate for the wicked
11:7a	Yahweh's love of the righteous
11:7b	Yahweh's fate for the righteous

Theological Focus

The righteous, when under siege by the wicked, are tempted to abandon God and the refuge he is, but they remain trusting of the divine royal judge, who hates wickedness and loves righteousness, and who will execute judgment—destruction for the wicked, and bliss for the righteous in the presence of God.

Commentary

Recommendation (11:1–3)

The text of 11:1c is ambiguous and can be read "flee [from] your mountain" (i.e., "flee *from* the secure mountain you thought Yahweh was, to a better sanctuary").[1] In light of 11:1a that shows the resolve of the psalmist, the designation of Yahweh as the psalmist's "refuge," and deity's presence in "His holy temple," i.e., the mountain of Zion (11:4a[2]), it makes sense to equate the "mountain" in 11:1c to the presence of God, from which the pessimists were urging the psalmist to flee.[3] Thus the *Recommendation* is for the psalmist to get far away from God—to any place other than Yahweh, apparently—as the beleaguered one attempts to fend off human

---

1. It could also be read "flee [to] your mountain" (i.e., "flee *to* your own secure mountain, away from Yahweh, to a better sanctuary"). In either case, it is a lack of faith in God.

2. Psalm 2:6 calls "Zion, My holy mountain" (also see 3:4; 15:1; 24:3; etc.).

3. The simile of birds fleeing to mountains was typically used in Assyrian analogies to compare defeated foes to escaping avians vainly heading to the mountains for refuge. For e.g., Esarhaddon (680–669 BC) declared: "I trusted in the god Aššur, my lord, (and) caught him [an enemy] like a bird from the midst of the mountains, and cut off his head" (Leichty, *Royal Inscriptions of Esarhaddon*, 28–29 [2.45–50]). Likewise, Tiglath-Pileser 1 (1111–1077 BC): "[The enemy peoples] flew like birds to ledges on high mountains" (Grayson, *Assyrian Rulers*, 18). So also Sennacherib (704–681 BC): "(As for) the populati[on living] inside it [an enemy city], [who] had flown away like [bir]ds to the peak of a [rug]ged mountain, [I pu]rsued them" (Grayson and Novotny, *Royal Inscriptions of Sennacherib*, 101 [53.1–5]). Birds fleeing to mountains are also seen in 1 Sam 26:20; Ezek 7:16.

attackers. These marauding foes, the "wicked," 11:2 tells us (in the voice of those recommenders), are ready to hunt down their prey even in the dark, with skullduggery and deception: "They have cocked their gun and are about to shoot."[4] Those cynical advisors continue[5] with a question of their own that, in effect, asserts that fleeing the mountain/Yahweh is the only option for the righteous, now that "the foundations are destroyed" (11:3). "Foundations [from שָׁתָה, *shatah*]" here is a *hapax* in the Psalter. Nevertheless, even the synonyms for "foundation" in the Psalms point to the primary location of deity in the mountains: 33:14 refers to the "foundation-place [מָכוֹן, *makon*]," the dwelling of God; 87:1 to the city God "founded [יְסוּדָה, *ysudah*]" on the holy mountains; and 89:14 and 97:2 to the "foundation [מָכוֹן]" of the divine throne. Quite possibly, then, the recommenders are alleging that the very mountain of God, Mt. Zion, his throne in his temple, has been compromised: it is in danger of being destroyed (or already has been). In other words, God has been defeated; there is no hope in him: "flee your [foundation-less] mountain, bird!" Perhaps this was a temptation that the psalmist himself was facing. In such a seemingly dire situation, what else could the righteous do? ask the detractors, rhetorically. "The psalm does not just offer an answer to this question, the psalm *is* the answer . . . a radical and countercultural expression of trust in the face of chaos," as we see in the psalmist's response to these pessimists' recommendation (11:4–7).[6]

Response (11:4–7)

In the *Response* of the psalmist, one thing is abundantly clear: God is still the only hope. Yahweh is the subject of the verbs in each of those verses, 11:4–7 (×6: 11:4c, 4d, 5a, 5c, 6a, 7b). Countering the naysayers' mistaken assumption about the collapse of Yahweh's dwelling (and of Yahweh's throne and perhaps even of his reign), the psalmist asserts that Yahweh is still in his temple and continues to occupy his throne (11:4ab): he is not defeated, he has not fled, he has not abdicated. And he alone has the sovereignty and authority, the power and right, and will and might, to rectify matters. In fact, it is not just that he is dwelling and sitting in those respective locations, he is actually *doing* something—judging (11:4c–5a). The sovereign King of the universe is the divine royal judge.

This divine arbitrator is testing and examining people ("children of humanity," 11:4cd). That he sees with his eyelids is, of course, hyperbolic, but it also promotes the notion that God can see with his eyes closed: he *never* stops seeing! Both the righteous and the wicked are tested, separating the faithful from the faithless (11:5a).

Subsequently, 11:5b–6 describes the judgment and punishment of the wicked by the divine umpire: they, the ones who "love" violence are the ones whom deity "hates." Upon them he "rains fire and brimstone," and a raging wind is their lot (11:6). "Fire and brimstone" was what was "rained" upon Sodom and Gomorrah, too (Gen 19:24); thus its depraved inhabitants are equated to the psalm's offenders, the lovers of violence and the objects of divine hate. This would be God's response to the oppression of the righteous by the wicked (and, indeed, even to the utterly faithless and fallible recommendation of the pessimists to the psalmist).

---

4. Goldingay, *Psalms*, 1:190.

5. I take the direct quote begun in 11:1c as extending to the end of 11:3: notice that כִּי, *ki*, begins both 11:2 ("for") and 11:3 ("if"); also the question of 11:3 is odd for the psalmist to be asking, after he has just protested the recommendation to flee ("how can you say . . . ?" in 11:1b).

6. deClaissé-Walford et al., *Book of Psalms*, 148.

But the fate of the righteous is quite different, even diametrically opposed to that of the wicked (Ps 11:7). Whereas the recommenders asked the psalmist hopelessly, "The righteous one, what can he do?" (11:3b), here the psalmist declares that Yahweh is the righteous one and that "righteousness he loves" (11:7; even as he hates the wicked, 11:5c). Surely he will take action and not be indolent in his heavens. The loves and hates of the wicked and of Yahweh form a parallel structure, A, B, C, and A', [B'], C', below—with Yahweh's righteousness at the center (and Yahweh's love of the righteous implied in B'). Besides, each trio forms an argument, both grounded in the righteousness of Yahweh. The fate of the wicked: because Yahweh is righteous, A results in B, and that culminates in C. And the fate of the righteous: because Yahweh is righteous, A', and therefore B', that culminates in C'.

> **A** Wicked "loves" violence (11:5ab)
>   **B** Yahweh "hates" the wicked (11:5c)
>   **C** Destruction of the wicked (11:6)
>
> **Yahweh is righteous (11:7a)**
>
> **A'** Yahweh "loves" righteousness (11:7b)
>   **[B'** Yahweh loves the upright/righteous]
>   **C'** Bliss of the upright/righteous (11:7c)

Whereas it was pointed out earlier to the psalmist that the "upright" are ripe for killing (11:2), here we are told in no uncertain terms that they are not: the "upright," instead will see the face of God, and dwell in safety and security in his presence, in his mountain (11:7c). When God's eyes "see" (11:4b), then the righteous can be assured that they, in turn, will "see" his face (11:7c). Thus, "reliance on Yhwh . . . [11:1] and being the object of Yhwh's beneficent look . . . [11:7] form a bracket" that blesses the faithful, their activity, and their end, and blasts the faithless, their activity, and their end.[7]

Sermon Map

I. Temptation of the Oppressed
    To defect because God appears defeated (11:1b–3)
    Move-to-relevance: When God appears to have lost

II. Discrimination by the Judge
    Deity in the temple, on the throne (11:4ab)
    Deity judging the righteous and the wicked (114c–5a)
    Move-to-relevance: Our failure to see God as never losing

III. Expectation for the Righteous
    Divine punishment for the wicked (11:5b–6)
    Divine presence for the righteous (11:7)

IV. *See the Face of the God Who Sees!*
    Specifics on individual trust in the royal judge when tempted to defect

---

7. Goldingay, *Psalms*, 1:194.

PSALM 12:1–8

Psalm of Disorientation

Words of God vs. Words of the Wicked

PSALM 12, A LAMENT, appears to be a conversation between God and psalmist. The problem is stated by the psalmist (12:1–4), including an aside to God's people in 12:3, and a direct quote of the wicked/unfaithful in 12:4. Yahweh responds with direct speech in 12:5. The psalmist then affirms his confidence in the faithfulness of God's words and their consequences for the righteous who are living in a world where evil abounds (see structure below).

Translation

12:1　Do deliver, Yahweh, for the devout one has come to an end,
　　　　for the faithful have disappeared from among humans.
12:2　Falsehood they speak, one to his fellow;
　　　　with the lip of smoothness, in a double heart, they speak.
12:3　May Yahweh cut off all lips of smoothness,
　　　　the tongue speaking big things—
12:4　[those] who have said, "With our tongue we will prevail.
　　　　Our lips are in our own [power]—who is lord over us?"
12:5　"Because of the devastation of the afflicted,
　　　　because of the groaning of the needy,
　　　now I will arise," says Yahweh;
　　　　"I will set in deliverance, the one who pants for it."
12:6　The sayings of Yahweh are clean sayings,
　　　　silver refined in a furnace on the earth, distilled seven times.
12:7　You, Yahweh, will keep them;
　　　　You will preserve him from this generation forever.
12:8　The wicked, they walk all around
　　　　as vileness is exalted by humans.

Structure

The structure of the psalm demonstrates an antithesis between the speech of the wicked (12:2–4) and the speech of God (12:5–7), with a statement about plight of the righteous (12:1, *Scattering*) and one about the power of the wicked (12:8, *Surging*) bookending the composition:[1]

A	Invisibility of the righteous (**12:1**) Faithful disappear among "humans" (7:1b)		**Scattering** (righteous)
	B Wicked's words (**12:2**) Wicked "speak" (×2); impure speech: false		**Speech** (wicked)
		C Psalmist's wish: punish wicked (**12:3–4**) Wicked "speak" and "say"; direct speech	
		C' Yahweh's resolve: protect righteous (**12:5**) Yahweh "says"; direct speech	**Speech** (God)
	B' Deity's words (and consequence) (**12:6–7**) Yahweh's "sayings" (×2); pure speech: faithful		
A'	Visibility of the wicked (**12:8**) Evil exalted by "humans" (12:8b)		**Surging** (wicked)

Theological Focus

The oppressed righteous, almost driven to non-existence amidst the exaltation of evil by the wicked—whose words, hollow and hubristic, deny the lordship of God—trust the deliverance of God, whose words, in contrast, are true and trustworthy, the fulfillment of those words ensuring God's protection of the righteous forever.

Commentary

Scattering of the Righteous (12:1)

As with most laments, Psalm 12 commences with the psalmist's supplication to Yahweh to deliver him (and them, his cohort of the righteous).[2] The reason: the invisibility of the righteous—the "devout" have scattered and the "faithful" have disappeared from among "humans"[3] (A above; 12:1), and the psalmist appears to be the only one left. The cause of this extinction is stated in the corresponding A' (12:8)—the surging and thriving of the wicked, who "walk all around," thereby exalting evil by "humans" and effectively suppressing

---

1. There is also the antithesis between the persecution of the righteous by the wicked (12:5ab) and the protection of them by God (12:7b).

2. The object of deliverance, "me"/"us," is absent. "But this fits with the fact that it does not relate to the speaker's own needs. Its background is the state of community life" (Goldingay, *Psalms*, 1:197). Also of note, the plea occurs in this psalm as an imperative entreating rescue (12:1a), as a jussive wishing recrimination (12:3a), and an imperfect affirming reliance (12:7a).

3. Here and in 12:8b, "humans" is literally "sons of man."

righteousness and its practitioners. Evil is winning! No doubt it is the oppression of the righteous by these wicked that has resulted in the former's elimination—perhaps by intimidation by the wicked, perhaps by the cowardice of the righteous (or their succumbing to alluring words, 12:2). Either desertion, defection, or death has caused them to be erased from the scene. In the final analysis, "humans" (12:1b, 8b), characterized here as evil (= the wicked), are prospering and dominating society, "walking all around" (12:8a), while the "devout"/"faithful" (= the righteous) are entirely eclipsed (12:1).

Speech (wicked); Speech (God) (12:2–7)

That there is some violent activity going on is obvious from 12:5: the afflicted are devastated and the needy are groaning. But the focus in this psalm is not particularly on the activity of the wicked but on their words (B, C; 12:2–4).[4] Countering the wicked's words are deity's words (C', B'; 12:5–7). Six of the eight verses of the psalm thus deal with speech and the consequences thereof (12:2–4, 5–7). Interestingly, while the psalmist quotes the wicked (12:4), Yahweh references the vocalizations of the suffering righteous (12:5b, 5d, the groaning of the needy and the panting of the afflicted).

The wicked's speech is characterized as "falsehood," uttered with "lips of smoothness" (12:2a, 2b, 3a; also see 12:4a, 4b), generated by a "double heart" (12:2b[5]) that powers the "tongue speaking big things" (12:3b). The deceit and guile they exercise further the wicked's grand ambitions. The sequence of the repeated mouthparts in 12:3–4 forms a chiasm, further emphasizing the synecdoche for speech: their words are thoroughly and totally evil:[6]

12:3a	"lips"	
12:3b		"tongue"
12:4a		"tongue"
12:4b	"lips"	

Effectively, in this psalm, we have not only lips and tongues, but also "heart" (12:2b) and, presumably, lungs (12:5d, where panting is noted). Their bearers are completely given over to wickedness.

The hubris of the wicked goes so far as to claim that they are the "masters of their fates" and the "captains of their souls":[7] "Who is lord over us?" (12:4b). They say what they want, and they are assured of the power of their words: "With our tongue we will prevail" (12:4a): evil unchecked, so much so, Yahweh is entreated to dismember those vile organs that produce those execrable utterances (12:2b, 3c). The psalmist's assurance that Yahweh will do exactly that is vindicated as deity responds.

---

4. In C, 12:3–4, the description of evil speech is couched in the psalmist's wish for God to expunge the wicked's words.

5. Literally, "a heart and a heart," suggesting two different and incongruent organs, i.e., hearts of deception (as with "double-mouthed" in English). The contrary, "with an undivided heart," translates the Hebrew "without a heart and a heart," in 1 Chr 12:33.

6. In 12:3 these evil words are part of the psalmist's wish; in 12:4 they are part of the wicked's direct speech being cited by the psalmist.

7. From *Invictus*, by William Ernest Henley (1875).

With God's speech, the speech of the wicked is directly and diametrically countered by the speech of God: they "say" (12:4), but *Yahweh* "says" (12:5). And his "sayings" alone will stand (12:6; see below). Yahweh had seen the "devastation of the afflicted" and heard the "groaning of the needy" (12:5ab); he is going to "arise,"[8] he promises, to "set in *deliverance*" (12:5cd) the suffering righteous, panting for relief. This is an explicit answer by God to the supplication of the psalmist, "Do *deliver*, Yahweh" (12:1a). God is responding, and he is responding "now" (12:5c)!

And God's speech, unlike that of the wicked, is "clean" (12:6a)—emphatically declared to be "distilled seven times" (12:6b), like silver in a furnace.[9] In other words, deity's speech is faithful—he *will* do as he promised, a fact the psalmist acknowledges in 12:7a (the "them" in 12:7a has as its nearest antecedent the "sayings" of God). And the consequence of a faithful God keeping his faithful words is that the righteous are protected (12:7b; the "him" in 12:7b likely refers to the singular righteous individual representing the community as a whole, as 12:5d also depicts). And this shielding of the righteous will be both "now" (12:5c) and "forever" (12:7b)! Yes, the faithful word of God and his fail-safe action will counter the false words of the wicked and their felonious actions.

Surging of the Wicked (12:8)

But the psalm ends, not on that positive note, but with another disheartening note about the surging of wicked and their evil in the world (12:8), matching the opening supplication about the scattering the righteous and their uprightness (12:1). "God had said he would arise . . . , and that true word could be believed. Protection was coming. Yet the reality of evil circumstances continued; the wicked still strutted about, their vile speech . . . exalted as if it were a divine word. It was not a change of circumstances which prompted the confidence of [12:7] but a conviction that God's word was pure and true."[10] Indeed, the defeat of the faithful and the triumph of the faithless seem to be bracketing the entire psalm, indicating that the suffering righteous are currently in the midst of their oppression, smack-dab in the real-life situation in which this lament was prayed. Yes, divine protection is certainly needed in an evil world, but the righteous need not be overly worried: a divine shield is assured, because of God's protective speech (faithful, true, and pure), unlike the pugnacious speech of the wicked (unfaithful, false, and vile). May we rest in the words of God, while we live in a restless world!

---

8. As has been noted, in the Psalms, God's arising bespeaks his intention to engage in a holy war as a divine warrior: Pss 3:7; 9:19; 10:12; 68:1; see also Num 10:35; Isa 33:10.

9. "By implication, the speech of wicked person is all dross, devoid of silver and gold!" (Craigie, *Psalms 1–50*, 138).

10. Craigie, *Psalms 1–50*, 139.

Sermon Map

I. Surging of the Wicked
   Increase of evildoers (12:2–4, 8), devastation (12:5ab)
   Wicked's speech (12:2–4)
   Move-to-relevance: How the wicked seem to have the upper hand

II. Scattering of the Righteous
   Decrease of the faithful (12:1), afflicted and needy (12:5ab)
   Move-to-relevance: How the righteous are few

III. Speech of God
   God's resolve (12:5–6)
   God's words (12:6)
   Protection of the righteous (12:7)
   Punishment of the wicked (12:3a)

IV. *Whose Speech Will You Trust?*
   Specifics on trust in divine words

PSALM 13:1–6

Psalm of Disorientation

How Long?

THIS BRIEF, SIX-VERSE LAMENT is an assertion of confidence in God, but it is set in a scene redolent with a sense of divine abandonment.

Translation

13:1 Until when, Yahweh? Will You forget me perpetually?
    Until when will You hide Your face from me?
13:2 Until when shall I take counsels [of worry] in my soul,
    [and have] sorrow in my heart daily?
    Until when will my enemy be exalted over me?
13:3 Look, answer me, Yahweh my God.
    Enlighten my eyes, lest I sleep [in] death,
13:4 Lest my enemy say, "I have overcome him,"
    [and] my adversaries jubilate because I totter.
13:5 But I—in Your lovingkindness I have trusted;
    my heart will jubilate in Your deliverance.
13:6 I will sing to Yahweh,
    because He has rendered [good] to me.

Structure

The structure is straightforward, with a *Complaint*, a *Claim*, and an expression of *Confidence*:

A	Yahweh unresponsive (**13:1**) "from me" (מִמֶּנִּי, *mimmenni*, 13:1b)		**Complaint** (13:1–2) [Yahweh]
	B Psalmist sorrowful (**13:3ab**) "sorrow in my heart" (13:2b)		[Supplicant] [Enemies]
		C "Enemy" triumphant (**13:2c**): exalted	**Claim** (13:3–4)
		D Yahweh appealed to (**13:3**) "look"; "answer"; "enlighten"	[Yahweh] [Supplicant]
		C' "Enemy" triumphant (**13:4**): joyful	[Enemies]
	B' Psalmist joyful (**13:5**) "my heart will jubilate" (13:5b)		**Confidence** (13:5–6) [Yahweh]
A'	Yahweh responsive (**13:6**) "to me" (עָלָי, *'alay*, 13:6b)		[Supplicant]

It begins with an almost confrontational address of *Complaint* to Yahweh: "Until when, Yahweh?" (13:1a), moves to a prayerful invocation and *Claim* made of Yahweh: "Answer me, Yahweh my God!" (13:3a), and ends with a joyful paean of *Confidence* in Yahweh: "I will sing to Yahweh" (13:6a). (These are also the only three instances of "Yahweh" in this psalm.) Not surprisingly, this final section (13:5–6) is notable for the absence of enemies.

The abrupt change in tone from *Complaint* and *Claim* to *Confidence* is striking, here and elsewhere in the laments of the Psalter. While it is unlikely the sufferer assumed God was going to change in the essentials of his character and attributes, the supplicant is certain he can be motivated to change. Therefore the righteous and his cohort appeal to God's reputation, his covenant, his relationship to the forefathers, his reign, his King, and so on. Particularly key in this rhetorical approach of the psalmist is the strategically located praise at the end of a lament. "An aggressive opening, followed by a demanding petition and concluded with extolling words comprises a well-rounded plea which intends to provoke a response from God.... At the end of the psalm neither the situation nor the mood of the psalmist has drastically changed. The rhetorical use of praise adds weight and substance to the appeal and informs God that God's assistance is required."[1] Of course, such an approach to God bespeaks considerable faith and trust in him and his potential willingness to deliver the suffering one(s).

Theological Focus

> The suffering righteous, tottering under the onslaught of the enemy, subjugated in a grave and grievous situation, trust God's lovingkindness, exult in their anticipated deliverance, and celebrate God as they expect him to turn things around for them.

---

1. Leiter, "Rhetoric of Praise," 48. Luther on Psalm 13 observed that herein "hope despairs and simultaneously despair hopes." See *Weimar Ausgabe, Schriften Band 3: Psalmenvorlesungen*, 25 (my translation from the German).

Commentary

Complaint (13:1–2)

Four times God is asked, "until when?" (or "how long?"). Notice that these questions are interspersed with timestamps both in 13:1[2] and 13:2: "perpetually" and "daily."

"until when"	**13:1aα**
"perpetually"	**13:1aβ**
"until when"	**13:1b**
"until when"	**13:2a**
"daily"	**13:2b**
"until when"	**13:2c**

The psalmist is in a dire situation indeed: seemingly he is "perpetually" forgotten and sorrowing "daily," with God's face hidden from him and the enemy exalted over him (13:1–2). The pangs were deeply felt "in my soul" and "in my heart" (13:2ab). It all seems interminable. So "until when?" echoes four times! As Westermann noted, "Here, time itself becomes a destructive force, wearing down a [person's] ability to hold out and intensifying the suffering to an inhuman level."[3] The questions are not requesting data, but function rhetorically, beseeching God to intervene *now*.

Claim (13:3–4).

The psalmist's three imperatives direct Yahweh to "look," "answer," and "enlighten my eyes" (i.e., restore him from the graveness of his situation[4]) (13:3). If God does not "look," "answer," and "enlighten," the enemy will have won (13:4a) and will be joyful (13:4b; when the psalmist is sorrowful, 13:2b) as the righteous supplicant "totters." As if to emphasize the dreadfulness of the situation the words used are assonant: "death" is מָוֶת (*mawet*, 13:3b) and "totter" is מוט (*mwt*, 13:4b). Whereas in his complaint, the psalmist was convinced God had "hidden" his face from him (13:1b), here in his claim, he wants God to "look" at him (13:3b)—effectively, to turn his, God's, face unto him.

---

2. "Taking counsels [of worry] in my soul" indicates a state of constant anxiety with self-directed conversations being conducted within this troubled individual.

3. Westermann, *Living Psalms*, 71. One is reminded of the speech "Our God Is Marching On," by Rev. Dr. Martin Luther King Jr., delivered on March 25, 1965, at the state capital in Montgomery, Alabama, at the conclusion of the Selma March. The remarkable oration is punctuated with "How long? Not long!" underscoring the truth that a lament, a desperate cry, is actually a fervent hope (see Brueggemann and Bellinger, *Psalms*, 79). For the text of King's speech, see http://americanradioworks.publicradio.org/features/prestapes/mlk_speech.html.

4. Bright eye = vitality and vigor: Deut 34:7; 1 Sam 14:27, 29; Ps 19:8. Dull eye = near death and denervation: Job 17:7; Pss 6:7; 38:10; Lam 5:17.

Confidence (13:5–6)

Quite emphatically, the confidence section commences with a (disjunctive) conjunction + a redundant pronoun: "But I." We are not clear whether the situation has changed, or what caused the psalmist's sudden confidence and music-making (as noted, it may well have been a rhetorical strategy: praise intended to motivate God). In any case, he has decided to trust divine lovingkindness (13:5a), and therefore can "jubilate" in God's deliverance (13:5b). Whereas it was the enemy that was previously "jubilating" because the psalmist was shaken (13:4b), the secure establishment of the latter in God's lovingkindness precludes his tottering, and so now it is his turn to be "jubilating" (13:5b). And whereas "my heart" was in "sorrow" earlier (13:2b), that same organ, "my heart," now exults with "jubilation." Deliverance is nigh (or here already)! And, in another contrast, whereas it was "over me" that the enemy was being exalted (עָלַי, 13:2c), now it is "to me" that Yahweh has rendered good (employing the same preposition, עָלָי, 13:6b). Cause for song, indeed!

Sermon Map

I. Tottering under the Enemy
    God's seeming abandonment (13:1–2b)
    Enemy's exaltation and exultation (13:2c, 4)
    Move-to-relevance: How God seems to be far away

II. Trusting in the Deity
    Expectation that God will see, answer, and restore (13:3)
    Trust in God's lovingkindness (13:5a)
    Joy in God's deliverance (13:5b)
    Celebration in God's goodness (13:6)
    Move-to-relevance: Why we find it difficult to trust God no matter what

III. *Trust, Don't Totter!*
    Specifics on trust in dark days

PSALM 14:1–7

Psalm of Disorientation

Refutation of the Fool

PSALM 14 IS MORE didactic than supplicatory. While the "fool" takes center stage (14:1a), the composition is, in fact, addressed to the righteous, members of God's community, to encourage them with the ultimate failure of the fool and his foolish conspiracies at the hands of a heavenly God. This composition reappears with alterations in Psalm 53. It is possible that in a prior existence, the two psalms were independently part of separate collections, but that would still make their functions discrete and the occasions of their use different. Psalm 14 has its focus on relieving the righteous, while Psalm 53 serves as a warning to the wicked.[1] The psalm does not directly address God, and there is no explicit plea though there is a wish (14:7); the wicked/fool is addressed in 14:6.

Translation

14:1 The fool has said in his heart,
 "[There is] no God."
 They act ruinously, they behave abominably in deed;
 [there is] not [one] who does good.
14:2 Yahweh, He has looked down from heaven
 upon the children of humanity,
 to see if there is anyone who understands,
 who seeks after God.

---

1. Differences between the two psalms include: use of יְהוָה, *yhwh*, in Psalm 14 (×4; and אֱלֹהִים, *ʾelohim*, ×3), and the exclusive use of אֱלֹהִים in Psalm 53 (×7)—both have seven instances of the divine name; and there are minor variations in the opening verses of the two psalms, and major variations between 14:6 and 53:5. Also some versions of the LXX and a few Hebrew MSS include more text in 14:1–3 (reflected in the citation of this psalm in Rom 3:10–18).

14:3 They have all turned aside,
         together they have become corrupt;
      [there is] not [one] who does good,
         not even one.
14:4 Have all the practitioners of harm not known—
         who eat up my people [as] they eat bread,
      [and] do not call upon Yahweh?
14:5 There they greatly dread,
         because God [is] with the generation of the righteous one.
14:6 The counsel of the afflicted one you put to shame,
         but Yahweh is his refuge.
14:7 Oh, may the deliverance of Israel come from Zion.
      When Yahweh restores the restoration of His people,
         Jacob will jubilate, Israel will rejoice.

Structure

The structure of the psalm may be depicted as follows:

14:1–3	**Description of the fool**	
	14:1	Fool's failed speech, faulty actions
	14:2–3	God's actions: Findings
14:4–6	**Destiny of the fool**	
	14:4	Fool's failed speech, faulty actions
	14:5–6	God's actions: Fate
14:7	**Deliverance of the faithful**	

It becomes obvious that even when the fool is being discussed (*Description* and *Destiny* of that individual), God's actions are the focus (findings regarding the fool and that one's fate). And those doings of deity cause the *Deliverance* of the faithful.

Theological Focus

The righteous, when afflicted by anti-God oppressors who do no good and do not seek God (and are only loathed by him), trust in God's presence with his people—a truth unrecognized by those foolish ones—for deity is a refuge from whom comes deliverance that is cause for celebration.

Commentary

Description of the Fool (14:1–3)

While the negation of deity by the fool could be an atheistic declaration, it is more likely a statement that "God can be discounted from everyday life," for all practical purposes.[2] Miller puts it well:

> The expression "there is no God" is not an ontological statement denying the reality or "being" of God. It means rather that God is not here or God is not present. As if one were to reach into one's pocketbook and exclaim, "There is no money" . . . . Or if one were to look into the pantry and say, "There is no food." In these cases one does not mean to say that money and food do not exist, but that one does not have any food or money.[3]

The question is whether God cares at all about the human condition and situation, and if he does, whether he cares enough to do anything about it. "If God is not present in the human situation, and if God is not powerful and manifests no power to redeem the human situation, then does any claim about the existence of God have any meaning or reality at all?"[4] To the question, "Does God make any difference in life?" the fool answers, "No!" Such people then proceed with life under the mistaken assumption that they themselves are responsible for their own welfare and destiny, and can engage in whatever it takes to accomplish those ends.[5] Effectively, "There is no God" (14:1b).

That the "fool" is representative of a group of like-minded individuals seems clear from the shift to the plural, in 14:1c and for the remainder of the psalm, to indicate the company of fools/wicked (except for the necessary rhetorical singulars in 14:3cd). On the other hand, the wise/righteous is depicted for the most part as an individual: in 14:1d (one "who does good"); 14:2cd (one "who understands," one "who seeks after God"); 14:3c (one "who does good"); 14:5b ("the righteous one"[6]); 14:6a ("the afflicted"); "his" (14:6b); and "Jacob" and "Israel" (14:7a, 7c). They show up as a cohort only in 14:4b ("my people") and 14:7b ("His people"). Perhaps this is an indication that fools abound; the righteous are scarce. "The fool is not a rare subspecies within the human race; all human beings are fools apart from the wisdom of God."[7] Indeed, even with God's wisdom about this matter freely available, most of humankind remain "fools" in this sense. This is true in all times and in all places, post-fall.

The negation of God by the fool in 14:1ab, "[there is] no God," is reciprocated in kind by God with repeated negations employing the same negative particle (אֵין, 'en, "not"): "[there is] *not* [one] who does good" (14:1d); "[there is] *not* [one] who does good" (14:3c); and "*not* even one" (14:3d).[8] It is God's judicial findings in the matter that give us this perspective on the absence of any righteous (14:2ab), and on the characteristics of a fool (14:2c–3)—one who fails to understand and to seek God, one who turns aside (from God), and one who has

---

2. Goldingay, *Psalms*, 1:213.
3. Miller, *Interpreting the Psalms*, 95.
4. Miller, *Interpreting the Psalms*, 98.
5. Needless to say, this company may even include believers in God, who act as though deity were uninvolved with them.
6. Even though it is the "generation of the righteous one" that is mentioned.
7. Craigie, *Psalms 1–50*, 147, 148.
8. This is hyperbole, of course: there is at least one person who meets God's criteria, the psalmist.

become corrupt. In sum, the fool is incapable of doing good, for the priorities of this person are atheistically scrambled. "The fool is not simply one lacking in mental powers; indeed, the fool may be a highly intelligent person. The fool is one whose life is lived without the direction or acknowledgment of God."[9]

The emphasis in 14:2–3 is on the pervasiveness of this anti-God thinking (and thus, the ubiquity of "fools"): "all" (14:3a; also in 14:4a) and "together" (14:3b)—plurals; "not [one] who does good" (14:1d, 3c) and "not even one" (14:3d)—singulars. Once again, the universality of this condemnation is emphasized. These "act ruinously," "behave abominably,"[10] and "become corrupt" incurring only the loathing of God (14:1c, 3b). Psalm 14:1–3 is "one of the strongest passages in the Bible about the complete depravity of the human race."[11]

In sum, the fool is one whose speech (denying God) has failed, and whose actions (becoming corrupt) are faulty. Guilty!

Destiny of the Fool (14:4–6)

Relating 14:4a and 4c, it appears that what the doers of harm have "not known" is Yahweh himself. Ignorant of him, disregarding him, they do as they please, oppressing the people of God (their faulty actions), never deigning to call upon God (their failed speech), for they lack any spiritual insight.[12] The consequence is expected: they become "practitioners of harm" (14:4a), with not a single one "doing good" (14:3c).

So their time is up. God is taking action again, on behalf of "my [the psalmist's] people" (14:4b; i.e., the cohort of the righteous) who are, in reality, *God's* people, as 14:7 makes clear with "Israel," "His people," and "Jacob." It is likely that those oppressors assumed that since God was not involved in the affairs of humans, he would neither bother to intervene in their corrupt actions. But they were wrong! And so, now it is the fate of the fool/wicked that deity is going to decree, because no one messes with God's people![13] And so "they [the wicked] greatly dread" (14:5a; literally, "they dread with dread"). But the righteous? God is with them (14:5b). So though the wicked oppress the "afflicted" (14:6a), and put them to shame (14:6a[14]), God is going to become their refuge (14:6b). What more does one need with the Creator of the universe on one's side, as one's champion?

---

9. Craigie, *Psalms 1–50*, 147, 148.

10. The root of the verb translated "behave abominably," תעב, *t'v*, is also the source of תּוֹעֵבָה, *to'evah*, "abomination," one of the most intense and fervent denunciations of anti-God things (e.g., Exod 8:26), activities (e.g., Lev 20:13), and people (e.g., Prov 3:32) in Scripture.

11. Ross, *Psalms*, 1:375. And Paul uses it to prove his case in Romans 3. The word translated "corrupt" (אָלַח, *'alach*, 14:3b) is elsewhere in the OT found only in Job 15:16; an Arabic cognate describes milk turning sour (Brown et al., "אָלַח," 47).

12. Again, this need not indicate an intellectual disbelief in the existence of God, only that these "fools" do not "know" him, ידע, *yd'*—in Scripture, this verb connotes intimate and personal knowledge.

13. Just as no one messes with Texas! (Post-script: That line was written when I was an inhabitant of that fair state. I have since moved.)

14. The "you" in 14:6a translates a second-person plural suffix, thus indicating the godless. How they shame God's people is unclear. Perhaps the latter are trounced in intellectual arguments of whether God is involved in affairs human, with those fools "proving" their case with evidence of the seeming unconcern of God for his own (or his incapacity to protect them). What answer could the righteous have for that, other than calling upon God for deliverance? And so they do, in 14:7.

Deliverance of the Faithful (14:7)

As is typical, this lament also ends in a note of confidence. God's "restoring the restoration" (14:7b) could be a hope for the return from exile or from the diaspora. With a careful scrutiny of the twenty-seven occurrences of שׁוּב שְׁבוּת, *shuv shvut*, "restore the restoration," in the Old Testament, Bracke shows that the phrase "is associated with promises which indicate Yahweh's reversal of his judgment, and the restoration of a condition of well-being. Additionally, the vision of restoration . . . often includes Yahweh's correction of that which led to his judgment."[15] Essentially, it is a removal of God's wrath and a return of God's favor upon his people (also see 53:6; 85:1; 126:1, 4). This may also be a hint, albeit subtle, that some guilt of God's people played a role in God's delay in delivering them. In any case, the nuance does not particularly make a difference for the reader (and preacher) today: the wish for deliverance, of one kind or another, has been universally voiced by the people of God of all times.

Notice the location of deity in this psalm: He is in "heaven" (14:2a), but he is also on earth, in the temple on Mt. Zion (14:7a). But most poignantly, he is with the righteous, his people (14:5b; see 14:4b, 7b). And that, brothers and sisters in Christ, is the most important truth about God, one that the fool was utterly ignorant of.

Sermon Map

I. The Fool
    Description (14:1–3)
    Destiny (14:4–6)
    Move-to-relevance: Atheistic oppressors today

II. The Faithful
    God's people (14:4b, 7bc)
    God's location: heaven, earth, but with them (14:2a, 7b; and 14:4b, 7bc)
    Expected joyful deliverance (14:7)
    Move-to-relevance: Why we find it difficult to believe God is with us

III. *Be Faithful, not Foolish!*
    Specifics on trusting God's presence and providence

---

15. Bracke, "*šûb šebût*: Reappraisal," 243.

PSALM 15:1–5

Psalm of Orientation

Criteria for Fellowship with God

PSALM 15 MARKS THE beginning of a set of ten consecutive psalms that are arranged chiastically:[1]

> **A**   Psalm 15 (entrance liturgy psalm: "Who may abide?" [15:1])
>   **B**   Psalm 16 (psalm of trust: "Yahweh ... my cup" [16:5])
>   **C**   Psalm 17 (lament psalm)
>   **D**   Psalm 18 (royal psalm: context of battle)
>   **E**   Psalm 19 (*Torah* psalm)
>   **D'**   Psalms 20–21 (royal psalms: context of battle)
>   **C'**   Psalm 22 (lament psalm)
>   **B'**   Psalm 23 (psalm of trust: "My cup overflows" [23:5])
> **A'**   Psalm 24 (entrance liturgy psalm: "Who may ascend?" [24:3])

This is clearly an intentional arrangement, but that need not necessarily bother the homiletician who preaches a single psalm for a particular occasion as dictated by the needs of the congregation. As with hymnbooks that have intentional (topical) organizations of their contents, so also does the Psalter (see Introduction). That is not a call to preach these psalms in sequence, of course, just as one would not necessarily pick songs from a hymnbook by moving sequentially from its first to its last entries.

Translation

> 15:1   Yahweh, who may stay in Your tent?
>   Who may abide on Your holy mountain?
> 15:2   One who walks with integrity,
>   and one who practices righteousness,
>   and one who speaks truth in his heart.

---

1. Brown, "'Here Comes the Sun!,'" 260.

15:3 He has not slandered with his tongue,
>   he has not done evil to his fellow,
>   and he has not taken up scorn against his neighbor.
15:4 Despised in his eyes is a reprobate,
>   but those who fear Yahweh, he honors;
>   he swears to [his own] calamity and does not change.
15:5 His silver he has not put out for interest,
>   nor a bribe against the innocent has he taken.
>   One who does these things will not totter, ever.

Structure

The structure of Psalm 15 is straightforward: a question is asked (15:1) that is subsequently answered (15:2–5b); and a closing assertion ends the psalm (15:5c). In between its introductory interrogation and its concluding declaration there is a back-and-forth positive/negative movement to the structure of Psalm 15:[2]

> Interrogation (**15:1**)
>   Three Positive Criteria–1 (**15:2**)
>   Three Negative Criteria–1 (**15:3**) (לֹא ×3)
>   Three Positive Criteria–2 (**15:4abcα**)
>   Three Negative Criteria–2 (**15:4cβ–5b**) (לֹא ×3)
> Declaration: Positive; Negative (**15:5c**) (לֹא)

Like the Decalogue, the psalm combines responsibilities of the righteous that are directed towards God and towards others.[3] Access into the presence of deity (fellowship with him) is clearly tied to both aspects of a holy, sanctified life.[4]

Theological Focus

> The person of God who is characterized by integrity in thought, word, and deed, demonstrating righteousness towards God and faithfulness to him, and doing right by fellowmen without exploiting them, will continue in fellowship with God, unshakable and steadfast.

---

2. The negative elements in their particular sections are all expressed with the particle לֹא, *loʾ*.

3. However, attempts to convert the nine items of the psalm to ten, to match the Decalogue, are unconvincing.

4. As in many other psalms, such holiness of life does not mean perfect righteousness, of course. Rather it points to a life committed to God. The fellowship with deity that such holiness results in is integral to the Christian life of sanctification, notwithstanding the perfect positional righteousness of the believer in Christ.

Commentary

Interrogation (15:1)

After a series of laments—psalms of disorientation—we turn now to what is almost a wisdom psalm that instructs: a psalm of orientation depicting what happens (or what ought to) in God's ideal world.[5] Essentially, it begins with the question of who may enjoy the presence of God and proceeds in the rest of its verses to provide an answer. Some have imagined it to be a "liturgy at the gate [of the temple], because it asks the question of who may enter the sanctuary to commune with the LORD and then provides the response."[6] While that may be the "story" behind the text, it is apparent that the psalm can be employed by all generations of readers everywhere who seek the intimacy of divine presence and fellowship.[7]

In the parallelism of the questions in 15:1a and 15:1b, the tent—originally the portable sanctuary in Exodus 25–40, later the covering for the ark (2 Sam 6:17; 1 Kgs 2:28–30; 8:4)—is equated with "Your holy mountain," Mt. Zion, i.e., the temple. Poetically, it indicates a place of refuge in the very presence of deity (Ps 61:4). So this psalm, in response to the questions of 15:1, is going to set out the conditions for a person to remain in God's presence, a haven of rest.

Three Positive Criteria–1; Three Negative Criteria–1 (15:2–3)

The trio of positive conditions in 15:2, all participles, describes one who is "walking" with integrity, "practicing" righteousness, and "speaking" truth (15:2). Speech and action are linked not only in this verse, but also in 15:3 ("slandering"/"scorning" and "not doing evil"), and in 15:4 ("swearing" and "not changing"[8]). But it is not just speech and action; attitude is also critical—"in his heart" (15:2).

The set of negative conditions in 15:3, all *qal* perfects, lists items to be avoided by the one seeking divine presence.

---

5. This world is, of course, not the eschaton, which might be called the era of the "ideal ideal" world, when evil is banished eternally and God's will is forever done. Life, post-fall and pre-eternity, is better described as an "ideal real" world—a world that, amidst evil abounding around and within, still runs according to divine precepts, priorities, and practices (at least among the people of God who are instantiating and actualizing God's ideal world). Both of those designations for worlds are terms borrowed and modified from Dworkin, *Sovereign Virtue*, 172–75.

6. Ross, *Psalms*, 1:386.

7. The fact that, unlike requirements for temple entry in the ancient Near East (and unlike the criteria set forth in Deut 23:1–6; Lev 21:17–21), "the psalm focuses exclusively on the *moral* requirements to the complete exclusion of cultic, physical, or sacrificial requirements" is a clear indication of the psalm's use and adaptability beyond the times and environs of ancient Israel. See deClaissé-Walford et al., *Book of Psalms*, 172. One must remember that these items are not "things to do" in order to enter into a relationship with God. That is a unilateral and entirely gracious initiative of deity. These elements in Psalm 15 (and the numerous divine demands in all of Scripture) relate to the responsibility of the people to God to the one who called them into relationship with him: relationship first, responsibility later. And such responsible obedience in the power of the Spirit results in blessing. See Kuruvilla, *Privilege the Text!*, 151–94.

8. I.e., acting as he had sworn to do, agreeing to negative consequences, "[his own] calamity," should he break his vow (15:4c).

In fact, one can discern that each of the three negatives here parallel each of the positive members in 15:2:[9]

Psalm 15:2abc	Psalm 15:3abc
"walks with integrity"	"has not slandered [gone about] with his tongue"
"practices righteousness"	"has not done evil"
"speaks truth"	"has not … taken up scorn"

While the three positive items in 15:2 seem to deal with attitudes, speech, and actions directed God-wards, the three negative items in 15:4 are directed other-wards—the third here explicitly said to be "against his neighbor" (15:3c). The subsequent collections of positive criteria (15:4a, 4b, 4cα) and of three negative ones (15:4cβ, 5a, 5b) are directed towards others.

Three Positive Criteria–2; Three Negative Criteria–2 (15:4–5b)

Though the righteous eschews evil towards neighbor in word and in deed (15:3), these persons will also "despise" reprobates and apostates who are not God-fearers; instead they "honor" those who do fear God (15:4ab). This is set forth in a chiastic structure, making the contrast stark:

> "Despised in his eyes
>   is a reprobate,
>   but those who fear Yahweh,
> he honors."

"Just as no evil man can be a guest in Yahweh's tent . . . , so the hospitality of the godly man does not extend to the wicked."[10] The one seeking divine presence is to abstain from participating in evil, by not performing it towards another (15:3abc), and by not tolerating it in another (15:4ab). This is fundamental to the *shalom* of community life, especially of a body that is in communion with a holy God who himself "hates all doers of harm" and "abhors" them (5:5, 6; 11:5). Indeed, the mark of a wicked person is that "evil he does not *reject*" (36:4; נִמְאָס, *nimʾas*, the same verb as in 15:4a). That the righteous person in divine presence is one who keeps one's word (15:4cα) without changing (15:4cβ), marks this individual out as one with integrity, who can be trusted and relied upon.

It is not surprising that money and wealth show up in the criteria for fellowshipping with God (15:5ab)—finances are definitely a spiritual issue in Scripture. Goldingay is right: "In monetary matters it is especially tempting not to be truthful . . . [15:2], to seek to wrong other people . . . [15:3] . . . , and to suspend moral standards in relation to other people . . . [15:4]."[11] In other words, all of the other requirements can come undone in the face of greed

---

9. The phrase "he has not slandered with his tongue" (15:3a) is literally "he has not gone about with his tongue" (לֹא־רָגַל עַל־לְשֹׁנוֹ, *loʾ-ragal ʿal-lshono*; the assonant link with רֶגֶל, *regel*, "foot" is obvious); thus the parallel with "walk" in 15:2a.

10. Dahood, *Psalms I*, 84.

11. Goldingay, *Psalms*, 1:222–23.

for filthy lucre. Usury was proscribed between Israelites in Deut 23:19–20, though pledges and securities for loans were permitted (24:6). "The presupposition of the Torah's attitude to lending is that it is a means of helping the needy fellow Israelite, not a means of the rich increasing their wealth . . . [see Exod 22:25–27; Lev 25:35–38]. It does not have in mind what we might call commercial loans (which may be what Deut 23:20 refers to). To lend at interest [perhaps presuming high rates of interest] is to take advantage of the needy."[12] Bribery was unequivocally prohibited: Exod 23:8; Deut 16:19. All of these manifestations of avarice of a rapacious kind are not becoming of one desiring intimacy with God. Godly living in community is critical for one desiring to live with God personally.

Declaration (15:5c)

And then the psalm concludes with: "One who does these things will not totter, ever!" (Ps 15:5c: a positive urging + a negative utterance). Whereas we had a not-to-be-"done" in 15:3b, we have a to-"do" here in 15:5c (both use the verb עשׂה, 'sh). Considering 15:5c as a bookend with 15:1 for the entire psalm, it may well be that there is an allusion once again to the temple: the righteous one who attains to the presence of God will be like the temple on God's "holy mountain," unshakable!

> From a human perspective, the psalmists were constantly shaken by their experience of human oppression and the vicissitudes of life, and so they issued their laments; but the only possibility of transforming lament into confidence or praise lay in the fact that there was an unshaken position transcending the vicissitudes of a shaken and uncertain life. That position was in the presence of God, whether in public worship or private devotion.[13]

Indeed!

Sermon Map

I. The Terminus
   The goal and desire: divine presence (15:1)
   Move-to-relevance: What fellowship with God means

II. The Terms
   Responsibility mandated by relationship
   Integrity and loyalty towards God (15:2ab, 4ab)
   Doing good to others and treating them fairly (15:3, 4c, 5ab)
   Move-to-relevance: How we fail to discharge our responsibility

III. *Be Upright, Don't Totter!*
   Specifics on being a person of integrity[14]

---

12. Goldingay, *Psalms*, 1:223.
13. Craigie, *Psalms 1–50*, 152.
14. One area listed in the psalm may be chosen to be the focus of application.

PSALM 16:1–11

Psalm of Orientation

Devotion to God

THE ONLY PLEA IN Psalm 16 is in 16:1a, but the verse in its entirety is more of a declaration of trust rather than an entreaty. In any case, 16:1–6 affirms Yahweh as the one upon whom the psalmist and the community of saints rely. No one else can take that place. But in the middle, 16:4 points a finger at others who take a different view, following after other deities. The psalm, therefore, has the tone of a polemic against such defectors though, of course, that, too, serves as an encouragement to the divine community. The rest of the poem, 16:7–11, is a statement of devotion to Yahweh, and the benefits that accrue therefrom.[1] There is only one deity worthy of reliance and devotion!

Translation

16:1 Watch over me, God,
    for I take refuge in You.
16:2 I said to Yahweh, "My Lord, You [are];
    my good, none besides You."
16:3 As for the holy ones who are in the land, they
    and the majestic ones—all my delight is in them.
16:4 Their pains will increase—those who espouse another [deity].
    I shall not pour out their libations of blood,
    and I will not take up their [deities'] names on my lips.
16:5 Yahweh is the portion of my share and my cup—
    You, the One who holds on to my lot.
16:6 The boundary lines have fallen to me in pleasant [places];
    yes, the inheritance is beautiful for me.

---

1. Therefore, I categorize Psalm 16 as a psalm of orientation.

16:7 I will bless Yahweh who has counseled me;
　　　yes, by night my innards correct me.
16:8 I have set Yahweh before me continually;
　　　because [He is] at my right hand, I will not be shaken.
16:9 Therefore my heart is joyous and my inner being jubilates;
　　　yes, my flesh will abide in safety.
16:10 For You will not abandon my soul to Sheol;
　　　You will not let Your devout one to see the grave.
16:11 You will make known to me the path of life;
　　　fullness of joy [is with] Your presence;
　　　pleasures in Your right hand perpetually.

Structure

The psalm is best seen as comprising two conceptually parallel sections, *Reliance on God* and *Devotion to God*:[2]

Reliance on God (16:1–6)
"Yahweh" (×2, 16:2, 5)
　Yahweh as exclusive object of reliance (**16:1–3**)
　　Grief of defectors (**16:4**; double negation: 16:4b, 4c)
　　　Yahweh as blesser of land (**16:5–6**)
　　　("pleasant" [נָעִים, *na'im*] 16:6a)

Devotion to God (16:7–11)
"Yahweh" (×2, 16:7, 8)
　Yahweh as exclusive object of devotion (**16:7–8**)
　　Joy of devotees (**16:9–10**; double negation: 16:10a, 10b)
　　　Yahweh as benefactor of life (**16:10–11**)
　　　("pleasures" [נָעִים, *na'im*], 16:11c)

Theological Focus

The one devoted to God, along with others in the divine community, seeks refuge in God, trusting exclusively in him and rejecting all false gods that bring only trouble, and finds satisfaction in the provision of God and even more in the presence of God, resulting in safety and abundance of joy.

---

2. From Botha, "True Happiness," 66–67, 70–71.

Commentary

Reliance on God (16:1–6)

Though "watch over" (שׁמר, *shmr*) can mean "keep" from harm (16:1a), making it an entreaty, that verse as a whole, as was noted, is unlikely to be a plea for protection from enemies; it is more a statement of trust, as 16:2 also makes clear. It is not just that Yahweh *provides* "good"; he *is* the psalmist's "good"—he, and no one else (16:2b).

After his twofold declaration about God in 16:2 (he is "my Lord" and "my good"), this devout God-loyalist affirms the community that also remains committed to this God, also described in twofold fashion: "holy ones"[3] and "majestic ones"[4] (16:3): both descriptors point to the same group, the community (and/or its leaders), with the connective "and" between the two terms perhaps being an explicatory "that is": "the holy ones . . . , that is, majestic ones." The two lines of both 16:2 and 16:3 are similar: the first line of each ends with an independent pronoun (16:2a, 3a: "You" and "they"), and the second line of each ends with a preposition + pronominal suffix indicating the same person referred to in the preceding line (16:2b, 3b: "besides You [i.e., God]" and "in them [i.e., holy ones]"):

16:2a	"My Lord"	"You"		
16:2b			"my good"	"besides You"
16:3a	"holy ones"	"they"		
16:3b			"majestic ones"	"in them"

In other words, the psalmist is closely identifying God with the people of God by describing them similarly. And the latter, he "delights" in (16:3b).

Then he quickly proceeds to take aim at those do not have such a commitment to Yahweh (16:4)—those who follow after "another" deity; their troubles are many.[5] The use of עַצְּבוֹתָם (*'atstsvotam*, "their pains," 16:4a) is a play on עֲצַבִּים, *atstsvim*, "idols":[6] "Their pains will increase" as their idols multiply! The blood offerings of the idolaters, the psalmist refuses to participate in (16:4b),[7] and these false worshipers, the psalmist despises, refusing even to mention their deities' names (16:4c). Thus a stark contrast is made between the ones who are committed to Yahweh (16:3) and the ones who are not (16:4).

The psalmist then returns to the motif of Yahweh being all he needs and all he yearns for: the poet (and his cohort) have God himself as their portion and destiny (16:5a).[8] With

---

3. While the term can indicate heavenly beings (89:5, 7), in the context of their being "in the land" these "holy ones" are members of the community of Israel, God's people (Num 16:3, 5, 7; Ps 34:9), and/or its leaders (2 Chr 35:3).

4. Likely nobility, as in Jdg 5:13; 2 Chr 23:20; Neh 3:5; 10:29.

5. "Another" (אַחֵר, *'acher*) for false deities is often employed in the OT, but only here and in Isa 42:8 is there an absence of the subsequent noun, "god" (to form "another god"); perhaps that is assumed. The meaning of מהר, *mhr*, in 16:4a is unclear; "espouse" comes closest to the only other use of the *qal* form of the verb in Scripture, in Exod 22:16 ("pay a dowry," thus to take as spouse).

6. As in 1 Sam 31:9; 2 Sam 5:21; 1 Chr 10:9; 2 Chr 24:18.

7. Such sacrifices were part of the OT sacrificial system (Exod 23:18; 34:25; Lev 9:18), legitimate when offered to Yahweh.

8. As in 73:26; 119:57; 142:5; Lam 3:24; also see Deut 10:9. For Israel as Yahweh's portion, see Deut 32:9; Zech 2:12.

16:6 it becomes clear that at least part of this divine portion involves land, and thus financial stability, for the supplicant and his posterity.⁹ With that affirmation, the poet demonstrates his total freedom from worry: he had his portion, his splendid allotment of land, because he was relying totally on Yahweh, rendering him free of "pains" (16:4a). The "beautiful" "inheritance" in 16:6b is, no doubt, the blessing of the land. But after having declared that "Yahweh is the portion of my share and my cup" (16:5a), one wonders if he, God, might well be the "inheritance [that] is beautiful for me"!

Devotion to God (16:7–11)

Because of all that he has said about God being his "Lord," his "good," his "portion," and his "cup" (16:2, 5), the psalmist intends to maintain an exclusive *Devotion to God*. A number of body parts with the first-person suffix show up: "my innards"[10] (16:7b), "my right hand" (16:8b), "my heart," "my inner being"[11] (16:9a), "my flesh" (16:9b), "my soul" (16:10a)—i.e., all of the psalmist, every part, will be committed to God. God is "before" the psalmist, i.e., in front of him, *and* "at [his] right hand" (16:8)—everywhere, and all around, surrounding every limb and member and appendage of the one devoted to God! No longer is it land, financial benefits, or other tangible assets that he sees as a gift of God, but the very presence of God himself.

> To set God before us is nothing else than to keep all our senses bound and captive, that they may not run out and go astray after any other object. . . . The meaning, therefore, is, that . . . [the psalmist] kept his mind so intently fixed on the providence of God, as to be fully persuaded, that whenever any difficulty or distress should befall him, God would be always at hand to assist him. . . . Amidst the various conflicts with which he was agitated, no fear of danger could make him turn his eyes to any other quarter than to God in search of succour. And thus we ought so to depend upon God.[12]

This dependence involves seeking Yahweh and his counsel and correction at all times, even "by night" (16:7b), "continually" (16:8a)—a lifelong devotion, marked by being "not . . . shaken" (16:8b), but by "jubilating" and by dwelling "in safety" (16:9).[13] That safety is explicated in 16:9b–11a, at the center (D, E, E', D') of the chiastic structure, below, of 16:8–11, as security for ever!

---

9. "Boundary lines" (16:6a) refers to the measuring ropes used to parcel out properties.

10. Literally, "my kidneys," perhaps equivalent to "mind."

11. Literally, "my liver" (amending כְּבוֹדִי, *kvodi*, to כְּבֵדִי, *kvedi*). This organ was often viewed in the ancient Near East as the source of human emotion, especially joy. In the "Ugaritic Poems about Baal and Anath" there is a description of the "liver [*kbd*]" of Anath (Baal's consort) swelling with laughter, and her heart filling with joy and her "liver" exulting (V AB B 25–27 [ANET 136]). Also see *Enuma Elish* I 31 that has Apsu the god declaring his "liver" was rejoicing (ANET 61).

12. Calvin, *Commentary on the Book of Psalms*, 1:228.

13. It is the "innards" doing the correction in 16:7b, but it is clear from the parallelism with 16:7a that Yahweh is working through the psalmist's mind to guide him.

```
A    "continually" (16:8a)
  B    "'my right hand" (16:8b)
    C    "joyous" (16:9a)
      D    "safety" (16:9b)
        E    "not abandon ... to Sheol" (16:10a)
        E'   "not let ... to see the grave" (16:10b)
      D'   "path of life" (16:11a)
    C'   "joy" (16:11b)
  B'   "Your right hand" (16:11cα)
A'   "perpetually" (16:11cβ)
```

Essentially, the protection is from (premature?) death, kept from Sheol and the "grave" (or the "pit")—synonymous terms (*E, E'*; 16:10). Instead, the "path of life" (16:11; *D'*), corresponding to "safety" (16:9b; *D*), is laid before the "devout" (חָסִיד, *chasid*; 16:10b), who is guarded, no doubt, by the lovingkindness (חֶסֶד, *chesed*) of God.[14] The consequence is a "fullness of joy" in the "presence" (literally, "face") of God, and enduring "pleasures" from the "right hand" of God.[15] The devout does not simply escape death and enjoy safety, but will revel in life in the divine presence, with divine pleasures.

> In the context of modernity, Christians are . . . inclined to distance God's involvement from the provision of everyday needs, because we can seem more in control of our environment and able to take provisions for granted. Psalm 16 knows that Yhwh is the God of this life and not just of the future life nor just of religious life, and provides for this life in abundance. It is one of the reasons why people should stay faithful to Yhwh.[16]

Amen!

---

14. The "making known" of the path of life (16:11a) is equivalent to the "counsel" of Yahweh and his correction of the psalmist via the mind (16:7). But "the 'path of life,' [is] not the afterlife, but the fullness of life here and now which is enriched by the rejoicing which emerges from an awareness of divine presence" (Craigie, *Psalms 1–50*, 158). The notion of an afterlife was not well-developed for most of OT history. Yet "most of these instances [that appear to speak of an afterlife: 9:13; 16:10; 30:3; 49:15; 71:20; 73:24; 103:4; 116:8] were also understood in terms of resurrection or eternal life, . . . as the [New Testament] application of Ps 16:10 in Acts 13:35 clearly show[s] . . . It is but a small step from here to the belief that death would not separate the believer from God" (Botha, "True Happiness," 71). One must also consider those references in Proverbs that suggest that a notion of the afterlife was not entirely absent from the thoughts of the ancients: 4:18; 14:32; 15:24; 23:13–14. On the whole, while a mention of a life of eternity with God is appropriate in the sermon, to be fair to the text and its divine and human A/authors, it is best to focus on the earthly blessings enjoyed by the devout, including physical safety. After all, the fact of such blessings in the here and now is, unfortunately, a neglected topic in Christian discussions and pedagogy. Note that the reference to 16:10 in Acts 13:35 is an *application* of the verse, not necessarily an explication thereof.

15. After several human body parts have been mentioned, the introduction of a couple of divine body parts (!) is apropos.

16. Goldingay, *Psalms*, 1:234.

PSALMS 1–44

Sermon Map

I. Reliance on God

   Trusting in his refuge and goodness (16:1–2)

   Move-to-relevance: Why we need God's refuge and goodness

II. Devotion to God

   Exclusively devoted to God (16:2)

   Keeping company with the devout (16:3)

   Rejecting all pseudo-deities (16:4)

   Move-to-relevance: How we fall in the thrall of false gods

III. Joy of God

   Material provisions from God (16:6)

   Divine presence—God all around; safety all around (16:7–8, 9b–11a)

   Resulting joy of God (16:9a, 11bc)

   Move-to-relevance: Forgetfulness of the necessity of God's provision

IV. *Our Only God!*

   Specifics on rejoicing in/blessing God for his abundance[17]

---

17. Considering the joy in the psalm (especially 16:9, 11) and the blessing of God (16:7), it might be best to take the application in that direction.

PSALM 17:1–15

Psalm of Disorientation

Defending Self and Seeking Protection

ALTOGETHER, PSALM 17 APPEARS to be the psalmist's defense of himself, perhaps to motivate God to deliver him from an attack by "deadly enemies" (17:9b). This prayer may have been uttered at night: note "night" in 17:3 and "awake" in 17:15.

Translation

17:1 Hear, Yahweh, a right [cause];
    attend to my lament;
    give ear to my prayer
    [which is] not from lips of deceit.

17:2 From Your face may my judgment come forth;
    may Your eyes behold equitably.

17:3 You have tried my heart; You have visited by night;
    You have tested me; You did not find [anything].
    I have purposed that my mouth will not transgress.

17:4 As for the deeds of mankind, by the word of Your lips
    I—I have kept from the ways of the violent.

17:5 My steps have held fast to Your tracks;
    my feet have not stumbled.

17:6 I—I have called upon You, for You answer me, God;
    stretch Your ear to me, hear my utterance.

17:7 Work wonders of Your lovingkindness,
    You who deliver
    those taking refuge
    from those who rise up
    by Your right hand.

17:8 Keep me as the precious pupil of the eye;
           in the shadow of Your wings hide me
17:9 from the face of the wicked who assault me—
           my deadly enemies around me.
17:10 They have closed their insides;
           their mouth, it has spoken arrogantly.
17:11 Now they have surrounded our steps;
           they set their eyes to stretch [us] out on the ground.
17:12 He is like a lion eager to rend in pieces,
           and as a young lion crouching in hiding.
17:13 Arise, Yahweh, be in front of his face, bring him to his knees;
           save my soul from the wicked with Your sword.
17:14 Kill them by Your hand, Yahweh,
           kill them from the world—their portion in life.
         But Your treasured one[s]—You fill their belly;
           they are satisfied with children,
           and leave their surplus to their babies.
17:15 I—in righteousness I shall behold Your face;
           I will be satisfied, when I awake, with Your likeness.

Structure

This psalm demonstrates a movement from the psalmist's *Assertion* of his innocence before God, his suffering an *Assault* from enemies, and his *Assurance* of God's recompense, each section comprising a plea to God and a prompt for God to act:

> **Assertion (17:1–5)** (emphatic "I" [אֲנִי, *'ani*], 17:4b)
> *Plea 1:* for attention (**17:1–2**)
> *Prompt 1:* faithfulness/innocence (**17:3–5**)
>
> **Assault (17:6–12)** (emphatic "I" [אֲנִי], 17:6a)
> *Plea 2:* for attention and action (**17:6–9**)
> *Prompt 2:* complaint/lament (**17:10–12**)
>
> **Assurance (17:13–15)** (emphatic "I" [אֲנִי], 17:15a)
> *Plea 3:* for action (**17:13–14b**)
> *Prompt 3:* confidence/satisfaction (**17:14c–15**)

Each move is also marked by the presence of an emphatic first-person pronoun, אֲנִי (17:4b, 6a, 15a), underscoring, respectively, the psalmist's assertion of innocence, his fear of the enemy assault provoking his calling out to God, and his assured confidence in Yahweh's aid.

PSALM 17:1–15

Theological Focus

Under oppression, the righteous seek divine attention and action, anticipating God's work as in the past: vindication of innocence because of a steadfast walk with God, protection from assault by the power of God, and recompense for enemies as God defends his people, culminating in their blessing as they abide in the intimate presence of their deity.

Commentary

Assertion (17:1–5)

What the psalmist wants of God first is attention (17:1), so that he might render justice in favor of the supplicant (17:2). This call for justice which came not from any deceit of his "lips" (17:1d) is a confident entreaty, for it is based on the fact that his life was grounded in righteous instruction by the "word of Your lips" (17:4). All this suggests that some sort of false accusation was being leveled against the sufferer. But he is quite certain of his innocence: divine testing has yielded no evidence of guilt (17:3ab), and an examination of his heart, "his thoughts, designs and disposition" has absolved him.[1] The threefold human plea in 17:1 ("hear," "attend," and "give ear") are matched by a threefold divine investigation in 17:3, comprehensive and exhaustive: "You have tried," "You have visited,"[2] and "You have tested," the result of which was "You did not find [anything]." As if to substantiate his claim, another triplet of affirmations is found in 17:4b–5: "I have kept,"[3] "my steps have held fast," "my feet have not stumbled"—all this in his avoidance of "the ways of the violent" (17:4b) and his adherence to "Your tracks" (17:5a) without dodging, without deviating, without drifting. There is a sense here in which "the suppliant walks in the tracks that have been made by Yhwh's feet"![4]

Needless to say, what the psalmist is claiming here (and in other psalms with similar assertions) is not total sinlessness: the particular contention is that, with regard to the context of some false accusation and enemy assault (see below), he is innocent.

Assault (17:6–12)

The second section of the psalm commences in 17:6 with a recurrence of "ear" and "hear" (as in 17:1a, 1c), as the psalmist's plea for attention is restated in the context of attacks from the enemy (17:9). So he also beseeches God to act against his enemies (17:7–9), with phrases redolent of the exodus: "work wonders" (verb פלא, *pl'*, in 17:7a; noun פֶּלֶא, *pele'*, in Exod 15:11), "lovingkindness" (Ps 17:7a; and Exod 15:12), "Your right hand" (Ps 17:7e; and Exod 15:13), and "those who rise up" (קום, *qwm*: hithpolel in Ps 17:7d; and *qal* in Exod 15:7).

---

1. Kwakkel, *'According to My Righteousness,'* 83.
2. Divine "visitation" has the sense of intense and concerned seeking here, on the part of God, as also in Gen 21:1; Exod 3:16; and Pss 8:4; 59:6 (to punish); 65:10 (to bless); 80:14; etc. That this visitation is "by night" (17:3a) might indicate that nothing can ever be hid from God.
3. An emphatic declaration, with a redundant pronoun: "I—I have kept . . . ."
4. Goldingay, *Psalms*, 1:240.

"The psalm asks that Israel's story becomes suppliant's story, asks for a personal exodus deliverance as someone who relies on Yhwh."[5] The same God who delivered Israel is the one that the psalmist appeals to in his distress under assault.

Notice the presence of "*by* Your right hand" in 17:7e—the multivalent preposition בְּ, *b* (here translated "by") linked to יְמִינֶךָ, *yminka*, "Your right hand." Mosca suggests that this rather flexible preposition is deliberately chosen, and the position of the word at the end of the verse purposefully set. Thus each of the four verbal elements of the verse (17:7a, 7b, 7c, 7d) that precedes בִּימִינֶךָ, *bimineka*, (17:7e) may be seen as being individually qualified by "Your right hand," with its prepositional prefix, בְּ, taking a unique valence in each case:[6]

Verbal Element	Preposition	Qualifier
"Work wonders of Your lovingkindness	with (בְּ)	Your right hand,
You who deliver	by (בְּ)	Your right hand
those taking refuge	at (בְּ)	Your right hand
from those who rise up	against (בְּ)	Your right hand."

"It is obviously impossible to capture the compressed force of the Hebrew . . . for no single English preposition has the required range."[7] And so we have a potent expression of divine power—i.e., God's right hand—capable of working all kinds of wonders on behalf of his people, as deity delivers those seeking refuge in him from the onslaught of enemies.

This brings us to another observation. As in Psalm 16, this psalm, too, is anatomically prolific, with a lot of body parts mentioned—the psalmist's, Yahweh's, and their enemies':[8]

Psalmist's	Yahweh's	Enemies'
lips (17:1d)		
	face (17:2a)	
	eyes (17:2b)	
heart (17:3a)		
mouth (17:3c)		
	lips (17:4a)	
feet (17:5b)		
	ear (17:6b)	
	right hand (17:7e)	
	eye (17:8a)	
	wings (17:8b)	
		face (17:9a)
		insides (17:10a)
		mouth (17:10b)
		eyes (17:11b)
		face (17:13aα)
		knees (17:13aβ)
	hand (17:14a)	
	face (17:15a)	

---

5. Goldingay, *Psalms*, 1:241.

6. From Mosca, "Note on Psalm 17:7," 390–91. Accordingly, I have split 17:7 into five lines.

7. Mosca, "Note on Psalm 17:7," 391.

8. There is also the "belly" of members of the psalmist's community in a closing comment in 17:14c.

What is striking is how the "body" of God permeates the psalm in its every section—and only his "body": the psalmist's is restricted to 17:1–5, and the enemies' to 17:9–13. The presence of God (which is what is indicated by "face" in 17:2a, 15a[9]) fills the entirety of the poem and, indeed, the "face/presence" of God effectively bookends the composition. Notice how the two instances of the "face" of Yahweh (17:2a, 15a) shuts in the two instances of the "face" of the enemy (17:9a, 13a). Also forming an *inclusio* are Yahweh's "right hand" in 17:7e and his "hand" in 17:14a: his upper limb, a metonym for his power, encloses and destroys the enemy, keeping those malefactors literally (and literally) away from the psalmist. That notion is further strengthened by the structuring of 17:7e–14a, God's upper limb bracketing off the balefulness of the enemies and their assault on the psalmist:

> A   "Your right hand" (17:7e)
>   B   "wicked" (17:9a)
>   C   "deadly" (בְּנֶפֶשׁ, *bnephesh*, 17:9b)
>   D   Enemy assault (17:10–12)
>   C'   "soul" (נֶפֶשׁ, *nephesh*, 17:13b)
>   B'   "wicked" (17:13b)
> A'   "Your hand" (17:14a)

No wonder the psalmist exclaims that he will be satisfied, upon waking, with "Your likeness" (תְּמוּנָה, *tmunah*, or "form," 17:15b[10]); after all, that "likeness/form" (or at least the anatomical parts thereof) has been verbally percolating all throughout this song!

A number of contrasts employing body parts are also discernible. While the psalmist entreated Yahweh that his "eyes" might see justice (17:2b) and that he, the psalmist, would be "kept" as the apple of the divine "eye" (17:8a),[11] the enemies' "eyes" were set to cast the godly community to the ground (17:11b). While the "mouth" of the psalmist would not transgress (17:3c), adherent as he was to the "word [דָּבָר, *davar*]" of God (17:4a), the "mouth" of the enemies was "speaking [דבר, *dbr*]" arrogantly (17:10b). While the "steps" of the psalmist held fast to divine paths (17:5a), the righteous' tread of those "steps" was now being surrounded by the wicked (17:11a). It was when the enemies sought to "stretch" out the godly ones upon the ground, casting them down (17:11b), that the psalmist appealed to Yahweh to "stretch" his ear to him (17:6b). When those oppressors crouched in "hiding" for their prey (17:12b), it would be Yahweh who "hid" his people under his wings (17:8b). Whereas the wicked "rose [קוּם]" to assault the righteous (17:7d), Yahweh would "arise [קוּם]" to defeat the violent (17:13a). Such a "keeping" by Yahweh (17:8a) of his devout is, of course, the consequence of the "keeping" by the psalmist to divinely directed paths (17:4b–5a).

Note, too, that the enemies' "insides" that they had closed (17:10a) is literally "fat," perhaps denoting impervious and calloused hearts.

9. Likewise the "face" of the enemies indicates their presence in 17:9a, 13a.

10. Like Moses who beheld the תְּמוּנָה of Yahweh (Num 12:8), so too would the psalmist!

11. Literally, "pupil, the daughter of the eye." Israel's "pupil" and Yahweh's "wings" show up together in Deut 32:10–11—another deliberate link of the psalmist's story with that of the community of God's people, implicitly present in the plurals of Ps 17:11, 14cde.

Assurance (17:13–15)

And so, in 17:13, the psalmist reasserts his hope and confidence, commencing again with a plea for divine action, and comprising four asyndetic imperatives: "arise," "be in front of his face," "bring him to his knees," "save my soul" (17:13).[12]

In 17:14–15, the "portion in life" of the "wicked"—death (17:14ab), and that of God's precious ones—abundant life (17:14cde) are contrasted. And just as the people of God were "satisfied" with their blessings (17:14d), so too is the psalmist—"satisfied" when he awakes, with the presence of God (17:15b). The "righteousness [צֶדֶק, tsedeq]" (17:15a), the basis of the psalmist beholding the divine face, no doubt refers back to the psalmist's "right [צֶדֶק] [cause]" in 17:1a—his expected vindication at the start is now accomplished at the end of the psalm. And so, after having commenced the psalm with an appeal that Yahweh "behold" (17:2b), the psalm now concludes with the psalmist "beholding" deity (17:15a).

While the "waking" in 17:15b could conceivably indicate a rising from death,[13] here it is most likely referring to the morning after a night of turmoil and apprehension. "The psalmist, having prayed himself as it were almost into an exhausted sleep, closes his eyes in the trusting confidence that the new day will dawn with hope—because all tomorrows are in the hands of the Lord."[14] After several pleas earlier in the psalm for attention and action relating to this life, it would be rather odd to see the psalmist launch into a confidence in the afterlife. Besides, the copious references to embodiment in this poem are an affirmation of the concrete (and traumatic) physicality of human existence this side of eternity. "Human lives are physical lives, not just spiritual ones, and the troubles that come to them affect the body and not just the spirit and psyche. Likewise, Yhwh is concerned not just about spiritual or psychological matters but also about the physical."[15] In any case, the "satisfaction" of the righteous (17:15b) is guaranteed!

---

12. The Hebrew of 17:14 is extremely difficult to translate, as the variety of English versions prove, perhaps indicating some textual corruption early in its provenance. Or perhaps the disorder is original: "The garbled phrases in the first line as we have it conveys the suppliant's incoherent spluttering, anxious fear, and bitter resentment" (Goldingay, *Psalms*, 1:244). With Craigie (*Psalms 1–50*, 160–61), I repoint the MT's duplicate מְמִתִים, *mimtim*, in 17:14ab as מְמִיתָם, *mmitam*, "kill them" (*hiphil* participle of מות, *mwt*, "die," with the third person masculine plural suffix). The presence of [ה]מיד [י]ממות, *mmwt[ym] myd[kh]* ("from those dead by your hand") in 11QPsᵃ also suggests a similar connection with the root מות. As for 17:14c, I accept the *qere*, וּצְפוּנְךָ, *utsphunka*, as a participle construct, "but your treasured one[s]."

13. As in 2 Kgs 4:31; Job 14:12; Isa 26:19; Jer 51:39.

14. deClaissé-Walford et al., *Book of Psalms*, 189.

15. Goldingay, *Psalms*, 1:245.

PSALM 17:1–15

Sermon Map

I. Rampage of Enemies
   Accusation (17:1–2, 6)
   Assault (17:9–12)
   Innocence of sufferer (17:3–5)
   Move-to-relevance: Our situations of similar suffering

II. Reality of God
   "Body" of God: his direct involvement (17:2, 4, 6–8, 13)
   Divine protection (17:7, 13); "hand" (17:7, 14)
   Recompense for enemies (17:13–14ab)
   Move-to-relevance: Our failure to see the direct involvement of God

III. Restoration of Sufferer
   Blessing of the community of God (17:14cde)
   Blessing of the person of God (17:15)

IV. *Hold His Hand!*
   Specifics on a confident trust in divine presence and power

PSALM 18:1–50

Psalm of Reorientation

God's Awesome Protection of the Righteous

PSALM 18 IS A fifty-verse-long testimony of thanksgiving to God's deliverance from enemy attack.[1] The first two and last two verses enclose "a first-person quasi-narrative" of this divine rescue mission.[2]

Translation

18:1   I love You, Yahweh, my strength.
18:2   Yahweh is my rock and my steadfastness and the One who saves me,
      my God, my cliff, I take refuge in Him;
      my shield and the horn of my deliverance, my haven.
18:3   The praiseworthy One, Yahweh, I called,
      and from my enemies I was delivered.
18:4   They encompassed me, the ropes of death,
      and the torrents of ungodliness terrified me.
18:5   The ropes of Sheol surrounded me;
      they confronted me, the snares of death.
18:6   In my distress I called upon Yahweh,
      and to my God I cried for help.
      He heard my voice from His temple,
      and my cry for help before Him [His face] came to His ears.
18:7   Then the earth shook and quaked;
      and the foundations of the mountains trembled,
      and were shaken, because He was angry.

---

1. Only Psalms 78 and 119 are longer.
2. Goldingay, *Psalms*, 1:252. Though not all of it reads "narratively," particularly 18:31–50.

18:8   Smoke went up from of His nostrils,
       and fire from His mouth, it devoured;
       coals blazed from it.
18:9   He spread the heavens also, and He came down,
       with thunderclouds under His feet.
18:10 He rode upon a cherub and flew;
       and He soared upon the wings of the wind.
18:11 He set darkness as His hiding place,
       around Him His canopy,
       darkness of waters, mists of clouds.
18:12 From the brightness before Him His mists passed through,
       hail and coals of fire.
18:13 And Yahweh thundered in the heavens,
       and the Most High gave forth His voice,
       hail and coals of fire.
18:14 And He sent His arrows, and He scattered them,
       And [sent] many lightning bolts, and He drove them.
18:15 Then channels of water appeared,
       and the foundations of the world were uncovered
       at Your rebuke, Yahweh,
       at the blast of the breath of Your nostrils.
18:16 He sent from on high, He took me;
       He pulled me out of many waters.
18:17 He rescued me from my strong enemy,
       and from those who hated me, for they were too strong for me.
18:18 They confronted me in the day of my calamity,
       but Yahweh was my support.
18:19 He brought me forth also into a broad place;
       He saved me, because He delighted in me.
18:20 Yahweh has rendered unto me according to my righteousness;
       according to the purity of my hands He has recompensed me.
18:21 For I have kept the paths of Yahweh,
       and not acted wickedly against my God.
18:22 For all His judgments were before me,
       and His statutes I did not put aside from me.
18:23 And I was blameless with Him,
       and I kept myself from my iniquity.
18:24 So Yahweh has recompensed me according to my righteousness,
       according to the purity of my hands before His eyes.

18:25 With the devout You show Yourself devoted;
> with the blameless one You show Yourself blameless;

18:26 with the pure You show Yourself pure,
> but with the perverse You show Yourself deceptive.

18:27 For You, indeed, deliver the afflicted people,
> but haughty eyes You bring down.

18:28 For You, indeed, light my lamp, Yahweh;
> my God brightens my darkness.

18:29 For by You I rush an army,
> and by my God I can leap a wall.

18:30 The [only] God—His path is blameless;
> the utterance of Yahweh is proven;
> He is a shield to all who take refuge in Him.

18:31 For who is God, except Yahweh?
> and who is a rock, besides our God—

18:32 the God who girds me with strength
> and makes my path blameless?

18:33 He makes my feet like deer's,
> and upon my high places stations me—

18:34 the One who trains my hands for battle,
> so my arms can bend a bronze bow.

18:35 You give me the shield of Your deliverance,
> and Your right hand upholds me;
> and Your response makes me great.

18:36 You broaden my steps under me,
> and my ankles do not give way.

18:37 I pursue my enemies and overtake them,
> and I do not turn back until they are finished.

18:38 I smite them, and they are not able to rise;
> they fall under my feet.

18:39 For You gird me with strength for battle;
> You subdue under me those who rise against me.

18:40 My enemies, You give me [their] neck,
> and those who hate me I annihilate.

18:41 They cry for help, but there is none to deliver,
> [even] unto Yahweh, but He does not respond.

18:42 Then I pulverize them as dust before the wind;
> as mud of the streets I empty them out.

18:43 You save me from the strivings of people;
    You place me as head of nations;
    a people I did not know serve me.
18:44 On hearing with the ear, they obey me;
    the children of foreigners cower before me.
18:45 The children of foreigners fall to ruin,
    and come trembling from their fortifications.
18:46 Yahweh lives, and blessed be my rock;
    and exalted be the God of my deliverance,
18:47 the God who executes vengeance for me,
    and subjugates peoples under me—
18:48 the One who saves me from my enemies.
    Yes, You exalt me above those who rise against me;
    from the violent man You rescue me.
18:49 Therefore I will give You thanks among the nations, Yahweh,
    and to Your name I will make music—
18:50 the One who gives great deliverance to His king,
    and shows lovingkindness to His anointed,
    to David and his descendants unto forever.

Structure

Considering the presence of "refuge" and "shield" in 18:2bc, 30c, and "rock" in 18:2a, 31b, one may divide the psalm into two major sections: *Refuge* (18:1–30: the righteous sufferer defended) dealing with an introductory praise and the preservation of the godly; and *"Rock"* (18:31–50: the righteous sufferer on offense: "for battle" in 18:34a, 39a) dealing with divine power, and concluding as the psalm began, with praise.[3]

> **REFUGE (18:1–30)** ["refuge," "shield" in 18:2bc, 30c]: **Defense**
>   Praise (**18:1–3**)
>   Preservation (**18:4–30**)
>   Distress (18:4–6) *[first-person verbs/suffixes]*
>   Deity (18:7–15) *[no first-person]*
>   Deliverance (18:16–30) *[first-person verbs/suffixes]*
>
> **ROCK (18:31–50)** ["rock" in 18:2a, 31b]: **Offense**
>   Power (**18:31–45**)
>   Training for battle (18:31–36) *[no first-person verbs]*
>   Triumph in battle (18:37–45) *[first-person verbs]*
>   Praise (**18:46–50**)

---

3. From Kuntz, "Psalm 18," 4–8; Ross, *Psalms*, 1:437; and deClaissé-Walford et al., *Book of the Psalms*, 192.

This psalm plumbs the abyss and scales the zenith of human experience in this life, literally describing life on a vertical scale:

> The antithesis of heights and depths runs through the psalm. Yhwh is a crag, fastness, and high haven (v. 2). Yhwh came down from the heavens to the earth, acting in such a way as to disturb the lowest depths (vv. 7–15). Yhwh reached down and drew me up (v. 16). The nemeses are people that rose up (vv. 39, 48), but Yhwh humbled lofty eyes (v. 27), and they will not be able to rise up again (v. 38). Yhwh stood me on high places (v. 33). I struck down and Yhwh struck down my enemies beneath my feet (vv. 38–39, 47). Yhwh made me head of nations/on high above my adversaries (vv. 43, 48). Nine times the psalm talks about enemies and adversaries and attackers, eleven times about Yhwh's delivering or rescuing or saving. One party thus goes from height to depths, the other from depths to height. And the key to these moves is God.[4]

Nonetheless, the context of the psalm is unclear; much of the section dealing with battles and triumphs appear to comprise the words of a leader of God's people (the king?). Nonetheless, the canonical text of the song in the hymnbook of Scripture is intended to have validity and relevance for all of God's people.[5]

Theological Focus

> The absolute commitment of God to preserve his people in distress, delivering them through the mighty deity's awesome theophany emanating straight from heaven, delegating power to his chosen, training them for triumph, is contingent upon his people's commitment to him, and is totally worthy of praise.

Commentary

Praise (18:1–3)

The opening element of *Praise* comprises several items that echo later and set the tone for the rest of composition: "save" in 18:2a and 18:43a, 48a (the participle, "the One who saves me," in 18:2a and 18:48a); "rock" in 18:2a and 18:31b, 46a; "deliverance" in 18:2c and 18:35a, 46b, 50a; "shield" in 18:2c and 18:30c, 35a; "enemies/enemy" in 18:3b and 18:17a, 37a, 40a, 48a ("from my [. . .] enemy/enemies" in 18:3b, 17a and 18:48a); "deliver" in 18:3b and 18:27a, 41a. Also there is a concentration of epithets for God in 18:1–3, many of them martial in tone, appropriate for the context of the psalm: "my strength," "my rock," "my steadfastness," "One who saves me," "my cliff," "my shield," "horn of my deliverance,"[6] "my haven," "praiseworthy

---

4. Goldingay, *Psalms*, 1:252.

5. While the psalm is no doubt written by an individual, with singularity prominent, a plurality referring to the delivered community of believers also shows up in 18:27.

6. Usually indicting the might of its owner; also see Ps 75:4–5, 10; 89:17, 24; 92:10; 112:9; 132:17; 148:14.

One." Almost all of these terms for Yahweh have a first-person linkage: "my."[7] No wonder the children of God can call upon their Lord and be committed to him, for he is theirs![8]

Preservation (18:4–30)

The *Preservation* section comprises the bulk of the psalm, recounting the sufferer's distress (18:4–6), the theophany of deity (18:7–15), and the deliverance accomplished (18:16–30; see structure above).

Distress (18:4–6) commences the seemingly historical recounting of Yahweh's preservation. The situation was apparently dire—four times the imminence of mortal danger is repeated (18:4a, 4b, 5a, 5b).[9] And as if to emphasize the "snare" and "ropes," in the Hebrew the verbs with first-person suffixes (A, A', A'', A''') and construct phrases (B, B', B'', B''') interweave and intertwine in an intricate double chiasm in 18:4–5:

A		"encompassed me"
	B	"the ropes of death"
	B'	"the torrents of ungodliness"
A'		"terrified me"
	B''	"the ropes of Sheol"
A''		"surrounded me"
A'''		"confronted me"
	B'''	"the snares of death"

"Each of the four nouns that are in construct . . . are plural. . . . The images could refer to any number of events. And that is the point—that the psalm is not looking back on any one event, but on the entire range and variety of distresses that a person or a people have been through. Each such distress is a microcosm of the cosmic battle with chaos."[10] All that to say, the literality is not what is emphasized; rather it is the rhetorical thrust and the magnitude of danger that is predominant. And if God, as we shall see below, is adequate for these lethalities afflicting his people, surely he can handle every other deadly contingency.

Then follows the appearance of deity—a theophany (18:7–15).[11] This section is marked by the absence of first-person constructions (unlike in 18:4–6): it is all about God, and what a mighty God he is! That it is a deliberate creation is obvious: without it, 18:6 could move

---

7. And for that matter, so does every instance of "enemy" in this psalm!

8. While there is undoubtedly an emotional component to it, "love" for God (especially with the verb רחם, *rchm*, as in 18:1, the only time in the Psalter that it is used in the *qal* and of the affections of humanity towards deity), "love" for a superior primarily indicates commitment and loyalty to him (see Levenson, *Love of God*).

9. "Ungodliness" in 18:4b is "Belial" (בְלִיַּעַל, *bliyya'al*) a name for Satan: see Nah 1:15; and in the NT, 2 Cor 6:15 (that has Βελιάρ, *Beliar*, a variant of Βελιάλ, *Belial*).

10. deClaissé-Walford et al., *Book of Psalms*, 197.

11. The theophany of 18:7–15 gives the confined earthly event a capacious cosmic dimension, employing language from ancient Near Eastern mythology—the conquering of chaos (see Craigie, *Psalms 1–50*, 173). The description is a deliberate escalation and amplification of the crisis that befell God's people.

seamlessly into 18:16.¹² Rhetorically emphasizing the majesty of deity's manifestation, the writer seems to be struggling for descriptors, finally resorting to a number of repetitions: "foundations" (18:7b, 15b); "nostrils" (18:8a, 15d); "fire" (18:8b, 12b, 13c); "coals" (18:8c, 12b, 13c); "hail" (18:12b, 13c); "hail and coals of fire" is repeated here¹³); "heavens" (18:9a, 13a); "wind/breath [רוּחַ, *ruach*]" (18:10b, 15d); "waters" (18:11c, 15a); "mist" (18:11c, 12a); "many" (18:14b, 16b). Indeed, "all the forces and elements of nature are involved in the LORD's presence to deliver," so loyal is he to his own.¹⁴

If the distress (18:4–6) was menacing and ominous to the people of God, no less is the theophany of deity (18:7–15) to those endangering his chosen. The remarkable image of God "spreading" the curtain of the heavens to "come down," "riding a cherub,"¹⁵ "flying," and "soaring upon the wings of the wind" (18:9–10) to aid his people is nothing short of inspiring!¹⁶ In 18:6, God is in his temple; in 18:9–10, he is coming down: Yahweh sees, Yahweh gets involved with all of his being and all of his creation, and Yahweh acts! In response to the "voice" of the righteous (18:6c), Yahweh now raises his "voice" (18:13b).

The deliverance subsection (18:16–30) returns to deploying first-person verbs and suffixes (as in 18:4–6, but absent in 18:7–15). The careful structure of 18:16–30 is remarkable:

A   *Yahweh delivers* (no reason given) (18:16–18)
          Yahweh delivers (because of the faithfulness of the righteous) (18:19–20)
  B   ["according to my righteousness, according to the purity of my hands, He has recompensed me," 18:20]
    C   **Faithfulness of the righteous** (no deliverance mentioned) (18:21–23)
          Yahweh delivers (because of the faithfulness of the righteous) (18:24–27)
  B'   ["Yahweh has recompensed me according to my righteousness, according to the purity of my hands," 18:24]
A'   *Yahweh delivers* (no reason given) (18:28–30)

"The effect is to underline the fact of Yhwh's deliverance, the fact of the worshipper's faithfulness, and the link between these; it puts the focus on the former in the [outer] prominent subsections [*A* and *A'*] and on the latter in the prominent central subsection [*C*], and interrelates them in the bridging [inner] subsections [*B* and *B'*, with their identical phrases]."¹⁷ It is certainly notable—though not at all new in Scripture—that the "delight" of God (18:19b) has a moral contingency: the psalmist's "righteousness," "purity of hands" (18:20), "keeping the paths of Yahweh," "not acting wickedly" (18:21), devotion to divine "judgments" and "statutes"

---

12. Besides, 18:7–15 has identical boundaries: foundations quake, smoke and fire are emitted by Yahweh, and "heavens" are mentioned at either end (18:7–9 [18:9a] and 18:12–15 [18:13a]).

13. "Coals of fire" is probably lightning. So 18:8, 12–13, 15 seem to depict Yahweh as a smoke-exhaling, fire-spewing, coal-kindling dragon-like Leviathan (Job 41:18–21), a theriomorphism that depicts his ferocity against the foes of his people.

14. Ross, *Psalms*, 1:447. "When he goes to war for Israel, it is holy war, and the battle by definition has a cosmic scope. . . . Thus his fighting is as his theophany, a powerful and disturbing entrance into history for Israel's own sake" (Kuntz, "King Triumphant," 167).

15. "Cherub" here might be a poetic description of a cloud?

16. Also see Ps 144:5; Isa 64:1.

17. Goldingay, *Psalms*, 1:265 (the figure is also modified from this source).

(18:22), "blamelessness," and "keeping myself from iniquity" (18:23).[18] This is further dilated upon in a series of gnomic statements about how Yahweh works, contrasting his activities on behalf of the righteous with his activities against the wicked (18:24–27).

The psalmist was in "distress" (18:6a), literally, "a place of narrowness"; but now, in 18:19a, Yahweh has brought him to a "broad place" (and, in addition, "broadened" his steps, 18:36a). It was from "on high" that Yahweh reached into the depths of "many waters"—the symbol of chaos—to accomplish his retrieval (18:16b).[19] Then, in a deliberate alternating sequence of positive and negative statements, the sufferer affirms his own faithfulness to God (18:21–23):[20]

A	"I have *kept* the ways of Yahweh" (18:21a)		+
B	"and not acted wickedly against *my God*" (18:21b)		−
C	"all His *judgments* were before me" (18:22a)		+
C'	"and His *statutes* I did not put aside from me" (18:22b)		−
B'	"I was blameless with *Him*" (18:23a)		+
A'	"I *kept* myself from my iniquity" (18:23b)		−

In essence, the righteous one here is claiming innocence: thus, the attack of the wicked was entirely unjustified. Then again, the justification for their assault may have been exactly that—this was a person who walked with God![21] On the other hand are those wicked ones who do not so walk and reap the consequences. With "perverse" in 18:26b, we have the first attestation to the immoral character of the enemy and God's response to that immorality: "Yhwh can match the faithless in the capacity to throw a curve ball or bend a free kick [or bowl a *doosra*]."[22] Such reciprocity from God, as shown in 18:25–26, ought not to come as a surprise—it is to be expected and anticipated, and to be thankful for, as the psalmist is!

All that to say, Yahweh is loyal and committed to the extent described in Psalm 18 only to those who are loyal and committed to him. Kuntz notes that the "gnomic quatrain" of 18:25–26 is the midpoint of the psalm, fulfilling "a crucial pivotal function": it directs

---

18. The NT is not silent about this either; see Col 1:10 that encourages the believer to "walk worthy of the Lord, in everything pleasing [Him], bearing fruit in every good work" (as well, 2 Cor 5:9; Eph 5:10; 1 Thess 4:1; 2 Tim 2:4; Heb 11:5; 13:16, 21; 1 John 3:22).

19. The phrase "pulled ... out of ... waters" in that verse occurs elsewhere in the OT (besides this psalm's parallel in 2 Sam 22:17) only in Exod 2:10, of the rescue of Moses.

20. Italics indicate similar elements in the corresponding lines.

21. It is worth noting that "devout" (חָסִיד, *chasid*, 18:25aα) and "devoted" (חסד, *chsd*, 18:25aβ) are related to חֶסֶד, *chesed*, "lovingkindness" (18:50). Thus these claims of walking with God that the psalmist makes is essentially that he has been aligning his character with that of God (becoming christiconic in his life, in post-cross terms).

22. Goldingay, *Psalms*, 1:270 (I was sorely disappointed that Goldingay, a native Britisher, picked baseball and soccer idioms rather than one from cricket, so I decided I would append comparable lingo from that noble game to his otherwise scintillating comment). It is notable that unlike in 18:25a, 25b, and 26a, it is not quid pro quo in 18:26b. God is not perverse to the perverse, but "deceptive" to them (the verb פתל, *ptl*, can also mean "wrestle," as in Gen 30:8). However, the two terms may not be that divergent: see Deut 32:5; Prov 8:8. Craigie, *Psalms 1–50*, 175, puts it well: "the twisted could expect tortuous returns." For more on how deception can be commensurate with divine action, see Chisholm, "Does God Deceive?" In the precise reciprocity depicted in this psalm, God from on "high" (מָרוֹם, *marom*, Ps 18:16a) brings down eyes that are high ("haughty," רום, *rwm*, 18:27b): thus God is himself "exalted" (רום, 18:46b) and in the process also "exalts" the righteous (רום, 18:48b). The "utterance of Yahweh" (18:30b) is perhaps God's promise to the sufferer that rescue was nigh.

the reader forward to 18:27–30 that concludes with the affirmation that Yahweh "is a shield to all who take refuge in Him" (18:30c), and further to 18:31–45 that depicts the power imparted by God to his faithful.[23]

The mention of "rock" in 18:31b links it to 18:2a and commences the latter half of the psalm ("rock" in 18:31b, 46a brackets this latter part; "shield" and "take refuge" in 18:2bc, 30c bracket the first half, the *Refuge* section of the psalm: the righteous sufferer defended by Yahweh). With that there is a turn in the "narrative" to more martial images, and the righteous sufferer goes on offense (in the power of Yahweh).[24]

Power (18:31–45)

That the power for victory is not intrinsic to the people of God but imparted by God is obvious. While God's "training [of the supplicant—leader? king?] for battle" is the primary focus of 18:31–36 (18:34a), it is also God (whose "path is blameless," 18:30a) who "makes my path blameless" (18:32b, linking this to the psalmist's own keeping the "path" of Yahweh in 18:21a).[25] In any case, God, the protagonist, is the primary subject of the verbs in 18:31–36; the righteous sufferer is the object.

In 18:37–45, how God's people are victorious is described. This is unlikely to be a recounting of historical events; rather it is the metaphorical conglomeration of how the faithful succeed against all manner of enemies. The description blends together what Yahweh does, what the faithful does, and what happens to the foes as a result. Because even thunderclouds were "under His feet" (18:9b; God's direct, insuperable power), so also the enemies would end up "under my feet" (18:38b; the sufferer's divinely delegated power). The ones who were "rising" against the faithful (18:39b) would not be able to "rise" (18:38a). The sufferer had cried to God for deliverance from the "enemy" and "those who hated me" (18:17); now these "enemies," those "who hate me," are annihilated by him (18:40). When all is said and done, this section is quite striking for its absoluteness and finality: God's people *will* triumph.

Foes in defeat would have called on *any* deity, so it is not surprising that non-Israelite enemies (see 18:44–45 that refers to them as "children of foreigners" [×2]) would try their luck with the Israelite God. But that was not going to work: Yahweh was not about to "respond" (18:41b; unlike in the case of the faithful, to whom he makes a positive "response," 18:35c). He heard the "cry for help" of his people in 18:6 (שׁוע, *shw'*, verb in 18:6b; and שַׁוְעָה, *shaw'ah*, noun in 18:6d), but not the "cry for help" (18:41a; שׁוע, verb) of the adversaries. Ultimately, however, even those (potential) opponents would submit to God's people; having heard of the latter's success, the former would do so lest the same catastrophe befall them as it did other enemies (18:43[26]).

"An intense personal feeling is deftly communicated" once again by the first-person suffix to three nouns and two participles ("*my* rock," "*my* deliverance," "*my* enemies," "the One who saves *me*," and "those who rise against *me*": 18:46, 48ab), two verbs ("exalt *me*" and

---

23. Kuntz, "Psalm 18," 19–20.

24. The two halves of the psalm "thus tell the same story from different perspectives, but the culmination is the same in both instances—deliverance and victory for God's servant" (Craigie, *Psalms 1–50*, 175).

25. Also see 18:23a, 25b (×2) for other instances of "blameless" applied to God and the psalmist.

26. The psalmist was likely a leader of the people of God, and his statement in 18:43–45 about foreigners submitting to, and serving, him, may be rhetorical: the divine community will be held in high honor even among non-God worshipers.

"rescue *me*": 18:48bc), and two prepositions ("for *me*" and "under *me*": 18:47[27]) (as in 18:1–3; see above). "Accordingly, the poet successfully recaptures the hymnic mood which had been struck at the outset of the poem.... We are led full circle."[28] Altogether, 18:46–50 summarizes the divine acts that permeated this psalm, with a return to the emphasis that delegated power is only ... delegated. It is God himself who ultimately accomplishes the rescue of his people. While the cosmic King is the center of gravity in this psalm, the poem ends with a notation about the human king, "David" (perhaps indicating the current Davidide), the representative of the cosmic regent. "The human king has victory [18:50], but only because the divine King grants victory as a sign of his covenant faithfulness 'toward his anointed.'"[29] God gives deliverance and shows lovingkindness to his people ... *forever* (18:50)!

Sermon Map

I. Distress

    Deadly situation (18:3b–5)

    Move-to-relevance: Our situations of lethal suffering

II. Deity

    Intervention sought (18:2–3a, 6)

    Intervention undertaken: theophany (18:7–15)

    Move-to-relevance: The amazing commitment of God to his people

III. Deliverance

    Rescue accomplished (18:16–19a)

    Contingency of rescue (18:19b–30)

    Divine power delegated and employed (18:31–48)

IV. *Faithfully Commit to a Faithful God!*[30]

    Specifics on a committing to (or remembering the faithfulness of) God

---

27. "Subjugate" translates a homonym of the verb דָּבַר, *davar*.

28. Kuntz, "Psalm 18," 15. "Yahweh lives" (18:46a) is the only such declaration of its kind in the Psalter (though "living God" is found in 42:2; 84:2).

29. Craigie, *Psalms 1–50*, 176–77.

30. While trust in and praise for God is appropriate, there should be a notable mention in the sermon of the contingency of divine help: it is extended only for the faithful, committed to God. The danger is in its overemphasis that could create the impression that one is suffering because of some unfaithfulness. It is fair to note that faithfulness/commitment is not sinlessness, but an overall lifestyle of loyalty to God.

PSALM 19:1–14

Psalm of Orientation

The Sun and the Servant

THAT PSALM 19 IS a work of great poetic artistry is incontrovertible. Though there are only six synonyms for God's word (see below), there are fourteen (7 × 2) descriptive aspects of the Torah in 19:7–10: "blameless," "restoring," "reliable," "making wise" (19:7), "right," "rejoicing the heart," "pure," "enlightening the eyes" (19:8), "clean," "enduring for always," "true," "righteous altogether" (19:9), "more desirable than gold," and "sweeter than honey" (19:10). Labuschagne points out that this multiple of seven corresponds to the seven cosmic elements/phenomena named in 19:1–6: "heavens," "sky" (19:1), "day," "night" (19:2), "earth," "the end of the world," and "sun" (19:4). Strikingly, the psalm also has seven instances of "Yahweh."[1]

Translation

19:1 The heavens declare the glory of God;
    and the work of His hands is announced by the sky.
19:2 Day after day it pours forth speech,
    and night after night it proclaims knowledge.
19:3 There is no speech, and there are no words;
    their voice is not heard;
19:4 [but] through all the earth their sound has gone out,
    and to the end of the world their utterances.
For the sun, He has placed a tent in them,
19:5   and it is like a bridegroom going out of his chamber.
It exults like a warrior to run his course;
19:6   its going out is from [one] end of the heavens,
and its circuit to the [other] ends of them,
    and there is nothing hidden from its heat.

---

1. Labuschagne, "Significant Compositional Techniques," 593.

19:7 The law of Yahweh is blameless, restoring the soul;
      the testimony of Yahweh is reliable, making wise the simple.
19:8 The precepts of Yahweh are right, rejoicing the heart;
      the commandment of Yahweh is pure, enlightening the eyes.
19:9 The fear of Yahweh is clean, enduring for always;
      the judgments of Yahweh are true, righteous altogether.
19:10 More desirable than gold, even than much fine gold;
      and sweeter than honey, even the flow [from] the honeycomb.
19:11 Also, Your servant is warned by them;
      in keeping them is much reward.
19:12 Who can discern errors?
      From those that are hidden acquit me.
19:13 Also from presumptuous [sins] withhold Your servant;
      let them not rule over me;
then I will be blameless,
      and I shall be acquitted of much rebellion.
19:14 May they be acceptable—the utterance of my mouth
      and the meditation of my heart—before Your presence,
Yahweh, my rock and my redeemer.

Structure

At first sight, the two parts of this psalm seem disparate: 19:1–6 talking about creation, and 19:7–11 talking about the law of God. But there are verbal links between them: "speech" (19:2a, 3a, and 19:14a); "hidden" (19:6c and 19:12b); and the notion of joy (19:5b and 19:8a [though employing different verbs]). And common throughout the psalm is the motif of speaking, either explicit or implicit: "declare," "announced" (19:1), "speech" (19:2a, 3a, 14a), "proclaim" (19:2b), "words," "voice" (19:3), "sound," and "utterances" (19:4). As well, there are six synonyms for divine speech ("law," "testimony," "precepts," "commandment," "fear,"[2] and "judgments"; 19:7–9).[3] "The dense occurrence of so many explicit references to speech firmly establishes speaking as the main poetic theme of the psalm."[4]

---

2. Likely indicating the result of divine speech, i.e., "[*God's word* that inculcates] fear."
3. Also related are "warned" (19:11a), "mouth," and "meditation" (19:14).
4. deClaissé-Walford et al., *Book of Psalms*, 206.

Thus, the structure of the psalm is as shown:[5]

> **"Utterance" about God (19:1–6)**
> By nature (19:1–4b)
> Divine order followed by the sun (19:4c–6)
>
> **Utterance of God (19:11–14)**
> By God (19:7–10)
> Divine order followed by the servant (19:11–14)

Theological Focus

The magnificence of nature, especially the astronomical creations of God, that speaks wordlessly but eloquently of divine order which they exemplify with total obedience and obeisance, models for God's people their submission to God's speech in his ineffable and beatific word, not straying to evil, but remaining blameless, as only God's word can guide them to be.

Commentary

"Utterance" about God (19:1–6)

The first verse of the psalm has two lines that are chiastic (19:1a, 1b[6]), each with a mention of nature, of proclamation, and of divine glory.[7]

"The heavens	Nature
declare	Proclamation
the glory of God;	Glory
and the work of His hands	Glory
is announced	Proclamation
by the sky."	Nature

Subsequently, the proclamation is expanded upon in 19:2–4b, and the role of nature (specifically that of the sun) in 19:4c–6.

The subsection on speech by nature (19:2–4b) has six verbal pronouncements of divine glory: "heavens declare" (19:1a), "announced by the sky" (19:1b), "it pours forth speech" (19:2a), "it proclaims knowledge" (19:2b), "their sound has gone out" (19:4a), and "their utterances [go out]" (19:4b). That is later balanced by six descriptors of divine revelation

---

5. Modified from deClaissé-Walford et al., *Book of Psalms*, 204.

6. "Sky" and "heavens" show up together in the OT only in Genesis 1 ("sky"/"expanse" in 1:6, 7, 8, 14, 15, 17, 20) and Psalm 19.

7. The paralleling of "glory of God" with "the work of His hands" (19:1) is best explained by seeing the latter as "the [radiance/splendor of the] work of His hands."

(19:7–9). Thus "the focus is not on creation qua creation, but rather on the *speech* with which creation lauds her Creator"—"*Utterance*" about God.[8]

But, curiously enough, this testimony in a section on utterances about God has "no speech," "no words," and "their voice is not heard" (19:3)—a surprising contradiction, as it comes right after 19:2a that affirmed that "day after day it pours forth *speech*."[9] But the thrust is clear: these declarations of nature are "speeches" without speaking. Notice that both time ("day after day" and "night after night," 19:2[10]) and space ("through all the earth" and "to the end of the world," 19:4) are encompassed in the declarations of 19:2, 4. The sound of this speechless, wordless, voiceless utterance goes out unremittingly and unceasingly throughout the cosmos as eloquent and universal witnesses—all of them silent![11]

Then, in the next subsection, 19:4c–6, the most impressive proclaimer and subject of divine revelation (at least from earthlings' point of view), the sun, takes center stage. That the activity of the sun is connected to what preceded is clear: "go out" (יצא, *yts'*), used in 19:4a of the "sound" and "utterances" of the heavens and skies, echoes in the description of the sun in 19:5a ("going out," יצא), and also in 19:6a ("going out," מוֹצָא, *motsa'*). And "*end* of the world" in 19:4a is reflected in "*end* of the heavens" and "*ends* of them" in 19:6.

There might be a polemic here against the exalted status of the sun god in the ancient Near East.[12] But in God's economy, "the sun is 'merely' an entity for which the real God provides overnight accommodation," attesting to his absolute sovereignty and indomitable order. Appropriately, then, this section begins with an introduction of God as the subject: he places a "tent" in the heavens/skies for the sun (19:4c), and "each morning the sun is like a groom emerging with a smile on his face from his room, ready for his wedding, or emerging with a smile from the marriage chamber."[13] The trajectory of the sun is as purposeful as a warrior's forward march, not hesitant or tentative, but running all the way through its appointed course (19:5b–6).

So why was the sun introduced here, and how does all this relate to Yahweh and his relationship to mankind?

Utterance of God (19:7–14)

The *Utterance of God*, divine revelation in his word, employs "Yahweh" seven times (six in 19:7–9). And this section is the first place in the psalm where that name shows up. Earlier it

---

8. deClaissé-Walford et al., *Book of Psalms*, 206.

9. Craigie called it "the paradox of 'inaudible noise'" (*Psalms 1–50*, 181).

10. The phrases "day after day" and "night after night" in 19:2 suggest a tremendous orderliness and an exacting conformity (or "obedience," if you will) of natural elements to divine design and intent, a state that has (so far) persisted since creation.

11. In the MT of 19:4, we have קָו, *qum*, "their measuring line," which does not seem to fit the context. It is better to read it as קוֹלָם, *qolam*, "their voice," as attested in the LXX (ὁ φθόγγος αὐτῶν, *ho phthongos autōn*).

12. Sarna demonstrates how in 19:1–6, there are "numerous, varied and striking parallels" to ancient Near Eastern sun-god literature that often depicted elements of nature rhapsodizing their maker; the sun was frequently viewed as a bridegroom, a denizen of the skies that joyfully ran its course in a fixed circuit, and having an all-pervasive effect upon the world it shone on (Sarna, "Psalm XIX," 173). In Egypt, the sun god was described as "runner, racer, courser," who was said to "race a course" each day (Sarna, *On the Book of Psalms*, 80–81).

13. Goldingay, *Psalms*, 1:289. "Chamber," חֻפָּה, *chuppah* (19:5a), can also indicate the bride's chamber (as in Joel 2:16).

was "God" (אֵל, 'el, 19:1a) who was revealed as Creator and sustainer of things in the heavens and skies. However, mankind is far away from such astronomical wonders. But now, with the introduction of divine law, that distance has been bridged by a deity who condescended to interact with humanity: it is exclusively "Yahweh" for the remainder of the psalm, that deals with matters of direct concern to the people of this deity.[14] *God* may be known through creation, but only his word can reveal the personal *Lord*, Yahweh. And with that, the revelation of divine will in Scripture, far more personal and precise than the revelation of sovereign power in nature, is introduced in its various forms.

In the subsection on the utterance by God (19:7–10), the six lines of 19:7–9 are parallel, each employing a synonym for Torah, the label "Yahweh," an attribute of divine revelation, and its effect on/relationship to human life.[15] These attributes of divine speech—"blameless," "reliable," "right," "pure," "clean," and "true"—are usually descriptors of persons elsewhere in the OT.[16] So here these adjectives must indicate that the word of God produces *people* who are blameless, reliable, right, pure, clean, and true. Commencing and concluding with absolute attributes, "blameless" (19:7a) and "righteous altogether" (19:9b), the comprehensive and exhaustive nature of divine law is laid forth.

Denninger notes the possibility that these six lines are set in two parallel triads, with the only plurals therein referring to divine revelation in the third and sixth lines (19:8a, 9b: "precepts"; "judgments"). He suspects that this is a deliberate allusion to the six days of creation which is itself divided into two triads: Gen 1:3–13, comprising the first three days and the creation of "compartments," with the third day having *two* creative acts, unlike the first two, and, significantly, God's speech mentioned *twice* (along with the blessing, "it was good," also twice); and Gen 1:14–31, comprising the next three days and the creation of elements to fill those compartments, with the sixth day also having two created acts, and again, God's speech mentioned *twice* (and "it was good," also twice). In addition, the sun and moon were created on the fourth day; correspondingly, perhaps, the fourth line here (Ps 19:8b) also mentions "enlightenment."[17]

---

14. Denninger, "Creator's Fiat," 142.

15. Each of the six lines has five words, perhaps alluding to the Pentateuch? See Bang, "Canonical Function of Psalms 19 and 119," 259.

16. E.g., Pss 7:10; 11:2; 15:2; 18:20, 23, 24; 51:10; 101:6.

17. Denninger, "Creator's Fiat," 160–62. See Kuruvilla, *Genesis*, 11.

Speech of God (Ps 9:7–9)	Acts of Creator (Gen 1:3–31)
FIRST TRIAD	
Singular: "law"	*One*: light–darkness (Gen 1:3–5)
Singular: "testimony"	*One*: waters–heaven (Gen 1:6–8)
Plural: "precepts"	*Two*: dry land, plants (Gen 1:9–13) "and God said" (×2; Gen 1:9, 11) "it was good" (×2; Gen 1:10, 12)
SECOND TRIAD	
Singular: "commandment"	*One*: sun–moon (Gen 1:14–19)
Singular: "fear"	*One*: fish–birds (Gen 1:20–23)
Plural: "judgments"	*Two*: land creatures, humans (Gen 1:24–31) "and God said" (×2; Gen 1:24, 26) "it was good" (×2; Gen 1: 25, 31)

This correspondence between the speech-acts and creation-acts of God underscore the significance of the former: they must be heeded, and heeded carefully!

Strikingly, a number of the descriptors pertaining to divine law were applied to the sun god in the ancient Near East. The "restoring of souls" (19:7a) was frequently understood as a property of the sun: in Egypt, "he maketh mortals to live"; in Mesopotamia, it was "the one who gives life"; among the Hittites, the sun was "life-giving." Just as the "testimony of Yahweh is reliable," an Egyptian eulogy to the sun-god declared that his "ordinances are permanent, . . . fast, . . . not destroyed," and whose "statutes fail not." Also, "right" (יְשָׁרִים, *ysharim*, 19:8a), echoed popular Akkadians epithets of the sun-god—"the one who directs aright [*muštešir*]," and "the lord of truth and right [*me-šari*]." Indeed, the offspring of the sun was called *mešaru*, the personification of rightness. Also of note, an Egyptian hymn declared: "Fine gold is not like [as good as] the radiance of thee"; and a Hittite song proclaimed that the sun god Istanu's "message is sweet to everyone." The link to 19:10 is obvious. Besides, in the ancient Near East, the sun represented the principle of cosmic justice, as the judge of the heavens and earth, of gods and men, and the supervisor of moral order: "thou establishest the custom and law of the lands"; it was considered the "maker of righteousness" (from a Hittite hymn and an Egyptian declaration, respectively).[18] But unlike these misconstruals of the sun, in Scripture, that yellow-dwarf star composed of hot plasma is merely one agent among many in divine hands, created to follow divine order. Instead, it is the one, true God, Yahweh, who is the only giver of life and the only one utterly righteous, the one who speaks law into effect.

Then comes the subsection on the servant of God following the divine order (19:11–14). And here, in 19:11, Yahweh is directly addressed for the first time in the psalm (the psalmist's self-references also show up here for the first time). The response of the servant of God to the impeccable word of God—in light of Scripture's blamelessness, reliability, rightness, purity, cleanness, truthfulness—is to be stricken with guilt! Not only is he aware of all his sins and seditions, and disobediences and delinquencies, there was always the danger of "errors . . . that are hidden" and "presumptuous [sins]," i.e., flagrant and willful "rebellion" (19:12, 13a, 13d). Just as the sun "hides" nothing, but exposes all (19:6c), the God-fearer also pleads to be acquitted from "hidden" sins (19:12b) exposed by the law of God. But—and

---

18. Sarna, "Psalm XIX," 173, 175, for sources of those ancient Near Eastern citations.

here is the crux—unlike the sun, the people of God are hopelessly "prone to wander."[19] Only the word of God (by the grace of God and by the Spirit of God) can bind wandering hearts to God, instructing them of the divine order that they are to adhere to.[20] And, lest we forget, there is "much reward" in keeping God's divine demand.[21]

All in all, the heavens with the sun placed "in them" (בָּהֶם, *bahem*, 19:4c), a created impersonal element faithfully and consistently following its divinely appointed course, is being paralleled in a human world with the God-fearer instructed "by them [the Scriptures]" (also בָּהֶם, 19:11a), a created personal being faithfully and consistently following (or supposed to follow) the divinely appointed course (the Scriptures). As a result of their conformity to divine law, both sun and servant express joy ("exult" in 19:5b; "rejoice" in 19:8a). Thus the cosmic order and moral order are related, stemming from the same divine source who is ordering, guiding, instructing, and appointing elements of creation, whether heavenly planets or human beings, to follow divine demand and abide by divine intent. Indeed, the law may well be "the extension of the cosmic order into human society."[22]

Coote pictures the cosmic drama, intended to become the human drama:

> If you watch them [the stars] marching across the sky all night long, you should find yourself impressed that despite their vast numbers and heavenly rank they show not a trace of unruliness, but have remained in exactly the same formation from dusk to dawn. You would think that floating individually in the spacious expanse of the nighttime sky these high and mighty warriors would show some individual initiative, or periodically regroup, or strike out on their own to prove their mettle against some exceptional challenge. But they don't. The next night, as darkness falls, the great sidereal march continues, and night after night, month after month, year after year they march, round and round, with no deviation, no alteration, no detour, no retreat, no backtracking, no failure of discipline, no disobedience.... What most impresses the psalmist is the straightness—the rectitude—of the sun's path. As the sun appears each morning, he is like a bridegroom emerging from his abode and setting his path straight in the direction of his bride with one thing only on his mind.... He maintains a steady, straightedge course, adhering strictly to God's orders and in this discipline accomplishing his assigned task of illuminating—and ruling—all. He is God's obedient and obeisant servant.[23]

So also should the *human* servant of God be, "obedient and obeisant"—"blameless" (19:13c). And only the "blameless" law of Yahweh (19:7a) can do that—God's instructions to guide God's people to become God's servants. Echoing this sentiment, in a final plea employing "mouth" and "heart," the God-fearing servant desires to be before Yahweh's "face" (translated "presence"), blameless, reliable, right, pure, clean, and true (19:14). "The psalmist moves in a climactic fashion from macrocosm to microcosm, from the universe and its glory to the individual in humility before God. But the climax lies in the microcosm, not in the heavenly roar of praise. For the heavens declare the glory of God, but the law declares the will of God

---

19. From "Come Thou Fount of Every Blessing," by Robert Robinson (1758).

20. The verb זהר (*zchr*, "warned," 19:11) can also mean "shine" like the sun (Dan 12:3).

21. "Blessed are those who hear the word of God and keep it," Jesus declared (Luke 11:28; also see John 15:10)—blessings here and now, not to mention eternal rewards in the future. See Kuruvilla, *Vision for Preaching*, 123–26.

22. Denninger, "Creator's Fiat," 194–95.

23. Coote, "Psalm 19," 87–88, 92.

for mankind, the creature."[24] And just as the astronomical entities perfectly and unceasingly submit to the will of their Creator and Sustainer, so also should humans do, blamelessly, righteously. For God has spoken! And if the sun can obey, why not us, humans?

Sermon Map

I. Speech about God

    By nature (19:1–4b)

    The sun: obedient and obeisant (19:4b–6)

    Move-to-relevance: The orderliness of the cosmos is amazing

II. Speech of God

    By God (19:7–9)

    The servant: blameless, reliable, right, pure, clean, true (19:10–11)

    Move-to-relevance: How Scripture makes one so

III. Speech to God

    By servant (19:12–14)

    Desire to be obedient and obeisant (19:13c–14)

    Move-to-relevance: Our failure to demonstrate divine order

IV. *I'll Follow the Sun!*

    Specifics on demonstrating divine order in our lives by Scripture

---

24. Craigie, *Psalms 1–50*, 183.

PSALM 20:1–9

Psalm of Orientation

Intercession for Success

For most of its verses Psalm 20 appears to be words uttered by the community of God's people to their leader who is getting ready to face an imminent crisis of some sort, perhaps military. "The rhetoric of the poem moves the speaker[s] into a solidarity of prayer with the individual in crisis."[1] But we are given no hint as to what that crisis may have constituted; neither are there are extended pleas for help, laments, complaints against God, or claims of innocence typical of such compositions. How God was expected to render aid in the critical situation is also not specified, leaving it open both for God to execute and for those praying in different times and spaces to anticipate.

Translation

20:1 May He answer you—Yahweh—in the day of distress.
   May the name of the God of Jacob secure you on high.
20:2 May He send you help from the holy place
   and from Zion may He sustain you.
20:3 May He remember all your grain offerings,
   and your burnt offering may He find acceptable.
20:4 May He give you according to your heart['s desire]
   and your every plan may He fulfill.
20:5 We will shout for joy at your deliverance,
   and in the name of our God we will raise banners.
   May Yahweh fulfill all your requests.
20:6 Now I know that Yahweh delivers His anointed;
   He will answer him from His holy heavens
   with the mighty deliverance of His right hand.

---

1. deClaissé-Walford et al., *Book of Psalms*, 219.

20:7   Some in chariots and some in horses,
          but we—in the name of Yahweh, our God we depend.
20:8   They—they bow down and they fall,
          but we—we rise and we stand firm.
20:9   Yahweh, deliver the king.
          May He answer us in the day we call.

Structure

There are two voices the psalm. The first five verses appear to be uttered by the community, interceding for the leader/king.[2] In 20:6 we meet a first person, the "I"—likely the leader/king responding to the community's intercession (and referring to himself in the third person). In 20:7–9, there is a return to the first-person plural of the members of the community.

Community 1 (20:1–5)
  Indirect intercession for leader (20:1–4)
  Declaration anticipating victory (20:5a)
  Indirect intercession for leader (20:5b)

Leader (20:6)
  Declaration anticipating victory (20:6)

Community 2 (20:7–9)
  Declaration anticipating victory (20:7–8)
  Direct intercession for leader (20:9a)
  Indirect intercession for community (20:9b)

There is also quite a diversity of forms of address: indirect intercessions by the community to God for aid ("may Yahweh/He . . ."), but addressed to the leader (employing "you/your"; 20:1–4; also 20:5); declarations uttered by the community and by its leader that anticipate victory (20: 6, 7–8); a direct intercession by the community to God for the leader's deliverance (20:9a); and another indirect intercession by the community to Yahweh for a positive response to their call ("may He . . ."), but reflexively addressed to themselves ("us," 20:9b). In sum, this is a psalm of direct and indirect intercession, interwoven with declarations that anticipate victory.[3]

---

2. The word "king" shows up in 20:9a. It is also possible that the speaker in 20:1–5 is the liturgical leader (priest) uttering these lines on behalf of the community.

3. But the sections are linked: the theme of divine "answer" shows up in each section (20:1a, 6b, 9b), as also does "name" of Yahweh (20:1b, 5b, 7b), and "deliverance/deliver" in 20:5a, 6a, 6c, 10a.

Theological Focus

> As the community of God's people intercede for victory in every undertaking for their leaders and for themselves, and as the former please deity with their faithful worship and submission to him, confident of success, the entire body grows in its understanding of God and in its exclusive trust of him as its personal deliverer.

Commentary

Community 1 (20:1–5)

A number of wishes for the leader/king are voiced by the community in 20:1–5: May God "answer you," "secure you on high" (20:1), "send you help," "sustain you" (20:2), "remember" and "find acceptable" the leader's/king's worship (20:3), "give you according to your heart['s desire]," "fulfill" his every plan (20:4), and "fulfill all your requests" (20:5).[4]

The "name of God" (20:1b) stands for the active presence of God with the summation of all his attributes (as in Exod 34:5–7), as well as the "deliverance" he was expected to accomplish, as the chiastic parallelism of Ps 20:5ab shows, equating "deliverance" with "name [presence] of our God":

> "We will shout for joy
> at your deliverance,
> and in the name of our God
> we will raise banners."

This was no random deity; this was "the God of Jacob," the God of their forefathers (20:1b). What they had heard of him and his deeds in the past, they expected him to demonstrate in their own situation, in their current crisis. But notice the subtle shift in who is being named as the psalm progresses in this section: it was "the name of the God of Jacob" in 20:1b; in 20:5b, it is "the name of *our* God" that is invoked. Clearly, in the process of traversing four verses, God has gone from being the deity of their forefather(s) to their own.[5]

Though the wish in 20:2 seeks divine intervention from the "holy place" and Zion (both earthly locations refer to the temple), in 20:6 the source of divine aid is "His holy heavens." They are not significantly different loci since "Zion [on earth] is itself the place where Yhwh decided to live, and it is a kind of outpost of Yhwh's home in heaven," the terrestrial counterpart of a celestial abode.[6]

A motivation for divine action, as introduced by the community, is the leader's/king's commitment and loyalty to God as evidenced by his cultic sacrifices (20:3). Such activities

---

4. Of these six verses, 20:2, 3, 4, and 5ab are each chiastic.
5. There will be another shift before the psalm concludes; see below.
6. Goldingay, *Psalms*, 1:304.

were, of course, acceptable to God only when accompanied by faith (1 Sam 15:22; Ps 40:6; Isa 56:6–7).[7] Sacrifices before war are noted in 1 Sam 7:9–10; 13:9–12.

> The king, who would be commander in warfare, offered sacrifices and the people joined him in words. The words which they spoke, addressed formally to the king, vocalized the prayer and desire of the king who was engaged in the activity of worship.... So the preparation for war was twofold. First, there must be practical and military preparation, for it would be impossible simply to sit back and wait for a miracle to happen. Second, there must be religious preparation, which is here reflected in Ps 20, for it would be equally irresponsible to hope that anything lasting could be achieved merely in human strength. The formal act of worship, prior to battle, which is reflected so clearly in Ps 20, would affect and influence the actual action on the battlefield which was to follow.[8]

And, anticipating victory when God had answered their prayers, the community fully expects to be whooping and hollering with joy, raising banners (flag-waving?), and generally celebrating a military triumph (Ps 20:5ab).

Thus, in this section, we have both cultic (20:2–3; also seen in 20:6b) and military terminology (20:5ab; also seen in 20:6c, 7–8), lending credence to the circumstances of the psalm as relating to liturgical activity before a martial engagement. This portion of the community's voice concludes in 20:5c with a return to another indirect intercession for the leader/king.

Leader (20:6)

The person speaking in the first person in 20:6 is presumed to be the leader/king that the community has been indirectly interceding for in 20:1–5. This is his response to what preceded, evident in the reuse of "deliver" and "deliverance" (20:6a, 6c; also "deliverance" in 20:5a), reference to the "holy" source of divine aid (20:6b; also in 20:2a), and the expectation of a divine "answer" (20:6b; also in 20:1a). Yet it is notable, though not unusual, that the speaker in 20:6 seems to be referring to himself in the third person ("His anointed" and "him").

The emphatic "now I know" (20:6a) as the leader/king begins his response could imply a time gap between 20:5 and 20:6.[9] Did the leader/king obtain some assurance of a divine answer after the indirect intercession of the community in 20:1–5? In any case, there seems to have been a movement forward from petition/intercession in 20:1–5 to trust/confidence in 20:6 (and in 20:7–8).[10]

Community 2 (20:7–9)

The speakers of 20:1–5 return in 20:7–9; in both sections the first-person plural is employed (20:5a, 5b and in 20:7b, 8b, 9b). Also reused is the verb זכר, *zkr*, "remember" in 20:3a; but when used with "in the name of" in 20:7b it signifies dependence upon the One

---

7. "Find acceptable" in 20:3b is literally "become fat," which is also the best portion of the animal sacrifices (Exod 29:13, 22–25; Lev 3:3–5).
8. Craigie, *Psalms 1–50*, 186, 188.
9. "Now I know" is also found in Gen 22:12 and Exod 18:11, for momentous declarations.
10. deClaissé-Walford et al., *Book of Psalms*, 219.

invoked—thus "depend" (20:7b; also זכר). In other words, God had "remembered" the commitment and faithful sacrifices of the leader/king (20:3a), so now, they reciprocate with "dependence" upon him (20:7b).

Notice another shift here with the "name" motif. Their *forefathers'* God ("the name of the God *of Jacob*," 20:1b), who became *their own* God ("the name of *our* God," 20:5b), had now become, after the confident assertions of their leader/king in 20:6, *their own covenant-keeping* God ("the name of *Yahweh*, our God," 20:7b). Obviously, the confidence of the community is waxing—and that even before the battle or military undertaking has commenced, let alone being concluded successfully.

20:1b	"the name of the God *of Jacob*"
20:5b	"the name of *our* God"
20:7b	"the name of *Yahweh*, our God"

This communal and corporate faith is underscored again in the emphatic (and redundant) pronouns employed in 20:7b, 8a, 8b. Unlike those who trusted in human (and animal[11]) contrivances, appurtenances, and paraphernalia, *this community* ("we—we . . . ," 20:7b) would trust only its God, the One who fought on their behalf. Outsiders ("they—they . . . ," 20:8a) would be suppressed and made to fall but, again, *this community* ("we—we . . . ," 20:8b) would rise and stand firm.

The very activity of corporate intercession (directly and indirectly) for victory (for their leader/king and for themselves) was imbuing the community with a deeper knowledge of, and a greater confidence in, the God, *their* God, who would fight for them.[12]

And then the psalm concludes, this time with a bipartite plea, one directly beseeching Yahweh that the king may be delivered (20:9a)—the only petition and imperative in the psalm—and the other indirectly interceding for themselves that Yahweh would answer them in the day they called (20:9b). This last element thereby forms an *inclusio* with 20:1a:

| 20:1a | "May He answer *you* | —Yahweh— | in the day | of distress." |
| 20:9b | "May He answer *us* | | in the day | we call." |

As Goldingay aptly noted, "If 'the day of trouble ['distress,' 20:1a]' becomes 'the day we call [20:9b],' it ceases to be the day of trouble."[13] And what began as "may Yahweh answer you"—i.e., the leader/king—becomes, at the end of the psalm, "may He answer us"—i.e., the community. Not only had the body's confidence grown, their corporality had intensified: what happened to their leader/king happened to them—his successes were theirs, his losses theirs.

---

11. The prohibition of Israelite kings from accumulating horses was an age-old notion: Deut 17:16.
12. Not to mention, strengthening the unity of the community, as it views itself as a single, integral unit.
13. Goldingay, *Psalms*, 1:308.

Sermon Map

I. Community Members
   Intercession (20:1–2)
   Name of God (20:1b)
   Move-to-relevance: The inadequacies of our intercession

II. Community Leaders
   Faithful worship and consequence (20:3–4)
   Confidence (20:6)
   Name of God (20:5b)
   Move-to-relevance: The inadequacies of leadership

III. Community Members
   Name of God (20:7b)
   Exclusivity of trust (20:7–9)
   Move-to-relevance: Spiritual growth through intercession

IV. *Progress by Praying!*
   Specifics on intercession for the body and its leaders

PSALM 21:1–13

Psalm of Orientation

Success of God's People

JUST AS WAS PSALM 20, Psalm 21, too, is about the community wishing their leader/king divine blessings, implicitly interweaving the destiny of both parties.[1] One might consider Psalm 21 the thanksgiving response to the success of the battle ("His *heart's* desire You have *given* him," 21:2a) that was prayed for in Psalm 20 ("May He *give* you according to your *heart*['s desire]," 20:4a).

Translation

21:1   Yahweh, in Your strength the king will be joyous,
        and in Your deliverance how greatly he will jubilate.
21:2   His heart's desire You have given him,
        and the request of his lips You have not withheld.
21:3   For You meet him with the blessings of good things;
        You set upon his head a crown of fine gold.
21:4   Life he asked of You; You gave [it] to him—
        length of days forever and always.
21:5   Great is his glory through Your deliverance;
        splendor and majesty You put on him.
21:6   For You set [upon] him blessings for always;
        You gladden him with joy through Your presence.
21:7   For the king trusts in Yahweh,
        and by the lovingkindness of the Most High he is not shaken.
21:8   Your hand finds out all Your enemies;
        Your right hand finds those who hate You.

---

1. Goldingay, *Psalms*, 1:311.

21:9 You set them like a furnace of fire
    in the time of Your presence;
Yahweh swallows them in His wrath,
    and fire consumes them.
21:10 Their offspring You destroy from the earth,
    and their descendants from among humans.
21:11 Though they spread evil against You
    [and] devise a plot, they do not succeed.
21:12 For You set them backwards [in retreat];
    with Your bowstrings You aim at their faces.
21:13 Be exalted, Yahweh, in Your strength;
    we will sing and make music of Your might.

Structure

Every verse mentions God in the second person, except for 21:7 (and the two lines 21:9cd) that mentions deity only in the third person. Incidentally, these are the only verses, or parts thereof, that actually mention deity by name, "Yahweh," predicating something about him. Of course, 21:1, 13, the first and last verses of the psalm, also employ "Yahweh," but in the vocative, directly addressing him. All that to say: this psalm is entirely about God!

> **Yahweh: Blessing of the King** (21:1–7)
> *King Rejoicing* (**21:1**): "strength"; "Yahweh" (vocative)
> > *Blessing of the King* (**21:2–7**): "Yahweh" (21:7a); "set" (21:3b, 6a)
>
> **Yahweh: Bane of the Enemies** (21:8–13)
> > *Bane of the Enemies* (**21:8–12**): "Yahweh" (21:9c); "set" (21:9a, 12a)
>
> *Community Rejoicing* (**21:13**): "strength"; "Yahweh" (vocative)

Theological Focus

God, in his divine strength and abundant grace, answers the requests of his community and its leader, far beyond what they expect, providing deliverance, long-lasting influence, and his very presence—blessings always—without which grace any endeavor is futile, and because of which grace the people of God joyously exalt him.

Commentary

Yahweh: Blessing of the King (21:1–7)

That blessing is of God, there is no doubt; it is articulated over and over. One sees the divine activity of blessing in almost every verse of this section, and always in a second-person address of God: "You have given," "You have not withheld" (21:2[2]); "You meet," "You set" (21:3);[3] "You gave" (21:4a); "You put" (21:5b); "You set," "You gladden" (21:6). Besides these, there are also divine attributes operating in the blessings: "Your strength" (21:1a), "Your deliverance" (21:1b, 5a), "Your presence" (21:6b), and "the lovingkindness of the Most High" (21:7b)—all directed towards the leader/king, thus blessing him with the presence of God. In a word (or three): Without God, nothing!

After the introductory proclamation of the king's joy at his deliverance, we find that this blessing had actually been requested by the leader/king: "his heart's desire" (21:2a), "the request of his lips" (21:2b), and "he asked" (21:4a).[4] But notice how the divine donation far exceeds what the human desire was for. Following after "Your strength" and "Your deliverance" (military metaphors) in 21:1, it is obvious that what the king had asked for was triumph in battle. And yes, God grants it to him: "You have given him" (21:2a) and "You have not withheld" (21:2b). But the heavenly giver goes further, favoring the king with "blessings of good things" (21:3a), including rulership, consummated with "a crown of fine gold" (21:3b)—over and above what was asked for (the "bonus" donations are in bold, below):

21:2aα	Human Desire: deliverance
21:2aβ	*Divine Donation: deliverance*
21:2bα	Human Desire: deliverance
21:2bβ	*Divine Donation: deliverance*
21:3	**good things; crown**
21:4aα	Human Desire: life
21:4aβ	*Divine Donation: life*
21:4b–6	**eternity; divine attributes blessings always; joy of divine presence**

This pattern is repeated in 21:4–5. The king had asked for "life" (likely related to military victory and battle survival), and God grants that to him, too (21:4a). But Yahweh goes further: it is not only life now that the king wins, but "length of days forever and always" (21:4b[5]),

---

2. As was noted, the king's "desire" was for deliverance, i.e., battle victory (see the connection with 20:4a).

3. In light of the martial context of this psalm, the crowning in this verse is most likely a symbol of divine approval, rather than an actual coronation.

4. I'm taking all of those human desires as being for deliverance, and all those divine donations as meeting those specific desires.

5. "It is best to assume that the king, prior to departing for battle, asked that his life be preserved in the time of conflict; on returning home alive, his prayer had been answered in the gift of 'life' and 'length of days.' The expression . . . ['forever and always,' 21:4b] in context, implies that such life would extend into the future as far as was conceivable, but there need be no implication of a future life or afterlife. . . . At most, it might imply the continuity which would exist through the continuation of the Davidic kings" (Craigie, *Psalms 1–50*, 191). And "short royal reigns are often symptomatic of nation[al] turmoil, and the common folk were

and "glory" and "splendor and majesty" (divine attributes; 21:5[6]), *and* divine "presence" (21:6; literally "face") (bonus donations in bold, above). This is nothing but God's amazing grace! So much so, the king's "being joyous [שׂמח, *smch*]" and "jubilating" (21:1) becomes his being "gladdened with joy [שִׂמְחָה, *simchah*]" (21:6b), a confluence of terms and a piling of synonyms: in short, the king is thrilled!

The reason for those divine donations? "For the king trusts in Yahweh" (21:7a). And the consequence? "By the lovingkindness of the Most High he is not shaken" (21:7b). "This [blessed] status is entirely the result of his close relationship with Yhwh," as 21:7 asserts. "The negative and contingent phrasing in the second part of the verse . . . suggest the very real possibility that were it not for חסד עליון [*chsd 'lywn*, 'the lovingkindness of the Most High,' 21:7b], the king might well collapse."[7] To emphasize this key verse, 21:7, it is constructed chiastically, with the king's action ("trust" in *A, B*) followed by the divine reaction (unshakability in *B', A'*):

> **A** "For the king trusts
> **B** in [בְּ] Yahweh ,
> **B'** and by [בְּ] the lovingkindness of the Most High
> **A'** he is not shaken."

Covenantal language—"trust" and "lovingkindness"—is employed here in 21:7. "There are two partners to the covenant, God and Israel (represented by the king); God's fundamental character in the covenant relationship is *lovingkindness* . . . , and the king's response was to be one of *trust*."[8] The former is unconditional, of course; however, the experience of God's unconditional lovingkindness is conditional; it can happen only with a constant maintenance of trust and a walk with God in order that the covenantal relationship may flourish.[9] The mention of "king" in 21:1 and 21:7 closes out the first half of the psalm.

Yahweh: Bane of the Enemies (21:8–13)

This section with its second-person addresses could be referring either to Yahweh (deity is referred to in the third person in 21:9cd) or to the leader/king. However, it is better to see God as being the "You" here, consistent with the earlier section of the psalm.[10] Besides, "right

---

just as likely to suffer in such times as were the nobility. Thus, the prayer that the monarch live long is at least equally a prayer in the people's own interest" (deClaissé-Walford et al., *Book of Psalms*, 224).

6. For "glory" pertaining to God, see Pss 19:1; 24:7–10; 26:8; 29:1–3; etc.; and for divine "splendor and majesty," see 45:3; 96:6; 104:1; 111:3; etc., respectively. The leader/king, bestowed with "glory" (21:5a), is "endowed here with supernatural attributes and becomes sort of superman" (Aster, "On the Place of Psalm 21," 314).

7. Aster, "On the Place of Psalm 21," 314.

8. Craigie, *Psalms 1–50*, 192.

9. For instance, Jude 21 exhorts: "Keep yourselves in the love of God." In other words, one *can* take oneself away from the experience of God's unconditional love towards his people and lose out on the blessings that accrue had one remained in divine love. This is, biblically, an integral part of sanctification and growth of the child of God into Christlikeness—a christiconic reading of Scripture. The loss, of course, is not of salvation. See Kuruvilla, *Privilege the Text!*, 211–68; Kuruvilla, *Vision for Preaching*, 131–48.

10. The third-person reference to Yahweh in 21:9cd is not surprising; we've already seen that in the previous section, in 21:7, while the rest of that portion referred to God in the second person.

hand" (21:8b) is most often employed of God in the Psalter.[11] It is significant that the term was employed with a divine referent in the previous psalm (20:6).[12] Also, the "fire" in 21:9a must be the same "fire" in 21:9d—this one is explicitly related to a divine operation. Likewise, "set" from 21:3b, 6a is repeated in 21:9a, 12a; no doubt, the same actant is performing all these "settings." And, needless to add, "presence" in 21:9b must be that of God, identical to the divine "presence" in 21:6b (both are literally "face").

What is striking is that, in such a reading, 21:8–12 makes no mention of the king performing any plucky military maneuvers on the field of conflict or undertaking dashing martial moves on the battlefield. No, any victory accomplished over the enemy is entirely Yahweh's doing (at least in the literary telling of it in this psalm). Enemies are merely fuel for the fire that will be kindled at the divine appearing ("in the time of your *presence*," 21:9): they and their descendants will be consumed (21:10). Just as we saw in 21:1–7, so also in 21:8–12 there is divine activity (of blessing earlier; of bane here) in almost every verse of this section, and always in a second-person address of God—it is God taking all the action: "Your hand finds out," "Your right hand finds" (21:8); "You set" (21:9a); "You destroy" (21:10a); "You set," "You aim" (21:12); there is also "Yahweh swallows" (21:9c).

In sum, no one can succeed in their propagation of evil against a holy God (21:11). Those who try are forced back into retreat, and enemies in the divine "face" (21:9b) will only have arrows shot at their own "faces" (21:12). The defeat of foes is graphic, signifying God's wrath (as well as his intense loyalty to his own—these latter are singed by the divine "face" ("presence," 21:9ab), unlike the adversaries, who are joyous at his "face" ("presence," 21:6b). In short, there is no contest here!

The psalm concludes with a reprise about "Your strength" (21:13a, recollecting 21:1a), the demonstration of which exalts God, as he delivers and blesses the community of Godfearers and its leader/king. Yes, indeed, trust in Yahweh does pay off!

Sermon Map

I. God's Strength

    Deliverance as requested (21:1–2)

    Blessing over and above what is requested (21:3–6)

    Move-to-relevance: Necessity for divine strength

II. God's Victory

    Utter defeat of enemies: God's commitment to his people (21:8–12)

    Trustworthiness of the personal, loving God (21:7)

    Move-to-relevance: Why we fail to trust God

III. *Praise for the Future!*

    The result of divine deliverance and blessing: exaltation of God (21:13)

    Specifics on trusting praise for God's future deliverance and blessing

---

11. Seventeen of the nineteen other references to "Your right hand" in the Psalms refer to deity's body part, as also do three of the five references to "h/His right hand."

12. Of the forty instances of "right hand" in the Psalms, only thirteen are not used of God: of the psalmist (and the needy): Pss 16:8; 91:10; 109:31; 121:5; 137:5; of enemies: 26:10; 89:42; 109:6; 144:8 (×2), 11 (×2); of the king: 45:9 (but, then again, this "king" is *the* King!).

PSALM 22:1–31

Psalm of Disorientation

Divine Presence in Deadly Persecution

PSALM 22 IS ESSENTIALLY an extended petition-lament concluding with praise. It is "gutsy, graphic, and grief-filled."[1] Yet it is grounded in a firm trust in the God of the fathers, a God who is now the sufferer's own. While personal to a poignant degree, there is clearly an awareness of the community of God's people in this psalm (22:3–5, 22–31): it may well have been prayed in their presence.

Translation

22:1	My God, my God, why have You abandoned me?	
	Far from my deliverance are the words of my groaning.	
22:2	My God, I call by day, but You do not answer;	
	and by night, but there is no silence for me.	
22:3	But You [are] the Holy One who sits [enthroned],	
	the great praise of Israel.	
22:4	In You our fathers trusted;	
	they trusted and You saved them.	
22:5	To You they wailed and they were liberated;	
	in You they trusted, and they were not ashamed.	
22:6	But I am a worm and not a human,	
	a reproach of mankind and despised by people.	
22:7	All who see me mock me;	
	they scowl the lip, they shake the head.	
22:8	"Commit to Yahweh; let Him save him;	
	let Him rescue him, for He delights in him."	

---

1. deClaissé-Walford et al., *Book of Psalms*, 139.

22:9   For You [are] the One who brought me out from the womb;
> making me trust upon the breasts of my mother.

22:10   Upon You I was cast from birth;
> from the womb of my mother my God You [were].

22:11   Be not far from me, for distress is near,
> for there is no one who is a helper.

22:12   They have surrounded me—many bulls;
> strong [bulls] of Bashan have encircled me.

22:13   They have opened their mouth at me,
> [like] a lion, tearing and roaring.

22:14   I have been poured out like water,
> And all my bones have been dislocated;

my heart has become like wax;
> it has melted in the middle of my insides.

22:15   Like a potsherd my strength has dried up,
> and my tongue—stuck to my palate,
> and in the dust of death You lay me.

22:16   They have surrounded me—dogs;
> a gang of evildoers has encompassed me;
> they gouged my hands and my feet.

22:17   I can count all my bones.
> They—they look, they stare at me;

22:18   They divide my garments among themselves,
> and for my clothing they cast lots.

22:19   But You, Yahweh, be not far;
> my strength, hasten to my help.

22:20   Rescue from the sword my soul,
> my only [one] from the hand of the dog.

22:21   Deliver me from the mouth of the lion,
> [and] from the horns of the wild oxen—
> You answered me.

22:22   I will recount Your name to my kindred;
> in the midst of the assembly I will praise You.

22:23   You who fear Yahweh, praise Him;
> all you descendants of Jacob, glorify Him,
> stand in awe before Him, all you descendants of Israel.

22:24   For He has not despised,
> and He has not detested, the affliction of the afflicted;

and He has not hidden His presence from him,
> but when he cried to Him for help, He heard.

22:25 From You [comes] my praise in the great assembly;
    I shall pay my vows before those who fear Him.
22:26 The afflicted will eat and be satisfied;
    those who seek Him will praise Yahweh.
    May your heart live for always.
22:27 They will remember and turn to Yahweh, all the ends of the earth,
    and they will worship before Your presence, all the families of the nations.
22:28 For to Yahweh is the Kingdom;
    and He rules over the nations.
22:29 They will eat and worship, all the prosperous of the earth;
    Before His presence they will bow, all those who go down to the dust
    and he [who] cannot keep his soul alive.
22:30 [Their] descendants will serve Him;
    it will be recounted of the Lord to the [future] generation.
22:31 They will come and they will announce His righteousness
    to a people who are to be born, that He has acted.

Structure

Structurally, it falls into three rounds of petitions: the first petition (unanswered) appended with declarations of trust and a lament; the second petition with only a lament; and the third petition (answered) with an appropriate paean of praise.[2]

Round 1 (22:1–10)
Petition unanswered (**22:1–2**) ("far," 22:1b; "You do not answer," 22:2a)
    Trust (**22:3–5**) ("but You," 22:3a; "trusted," 22:4b)
        Lament (**22:6–8**) ("but I," 22:6a)
    Trust (**22:9–10**) ("for You," 22:9a; "trust," 22:9b)

Round 2 (22:11–18)
Petition (**22:11**) ("be not far," 22:11a)
    Lament (**22:12–18**)

Round 3 (22:19–31)
Petition answered (**22:19–21b**) ("be not far," 22:19a; "You answered," 22:21b)
    Praise (**22:21c–31**) ("praise," 22:22b, 23a, 25a, 26b)

---

2. The first has "deliver" in 22:1b, and the third has "deliverance" in 22:21a. The second has "helper" in 2:11a, and the third has "help" in 22:19b.

Theological Focus

Seemingly abandoned by God, the people of God persist in petitioning deity—on the basis of their past trust and resulting deliverance from God—for rescue from deadly assaults from enemies, but especially for assurance of divine presence in dire situations, promising praise when delivered: communal praise of the cosmic ruler that achieves universal and omnitemporal dimensions.

Commentary

Round 1: Petition–Trust–Lament–Trust (22:1–10)

The first round commences with a petition that is almost a lament: thrice calling upon "My God" (22:1a [×2], 2a), the petitioner considers deity to have abandoned him, and his deliverance far from his groaning—there is apparently no answer to his entreaties (22:1–2).[3] We have abandonment in 22:1a resulting in distance in 22:1b and silence in 22:2a, with loudness of agitation in 22:2b. All that to say, suffering is near, but God is far; suffering is loud (there is "no silence" for the sufferer), but God is silent. "When the Psalmist speaks of being forsaken and cast off by God, it seems to be the complaint of a man in despair; for can a man have a single spark of faith remaining in him, when he believes that there is no longer any succour for him in God? And yet, in calling God twice his own God, and depositing his groanings into his bosom, he makes a very distinct confession of his faith."[4] Goldingay observes that "'My God' [twice!] and 'abandon' do not fit easily in the same sentence."[5] But even such a question, almost a lament, is, at its core, trust. Interestingly enough, the petition is not actually a plea for help, but for understanding: "Why?" (22:1a).

> The worshiper begins by expressing the darkest mystery of his suffering, namely the sense of being forsaken by God. It is a mystery because it appears to be rooted in a contradiction, namely the apparent contradiction between theology and experience. Theology, based upon the tradition and experience of the past, affirmed unambiguously that *trust* (the verb is used three times, for emphasis, in . . . [22:4–5]) resulted in deliverance . . . But experience was altogether at odds with theology; whereas the fathers trusted and were delivered, the essence of the psalmist's complaint . . . ["my groaning" (22:1b)] was "the distance of my salvation" ["far from my deliverance," 22:1b]. The God of covenant, who was believed not to have deserted his faithful people, appeared to have forsaken this worshiper . . . And it was the sense of being forsaken by God that was the fundamental problem—more grave than . . . the threat of death.[6]

---

3. This first round is bookended by "my God"—thrice in 22:1–2, and once again in 22:10b (אֵלִי, *'eli*, ×3 in 22:1a, 10b; אֱלֹהַי, *'elohay*, in 22:2a).

4. Calvin, *Commentary on the Book of Psalms*, 1:357.

5. Goldingay, *Psalms*, 1:324. As was noted, "my God" resounds thrice in two verses, marking the depth of despair and the intensity of need.

6. Craigie, *Psalms 1–50*, 198–99.

"But You" voices a protestation in 22:3–5. The forefathers "trusted" (22:4a, 4b, 5b[7]) and they were saved.[8] "But I" (22:6a)—balancing the "but You" of 22:3a—am reduced to nothing, despised, and mocked (22:6–8, the lament).[9] God had "saved" the fathers (22:4b), but now the psalmist was being taunted: "let Him [Yahweh] *save* him" (22:8a). For the supplicant, "the past deliverance was as real as the present abandonment."[10] The picture of God enthroned on the "great praise of Israel" (22:3[11]) carries the protest further: "Then the fathers trusted and they crowned You with praise. How can I do that now? And I've trusted You for ages"—as 22:9–10 emphasizes. "To You [אֵלֶיךָ, 'eleka]" the fathers cried (22:5a); "upon You [עָלֶיךָ, 'aleka]" the psalmist was cast (22:10a).[12]

The two verses 22:4–5 have, in each of their lines, "trusted"; "trusted" and "saved"; "wailed" and "liberated"; "trusted" and "not ashamed." The deliverance of the fathers by God, that had rendered them "not ashamed" (22:5b), suggests that the current crisis, aggravated by the mocks and scorns of others—shaming—meant that Yahweh did *not* delight in him (22:7), compounding inherent human powerlessness in the face of seeming divine rejection. Notice that at least in this first round (22:1–10) the pain is not so much caused by the suffering as much as by the abandonment by God and the derision and shame at the hand of fellow humans. The mockery, of course, brings back the idea of God's apparent neglect; thus, there apparently is a ring of truth to what the detractors are claiming as they scoff about God's absence. The psalmist seems to concur, dejectedly, despairingly.

In any case, the resounding motif of the trust of the forefathers in this first round is intended not only to bolster the sufferer's own faith, but even more to motivate God to respond to the present agonies, just as he had done for them in the past, a *modus operandi* quite common in the lament psalms. Miller's words in this regard are apropos:

> [These words of the psalmist] assume a theological perspective that is fairly widespread in the Old Testament, that is, that God's purpose and action are involved with and affected by the purposes and actions of those whom God has created. God is independent of human control but has chosen to be responsive to the human situation. There is a kind of openness, a room for maneuvering, not just a willingness but an intention on God's part to be accessible to and responsive to the creation without being dependent upon it and controlled by it. This openness does not introduce whimsicality, capriciousness, and inconsistency into the divine activity; nor do the motivational sentences of the psalmists seek such. It is necessary to recognize . . . that in the laments the psalmists are urging God to act according to what is in fact God's will and purpose. It is precisely because God's way and manner in the past have been discerned to be merciful to the suffering and delivering of the

---

7. The phrase "in You [. . .] they trusted," shows up in 22:4ab, 5b.

8. It is likely that an allusion is being made in this first round to the deliverance of the Israelites in the exodus: אֵלִי occurs only fourteen times in the OT, twelve of them in the Psalms, once in Exod 15:2 (the Song of Moses), and once in Isa 44:17 (of a false god).

9. The image of a worm (22:6a) creates disgust in the minds of readers, accosting them with images of death and decay, smells and rottenness.

10. Goldingay, *Psalms*, 1:327.

11. The plural, "praises," is best read as an intensive, "great praise."

12. The repetition again intensifies the sufferer's cry: "from the womb . . . of my mother" is מִבֶּטֶן . . . אִמִּי (*mibaten* . . . *'immi*, 22:9ab); "from the womb of my mother" is מִבֶּטֶן אִמִּי (*mibeten 'immi*, 22:10b). Also note that "womb" is בֶּטֶן (*beten*, 22:9a, 10b) and "trust" is בָּטַח (*batach*, 22:9b, also in 22:4a, 4b, 5b): the wordplay is obvious. The poet's was a longstanding trust in God, seemingly not reciprocated by deity's deliverance.

oppressed that the psalmist can know it is right to cry out in the present. The petitions and the motivational expressions are consistent with what God has revealed about the divine nature. So the psalmist's prayer and urgings are in fact that the will of God be done. They are an urging that God act as God.[13]

The chiastic shaping of 22:9–10 is trenchant, focusing upon the God whom the sufferer has trusted in, from his days as a neonate:[14]

```
A    "For You [are]
  B    the one who brought me
    C    out from the womb;
      D    ... trust upon the breasts of my mother.
      D'   Upon You I was cast from birth;
    C'   from the womb of my mother
  B'   My God
A'   You [were]."
```

"For so long I have trusted you, as our fathers did. Would you, therefore, not do for me as you did for them?"

Round 2: Petition–Lament (22:11–18)

While 22:1–2 bore an implicit petition (unanswered), an explicit petition is found for the first time in this psalm in 22:11, introducing the substantial lament that follows in 22:12–18. This plaint of 22:12–18 alternates between the "they" (enemies) and the "I" (sufferer)—the anguish is palpable:

22:12–13	"They"
22:14–15	"I"
22:16	"They"
22:17a	"I"
22:17b–18	"They"

But in addition to the "they" and the "I" that punctuate this section, there is also a "You," referring to God, in 22:15a. Besides not being available to help (22:11—"there is no one," not even God!), it appears to the complainant that God is himself implicated in his sufferings: "in the dust of death You lay me," i.e., "You are killing me!" "The psalm began with God distressingly absent and inactive; worse, it continues with God distressingly present but active in a death-bringing way."[15] God was responsible! This in no way involves God in the direct infliction of evil, but simply understands him as totally sovereign over all that happens.

---

13. Miller, *Interpreting the Psalms*, 103.
14. Modified from Kselman, "'Why Have You Abandoned Me?,'" 177.
15. Goldingay, *Psalms*, 1:333.

Again, as in the previous section, the primary need is of divine presence (a reversal of divine absences and abandonment): 22:11 reiterates the word "far" from 22:1b. "More than anything else, the worshiper requires to know once again the intimate presence of God. If such presence brought with it healing, so much the better, but even if it did not, sickness and death could be faced squarely in the presence of God, who would be a helper."[16] Whether the morbid lament of 22:12–18 relates to a deathly illness or a severe persecution is unclear.

> Because of Psalm 22's metaphorical and hyperbolic language, the precise nature of the distress suffered by the individual who cries out to God for help remains open to multiple interpretations. The psalm describes a world filled with jeering, bestial enemies—portrayed as enraged bulls, ravening lions, and hounding dogs—whose threatening gestures cause the psalmist to be poured out like water and his heart to melt like wax within his breast, until he lays in the very dust of death. The suggestive vagueness of this stereotypical imagery appears to be a deliberate strategy that allows people facing any number of horrors to adopt the psalm for ritual [or personal] use.[17]

A number of denizens of the animal kingdom make an appearance in this psalm: "worm" (22:6a), "bulls" (22:12a, 12b), "lion" (22:13b, 21a),[18] "dogs" (22:16a, 20b), and "wild oxen" (22:21b), testifying to the ferocity and lethality of the psalmist's distressing experience. Interestingly enough, there is a chiastic organization in the appearance of several of these beasts, further intensifying the threat:[19]

> **A**   "Bulls" (×2, 22:12)
>   **B**   "Lion" (22:13b; and "mouth," 22:13a)
>   **C**   "Dogs" (22:16a)
>
>   **C'**   "Dog" (22:20b)
>   **B'**   "Lion" (22:21a; and "mouth," 22:21a)
> **A'**   "Wild oxen" (22:21b)

The plight of the psalmist is so threatening that he is unable to hold himself together (22:14–15): he is disintegrating, being poured out like water, bones dislocating, heart melting, strength drying, tongue paralyzing, lying in the dust of death. As if that weren't enough, the onslaught of beasts continues: dogs, i.e., a band of evildoers, gouge out (gnaw? bite?) the sufferer's hands and feet (22:16);[20] all his bones are visible; he is considered dead and gone (22:17)—his persecutors have already divvied up his clothing (22:18).

16. Craigie, *Psalms 1–50*, 199.

17. Menn, "No Ordinary Lament," 308.

18. Both lions and sufferer emit the same sound—"roaring" in 22:13b and "groaning" in 22:1b translate the same word, שׁאג. That is to say, it is the "roaring" of the lions that causes the "groaning" of the sufferer!

19. Modified from Kselman, "'Why Have You Abandoned Me?,'" 188. "This chiastic arrangement is a good example of how structure can mirror and reinforce meaning. The reversal of the animal names . . . [in 22:20–21] prepares for the coming reversal of the poet's situation (from lament to thanksgiving) . . . [in 22:23–32]" (Kselman, "'Why Have You Abandoned Me?,'" 188).

20. The MT's כָּאֲרִי, *ka'ari*, is translated "*like a lion* my hands and my feet," but that is grammatically awkward in the context. The most reasonable emendation of the text is to read the consonantal כארי, *k'ry*, as כָּארוּ, *ka'ru*, or כָּרוּ, *karu*, the *qal* perfect third-person common plural of כָּרָה, *karah*, "to dig/gouge" (as in

Round 3: Petition–Praise (22:19–31)

After the utter helplessness expressed in the closing verses of Round 2, this round begins, "But You . . . [וְאַתָּה, *w'attah*]" (22:19). That (disjunctive) conjunction + pronoun suggests that the psalmist has given up hoping in his deity. "My enemies, they torment me. But You, Yahweh, do not abandon me." What exactly the sufferer expected God to do is unexpressed, leaving it up to God (and thereby enabling the reuse of the song by God's people in a variety of similar dire situations). In any case, this is the first direct address to God using the vocative "Yahweh" in this psalm (his name had been employed derisively by the opponents in 22:8). He pleads for protection from "the hand of the dog," "the mouth of the lion," and "the horns of the wild oxen" (22:20b, 21a, 21b). In 22:8b the detractors had mockingly implied that God would not "rescue" him; here in 22:20a, such a "rescue" is exactly what is petitioned for.

And as if on cue, 22:21c affirms: "You answered me!" (in contrast to "You do not answer," 22:2a).[21] Perhaps there is a time gap between 22:21ab and 22:21c wherein the petitioner received an oracle or some assurance of divine response (from a prophet? priest?). Thus we have here a plea for help in 22:21ab, a profession of confidence in 22:21c, and a promise of praise in 22:22. In that chiastic verse, 22:22,[22] the psalmist pledges to "recount" (i.e., tell of) the deliverance obtained in God's name. The psalmist, earlier, could "count" his bones (ספר, *sphr*, 22:17a); now he will "recount" (also ספר, 22:22a, and likewise in 22:30b) the deeds of God in order to praise him.

It is unlikely that God had already delivered the sufferer in 22:22–31, but his faith is evident: God has answered (with a promise of deliverance?) and God *would* keep his word, so everyone can rejoice already! Indeed, once "despised" by his enemies (22:6b), the sufferer is now the child of a God who "has *not* despised" the sufferings of his people (22:24a): he cares for them and for their woes. No, God had not "abandoned" the sufferer (22:1)—this God "has not hidden His presence [face]" (22:24c) and he has "heard" the petitioner's cry for help (22:24d). The psalmist shifts to address God in 22:25a, perhaps moved by his claim that when he had cried to God for help, God had heard (22:24d). "From You [comes] my praise,"

Gen 26:25; 50:5; Pss 7:15; 57:6; 94:13; 119:85; etc.), the former with the addition of א,', an archaic fuller/ *plene* spelling. The ו to י (*w* to *y*) alteration is not an uncommon scribal error, especially in a day when these two manuscripted letters were not as distinguishable as they are now. In any case, with the emended כָּאֲרוּ, we have "they gouged/pierced my hands and my feet." The LXX, concurring, has the aorist active indicative third-person plural ὤρυξαν, *ōryxan*, from ὀρύσσω, *oryssō*, "to dig" (as in Ps 57:6, where כָּרוּ is translated in the LXX with ὤρυξαν). Validating our emendation is the fact that otherwise 22:16 would be the only locus where a Hebrew non-verb, the MT's כָּאֲרִי, "like a lion," is translated with a verb ὀρύσσω. Remarkably, in the last three decades, the text of 5/6 Ḥev Psalms Scroll, one of three mid-first-century Psalms scrolls discovered outside the Qumran area, containing portions of Psalms 7–18, 22–25, and 28–31, has been found to have כארו, *k'rw*, in Ps 22:16 (column XI, fragment 8, line 12) instead of the MT's כארי, thus substantiating the emended reading proposed here. See Gren, "Piercing the Ambiguities," 292–93; and Flint, "Preliminary Edition," 31. With regard to later Hebrew manuscripts, Ross notes that Kennicott MS 39 also has ו instead of the final י, and that DeRossi MS 337 has a *Ketiv-Qere* reading attesting to both forms (Ross, *Psalms* 1:523–24n9). All that to say, the sense of "piercing" that is redolent of Christ's sufferings in the NT is not misplaced; while that is not the *meaning* of this text, it is certainly a valid *application* thereof, as also are the NT citations of 22:7–8, 17–18. The psalm as a whole is unlikely to be prophetic, for the sufferings described herein do not match with much precision those of the Savior. Nonetheless, the idioms and memes of sufferings in Psalm 22 are applicable to a number of agonizing situations in the life of God's people (and of God's Son).

21. The verb ענה, *'nh*, a fientive *qal* perfect, is best read as "You answered" or "You have answered."
22. "I will recount Your name / to my kindred; // in the midst of the assembly / I will praise You."

he exclaims in 22:25a, meaning that the delivering acts of God deserved praise in the public gathering; the "vow" in 22:25b is likely a vow to praise God in that setting.[23]

Perhaps matching the profusion of the lament of 22:12–18, the following subsection, 22:22–31, is "one of the most effusive and extravagant songs of thanksgiving in the Old Testament."[24] There is a constant back-and-forth oscillation here between praise (22:22–23, 25, 26b–27, 29–31bα) and the reason for that praise (22:24, 26a, 28, 31bβ). Quite evident here is the emphasis on community ("kindred" and "assembly" in 22:22; also "assembly" in 22:25, besides the various references to, and descriptors of, the body of God's people in 22:23, 25, 26, 30: God fearers, descendants of Jacob, descendants of Israel, those who seek God).[25] The praise of God is always a corporate undertaking, as it glorifies God before others.

> [This song of thanksgiving] brings the singers of the psalm from the deepest depths to the highest heights as it closes with a crescendo of praise to the God who is present to deliver. There is a movement outwards, however, as well as upwards as a great ripple, yea a wave of praise, spins out from God's deliverance of this one person. . . . The utterly desolate and isolated individual who felt [like] a worm, nothing, mocked by everybody, has moved to the center of a universal circle of praise and worship of the Lord.[26]

That universalizing is also chiastic. On either side of the declaration of Yahweh's kingdom and his rulership (22:28[27]) stand the responses of the reigned: they remember, they turn to Yahweh, they worship (22:27), and they eat and worship, and bow before him (22:28).

"remember," "turn," "*worship*" (22:27bα)
"nations" (22:27bβ)
Yahweh's kingdom and rulership (22:28a)
"nations" (22:28b)
"eat," "*worship*," "bow" (22:29aα)

The specific desolation and deliverance of this individual, the psalmist, should be considered on the broader tapestry of Yahweh's dominion and regency (22:28).[28] Psalm 22:25–30 offers an almost "apocalyptic vision of God being praised the world over by both the living, the dead, and posterity," with a prospective, rather than a retrospective view.[29] Both the prosperous (22:29a) and the afflicted and those close to dying (22:29bc) would join in worship of God. The note about near death in 22:29c (and implied in 22:26c) is striking. Even these, terminal

---

23. God returns to the third person in 22:25b. An equally sudden shift in address is also found in 22:26c: the "your" (plural) refers to the afflicted and the God-seekers of 22:26ab. The psalmist's "heart" was melting like wax once (22:14cd), but the "hearts" of God's people would live forever! Craigie suggests that in the context of the communal meal (22:26a, 29ab), this might be "a toast to his fellow diners—a significant toast from one who stood so recently on the threshold of death!" (Craigie, *Psalms 1–50*, 201).

24. Miller, *Interpreting the Psalms*, 107.

25. Notice also the communal meal, denoted by "eat" in 22:26a, 29a (an activity engaged in by the community and, one day, by all people).

26. Miller, *Interpreting the Psalms*, 108.

27. Also noted in 22:3, with the mention of God's enthronement.

28. See Craigie, *Psalms 1–50*, 201.

29. Boulton, "Forsaking God," 71.

in state, as was the sufferer in this psalm (22:12–21), would, perhaps post-deliverance, be able to eat and worship in the company of God's people. In sum, the praise of 22:22–31 is to be performed both by the community (22:22–26, all Israel) and by people worldwide (22:27–31, all Gentiles). And not only that, their descendants and future generations, those yet to be born, would continue to praise (22:30–31), a vision transcending both time and space!

Sermon Map

I. Abandoned by God?
   Divine non-response (22:1–2)
   Deathly peril (22:6–8)
   Dire situation (22:12–18)
   Move-to-relevance: Our sense of divine abandonment

II. Trusting in God
   Community's trust in the past (22:3–5)
   Individual's trust in the past (22:9–10)
   Move-to-relevance: The importance of remembering

III. Praying to God
   Individual's petition for divine presence (22:11, 19–21b)
   Move-to-relevance: Prayer as a manifestation of trust

IV. Praise unto God
   Individual praise (22:22–25)
   Community praise (22:26–31)
   Move-to-relevance: Our lack of communal praise to God

V. *Pray for Presence; Praise in Public!*
   Specifics on prayer and praise remembering past, and expecting future, divine intervention

PSALM 23:1–6

Psalm of Orientation

Guided by the Shepherd; Going to the King

THERE IS NO EXPLICIT plea in this popular psalm; it is an unremitting song of trust that is almost entirely symbolic and pictorial, with the only concrete realities being Yahweh and the psalmist in 23:1–4c, and Yahweh, the psalmist, and enemies in 23:4d–6. "The preciousness of the psalm derives in large part from its lyricism, which is part of what also makes us unable to tie it down."[1]

Translation

23:1 Yahweh is my shepherd;
    I will not lack.
23:2 In grassy pastures He makes me lie;
    by restful waters He leads me.
23:3 My soul He restores;
    He guides me in tracks of righteousness
    for the sake of His name.
23:4 Even though I walk in the valley of the death-shadow,
    I do not fear evil,
    for You are with me;
Your rod and Your staff,
    they—they comfort me.
23:5 You prepare a table before me
    in the presence of my enemies;
You refreshed my head with oil;
    my cup is overflowing.

---

1. Goldingay, *Psalms*, 1:345.

23:6 Surely goodness and lovingkindness
will pursue me all the days of my life,
and I will dwell
in the house of Yahweh for long days.

Structure

"Yahweh" shows up only twice in Psalm 23, at its beginning and its end (23:1a, 6d), and the forms of address (*about* Yahweh and *to* Yahweh) are arranged symmetrically, giving the whole poem a sense of balance.[2]

23:1–4b	*Shepherd* (**23:1–3**)	About Yahweh
	God (**23:4ab**)	To Yahweh
23:4c	"For You are with me" (**23:4c**)	
23:4d–6	*King* (**23:4d–6b**)	To Yahweh
	God (**23:6cd**)	About Yahweh

In sum, 23:1–3 commences with the *Shepherd* metaphor but transitions into one more explicitly about *God* in 23:4ab. The center of the poem is 23:4c, affirming the presence of God, and this is preceded and followed by twenty-six Hebrew words (disregarding the *maqqeph*, akin to a hyphen).[3] In 23:4d–6b, the metaphor is that of a *King*, but that too transitions into a more direct focus on *God* (and his house) in 23:6cd. One should also note the metaphor of a journey that is prominent in 23:1–4b ("leads," 23:2b; "guides," 23:3b; "I walk," 23:4a; and the allusions to the exodus [see below]), with a destination prominent in 23:4d–6 (the palace of the King—"the house of Yahweh"; 23:6d).

Theological Focus

The people of God undertake the journey of life with God who, as their Shepherd, cares for their every need as he guides them on his paths, protecting them from evil; and who, as their King, prospers them and blesses them abundantly, as they move to their destination—in and with divine presence forever.

---

2. Also in the commencing and concluding verses are first-person singular verbs making assertions about the supplicant's situation in the presence of God: "I will not lack" (23:1b) and "I will dwell" (23:6c), respectively.

3. Van der Lugt, "Mathematical Centre," 643. And he also notes that, intriguingly, the numerical value of the letters constituting "Yahweh" add up to twenty-six: י + ה + ו + ה ($y + h + w + h$) = 10 + 5 + 6 + 5 = 26.

Commentary

Shepherd–God (23:1–4c)

God as a shepherd is a common motif in the Bible, and Psalm 23 is a paramount example of such a depiction.[4] But this motif is also linked to the exodus in the opening section, 23:1–3: both "lead" (נהל, *nhl*; 23:2b) and "guide" (נחה, *nchh*; 23:3b) show up in Exod 15:13;[5] the absence of lack (לֹא אֶחְסָר, *lo' 'echsar*, Ps 23:1b) is noted in Deut 2:7; 8:9; Neh 9:21 (referring to the wilderness wanderings); "pastures" (Ps 23:2b) is mentioned in Exod 15:13 (also see Jer 23:3; 31:23; Ezek 34:14–15, that also has "lie down"); likewise, "waters" (Ps 23:2b) is employed in Exod 15:22–27; 17:1–7; Pss 78:20; 105:41; etc. Besides, "for the sake of His name" (23:3c), i.e., for God's reputation and glory, is also found in relation to the exodus in 106:8.[6] Thus, a familiar and traditional context is hinted at in Psalm 23, to reassure the flock of God's faithfulness in the past, with previous journeys of moment encapsulated into the "journey of life" in this psalm.[7] And in this passage, "Yahweh is *my* shepherd" makes the entire declaration personal, individual, intimate.

Thus, in the first two verses, with its *Shepherd* motif, there is no lack for the sheep; there is ample provision as indicated by their lying down by grassy pastures without needing to seek further food; they are secure by restful, not roiling, waters. The Shepherd-God is sufficient for all things, because with him there is "no lack" (23:1b). He provides for all the needs of all his flock, his people.[8]

But this shepherding motif begins to lose specificity with the addition of the moral emphases of 23:3 that affirm the restoration of souls and guidance in the paths of righteousness for the sake of God's name, clearly moving from a pastoral metaphor to one that is more explicitly and exclusively identified with Yahweh as deity. Indeed, the verb נחה ("guide"; 23:3b) is never used of animals, but often denotes divine direction.[9] So also "tracks" (23:3b) often indicates the paths of God.[10] "Restoration" of the "soul" (23:3a) was already encountered in 19:7 as a function of the *Torah*. In light of the collection of Psalms 15–24, within which Psalms 15, 19, and 24 (the two outer and central psalms[11]) are united in their understanding

---

4. See, in the Psalter, 28:9; 78:52; 79:13; 80:1; 95:7; 100:3. Likewise, in the ancient Near East, gods were often referred to as shepherds: see, for e.g., the "Akkadian Creation Epic" VI, 108; VII, 72, 148; the "Akkadian Ritual of *Kalū*-Priest," Text D, 31; the "Sumero-Akkadian Hymn to the Sun-God," i.26, 33 (*ANET* 69, 71, 72, 337, 387–88, respectively).

5. Also see Pss 31:3; 77:20.

6. There may be related allusions to the Israelites' return from exile, too, another journey that took on pastoral motifs: Jer 50:19; Isa 40:11 (with "comfort" in 40:1, as in Ps 23:4e); Ezek 34:12–15, 25–27; Zechariah 10–11.

7. Botha, "Following the Tracks," 289.

8. It behooves the reader to acknowledge that "the shepherd image thus applies naturally to the people as a whole rather than to individuals, to a flock rather than an individual sheep" (Goldingay, *Psalms*, 1:348). Though the psalm is addressed in an individual's voice, it is the community that is the flock, not any one member thereof. Yet, as was noted, "Yahweh is *my* shepherd" (23:1a), so perhaps both "mine" and "ours."

9. See Pss 5:8; 27:11; 43:3; 139:24; 143:10. It is also found in the account of the exodus: Exod 13:17, 21; Deut 32:12; Neh 9:12; Pss 78:14, 53; 107:30. Tanner, "King Yahweh," 275n40, notes that the verb occurs thirty-nine times in the OT; thirty-three times the subject is God.

10. See Pss 17:5; 65:11; Prov 4:11; and Prov 2:9 has "righteousness" linked with "tracks" just as in Ps 23:3b.

11. See on Psalm 15.

of the supremacy of ethical conduct and *Torah* piety, there is a "predominately morally oriented context for understanding Ps 23:3b."[12] Likewise, the link between "His name" (23:3c) and divine glory, as noted earlier (and see 31:3). All that to say, the restoration of souls and the guidance by God in divine paths of righteousness indicate deity's superintendence of the course of the lives of his people as they undertake that "journey of life." And even if such journeys involve traversing "the valley of the death-shadow" (23:4a; perhaps some imminent threat of death), the flock of God "do not fear evil" (23:4b).

The reason for this absence of panic follows: "For You are with me" (23:4c). This affirmation of divine presence with the child of God in the "journey of life" forms the centerpiece of this poem. It also marks a shift indicated by an alteration of address: 23:1–3 was *about* Yahweh (speaking of him in the third person); 23:4 is *to* Yahweh (speaking to him in the second person).

Thus in 23:1–4c, the "journey of life" is being undertaken, with Yahweh as Shepherd-God. Where is this journey headed? The destination becomes clear in 23:4d–6, with Yahweh now portrayed as King-God.

King-God (23:4d–6)

Notice that 23:1ab had introduced the motif of Yahweh as *Shepherd*; here 23:4de introduces, via "rod" and "staff," the motif of Yahweh as *King*. Traditionally, these latter implements have been considered shepherdly instruments, continuing the metaphor of God the Shepherd from 23:1–4b. However, שֵׁבֶט (*shevet*, "rod") is often an accompaniment of a king's authority (23:4d).[13] And, of course, the patriarch Jacob promised his son Judah that the insignia of regency, a scepter (שֵׁבֶט) and staff, would be his forever (Gen 49:10). "This scepter or rod never carries the sense of providing security or comfort, nor is it used as a word for an actual shepherd's staff.... This is the insignia for the king-god who will judge the earth."[14] The second implement מִשְׁעֶנֶת (*mish'enet*, "staff") also seems to connote power and might (a broken staff indicated destroyed nations: 2 Kgs 18:21; Isa 36:6; Ezek 29:6).[15] Thus the "rod" and "staff" of Ps 23:4d are "certainly not the accouterments of simple shepherds but carry a meaning of power and judgment.... These are the implements of a just and righteous king, who rules with equity.... The 'comfort' [emphasized in 23:4e with "they—they comfort me"], then, is not only of God's presence [23:4c] but also of God's righteous reign that will maintain order."[16] Besides all this, there is also the fact that God's people receive "comfort"

---

12. See Abernethy, "'Right Paths,'" 316 (and see 304n14, 313, 318).

13. See the following verses, all of which depict the bearer of the "rod" as one with authority, whether it be king or parent: 2 Sam 7:14; 18:14; Pss 2:9; 45:6; 89:32; Prov 13:24; 22:8, 15; 23:13, 14; 26:3; 29:15; Isa 9:4; 10:5; 11:4; Ezek 20:37; Amos 1:5; Mic 7:14; Zech 10:11. The neo-Babylonian king Nabonidus (who reigned 556–539 BCE) prayed that he would possess forever the "scepter and reliable staff that you put in my hand." See Langdon, *Die neubabylonischen Königsinschriften*, 226 (Nabonidus I, column III, 20–21; German translation, 227; my English translation from the German).

14. Tanner, "King Yahweh," 278.

15. Though it also is used of a walking stick (2 Kgs 4:29, 31; Zech 8:4).

16. Tanner, "King Yahweh," 279. Evidence of kings employing these pastoral paraphernalia are also found in an ancient Sumerian Legend of Etana; scepter and staff are particularly noted (Kinnier-Wilson, *Legend of Etana*, 30; Tablet 1/A, 10–11). Of note, shepherding and ruling are often conflated in Scripture: 1 Sam 17:34–36; Ps 80:1 (divine shepherd); Isa 44:28 (of Cyrus). Neither was this uncommon in the ancient Near East generally, where great kings were referred to as shepherd: See "Prologue to the Code of

(23:4e) from their rod-and-staff bearer, signaling the shift to a non-pastoral metaphor, for sheep are only cared for, never comforted. All that to say, Yahweh is depicted here as a regent with authority, the King—the prosecutor of justice and righteousness—who comforts his people with the assurance of his dominion over mankind and all of creation.

The regal image is continued in 23:5, with a king's banquet and a "table [שֻׁלְחָן, *shulchan*]" and a "cup" in view, perhaps parallel to the "pastures" and "waters" in 23:2. As well, there is an "overflowing" (23:5d) that is akin to the absence of "lack" (23:1b).[17] The "refreshing . . . with oil" (23:5c; literally "making fat") is not an anointing, but a gesture of hospitality from a host toward guests. In Prov 15:30 such an act is parallel to "cheering the heart." In sum, the psalmist is describing a flourishing at the hands of the divine host, Yahweh the King—the promoter of the gladness of his people.[18] And with Ps 23:5, the destination of the "journey of life" that began the psalm becomes more distinct: the King's palace (more clarity comes as the psalm progresses).

But one glimpses the most unexpected guests at this royal banquet—"enemies" (23:5b). Then again, these foes are to be expected after the "rod" and "staff" of the monarch—his justice and righteousness—were mentioned. It might be that these adversaries are only observing the overwhelmingly benevolent blessing of God upon his people, and are thus put to shame publicly (as in Ps 86:16–17; Mic 7:16–17).

Again, as in the first half of the psalm with the metaphor of the *Shepherd*, the metaphor of the *King* also begins to lose specificity. "Goodness" and "lovingkindness" (Ps 23:6a) are elsewhere in the Psalter moral characteristics of Yahweh and Yahweh alone,[19] and it is more than likely that it is from Yahweh that "goodness and lovingkindness" proceed to follow the supplicant.[20] Usually it is enemies who "pursue" (7:1, 5; 31:15; 35:3; 109:16; etc.), but here it is Yahweh's "goodness and lovingkindness" that are in pursuit of the psalmist.[21] The world and the flesh and Satan chase us to cause us to fret and to fall. God chases us towards himself, to free and to fulfill us. "Evil" in 23:4b is thus transformed to "goodness" in 23:6a,

---

Hammurabi" i.60; "Epilogue" (reverse xxiv) 10–42 (*ANET* 164, 177–78). A number of contemporary portrayals of monarchs with scepter and staff attest to the regal nature of these implements. See, for e.g., Wiseman, "New Stela," 24–44; plates II, III, VII.

17. For שֻׁלְחָן referring to a king's "table," see Jdg 1:7; 1 Sam 20:34; 2 Sam 9:7, 10, 11, 13; 19:28; 1 Kgs 2:7; 4:27; 10:5; 13:20; 18:19. Yahweh has a victorious "table" laid out in Ezek 39:17–20; there was also a "table" of Yahweh in the temple (Ezek 41:22; 44:16; etc.). The Neo-Assyrian king Sargon II (reigned 722–705 BCE) boasted that he had "a magnificent table set up" before his guest (Thureau-Dangin, *Une relation*, 12 [line 62; French version, 13; my translation from the French]).

18. Also see as in Prov 11:25; 13:4; 28:25. That such a generous treatment of guests was performed by a king is evidenced in the claim of the Neo-Assyrian king Esarhaddon (reigned 681–669 BCE) to have "caused excellent oil . . . , oil to wet their heads," i.e., of guests at a festive meal (Borger, *Die Inschriften*, 63: §27 A, VI 49–53; my translation from Borger's German version).

19. See Pss 25:7; 63:3; 69:16; 86:5; 100:5; 106:1; 107:1; 109:21; 118:1, 29; 136:1; also see "goodness" related to Yahweh's "house," 65:4.

20. I keep 23:6ab with what preceded, as a continuation of an address *about* Yahweh: the dual nouns, "goodness and lovingkindness" parallel the earlier pair in 23:4d, "Your rod and Your staff." The effect of the latter pair—"they comfort me" (third-person plural, with a first-person suffix; 23:4e) is also parallel to the verb describing what the former pair do—"[they] will pursue me" (another third-person plural, with a first-person suffix; 23:6b). And just as 23:4ab concludes the first half of the psalm, so also does 23:6cd; also, both commence with a conjunction ("even though [כִּי גַם, *gam ki*]" and "and [וְ, *w*]," respectively).

21. There may be an allusion here to the "overtaking" (נשׂג, *nsg*) by divine blessings (or curses) in Deut 28:2, 15; this verb is used in parallel with "pursue" (רדף, *rdph*), in 28:45.

and "death" in 23:4a to "life" in 23:6b. God, the divine cause of prosperity and flourishing, has blessed his people!

And so the psalmist is certain that for "long days," i.e., all his life, he will "dwell" in the presence of Yahweh, simply because this God and his goodness and lovingkindness will see to it that he, and the rest of God's people, do.[22] With that we finally arrive at the destination of the "journey of life"—the "house of Yahweh," into the very presence of God. The journey began with "Yahweh" (23:1a) and it ends with "Yahweh" (23:6d). This transit is likely to be a recurrent pursuit of God, toward God and his house, for temptations to hurtle in the opposite direction never cease to accost us in this life. But one day . . . .

Sermon Map

I. The Journey of Life

    Move-to-relevance: Our needs in the journey of life

II. Shepherd–God

    Journey of life: He rests, leads, restores, guides, protects (23:1–4c)

    Move-to-relevance: The restfulness of knowing the Shepherd–God

III. King–God

    Journey of life: He controls, comforts, honors, blesses (23:4d–6b)

    Move-to-relevance: The comfort of knowing the King–God

IV. The Destination of Life

    The presence of God (23:6cd)

    Move-to-relevance: Our constant move towards the destination

V. *Go with God; Go to God!*

    Specifics on traveling with/to God

---

22. The verb וְשַׁבְתִּי (*wshavtti*, from שׁוב, *shwv*, "return") does not fit the context and is best emended either to וְשִׁבְתִּי, *wshivtti*, an infinitive construct, or to וְיָשַׁבְתִּי, *wyashavtti*, qal perfect first-person singular from ישׁב, *yshv*, "to dwell." "Dwelling" in the "house of Yahweh" is also mentioned Pss 27:4; 65:4; 84:10. Yet another Neo-Assyrian king, Ashurbanipal (reigned 669–631 BCE), pled in a dedication to the goddess Ninlil: "Give me, Ashurbanipal, who fears your great deity, a life of long days and wholeness of heart, and may my feet age walking in your temple" (Streck, *Assurbanipal*, 2:276 ["Dedication to the goddess Ninlil," lines 16–18; German translation, 2:277; my translation from the German]).

PSALM 24:1–10

Psalm of Reorientation

Order Consummated over Chaos

AT FIRST GLANCE THERE appears to be three different sections in Psalm 24; 24:1–2 (a statement about God's creation), 24:3–6 (a question-and-answer revealing who has the privilege to be in the divine presence), and 24:7–10 (that appears to be an antiphonal liturgical chant). But an appreciation for poesy and an interpretive tack in the direction of authorial *doings* reveal that all the sections are united under the aegis of God's workings between the moment after creation and the instant of the inauguration of the eschaton.[1]

Translation

24:1   Yahweh's is the earth, and what fills it,
         the world, and those who dwell in it.
24:2   For He—upon the seas He founded it
         and upon the rivers He established it.
24:3   Who may ascend into the hill of Yahweh,
         and who may stand in His holy place?
24:4   The innocent of hands and the pure of heart,
         who has not lifted up his soul to emptiness
         and has not sworn to deception.
24:5   He shall take away a blessing from Yahweh,
         and righteousness from the God of his deliverance.
24:6   This is the generation of those who seek Him,
         those who look for Your presence—Jacob.
24:7   Lift up your heads, gates,
         and be lifted up, doors of eternity,
         that the King of glory may come in.

---

1. Eschaton, i.e., the consummation of all things in the last days in Christ, as Eph 1:9–10 describes.

24:8 Who is this King of glory?
   Yahweh powerful and mighty,
   Yahweh mighty in battle.
24:9 Lift up your heads, gates,
   and lift up, doors of eternity,
   that the King of glory may come in.
24:10 Who is He, this King of glory?
   Yahweh of Armies,
   He is the King of glory.

Structure

The structure of the psalm may be delineated as follows, relating both to the eschaton (preparation for, motion towards, and consummation of) and to the depiction of God (as Creator, as the Holy One, and as King):

Preparation for the Eschaton (**24:1–2**)
   God the Creator
   "Yahweh" ×1 (24:1a)

Motion towards the Eschaton (**24:3–6**)
   God the Holy
   "Yahweh" ×2 (24:3a, 5a)

Consummation of the Eschaton (**24:7–10**)
   God the King
   "Yahweh" ×3 (24:8b, 8c, 10b)

Theological Focus

God's people are privileged to partner with the Creator who prepares for the eschaton as he sets apart, from the surrounding chaos, a space for inhabited life; and with the King who will one day consummate the eschaton with his final victory over chaos, opening the portals to an eternity with him—all by serving the Holy One who sets apart his people to move towards the eschaton by rejecting chaos/evil and choosing order/holiness.

Commentary

Preparation for the Eschaton: God the Creator (24:1–2)

The emphatic positioning of "Yahweh's [לַֽיהוָ֗ה, *layhwh*]" at the commencement of 24:1a and the equally emphatic (and redundant) pronoun at the head of 24:2a ("for He . . . He . . .") make the identity of God the Creator a central focus of 24:1–2. But what he created also is given prominence with the sonic echo of *-ah, -ah, -ah,* and *-ha* at the end of each line of the first two verses: וּמְלוֹאָ֑הּ, בָ֗הּ, יְסָדָ֑הּ, and יְכוֹנְנֶֽהָ (*umlo'ah, vah, ysadah,* and *ykonneha*)—all third-person feminine singular suffixes referring to the "earth" and the "world" ("what fills it," "in it," 24:1; "He founded it," "He established it," 24:2). The "founding" and "establishing" of the "earth" and "world" are reminiscent of the construction of a house or a temple, a constrained space within the cosmos, where dwellers could experience fulfillment as intended by the Creator, apart from the disorder without—a separation of sorts.[2] That separating constraint was necessary because outside this created station of order was a prior situation of chaos that had to be restrained at creation.[3] Thus, God's work as Creator has for a backdrop the unruly "seas [יַמִּ֑ים, *yammim*]" and turbulent "rivers [נְהָרֽוֹת, *nharim*]" upon which he founded/established *terra firma* (24:2). These fluid entities were well-known, both in Hebrew and in Ugaritic literature, as a nefarious pair of actors. For instance, in Isa 50:2 and Hab 3:8, they are enemies of Yahweh, symbols of the chaos he had to subdue in the creation of the "earth"/"world" for humans.[4] However, there is no hint in Scripture that those chaotic forces were annihilated at the time; God's work at creation was only a neutralization and not a final defeat, a constraining but not an exterminating—that final disposition will happen only in the eschaton. All that to say, creation is thus a preparation for those last days, a preliminary set up for the end, a first step to enable humanity to thrive on this side of eternity in a separated locus, the "earth"/"world." But the continued presence of the not-yet-eliminated chaos points to a contingent fallibility in the here and now: demonic disorder constantly threatens to overwhelm and break through into divine order. And, of course, in the fall, that threat became reality: God's creation was invaded by the disorder and chaos of sin and evil.

In sum, post-creation (or better: with creation), deity established a separated space, the "earth"/"world," for its inhabitants to flourish in his presence. What would God do, post-fall, now that the evil of chaos had infested and infected that space? The answer: a further constraint—another separation—as the next section, Ps 24:3–6, portrays.

Motion Towards the Eschaton: God the Holy (24:3–6)

The "drama" of Psalm 24 takes a sudden turn in 24:3–6.[5] But there is logic in the obliquity . . .

---

2. For the notions of God's creation in its entirety as a temple in which he chooses to dwell, with the primordial garden as its Holy of Holies, see Kuruvilla, *Genesis*, 39–49, 56–61 (and see below). Separation, of course, is the main characteristic of divine creation (see Kuruvilla, *Genesis*, 17–20).

3. No doubt the infernal activities of Satan and his demonic horde are implicit in the origination and perpetuation of these chaotic, anti-God phenomena.

4. In Ugaritic mythology, they were enemies of Baal. *Yam* ("sea") and *Nahar* ("river") "represented a threat to order in Canaanite mythology; the conquest of Yam by Baal represented the subjugation of chaotic forces and the establishment of Baal's kingship" (Craigie, *Psalms 1–50*, 212).

5. Sudden turn notwithstanding, 24:1–2 and 24:3–6, as well as 24:7–10, show similarities. They are linked by the presence of demonstrative pronouns in the last verses of each of the three sections: "he [הוּא,

Notice a dual specification that is depicted in this section: the "earth"/"world" of 24:1 is narrowed to a particular "hill of Yahweh"/"His holy place" (24:3⁶), and "those who dwell in it" is narrowed to one particular group of people, "generation" of God-seekers/"Jacob," i.e., the people of God (24:6). Creation itself was a constraining act to separate chaos from God's order; now, post-fall, with the invasion of chaotic evil, we see another constraint applied, another separation, and for the same purpose: to stave off further encroachment by chaos and evil. The blessing of God would no longer be open to everyone (as it was at creation: Gen 1:27–28), but only to certain individuals (the *people of blessing*); and the locus of blessing would no longer be everywhere in God's creation (all of which was originally declared by him to be "good"), but only in the special space of divine presence (the *place of blessing*).⁷

The *people of blessing*, the ones who will be blessed (as stated in 24:5), are described in 24:4 as having four characteristics, together forming a chiastic pattern of qualities that are outwardly visible or invisible,⁸ positive or negative.

24:4aα	"the innocent of hands"	visible	+
24:4aβ	"the pure of heart"	invisible	+
24:4b	"who has not lifted up his soul …"	invisible	−
24:4c	"who has not sworn to deception"	visible	−

This is the responsibility God lays on his people that they may, in partnership with him, stem the tide and parry the advances of demonic disorder over divine order. And, needless to say, the discharge of this human responsibility to live in accordance with divine demand for holiness is to be ongoing in the lives of God's people in the here and now, if chaos/evil is to be rebuffed and removed far from the people of God and the kingdom of God.

The *place of blessing* is clearly the presence of God, where God is—at "the hill of Yahweh" and in "His holy place" (24:3). Other places on earth are represented as low ("earth," "world," "seas," "rivers" in 24:1–2), while God's locus is high: those who would be in his presence have to make an ascent (note "ascend" and "hill" in 24:3a⁹). Therefore, those who desire to "ascend" from the foot of the "hill of Yahweh" to the top of his mountain to be in the presence of the holy God (moving from utter chaos to supreme order) must themselves be aligned to

---

hu']" in 24:2a; "this [זֶה, *zeh*]" in 24:6a (and in 24:8a); and both in 24:10 (הוּא twice, 24:10a, 10c).

6. What is remarkable with this narrowing localization of space is that God, who was implicitly described in 24:2 as being transcendent, i.e., spatially over the earth/world (implied in his establishment of the earth/world "upon" [עַל, *'al*; ×2] the waters of seas and rivers), has now become immanent, i.e., situated within the specific location of a "hill" and a "holy place" (implied by the preposition "into/in" [בְּ, *b*; ×2] qualifying these loci; 24:3).

7. Sumpter, "Coherence of Psalm 24," 47. Of course, anyone could choose to become part of the people of God.

8. Botha, "Answers Disguised," 541. The text of 24:4b has "my soul [נַפְשִׁי, *naphshi*]" in Hebrew, better read as "his soul [נַפְשׁוֹ, *naphsho*]," as does the LXX (τὴν ψυχὴν αὐτοῦ, *tēn psychēn autou*). This "lifting up" of one's soul to "emptiness" could either be dealing with false speech (as in 12:2), particularly in light of the swearing mentioned in the next line (24:4c), or with declaring allegiance to false gods (as in 31:7, as opposed to what is in 25:1; also see Exod 20:7; Deut 5:11—all have שָׁוְא, *shaw'*, "emptiness," as also does Ps 24:4b).

9. This ascent ("ascend," 24:3a) leads to a stance ("stand," 24:3b) before deity. One notices the resounding of the stem קום, *qwm*, "rise," in both יָקוּם (*yaqum*, "stand") and מָקוֹם (*maqom*, "place") in 24:3b. By the grace of God, (believing) humanity gets to *stand* in that divine *place*, with God and in his presence, made possible by his choice and redemption of a people in Christ for his own possession (1 Pet 2:9).

the divine order of holiness. In other words, they should partner with God in the distancing of chaos/evil by donning order/holiness in their lives (24:4). Thus there is a sense in which "God constantly becomes king as chaos is defeated—and humanity has a role in this process," a process that is daily, ongoing, and incessant, until the eschaton.[10]

In the past, God created a constraining space (everywhere in the "earth"/"world") for humanity (everyone) to be kept from chaos. This was the preparation for the eschaton and the final elimination of chaos (24:1–2). Then came the fall. So God made another constraint—a people for blessing (*not* everyone: only those manifesting divine holiness), in a place for blessing (*not* everywhere: only in the presence of God). These specifications of people and place are not two different features: when the people of God manifest the holiness of God, practicing godliness and being conformed to Christlikeness in the power of the Spirit, they are in the place/presence of God in a special way. In other words, living holy lives locates the people of God in the place of blessing, in a microcosm of the kingdom of God of which they are true citizens, ruled by the heavenly King.[11]

This was the movement towards the eschaton—the setting apart of a people of God to be holy and to abide in his presence (24:3–7), to become an orderly, deity-governed nucleus of God's people, an outpost of the kingdom of God in a foreign land. "Through honest action, admirable thought, and sincere speech, humans diminish primordial chaos. Through the opposite, people add to it, making creation itself less firm and detracting from God's status as king." In other words, "[godly] human behavior generates the environment in which God can become king with an earthly home."[12] This movement towards the eschaton and perfection has been what God has been up to post-fall, until a time when his kingdom is established—God's ideal world! Though that day is "not yet," a movement towards the eschaton has begun "already," as the people of God, epitomizing holiness, godliness, and Christlikeness, abide in the place/presence of God, living in—and thereby creating—the world as God desires.

There are consequences for those who choose to so live with God, for him, like him: "blessing" (including "righteousness"[13] and "deliverance"; 24:5). Note that "take away" in 24:5a translates נשא, *nsʾ*, the same verb translated "lifted up" in 24:4b. The children of God do not "lift up [נשא]" themselves to unholy behavior and, as a result, they "take away [נשא]" divine blessing/righteousness/deliverance. It is such privileged ones who are the true God-seekers, those who look for God's presence (literally, "face") and favor—the true "Jacob," righteous Israel: the people of God. The chiastic structure of 24:6 makes this clear:

> "This is the generation of
> those who seek [*participle*] Him,
> those who look [*participle*] for Your presence—
> Jacob."

---

10. Sommer, "Commentary on Psalm 24," 514.

11. Needless to add, this microcosm will one day become a macrocosm—that was God's intent from the beginning.

12. Sommer, "Commentary on Psalm 24," 514, 515.

13. "Righteousness" indicates an "element of mutual covenant responsibility"—"just as those who enter Yhwh's presence for blessing must be righteous—i.e. live according to what is right—so Yhwh displays his righteousness," providing for their every need, enabling their growth in holiness, abundantly blessing them (Sumpter, "Substance of Psalm 24," 144).

And thus, chaos is held at bay even more, and holiness begins to reign, at least in *this* microcosm (and in multiple iterations of this microcosm in this age) and for *this* time, involving *these* (believing) humans acting in holy partnership with their God (in the presence of God) against the forces of evil.[14] In other words, 24:3–6 is an "already" motion towards the "not-yet" eschaton. And, as noted, by living by kingdom standards, God's people are actualizing, "realizing," and instantiating the kingdom of God in the here and now: the people of blessing are living in his presence, the place of blessing.

So what about the eschaton, where all this is headed?

Consummation of the Eschaton: God the King (24:7–10)

Yet another abrupt shift seems to have occurred with this final section of the psalm.[15] But, again, it all turns out to be cogent and coherent . . . .

The sequencing of the acts of the "drama" of Psalm 24 runs into an obvious problem in the text of 24:7–10: Yahweh, who seemed have been located within the temple with his people seeking him there (in 24:3–6), is now apparently waiting outside seeking to be let in. Obviously then, those "gates" and "doors" of 24:7ab, 9ab cannot be temple entrances. Considering שַׁעַר (*sha'ar*, "gate" in 24:7a, 9a) and פֶּתַח (*petach*, "door" in 24:7b, 9b), Sumpter points to parallels in Gen 28:17 (שַׁעַר הַשָּׁמָיִם, *sha'ar hashshamayim*, "gate of [leading to] the heavens") and in Hos 2:15 (פֶּתַח תִּקְוָה, *petach tiqwah*, "door of [leading to] hope") that strongly suggest that the שְׁעָרִים and פִּתְחֵי עוֹלָם, *pitche 'olam*, the gates and doors (Ps 24:7ab, 9ab) indicate portals into eternity. After all, God is himself a God of eternity.[16] So the earthly temple to which humans "ascend" (עלה, *'lh*) in 24:3a[17] is only symbolic of the final, all-encompassing sanctuary of God and *its* gates and doors (of "eternity"), to which Yahweh has "come" in 24:7c, 9c, and which he opens, 24:7–10. In a sense, then the scene has shifted from the general to the very specific: earth/world (24:1–2) → a particular mountain (24:3–6) → a specific set of gates/doors into a special locus (24:7–10). All that to say, what is happening in 24:7–10 is the inauguration of eternity.[18] The eschaton is here . . . because the King is here at its gates: let the doors open, let eternity begin!

That these entrances are commanded to "lift up" their "heads" (= lintels; 24:7a, 7b, 9a, 9b) indicates "a God who is of massive proportions."[19] This comes as no surprise, for he is, after

---

14. Yet, this role of humans, important though it is, is subordinated by that of Yahweh: 24:3–6 is bounded on either side by an explicit focus on Yahweh (24:1–2 and 24:3–7). Besides, humankind's actions are still conditional and future, yet unrealized (and not to mention, still fallible), whereas those of God are depicted as done and dusted in both those outer sections of this psalm.

15. Perhaps not! There are a number of similarities between 24:3–6 and 24:7–10: both are antiphonal (questions in 24:3a and 24:8a, 10a, with corresponding answers in 24:4 and 24:8bc, 10bc); both employ the root נשא ("lift" in 24:4b, 7a, 7b, 9a, 9b; "take away" in 24:5a), the interrogative "who" (24:3a, 3b, 8a, 10a), and the demonstrative pronoun "this" (as was noted above); and both emphasize the identity of the one entering or attempting to enter a specific locus. Besides, both describe this ingress-seeking person in terms of characteristics (24:4; and 24:8bc, 10b), destination ("hill of Yahweh/His holy place," in 24:3; and eternity in 24:7b, 9b), and destiny ("blessing" in 24:5a; "glory" in 24:7c, 8a, 9c, 10a, 10c).

16. Pss 9:7; 10:16; 29:10; 41:13; 45:6; 48:14; 90:2; 92:8; 93:2; 102:12; 145:13; 146:10.

17. This includes, in this age, the church, the body of Christ, the temple of God the Spirit (1 Cor 3:16).

18. In which case, perhaps those "gates" and "doors" are approaches to the eternal temple of God, that also represents the final age of consummation.

19. Sumpter, "Substance of Psalm 24," 147. Ugaritic texts note the encouragement of Baal to other gods who are stricken with terror to "lift up their heads," as he prepares to address the forces of chaos, Yamm ("sea") and Nahar ("river") ("Poems about Baal and Anath," c. III AB B, lines 25–29 [*ANET* 130]).

all, the "King of glory" (the glorified One;[20] 24:7c, 8a, 9c, 10a, 10c) and "Yahweh of Armies" (24:10b), the one "powerful and mighty" and "mighty in battle" (24:8bc). All these epithets are directly related to the victories deity has won over the forces of chaos (24:8bc, 10b). Indeed, appearing at the zenith of the poem, and in light of the symbolism of gates and doors, "King of Glory" and "Yahweh of Armies" function as the passwords (or Face ID, if you will) that unlock these final access points to eternity, the consummated eschaton.[21]

In summary: As one follows the drama and sequencing of the psalm, one realizes that chaos is still present in the *hic et nunc* (pointing to contingent fallibility after creation in 24:1–2 which was a *preparation for the eschaton*), and that humans are called to eschew the chaos/evil and follow divine order/holiness and abide in God's place/presence (promising a conditional blessing in 24:3–6 for holiness in a less-than-ideal world, a *motion towards the eschaton*). And now, in the last act of the play, we have the divine warrior, returning from battle, after having once and for all annihilated chaos and quelled evil, unlocking the doors of eternity so that "Jacob" (24:6b)—God's people of all time and space—can enter with him (thus pronouncing a comprehensive finality to the narrative of God's work in 24:7–10: the *consummation of the eschaton*).[22]

The Drama of Psalm 24			Chaos
24:1–2	Created Order	*Preparation for the Eschaton*	+
24:3–6	Human Order	*Motion towards the Eschaton*	+ / −
24:7–10	Divine Order	*Consummation of the Eschaton*	−

And so the psalm ends as it began: "Yahweh" in both 24:1 and 24:10. Yes, "Yhwh will certainly enter, but will he have a Jacob to enter with him?"[23]

Sermon Map

I. Created Order: Preparation for the Eschaton

God the Creator: order from chaos for habitation (24:1–2)

Move-to-relevance: God's intention all along—order out of chaos

II. Divine Order: Consummation of the Eschaton

God the King: final elimination of chaos for eternity (24:7–10)

Move-to-relevance: The endpoint of all time, all history

III. Human Order: Motion towards the Eschaton

Serving God the Holy: rejecting chaos and choosing order (24:3–6)

Move-to-relevance: Importance of our partnership with God *now*

IV. *Make the Then-and-There Here-and-Now!*

Specifics on choosing order/holiness in light of the eschaton

---

20. Glory is God's destiny, so to speak, as he enters a location (24:7–10), as opposed to the destiny of God-seekers who enter the location of his presence (24:3–6): blessing/righteousness/deliverance.

21. Sumpter, "Substance of Psalm 24," 145.

22. Or if one prefers, the three sections may be sloganized as: *Ready!* (24:1–2), *Set!* (24:3–6), and—praise God!—*Go!* (24:7–10).

23. Sumpter, "Substance of Psalm 24," 158.

PSALM 25:1–22

Psalm of Disorientation

Hope from Hopelessness

LIKE PSALMS 9–10, PSALM 25 is also an incomplete acrostic: here the ו *Waw* and ק *Qoph* segments are missing, the ר *Resh* segment is duplicated, and an additional פ *Pe* segment has been added at the end. Yet the total number of verses is maintained at 22, corresponding to the number of letters in the Hebrew alphabet, suggesting that there is design even in its "incomplete" status.

Translation

25:1 [א ALEPH] To You, Yahweh,
 I lift up my soul, my God.
25:2 [ב BETH] In You I trust, let me not be ashamed;
 let not my enemies exult over me.
25:3 [ג GIMEL] Indeed, all who hope in You will not be ashamed;
 they will be ashamed—those who act unfaithfully without cause.
25:4 [ד DALETH] Your paths, Yahweh, make me know;
 Your ways, teach me.
25:5 [ה HE] Guide me in the path of Your truth
 and teach me, for You are the God of my deliverance;
 in You I hope all the day.
25:6 [ז ZAYIN] Remember Your compassions, Yahweh,
 and Your lovingkindnesses, for they are from eternity.
25:7 [ח CHETH] The sins of my youth and my rebellions, do not remember,
 according to Your lovingkindness, You—do remember me,
 because of Your goodness, Yahweh.
25:8 [ט TETH] Good and upright is Yahweh;
 therefore He instructs sinners in the path.

25:9	[י YODH]	He guides the path of the humble in ordinances,
		and He teaches the humble His path.
25:10	[כ KAPH]	All the ways of Yahweh are lovingkindness and truth
		to those who preserve His covenant and His decrees.
25:11	[ל LAMED]	Because of Your name, Yahweh,
		pardon my iniquity, for it is great.
25:12	[מ MEM]	Who, then, is the one who fears Yahweh?
		He instructs him in the path he should choose.
25:13	[נ NUN]	His soul remains in goodness,
		and his descendants possess the land.
25:14	[ס SAMEKH]	The counsel of Yahweh is for those who fear Him,
		and His covenant He makes them know.
25:15	[ע AYIN]	My eyes are constantly toward Yahweh,
		for He—He brings forth my feet from the net.
25:16	[פ PE]	Face towards me and be gracious to me,
		for alone and afflicted I am.
25:17	[צ TSADE]	The distresses of my heart are increased;
		from my straits bring me forth.
25:18	[ר RESH]	Look upon my affliction and my trouble,
		and forgive all my sins.
25:19	[ר RESH]	Look upon my enemies, for they are many,
		and with violent hatred they hate me.
25:20	[ש SHIN]	Guard my soul and rescue me;
		may I not be ashamed, for I seek refuge in You.
25:21	[ת TAW]	May integrity and uprightness preserve me,
		for I hope in You.
25:22	[פ PE]	Redeem Israel, God,
		out of all its distresses.

Structure

The psalm is carefully structured with a petition (to Yahweh), and significant portions dealing with penitence (also directed towards Yahweh) and ancillary instruction (to others in the community).[1]

---

1. Modified from Craigie, *Psalms 1–50*, 217–18. In this psalm there is a high concentration of verbs related to instruction and teaching that have God as the subject: 25:4a, 4b, 5a, 5b, 8b, 9a, 9b, 12b, 14b. The occurrence of both "enemies" and one's own sins in this psalm, functioning as landmines and IEDs along the paths and courses of life, justify the composition's petitionary and penitential character.

> **A** To Yahweh: Petition 1 **(25:1–3)**
> "my soul" (25:1b); "ashamed" (25:2a); "my enemies" (25:2b); "hope" (25:3a)
>
>> **B** To Yahweh: Penitence 1 **(25:4–7)**
>> "sins of my youth" (25:7a)
>
>>> **C** To Others: Instruction **(25:8–10)**
>>> "He instructs ... in the path" (25:8b); "His covenant" (25:10b)
>
>>>> **D** To Yahweh: Penitence 2 **(25:11)**
>
>>> **C'** To Others: Instruction **(25:12–15)**
>>> "He instructs ... in the path" (25:12b); "His covenant" (25:14b)
>
>> **B'** To Yahweh: Penitence 3 **(25:16–18)**
>> "my sins" (25:18b)
>
> **A'** To Yahweh: Petition 2 **(25:19–22)**
> "my enemies" (25:19a); "my soul" (25:20a); "ashamed" (25:20b); "hope" (25:21b)

Theological Focus

In times of distress, whether caused by external enemies or internal iniquities, the people of God remain steadfastly hoping in God who alone can provide deliverance and long-term stability in life, in keeping with his gracious character, as they seek to walk in the paths of God, learning his ways.

Commentary

To Yahweh: Petition 1 (25:1–3)

The psalm commences with two vocatives used to address deity: "Yahweh" and "my God" (25:1), a double invocation, as it were, as the first three verses petition God to not let the supplicant down in his distress at the virulence of enemies. "To you ... I lift up my soul" (25:1) likely indicates a posture of trusting worship. But it is a confidence tinged with anxiety. The potential of being "ashamed" that the supplicant fears (25:2a) involves his current apparent abandonment by God, thus giving enemies a reason to rejoice over his failures, illnesses, bereavements, disasters. Yet he reaffirms his confidence that the tables will be turned: those who hope in God will *not* be "ashamed" (25:3a); instead, it will be those adversaries, unfaithful ones, who will be "ashamed" (25:3b) for failing to trust in God themselves.[2]

---

2. The verb translated "hope" is קוה, *qwh*, and may also be translated "wait," but a cognate of the verb, תִּקְוָה, *tiqwah*, is often translated "hope" in the OT.

This motif of life-situation reversal is remarkably demonstrated by a literary-structure reversal in the chiasm of 25:3:

Conjunction	"Indeed,
Participle	all who hope in You
Verb	will not be ashamed;
Verb	they will be ashamed—
Participle	those who act unfaithfully
Adverb	without cause."

Thus "hoping in You," i.e., waiting and trusting in God, is the antithesis of "acting unfaithfully." All that to say, as long as there is God, there is hope!

To Yahweh: Penitence 1 (25:4–7)

While there were "enemies" in 25:1–3, there are also the supplicant's own failures he has to contend with in 25:4–7. Dangers and disasters along the path of life are constituted not by external enemies alone, but also by internal iniquities—one's own "sins," (25:7a; also 25:18b), "rebellions" (25:7a), and "iniquity" (25:11b). It is best to see both 25:4–5 that petitions God for teaching and instruction, and 25:6 that asks God for compassion and lovingkindness, in the light of those failures. Because the supplicant is veering off the paths of God, he seeks guidance (25:4–5), and because he has been doing so from his youth as a sinner, he seeks God's forgiveness (25:6).[3] That hoped-for "deliverance" (25:5b) from both malefactors external and misdeeds internal, only God can provide, so "in You I hope all the day" (25:5c). Thereby the motif of hoping, introduced in 25:3a, returns in 25:5c.

The repetition of "remember" in 25:6a, 7a intensifies the plea: God is to "remember" his own "compassions" and "lovingkindnesses" (both nouns are plural) which are longstanding—eternal; but God is *not* to "remember" the psalmist's "sins" and "rebellions" (both these are plural, too) which are also longstanding—from his youth. And, the sufferer adds, "remember me" (25:7b) in proportion to God's "lovingkindness" and "goodness" (both singular, 25:7bc). Thus "lovingkindness*es*" and "compassion*s*" for "sin*s*" and "rebellion*s*" (all plural: 25:6–7a) are to be accompanied by "lovingkindness" and "goodness" toward "me" (all singular: 25:7bc). "His prayer, in effect, separates sin from the sinner; he prays 'do not remember the sins' . . . , but 'please remember me' (the sinner)" because of who you are, gracious and good!"[4]

In this section, we also witness the first disruption of the acrostic, with the missing ו *Waw* segment that should have followed the ה *He* segment in 25:5. Interestingly enough, 25:5 is the first of two tricola in this psalm; in tricola, often the third line, breaking the standard bicola pattern, calls attention to itself. Here, in 25:5c, one finds the verb קוה ("hope") that contains both ו, *w*, and ק, *q*, the two letter segments missing in the acrostic of this psalm (more on this below). In any case, whether the turbulence in life is created by perfidious enemies or caused by personal sins (or both), hoping and waiting in God is the only solution.

---

3. Hence, my label of this section, *Penitence*.

4. Craigie, *Psalms 1–50*, 220. And 25:7b is emphatic with a redundant pronoun, "You," that is already implied in the (second-person) imperative verb, "do remember."

To Others: Instruction (25:8–10)

And this solution is now addressed to the community in words of instruction. Because of his "goodness" (and lovingkindness; 25:6–7) Yahweh forgives, and because he is "good" (and upright) he also guides sinners (25:8) and the humble (25:9) to get back on track with him.[5] God's "lovingkindness" and his "truth" (25:10a; also 25:5a, 6b) are the two qualities that characterize the "ways of Yahweh" for those who seek his word for direction and guidance (i.e., God's "ordinances," "covenant," and "decrees," 25:9a, 10b). That is to say, keeping the ways of Yahweh will result in the experience of divine lovingkindness and truth.[6]

To Yahweh: Penitence 2 (25:11)

And thus we come to the center of the psalm that beseeches Yahweh "because of Your name," i.e., for the sake of his reputation and nature (25:11; akin to "according to Your lovingkindness," 25:7b, and "because of Your goodness," 25:7c), to "pardon" the supplicant's "great" iniquity. He had already asked God to "not remember" his sins in 25:7a, and later he will also implore God to "forgive" (25:18b). Thus, throughout the psalm, there is a personal sense of having violated divine norms and strayed off God's path. Perhaps that is why the focus on "path(s)" in this psalm is considerable: the noun (דֶּרֶךְ, *derek*) shows up in 25:4a, 5a, 8b, 9b, 12b; and the verb (דרך, *drk*, "guides the path") in 25:9a. In addition, there is the synonym "way(s)" (אֹרַח, *'orach*) in 25:4b, 10a. Notice also the many expressions for divine pedagogy; "teach" in 25:4b, 5b, 9b; "make me know" in 25:4a (and "make them know" in 25:14b); "guide" in 25:5a, 9a; "instructs" in 25:8b, 12b. For one who acknowledges personal "iniquity, for it is great," such an emphasis on getting right with God, on his path, as directed by him, is appropriate and necessary.[7]

To Others: Instruction (25:12–15)

The psalm now returns to a second instruction section, paralleling that in 25:8–10: God "instructs" sinners "in the path" (25:8b), and God "instructs" the God-fearer "in the path" (25:12). Just as the "sinner" in 25:8 is equated with the "humble" willing to take correction (25:9), so also the sinner becomes the God-fearer willing to follow divine demand (25:12). The result is

---

5. The word עָנָו, *'anaw*, generally indicates the afflicted, but here in the context of the sins of the supplicant, it denotes those "humble," the ones willing to accept divine correction (25:9a, 9b). Notice the psalmist identifying himself with this cohort: "Yahweh ... teach *me*" in 25:4b has its parallel in "He teaches the *humble*" (25:9b).

6. This, as happens frequently in the Psalms, is not to assert that only with absolute obedience will God's lovingkindness be offered. Not at all, for that would not be grace, but a commercial, contractual exchange of chattel. Rather, in the Psalms, it indicates more an ongoing commitment to God and a demonstration of *relative* integrity and uprightness in the past. And such integrity and uprightness is necessary for the conditional experience of God's unconditional love (as Jude 21 also reminds us: "Keep yourselves in the love of God"—i.e., it is possible to take ourselves out of the love of God).

7. In connection with "covenant and testimonies," signifying the *Torah* (25:10b), and "covenant" parallel to "counsel" in 25:14, it is likely that "paths" and "ways" in this psalm (25:4a, 4b, 5a, 8b, 9b, 12b) also generally refer to divine revelation (as in Deut 5:33 which follows the Decalogue). This is also substantiated by the parallel "Your *paths*, Yahweh, make me know" (Ps 25:4a) and "His *covenant* He makes them know" (25:14b), as well as the paralleling of "ordinances" with "path" in 25:9. See Abernethy, "God as Teacher," 342–43.

that God's "goodness" (25:7c; see also "good" in 25:8a) becomes the state of "goodness" of the one obeying God (25:13a), with long-term stability guaranteed ("his descendants possess the land," 25:13b).[8] He had earlier beseeched Yahweh to "make me know" his paths (25:4); now in 25:14 he declares that God "makes them [God-fearers] know" his covenant.[9]

In 25:15 there is a slight shift in tone: though addressed to others, the supplicant makes his case personal (which he had not done thus far in the earlier *To Others* section [25:8–10], or in this one until 25:15). The mention of "net" in 25:15b suggests that enemies are again in focus. In any case his confidence is sure: "My eyes are constantly toward Yahweh" (25:15a) who will be his deliverer. Once again this is the image of hoping and waiting upon God and God alone.

To Yahweh: Penitence 3 (25:16–18)

The notion of penitence, a deep awareness of one's own failings, reappears ("sins," 25:18b; earlier there were "sins" and "rebellions," 25:7a; "sinners," 25:8b; and "iniquity," 25:11b). But while there is a focus on personal sins in 25:18b (as the parallel sections of *Penitence 1* in 25:4-7 and *Penitence 2* in 5:11 also substantiate), the "distresses of my heart" and "my straits" (25:17[10]), and "my affliction" and "my trouble" (25:18a) are likely to be related to the enemies, as hinted at by the "net" in 25:15b. And so the poet's confidence that God "brings forth [יצא, *yts'*]" his feet from that trap (25:15b) is continued in his petition in 25:17b to "bring him forth [יצא]" from his dire circumstances. Also notice how "my eyes are constantly *toward* [אֶל, *'el*] Yahweh" (25:15) becomes a plea to Yahweh to "face *towards* [אֶל] me" (25:16a): he looks to Yahweh, and he desires that Yahweh look to him—the imperative "look" in 25:18a emphasizes this request.[11]

So this *Penitence* section concerns more than just the sufferer's own evildoing; his enemies are part of his bane. Nonetheless, personal "sins" have not been overlooked (25:18b); they are indeed multiplying his "affliction" (25:18a; and making him "afflicted," 25:16b), and he is left all "alone," bereft of aid (25:16b). "The acuteness of the loneliness and the sense of distance from God are amplified by their dual source; they are partly a consequence of the psalmist being surrounded by enemies who create trouble and partly a consequence of the awareness of sin within."[12] And so not only does Yahweh have to deliver him from enemies, he has to "forgive all my sins" (25:18b). At the beginning of the psalm, this individual had "lifted [נשא, *ns'*]" up his soul to God (25:1b); now a reciprocation is appealed for: Would that God would "forgive [also נשא]" his sins (25:18b)—all of them! There is here, unlike in the previous sections, a seeming sense of unmitigated hopelessness, but that would be a misreading of these verses....

---

8. Though the distressed supplicant lifted up his "soul" to God (25:1b), he is confident that the God-fearer's "soul" will remain in goodness, i.e., without sinning (25:13a), because God answers his subsequent plea to guard his "soul" (25:20a).

9. Fearing God shows up in 25:12a, 14a; it is the attitude of the sinner who is humble enough to accede to the demand of a holy God.

10. An interesting play of words occurs in 25:17: "straits" is מְצוּקָה, *mtsuqah*, that has the sense of narrowing. But the psalmist complains that his distresses are "increased," רחב, *rchb*, which also has the sense of broadening. Thus "the distresses of my heart are *broadening*; from my *narrowing*, bring me out"!

11. But the repeat of "look" in 25:19a is for Yahweh to also "look upon *my enemies*"—obviously not with favor. Also note the theme of vision in 25:15a: "My eyes are constantly toward Yahweh."

12. Craigie, *Psalms 1-50*, 221.

It is after 25:17 (the צ *Tsade* segment) that the ק *Qoph* segment goes AWOL. Earlier, after 25:5 (the ח *Cheth* segment), it was the ו *Waw* segment that had disapparated. It was also pointed out earlier that the third line of the first of the only two tricola in this psalm, 25:5c, contained the verb קוה, "hope" (it also occurs in 25:3a, 21b). That these missing letter-segments in the acrostic, ו *Waw* and ק *Qoph*, are also the key letters of the word קוה, suggest a critical role for "hope" in Psalm 25.[13] Besides, those very letters ו and ק show up together in מִמְּצוּקוֹתַי, *mimmtsuqotay*, "from my straits" (25:17b). Thus this word indicating *hope*lessness contains within it the word signaling *hope* (coded by its two key Hebrew letters)! Indeed, the phrase "from my straits bring me forth" (25:17b) could well be a poetic wink directing us to extract ("bring . . . forth" or "bring out") hope (the letters ו and ק) from hopelessness ("from my straits").

Note also that קִוִּיתִי, *qiwwiti*, "I hope," occurred in 25:5c, right before the missing ו *Waw* segment (i.e., hoping in vain all day for something not there), and likewise מִמְּצוּקוֹתַי, with its inbuilt ו and ק (25:17b), is positioned right before the missing ק *Qoph* segment. In any case, the message of this psalm is "hope in God, even when it looks like all is lost. So in 25:17b, ממצוקותי, *mmtswqwty*, "a word which has hope embedded within distress, sums up the entire message of this acrostic."[14] Indeed, all is not lost—as long as there is God, there *is* hope! (Needless to add, this is ingenious inscription at its inspired best!)

To Yahweh: Petition 2 (25:19–22)

And so, the sufferer yields his turmoil to God in the final petition in 25:19–22. "Enemies" show up again in 25:19a (as in 25:2b). But, as has already been observed, external impeachers *and* internal impieties are significant in this psalm: the supplicant's iniquity is "great" (רַב, *rav*, 25:11b), and his enemies are "many" (רבב, *rbb*, 25:19a)—no wonder the distresses of his heart are "increased" (רחב, 25:17a). The psalm that began with a petition that the sufferer "not be

---

13. The first two letters of קוה show up in all its forms and conjugations; the final ה (a guttural consonant, that renders קוה a "weak" verb) can drop out in certain forms of the verb—a process called apocopation. It is possible that the original tri-radical root of this verb had י, *y*, instead of ה, *h*, in the third position. In that case, ה might be functioning in קוה simply as a *mater lectionis*, a sort of placeholder for the vowel that preceded the absconding י. I am grateful to John Hilber for his input on this discussion (December 21, 2022).

14. Benun, "Evil and the Disruption of Order," 12 (also see 26n34, 26n35). Validating this interpretation is the fact that in the first acrostic of the Psalter, Psalms 9–10 (also incomplete, as is Psalm 25), it was the *appearance* of the ו *Waw* and ק *Qoph* segments that restored order in 9:7 and 10:12, respectively (*hope*—or its code—appears and order is regained); here in Psalm 25, it is the *disappearance* of those same letters and segments that signals disruption (the code for *hope* disappears and all order is lost). That these two acrostics, Psalms 9–10 and 25, are working off each other is clear: 9:3 has the psalmist "exulting" in Yahweh; 25:2 has the psalmist requesting that his enemies not "exult" over him. The employment of this rare verb (עלץ, *'lts*; elsewhere in the Psalter only in 5:11 and 68:4; and only four more times in the rest of the OT) indicates purposeful design. As well, "net" shows up in 10:9 (the wicked hoping to trap the righteous in it) and in 25:15 (God rescuing the righteous from it). These, and the occurrence of "net" in 9:16, are the first three instances of the word in the Psalter—all in the first two acrostics of the book, Psalms 9–10 and Psalm 25. One notices other similarities in those acrostic textual loci. In both Psalm 10 and 25 the victim is the "afflicted" (10:9b; 25:16b); and in both, "eyes" are involved (10:8, those of the wicked watching for the righteous; 25:15, those of the righteous watching for God). All that to say that the first and second acrostic in the Psalms evidence careful organization and arrangement, making it extremely likely that the ו and ק interplays between them are deliberate. See Benun, "Evil and the Disruption of Order," 12–13. One could also conceive of the "increase" in distresses in 25:17 as the cause of the subsequent disorder and disappearance of ק *Qoph* segment; and the double "look upon" in 25:18a, 19a as resulting in (or necessitating) the duplication of the ר *Resh* segment.

ashamed" (25:2b) ends with a similar appeal ("may I not be ashamed," 25:20b).[15] His confidence that his "integrity and uprightness" will "preserve" him (25:21a) marks him as one of those who "preserve" God's covenant and decrees (25:10b). Yet his final hope is in God alone and therefore he "hopes" in him (25:21b), making the closing entreaty for the redemption of the entire community from "all its distresses" quite appropriate (25:22).[16] God will act, not just for the psalmist, but for all who "hope" in him, with "integrity and uprightness" (25:21).

The final verse, 25:22, a second פ *Pe* segment, appears to be out of place at the end of the acrostic.[17] But thereby the first word of the opening א *Aleph* segment, the first word of the middle ל *Lamed* segment, and that of the closing פ *Pe* segment begin (obviously) with א, ל, and פ (', *l*, and *p*) respectively, hinting at the verb אלף, *'lp*, "learn" (as in Prov 22:25).[18] Indeed, we must *learn*, about *hope* in *hope*less times!

Sermon Map

I. Hopelessness of Life
    External enemies (25:1–3; 19–22)
    Internal iniquity (25:4–7, 11, 16–18)
    Move-to-relevance: Hopelessness in our lives

II. Hopefulness with God
    The distortion and reordering of the acrostic
    Waiting on God (25:3, 5, [17], 21)
    Move-to-relevance: How God is our hope

III. Honorableness in Godliness
    God's guidance (25:8–10, 12–15)
    Move-to-relevance: Hopefulness involves honorableness (faithfulness)

IV. *Wait and Pray!*
    Specifics on waiting upon God with faithfulness to him

---

15. Mentions of "my soul" (25:1b, 20a) and "hope" (25:3a, 21b) also are parallel.

16. Also note that in 25:8a it was God who was called "upright"; now in 25:21a, the psalmist lays claim to his own "uprightness," no doubt because he was keeping divine demand (with divine help).

17. This is not unique in an acrostic psalm: Psalm 34 also ends with a second פ *Pe* segment. Interestingly, the פ-words that commence both 25:22 and 34:22 are derived from the same root, פדה (*pdh*, "redeem"). "It is clear that a deliberate program of alteration and adaptation has taken place in both cases" (Freedman, "Patterns in Psalms 25 and 34," 127).

18. Brug, "Biblical Acrostics," 288. The duplication of פ, *p*, could also have been a historical idiosyncrasy akin to the Greek alphabet that has both π and φ (*p* and *ph*).

PSALM 26:1–12

Psalm of Disorientation

Plea of the Committed

THE LOCATION OF THIS psalm after Psalm 25 makes sense, as 26:1a refers to the supplicant's "integrity" and "trust" (linking to 25:2a, 21a), and 26:3 points to Yahweh's "lovingkindness" and "truth" (linking to 25:10). The petition for redemption in 26:11b also harks back to the closing request in 25:22a. "Like Ps 25, it lacks any lament or the urgency that suggests a current crisis in the supplicant's life, and rather suggests a prayer that people could pray at any time."[1] But unlike the previous psalm with a consciousness of personal sin, the psalmist here is confident about his commitment to Yahweh and grounds his petition for help in that certainty, adopting a self-vindicating posture.[2]

Translation

26:1 Judge for me, Yahweh, for I—in my integrity I walk,
 and in Yahweh I trust; I will not waver.
26:2 Try me, Yahweh, and test me;
 refine my innards and my heart.
26:3 For Your lovingkindness is before my eyes,
 and I walk in Your truth.
26:4 I do not sit with deceitful people,
 and with the treacherous I will not go.
26:5 I hate the assembly of evildoers,
 and with the wicked I will not sit.
26:6 I shall wash my palms in innocence,
 and I will go around Your altar, Yahweh,
26:7 That I may cause to be heard, with the voice, thanksgiving,
 and declare all Your wonders.

---

1. Goldingay, *Psalms*, 1:380.
2. Which does not obviate divine grace, of course (see 26:11).

26:8   Yahweh, I love the habitation of Your house
           and the place where abides Your glory.
26:9   Do not take away with sinners, my soul,
           and with people of bloodshed, my life.
26:10 In whose hands is a wicked plan,
           and their right hand is full of bribery.
26:11 But I—in my integrity I will walk;
           redeem me, and be gracious to me.
26:12 My foot stands on a level place;
           in the assemblies I will bless Yahweh.

Structure

Psalm 26 may be visualized chiastically, with sections on *Challenge to God*, *Worship of God*, and *Pledge to God* (with no evildoers mentioned) surrounding sections dealing with *Claim against evildoers* and *Plea against evildoers* (with no Yahweh mentioned):[3]

A   *Challenge to God* (**26:1–3**): "Yahweh" (×3) [no evildoers]
           "integrity I walk," "not waver" (26:1)

  B   *Claim against evildoers* (**26:4–5**): dissociation from four groups
             "deceitful," "treacherous" (26:4)
             "evildoers," "wicked" (26:5)

    C   *Worship of God* (**26:6–8**): "Yahweh" (×2) [no evildoers]

  B' *Plea against evildoers* (**26:9–10**): dissociation from four groups
             "sinners," "people of bloodshed" (26:9)
             "wicked plan[ners]," "bribe[rs]" (26:10)

A' *Pledge to God* (**26:11–12**): "Yahweh" [no evildoers]
           "integrity I will walk" (26:11); "foot stands on a level place" (26:12)

Effectively, the psalm is a defense of the supplicant, adducing his nearness to Yahweh and his distancing from evildoers. Both these exculpatory postures permeate the psalm.

Theological Focus

> The people of God, faithful to him—and dissociating themselves from those who are not—are confident that God will intervene on their behalf, because of their commitment to him in all things, including worship, and because of divine grace, that also leads them to promise ongoing faithfulness to God in the future.

---

3. Modified from Mosca, "Psalm 26," 212–37; and Bellinger, "Psalm XXVI," 460.

Commentary

Challenge to God (26:1–3)

While this section commences with a plea—"judge for me, Yahweh" (26:1a)[4]—it is actually a challenge to God: "Help me, for I've been committed to You and I trust You unwaveringly." The supplicant is the subject of three verbs in 26:1: "I walk," "I trust," and "I will not waver."[5] Correspondingly, after the opening lines in 26:1, Yahweh is also challenged to do three things and is the subject of three verbs (with the supplicant as the object): "Examine me," "try me," and "test my innards [literally, 'kidneys,' equivalent to the modern 'mind'] and my heart" (26:2).[6] The psalmist is confident about "my integrity," "my innards," "my heart," and "my eyes" (26:1a, 2b, 3a; and later, "my palms" [26:6a] and "my foot" [26:12a]): these body parts have remained faithful to Yahweh, therefore, he implies, Yahweh needs to be faithful to him in return. There seems to be a deliberate movement from the core of his being (26:2b) to his eyes (26:3a) and down to his hands (26:6a), and his feet (26:12a).[7] The entirety of his being has been marked by "integrity" (26:1a, 11a) and is committed to God![8] This emphasis on his own innocence is underscored by reference to himself in the psalm twenty-nine times—in pronouns, and verb and nominal suffixes. "The speaker's individuality is not, however, a goal in itself, for the 'I' is defined by its proper relationship with and its dependence on the divine 'you.'"[9] Indeed, in 26:3 one finds the following structure comprising first-person suffixes (referring to the supplicant) balanced by (and ensconced by!) second-person suffixes (referring to God):

> "Your lovingkindness"
> "my eyes"
> "I walk"
> "Your truth"

This balance holds steady even when the psalmist makes a claim to integrity: He "walks" in *his* integrity (26:1a), but he "walks" in *God's* truth (26:3b), rendered chiastically again.

---

4. The "judgment" sought suggests a forensic setting, which indicates that some sort of injustice was plaguing the supplicant: he had to petition God to render a ruling to vindicate him.

5. And there is an emphatic (and redundant) first-person pronoun in 26:1a: "*I*—in my integrity I walk."

6. "Examine" and "test" are smelting terms, used of the refining of precious metals.

7. Perhaps feet are implied in "walk" as well, in 26:1a, 3b, 11a (and maybe even in "go," 26:4b). There is also "voice" and "heard" (in 26:7a), suggesting mouth and ears, respectively, though the latter is that of the community. As well, "my soul," equated to "my life" in 26:9. (If I were a smart aleck, I'd also point out "sit" in 26:4a, 5b and relate that to a body part. But I'm not!)

8. Mosca, "Psalm 26," 222. As elsewhere in the Psalms, this is not an affirmation of absolute sinlessness, but only a relative integrity and commitment to God. (I acknowledge my debt to Mosca, from whom I have borrowed liberally for my commentary on this psalm.)

9. Mosca, "Psalm 26," 221, 224.

PSALM 26:1-12

"in *my* integrity I walk"	**26:1a**
...	
"I walk in *Your* truth"	**26:3b**

At least one basis for praying that God would act is the supplicant's own commitment to God, the grace of God aiding and facilitating that individual's integrity.

Claim against evildoers (26:4–5)

This section continues the focus on the psalmist and his activities. Four groups of nefarious characters are named here: "deceitful people," "the treacherous," "the assembly of evildoers," and "the wicked" (26:4–5), and from all of them the supplicant claims to keep distance.[10] The comprehensiveness of the supplicant's claim to be unlike evildoers is depicted in the double chiasm of 26:4–5, with the wicked at the center of each and the psalmist's assertions of independence from them bounding each core pair:

"I do not sit" "deceitful people"	**26:4a**
"the treacherous" "I will not go"	**26:4b**
"I hate" "the assembly of evildoers"	**26:5a**
"the wicked" "I will not sit"	**26:5b**

These activities include both dynamic lifestyle elements: "I walk" (26:3b), "I will not go" (26:4b); and static ones: "I do not sit" (26:4a), "I hate" (36:5a), "I will not sit" (26:5b). As well, they include both present actions ("I do not sit," "I hate") and future ones ("I will not go," "I will not sit"). All because "Your lovingkindness is before my eyes" (26:3a), an assertion that forms a sort of heading for the list.

Neither in 26:4–5 or later in 26:9–10 (that displays another quartet of evildoers) are the psalmist and the wicked directly connected, morally (in real life) or even literarily (in the text): in this psalm, the latter are not shown doing anything to the former, and vice versa. They are, as the psalmist is at pains to affirm, entirely separate, incongruent and irreconcilable. "The only connections directly affirmed are between the 'you' [Yahweh] and the 'I' [psalmist]; the only connections explicitly denied [in 26:4–5] are between the 'I' and the 'they.'"[11] Thus while the first section (*Challenge to God*, 26:1–3) stressed the *association* between supplicant and deity, here in *Claim against evildoers* (26:4–5), it is all about *dissociation* of supplicant and

---

10. Later, in the corresponding section dealing with evildoers (26:9–10), four more arrant gangs are named and dissociated from.

11. Mosca, "Psalm 26," 221.

wicked. And as is visible in the structure of Psalm 26, 26:1–3, 26:6–8, and 26:11–12 (*A*, *C*, and *A'*; see structure above) make no mention of evildoers, while, correspondingly, the other two sections, 26:4–5 and 26:9–10 (*B* and *B'*) make no mention of Yahweh.[12] So it is not just that the wicked are dissociated from the righteous one, but they are disjoined when the psalmist is associated with Yahweh. The loyalties of the people of God are clear and lines are strictly maintained, an integral part of their commitment to God!

Worship of God (26:6–8)

If 26:4–5 emphasized what the supplicant would *not* do, 26:6–8, the central core of the psalm (*C*), details all that he *will* do, as we are returned to a section dealing once again with his *association* with God, the one the psalmist is committed to.

It is obvious that progress has been made as the psalm moved from 26:1–2 to 26:6–8: the many first-person suffixes (referencing the "I" of the supplicant) have given way here to second-person suffixes (referencing the "You" of deity): the focus has shifted prominently to God and divine verities: "*Your* altar," "*Your* wonders," "*Your* house," and "*Your* glory" (26:6–8). He had earlier declared his "hatred" of the assembly of evildoers (26:5a); now he pronounces his "love" for the habitation of Yahweh's house, the temple, "the place where abides Your glory" (26:8). This is the first mention of a location in the psalm; thus far we have seen only persons. All that to say, whereas the supplicant had stated his moral commitment to God in 26:1–2, now it is his cultic/religious commitment to deity in the presence of God that is in view.[13]

The cultic activities engaged in by the psalmist include: ablution of hands "in innocence" (an outward declaration of guiltlessness[14]), going around the altar (to make the sacrifices at God's table, where the presence of deity was felt and his fellowship enjoyed), giving thanks, and proclaiming God's deeds (26:6–7[15]). "Only here [in 26:6–8] do we find that the references to the divine 'you' outnumber and, by the end of the section, even dwarf the speaker's 'I.' If in [this section] this 'I' circles around 'your altar,' it is also fair to say that the poem itself circles around [these verses, 26:6–8, textually]. At its center is the temple, the appointed meeting-place of 'you,' God, and 'I.'"[16]

Strikingly, 26:6b is the only place in the OT where "go around" and "altar" are juxtaposed; access to the altar was always strictly limited to appropriate cultic officiants.[17] But perhaps this is not surprising in Psalm 26, where the innocence of the supplicant has already been

---

12. Creating an equally delicate balance is the "and with [וְעִם, *w'im*]" (in 26:4b, 5b, and 9b) and עִם, *'im*, "with" (in 26:4a, 9a)—found only in those parallel sections dealing with evildoers—once again denoting dissociation between supplicant and wicked. Instead, the preposition in the other three sections dealing with the psalmist and Yahweh is always בְּ, *b*: "*in* my integrity," "*in* Yahweh" (26:1), "*in* Your truth" (26:3b); "*in* innocence" (26:6a), "*with* the voice" (26:7a); and "*in* my integrity" (26:11a), "*on* a level place," "*in* the assemblies" (26:12) (see Mosca, "Psalm 26," 226).

13. If the psalmist so loves God's habitation (26:8a), how much more must he love God himself!

14. This cleanness of "palms" (26:6a) is in contrast to the upper extremities of the wicked that bear evil plans and foul bribes (26:10a, 10b; each of these three instances of upper limb parts translates a different Hebrew noun).

15. There is a sonic resonance between קוֹל, *qol*, "voice" (26:7a), and כֹּל, *kol*, "all" (26:7b), emphasizing the proclamation by the psalmist of the prominence of Yahweh.

16. Mosca, "Psalm 26," 228–29.

17. Mosca, "Psalm 26," 230.

vigorously proclaimed; indeed, the fact of his proximity to the altar further substantiates his claim to blamelessness and commitment to God.

Plea against evildoers (26:9–11)

Once again, the dissociation of the supplicant from evildoers is described—here, too, four groups of the thugs are named: "sinners," "people of bloodshed" (26:9), and those "in whose hands is a wicked plan," whose "right hand is full of bribery" (26:10). But this is dissociation of a different kind: earlier it was the poet himself doing the distancing; here the psalmist wants *God* to keep him clear of these malignant ones, lest he get caught up in their punishment at the hand of deity. While this plea may reiterate the sufferer's innocence, it may also depict him as being conscious of some guilt,[18] but seeking relief as he throws himself upon the mercy of God. In any case, he is acknowledging that his integrity was (and is), first and foremost, a matter of God's gracious protection. Which leads him to his final plea, couched in a promise....

Pledge to God (26:11–12)

Going from a perfect verb ("I walk") in 26:1a to an imperfect form ("I will walk") in 26:11a, the supplicant promises to live "a complete life, beginning in the past, and carrying on into the future," a comprehensive commitment to God.[19] This is expressed emphatically again in 26:11a (as in 26:1a) with a redundant first-person pronoun: "But I—in my integrity, I will walk." Whereas earlier he had declared he would "not waver" (26:1b), here his pronouncement is that his "foot stands on a level place" (26:12a)—no doubt unwavering, unshakable, steadfast, and solid. And rather than associate with the "assembly of evildoers" (26:5a), he vows to bless Yahweh in the "assemblies," likely of the righteous (26:12b). Though the psalmist incurs a duty here, there is also a plea in 26:11b that recognizes divine deliverance and divine grace. Appropriately enough, with this consciousness, 26:11–12 begins with "I" and ends with "Yahweh."

> [Psalm 26] reminds us that, ideally, people who pray need to be able to claim moral integrity and religious commitment, and must dissociate themselves from the faithless. The psalm surely presupposes that God's relationship with us is based first on God's acceptance of us, not on our deserving, but this underlines rather than undermines the need for people of whom God takes hold to commit themselves in integrity and trust.... People who lack moral integrity and trust in God can still pray for God to deliver them and may well find that God responds, but people who can claim moral integrity and trust in God have more basis for leaning on God to do so.[20]

And may the people of God, therefore, be both morally upright and spiritually trusting!

---

18. Or at least aware of the potential of his succumbing to the wiles of these villains.
19. Botha, "Poetry and Perlocution," 38.
20. Goldingay, *Psalms*, 1:388.

Sermon Map

I. Walking with God
   Personal integrity (26:1–2, 12a)
   God's help for personal integrity (26:3, 11b)
   Move-to-relevance: What integrity looks like

II. Withdrawing from the Ungodly
   Distancing from evildoers (26:4–5)
   God's help for distancing from evildoers (26:9–10, 11b)
   Waiting on God (25:3, 5, [17], 21)
   Move-to-relevance: What distancing looks like

III. Worshiping with the Godly
   Commitment to God (26:6–8)
   Pledging allegiance (26:11a, 12b)
   Move-to-relevance: What worship looks like

IV. *Confidently Call on God, Committed to Him!*
   Specifics on developing confidence in prayer

PSALM 27:1–14

Psalm of Disorientation

Hoping in the Divine Presence

THIS PSALM IS MARKED by alternating professions of trust and petitions for deliverance. The professions have God in the third person; the petitions, in the second person. Overall, professions predominate (nine of fourteen verses), and the psalm begins and ends with these affirmations of confidence. Indeed, the first and last word of the psalm is "Yahweh" (27:1a, 14c)

Translation

27:1   Yahweh is my light and my deliverance—
          whom shall I fear?
       Yahweh is the stronghold of my life—
          whom shall I dread?
27:2   When evildoers came upon me
          to devour my flesh,
       my adversaries and my enemies against me—
          they—they stumbled and they fell.
27:3   If an army camp encamp against me,
          my heart will not fear;
       though war rise against me,
          [even] in this I am trustful.
27:4   One thing I have asked from Yahweh—
          that I shall seek:
       for me to dwell in the house of Yahweh
          all the days of my life,
       to behold the beauty of Yahweh,
          and to contemplate in His temple.

27:5   For He will conceal me in His shelter in the day of evil;
         He will hide me in the hiding place of His tent;
         on a rock He will lift me high.
27:6   And now my head will be lifted high
         above my enemies all around me,
         And I will sacrifice in His tent sacrifices with shouts of joy;
         I will sing and I will make music to Yahweh.
27:7   Hear, Yahweh; with my voice I cry,
         and be gracious to me and answer me.
27:8   On Your behalf my heart says, "Seek My face."
         Your face, Yahweh, I seek.
27:9   Do not hide Your face from me,
         do not turn aside, in anger, Your servant;
       My help You have been.
         Do not abandon me and do not leave me,
         God of my deliverance.
27:10 For my father and my mother have left me,
         but Yahweh will take me in.
27:11 Teach me, Yahweh, Your path,
         and lead me on a level way.
       Because of my watchful foes
27:12   do not give me over to the desire of my adversaries;
       for false witnesses have risen against me,
         those breathing out violence.
27:13 Unless I had believed in seeing the goodness of Yahweh
         in the land of the living . . . .
27:14 Hope in Yahweh;
         be strong and let your heart take courage;
         and hope in Yahweh.

Structure

Professions alternating with petitions form the structure of the psalm:

27:1–6	**Profession 1** (God: third person)	
	27:1–3	*Confidence*
	27:4–6	*Concealment*
27:7–9	**Petition 1** (God: second person)	
27:10	**Profession 2** (God: third person)	
27:11–12	**Petition 2** (God: second person)	
27:13–14	**Profession 3** (God: third person)	

PSALM 27:1–14

Theological Focus

God's people hope in God without fear even in times of great oppression, seeking divine presence and guidance all their days, for God, in his goodness, has never abandoned and will never do so.

Commentary

Profession 1 (27:1–6)

The psalm (and its first profession) begins with "Yahweh," described as "my [the supplicant's] *light* [אוֹרִי, *'ori*]" and "deliverance" (27:1a). Therefore "whom shall I *fear* [אִירָא, *'ira'*]?" (27:1b). The paronomasia makes the rhetorical question poignant and the answer obvious: "No one!" For, the "light" that Yahweh is driveth out all "fear." In a second rhetorical question with "whom?" another affirmation is made: neither will the supplicant dread anyone, because Yahweh is his life's "stronghold," his fortress, his bastion (27:1cd). "Evildoers," "adversaries," and "enemies" may have "come upon" him, they may have "devoured" his flesh, and been arrayed "against me," but their fate was sealed: "they—they stumbled and they fell" (note the emphatic pronoun), weak and confused (27:2).[1] The implication is that Yahweh caused this collapse.

And so, because of what Yahweh had done in the past (27:2), the psalmist can trust him for the future (27:3). "Evildoers," "adversaries," and "enemies" had been summarily dispatched once. So now even if a whole "army camp encamps" against the single individual that the supplicant constitutes, waging war against this besieged soul, "my heart will not fear" (27:3abc). Of his deliverance, he has no doubt—he is "trustful" (27:3d). One also notices that the first two verses have *five* mentions of Yahweh or of a metaphor relating to him: "Yahweh" (×2; 27:1a, 1c), "my light," "my deliverance" (27:1a), and "the stronghold of my life" (27:1c). More than adequate for the *five* mentions of foes in 27:2–3: "evildoers" (27:2a), "adversaries," "enemies" (27:2c), "army" (27:3a), and "war" (27:3c; war is personified as a "rising" foe).

All this talk of armies, camps, encampments, and war (27:3; perhaps all metaphorical[2]) pictures the psalmist on a battlefield, out in the open, all alone, with hordes of soldiers and phalanxes of combatants encamped against him ("all around," 27:6b). The wordplay makes this threat in the open space particularly intense: "army camp" is מַחֲנֶה, *machaneh*, and "if . . . [they] encamp" is אִם־תַּחֲנֶה, *'im-tachaneh* (27:3a). Appropriately, what the supplicant does next is seek refuge, avoiding this open space packed with antagonists, and heading to the "house of Yahweh," not just during the current crisis, but "all the days of my life" (27:4).[3] And that's all he wants—to dwell in the presence of his God (27:4a–d; see below). In a sense, then, this

---

1. Goldingay, *Psalms*, 1:392, notes that the postponing of the verbs that describe the fate of these variously labeled foes, "they stumbled and they fell," to the end of the line, "builds suspense." But no surprise here: with Yahweh as one's light, deliverance, and stronghold, this is an expected coup!

2. Later it is "false witnesses" who "rise" against the psalmist (27:12b). The lack of concrete detail as to what exactly was the torment being suffered by the psalmist, and who exactly was against him, lends this psalm the capacity for reuse by believers in equally dire, but different, circumstances.

3. Levine, "Symbolic Sukkah," 263.

relocation is a concealment under the protection of Yahweh and in his presence ("conceal," "shelter," "hide," and "hiding place" show up in 27:5ab).

The "beholding" of the "beauty of Yahweh" (27:4e) is not simply a gaze upon deity, something that the OT is very reluctant to endorse as being possible for a human. But the parallel construction found in 27:4f and 27:13a gives us a sense of what 27:4e might mean:[4]

	Preposition	Verb	Preposition	Object
27:4e	לְ, l "to"	חזה, chzh behold	בְּ, b [untranslated]	נֹעַם־יְהוָה, noʿam-yhwh the beauty of Yahweh"
27:4f	לְ "to"	בקר, bqr contemplate	בְּ in	הֵיכָלוֹ, hekalo His temple"
27:13a	לְ "in	ראה, rʾh seeing	בְּ [untranslated]	טוּב־יְהוָה, tov-yhwh the goodness of Yahweh"

The syntax is identical and the verb in each case is a form of perception: "to behold," "to contemplate," and "to see." The objects of these perceptive verbs are likely to be related: "beauty" of Yahweh, "temple" of Yahweh (indicating the physical locus of divine presence), and "goodness" of Yahweh. It appears, then, that proximity to the presence of God—exemplified by the beholding of his beauty, the contemplation of his dwelling, and the seeing of his goodness—is the psalmist's *summum bonum* and desire for "all the days of my life" (27:4d).[5]

That nearness of God is underscored by a number of equivalent locations noted in 27:4–5: "house of Yahweh" (27:4c), "His temple" (27:4f), "His shelter" (27:5a), "His tent" (27:5b, 6c), and perhaps even the "rock" (27:5c) on which the psalmist is lifted high by God. The "rock" may, in fact, refer to God himself, as in 28:1; 31:2, or a place of divine protection and goodwill: outside is the "*day* of evil" (27:5a), but inside the temple, in the proximity of the presence of Yahweh, is the beauty (and goodness of Yahweh, 27:13a), not just for a singular "day," but for "all the *days* of my life" (27:4de). And as a result, not only is the sufferer himself "lifted high" on a protective rock or crag (27:5c), away from the depredations of the violent, but his head is also "lifted high"—exalted and honored before those very enemies (27:6ab). In any case, this realization of God's blessings in divine presence and the consequential divine protection leads the supplicant to thanksgiving (27:6cd).

When 27:1–3 is compared with 27:4–6, one discerns a parallel sequence of protagonists, with one difference: the enemies against the psalmist (27:2) are replaced by Yahweh for him (27:5; both in bold, below), thus providing the reason for his lack of fear and his obtaining of victory.[6]

---

4. The untranslated preposition בְּ in 27:4e, 13a may be intensifying those verbs: *intensely* "behold" and "see."

5. Hartenstein, "Iconicity of the Psalms," 337. Elsewhere, 63:2–3 also has the psalmist "beholding" Yahweh in his sanctuary, seeing his power and splendor. As well, 90:17 wishes for the "favor [נֹעַם, the same word translated 'beauty' in 27:4e] of the Lord our God" to be upon his people. All of these are related to, or are the consequences of, the proximity of the psalmist to the very presence of God.

6. From van Grol, "Psalm 27:1–6," 34.

27:1	I (with Yahweh)	I (with Yahweh)		**27:4**
27:2	**Enemy** (against me)	**Yahweh** (for me)		**27:5**
27:3	I + "my heart" (unafraid)	I + "my head" (victorious)		**27:6**

Yes, Yahweh makes *all* the difference!

Petition 1 (27:7–9)

The psalm moves to petition in 27:7–9, but progress has been made since the beginning of the prayer. To the psalmist's plea that God hear him, that God be gracious to him, and that God answer him (27:7), apparently God has responded. The heart of the supplicant has spoken "on Your behalf" (literally, "for You," i.e., echoing God's voice; 27:8a): "*Seek* My face."[7] This is a divine reaffirmation of what the poet had affirmed he was doing: "I shall *seek* . . . to dwell in the house of Yahweh" (27:4bc). "Yes, indeed," God is apparently saying, "that's exactly what you need to be doing: seek My face!" (27:8a). And the psalmist, in turn, then re-reaffirms God's reaffirmation: "Your face, Yahweh, I *seek*!" (27:8b). Thus, the three parallel phrases that were looked at in 27:4e, 4f, 13a (see earlier figure) are tightly condensed into this primary injunction to abide in divine presence: "Seek My face," for it is in doing so that one beholds divine beauty, one contemplates divine presence, one glimpses divine goodness. In sum, the seeking of God's face is an exhortation to abide in the divine presence. And that, according to God, and acknowledged by the psalmist, is what God's people need to be doing in times of crisis. And so to God—whose "face" he was called to seek (27:8ab), and who the psalmist is sure will "*hide* me in the *hiding* place of His tent" (27:5b)—the petition is explicitly voiced, bringing those elements together: "Do not *hide* Your *face* from me" in anger (27:9ab).[8] Perhaps the psalmist was remembering his own failings in life and throwing himself at the mercy of God (he had already entreated deity to "be gracious to me" in 27:7b). After all, the supplicant was "Your servant" (27:9b).

Profession 2 (27:10)

Perhaps it is the use of the verb "leave [עזב, *'zv*]" in 27:9d that reminds the psalmist to make a profession before his community. That declaration in 27:10 also employs עזב: everyone, including his parents, have "left" him, but Yahweh will not; rather, deity "will take me in." Yahweh is more to him—and to all God's people—than father or mother!

---

7. This is perhaps an internal voice uttering, for God/on God's behalf, the imperative to the psalmist. Both the verb, "seek" in 27:8a (but not in 27:8b), and the object, "face," in 27:8a and 27:8b are plural; that might simply be idiosyncratic (or a transcriptional error), for the focus remains on the psalmist as a single individual and upon God's singular face.

8. There are four negative pleas to God in 27:9: "do not hide Your face," "do not turn aside," "do not abandon," and "do not leave."

Petition 3 (27:11–12)

And after raising that momentary pedagogical point and testimony in 27:10, the supplicant returns to petition in 27:11–12, this time combining a request not to be handed over to his foes with a plea that he be led by Yahweh on a "level," smooth, non-turbulent path of life (27:11b).

Profession 3 (27:13–14)

A final profession of faith by the supplicant (27:13) is left incomplete. "By saying 'unless' the supplicant strongly implies the reality of trust without declaring it, as in the form of an OT oath that similarly lacks an apodosis."[9] And, following up with an urging of confidence in Yahweh on part of his community (27:14) the psalm concludes.

Clearly, the petitions in this psalm for relief (from whatever oppression and turmoil) are grounded in this life: he expects his trustworthy God to act on his behalf here and now. God, the "stronghold of my *life*" (27:1c), he anticipates, will work wonders and demonstrate his goodness "in the land of the *living*" (27:13b), enabling the supplicant to live peacefully, dwelling in presence of Yahweh "all the days of my *life*" (27:4d).

The community-directed profession (and exhortation) in 27:14 lists four (with one repeated) ways of saying "seek My face" (27:8a): "hope in Yahweh," "be strong," "let your heart take courage," and "hope in Yahweh" (reiterated).[10] The psalm had begun with mentions of "fear" and "dread" (27:1b, 1d); it now ends with "be strong" and "take courage."[11] And: "Hope in Yahweh!" Yes, we must!

Sermon Map

I. Seeing Disaster
   Times of trouble (27:2–3c, 9, 10a)
   Move-to-relevance: Dire circumstances in our lives

II. Seeing Deity
   Confidence (27:1, 3d–4, 10b, 13)
   Deliverance (27:5–6)
   God's advice (27:7–8)
   Move-to-relevance: The presence of God

III. *See God, not Gloom!*
   Appeal (27:11–12, 14)
   Specifics on developing God-sight

---

9. Goldingay, *Psalms*, 1:399. The sentence of 27:13, left incomplete, is rhetorically labeled an aposiopesis—to convey the psalmist's intensity of emotion. Thus the ellipsis in my translation of 27:13. The presence of *puncta extraordinaria*, dots over letter (predating the Masoretes) found with לׅוּלֵׅאׅ, *lule'*, "unless" (27:13a), perhaps indicates some scribal uncertainty of the sentence in its incomplete form, but it does make good sense as it stands.

10. Together this makes another quintuplet after the fivefold description of Yahweh in 27:1 and that of the enemies in 27:2–3 (see above).

11. Especially see 27:3b: "my *heart* will not fear"; and here in 27:14b: "let your *heart* take courage."

PSALM 28:1–9

Psalm of Disorientation

The Shepherd Hears

PSALM 28 IS ANOTHER combination of petition and praise, without much lament, but unlike Psalm 27, the petition precedes the praise. Within the psalm the address to God proceeds from direct (second person, 28:1–4), to indirect (third person, 28:5 and 28:6–8), and then back to direct address (second person, 28:9).

Translation

28:1 To You, Yahweh, I call;
     my rock, do not be deaf to me,
   lest You be silent to me,
     and I become like those who go down to the pit.
28:2 Hear the voice of my supplications [for grace]
     when I cry to You for help,
   when I lift up my hands
     to Your holiest place.
28:3 Do not drag me off with the wicked
     and with those who do harm—
   those who speak peace with their neighbors,
     while evil is in their hearts.
28:4 Give to them according to their doings
     and according to the evil of their practices;
   according to the work of their hands give to them;
     return their recompense to them.
28:5 For they do not consider the doings of Yahweh
     or the works of His hands;
   He will tear them down and not build them up.

28:6 Blessed be Yahweh,
       Because He hears the voice of my supplications [for grace].
28:7 Yahweh is my strength and my shield;
       in Him my heart trusts, and I am helped.
      So my heart exults,
       and with my song I will give Him thanks.
28:8 Yahweh is to them strength,
       and a stronghold of deliverance to His anointed.
28:9 Deliver Your people and bless Your inheritance;
       shepherd them and carry them unto forever.

Structure

Petition and praise constitute the composition:[1]

Petition (28:1–5)
28:1–2   For God to listen ["lift up," נשׂא, *nsʾ*]
28:3–5   For God to punish the wicked

Praise (28:6–9)
28:6–8   For God's preservation of the righteous
28:9   For God to liberate ["carry," נשׂא]

Theological Focus

In times of intense crisis—particularly those inflicted by opponents who have no concern for God and his deeds, only their own—God hears the desperate pleas of grace of his people, requites evildoers appropriately, and blesses those who trust him, resulting in the praise of their strong and delivering God who shepherds his flock forever.

---

1. See Craigie, *Psalms 1–50*, 237. Obviously these demarcations are rather porous, and one might choose to structure the psalm according to how God is addressed/referred to. In the *Petition* section, we see God being addressed in the second person in 28:1–4, and then being referred to in the third person in 28:5, in an address to the community. (Though less likely, perhaps that shift in address in 28:5 may indicate a response made by a different individual, a temple official.) Likewise, in the *Praise* section, God is addressed in the third person in 28:6–8, in what appears to be an address to the community, only to return to a direct address to God in the second person in 28:9. Overall, the structure depicted above seems to be the most satisfactory, though it introduces what appears to be a plea (28:9) in the *Praise* section (28:6–9). But that entreaty is best seen as giving reasons for (future) praise: God's deliverance, blessing, shepherding, and carrying his people—his ongoing lovingkindnesses directed to his people.

Commentary

Petition (28:1–5)

The *Petition* is divided into a plea for God to listen (28:1–2), followed by a request for God to punish the wicked (28:3–5). The situation that the supplicant was in appears to have been dangerous enough that he contemplated the possibility of death (28:1d), though, as is often the case in the laments, the precise circumstances of the crisis are vague. That also suggests that the labels of the evildoers—"wicked" and "those who do harm" and "those who speak peace . . . while evil is in their hearts" (28:3)—are also intended to be generic, including all manner of nefarious practitioners and their malevolent oppositions.

Notice that 28:1 and 28:2 follow a similar pattern, ABB^+ and BAA^+: A relates to the call; B to the beckoning of divine attention; and the "+" is an added-on element to A and B that deals not only with another aspect of the call and the request of God's attention, respectively, but also involves a location in each case (see below): "grave" in 28:1d (forming B^+) and "Your holiest place" in 28:2d (forming A^+).[2]

28:1
A	28:1a	Call ("I call")
B	28:1b	Hear ("do not be deaf")
B+	28:1cd	Hear ("lest You be silent") + **"pit"**

28:2
B	28:2a	Hear ("the voice of my supplications [for grace]")
A	28:2b	Call ("I cry")
A+	28:2cd	Call ("I lift up my hands") + **"Your holiest place"**

It is a literary portrayal (i.e., a text-pictorial depiction) of the intensity of the supplicant's plea: "I call [A], and please hear me [B]—hear me, lest I end up in the pit [B^+]; so please hear me [B] when I call [A]—I call to Your holiest place [A^+]." There may also be a hint that the pleader has access to "Your holiest place," thus making him one of the faithful, committed to Yahweh, and (relatively) blameless and virtuous, unlike those "vicious" ones mentioned immediately following, in 28:3–4, who have "evil . . . in their hearts." In the psalmist's mind, only by God's grace can he expect a response to his "supplications [for grace]" (28:2a; תַּחֲנוּן, *tachanun*, is derived from חֵן, *chen*, "grace," and חַנּוּן, *channun*, "gracious").

The lifting up of one's hands in prayer (28:2c) was a common posture in approaching God and can be considered to be part of the psalmist's call (Pss 63:4; 134:2; Lam 2:19; 3:41; etc.), but in light of the mention of "pit [בּוֹר, *bor*]" in Ps 28:1d (i.e., "grave"), this paints a poignant picture: "The psalmist is also like one standing on the edge of the pit of death in danger of falling in, and his hands are stretched out in desperation. If God would only answer his prayer, it would be as though he [God] had taken his [the sufferer's] hands and rescued him from that threatening abyss."[3] Yes, grace is necessary—absolutely necessary!

---

2. "Pit" is a cistern, hole, or dungeon, effectively a grave. "The blessing of life was fellowship with the living God, but if in life's crises God were silent, then for all practical purposes the psalmist [would become] like the deceased" (Craigie, *Psalms 1–50*, 238).

3. Craigie, *Psalms 1–50*, 238.

The psalmist then moves to petition God to punish the wicked (28:3–5). He begins with a nudge, a plea to God that he not be treated like evildoers (28:3). Perhaps this arose from God's apparent "deafness" and "silence" (28:1bc): "Since God does not hear the prayers of the wicked and the sinner (Isa 59:2), the psalmist was afraid that he was being treated as if he were ungodly too."[4] May that not be, he prays, pleading that God not act as if he, the supplicant, were also one of the unrighteous, those unfavored ones who have "evil" in their hearts (in their attitudes: Ps 28:3d), and "evil" on their hands (in their actions, "practices": 28:4bc)—they were comprehensively evil!

It is made abundantly clear that these "who *do* harm" (28:3b) and who are worthy of commensurate punishment "according to their *doings*" (28:4a), are the ones who do not consider the "*doings* of Yahweh" (28:5a; all from פעל, *p'l*): the wordplays are pungent. These malefactors have no respect, concern, or regard for God (and his doings) at all. The terms "work of hands" and "doings" pertaining to both the depraved and to deity are deliberately arranged in 28:4–5:

Wicked's	"doings" (28: 4a)
	"work of their hands" (28:4c)
Yahweh's	"doings" (28:5a)
	"works of His hands" (28:5b)

All that to say, to evildoers will be "returned their recompense" (28:4d). The result of their dismissal of Yahweh's "doings" and "works" is that Yahweh will "tear them down and not build them up" (28:5abc), the punishment of destruction (or deconstruction) of their endeavors. Strikingly, "they do not consider" is לֹא יָבִינוּ (*lo' yavinu*, 28:5a), and "He will . . . not build them up" is לֹא יִבְנֵם (*lo' yivnem*, 28:5c). The paronomasia once again demonstrates that the wicked ones are getting their just deserts. These descriptions of the wicked's praxis and their payment in kind "picture the faithless as being like people doing a hard week's work, and the point is underlined in the fourth colon [28:4d] by the use of the word 'recompense.' The supplicant wants to see these dedicated laborers properly compensated," "according to," commensurate with, their evildoing—the preposition כְּ echoes thrice: 28:4a, 4b, 4c.[5] And they will be (re)paid, for God is just. Appealing further to divine justice, the distinction between the psalmist and these noxious ones is maintained: his "hands" are calling upon God (28:2cd), while their "hands" are engaged in iniquity and evil (28:4c).

Praise (28:6–9)

Following the *Petition* for God to hear and for God to punish the wicked, the psalmist understandably moves to thanksgiving and praise; after all, condemnation of the wicked is simultaneously vindication of the righteous, and for that the psalmist is thankful. The petition had begun with "hear the voice of my pleas for grace" (28:2a); the praise now begins with "He hears the voice of my pleas for grace" (28:6b). God hears! God be praised!

This section is structured to center on the declaration "I am helped" by the blessed Yahweh (28:6a), who hears the plea of his servants (28:6b), who strengthens and protects

---

4. Ross, *Psalms*, 1:641.
5. Goldingay, *Psalms*, 1:406.

the psalmist (28:7a), in whom the psalmist trusts (28:7b), and to whom the psalmist gives thanks (28:7bc). But the last two lines of the structure extend this confidence beyond the individual to the entirety of the community that is also strengthened by Yahweh (28:8a), rendering them blessed (28:9a):[6]

28:6a	"blessed"	Supplicant to Yahweh
28:7a	"Yahweh … strength"	Strength of supplicant
28:7bα	"my heart trusts"	
28:7bβ	**"I am helped"**	
28:7c	"my heart exults"	
28:8a	"Yahweh … strength"	Strength of community
28:9a	"bless"	Yahweh to community

And so, while the doers of iniquity had only evil in their "hearts" (28:3d), the supplicant's "heart" trusts God (28:7b), and his "heart" exults (28:7c). Indeed, he who is "my strength" (28:7a) is also "to them [the community] strength" (28:8a).[7] Surely the "stronghold of *deliverance*" that Yahweh is for his people (28:8b) will "deliver" them (29:9a). Thus the blessed God blesses his people with deliverance! These rhetorical twists of fate bear witness to

> the existential reversal that the psalmist has received at the word of God. This reversal is further expressed poetically by the shift from words and images of mournful prayer … [in 28:1–5] to words and images of music-filled praise [28:6–9]. … The motif completes a movement in the psalm from the original position in which the psalmist cried out, because God was *silent* and did not hear, to the new position in which the psalm sings forth, because God has heard.[8]

Addressing Yahweh directly in 28:9 with a final request for the community—comprising a quartet of imperatives: that God deliver his people, bless his inheritance, shepherd his flock, and carry them forever—the psalm concludes. In his petition, the psalmist had earlier "lifted up [נשׂא]" his hands in prayer and supplication (28:2c); now, he asks that God "carry [נשׂא]" his people (28:9b), as would a shepherd his sheep (and as he bore them in the days of the exodus: Exod 19:4; Deut 1:31; 32:11—the same verb is employed here). This strong and delivering God certainly will!

---

6. From Girard, *Les Psaumes*, 1:230.

7. "Them" in 28:8a is plural, but the parallel "anointed" is singular in 28:8b, suggesting not that the latter is one specific individual, but that that particular person represents many similarly anointed (see Pss 18:50; 105:15; etc.). No doubt "anointed" can apply to Christ; but so can it apply to each and every believer, those indwelt, and thus anointed, by the Holy Spirit (2 Cor 1:21).

8. deClaissé-Walford et al., *Book of Psalms*, 278 (emphases original).

Sermon Map

I. God Is not Unhearing
  Intense crisis and the seeming deafness of God (28:1–2)
  Move-to-relevance: When we feel God is silent to pleas

II. Wicked Are not Unpunished
  God visits the wicked with justice (28:3–5)
  Move-to-relevance: When we feel God is apathetic to the wicked

III. Faithful Are not Ungrateful
  God attends to the faithful appropriately (28:6–7b, 8–9)
  Thankfulness of the flock (28:6, 7cd)
  Move-to-relevance: When we feel God is cool to the faithful

IV. *Sustained by the Shepherd!*
  Developing trust in the caring, carrying Shepherd

PSALM 29:1–11
Psalm of Orientation

The Voice of the Victor

PSALM 29 DOES NOT address God at all. Rather it is directed to the community of God's people, characterizing their God, particularly distinguishing him from the gods of the surrounding peoples. Indeed, humankind is never mentioned until the last verse. Thus, Psalm 29 is entirely praise, a song of orientation.

Translation

29:1 Ascribe to Yahweh, heavenly beings,
  ascribe to Yahweh glory and strength.
29:2 Ascribe to Yahweh the glory of His name;
  worship Yahweh in [His] holy majesty.
29:3 The voice of Yahweh is upon the waters;
  the God of glory thunders—
  Yahweh upon great waters.
29:4 The voice of Yahweh in power,
  the voice of Yahweh in majesty.
29:5 the voice of Yahweh breaks the cedars;
  Yahweh thoroughly breaks the cedars of Lebanon.
29:6 And He makes Lebanon skip like a calf,
  and Sirion like a young wild ox.
29:7 The voice of Yahweh splits flames of fire.
29:8 The voice of Yahweh quakes the wilderness;
  Yahweh quakes the wilderness of Kadesh.
29:9 The voice of Yahweh quakes the large trees
  and strips the forests [bare].
  And in His temple everyone says, "The glory

29:10   [of] Yahweh sits [enthroned] at the flood;
        And Yahweh, King, sits [enthroned] forever.
29:11 Yahweh, strength to His people He gives;
        Yahweh, He blesses His people with peace."

Structure

The psalm is structured as a *Call to Praise* (29:1–2; location: heavens); a *Cause for Praise*—the divine "voice" (29:3–9b; location: earth[1]); and a *Conferral of Praise* (29:9c–11; location: heavens):[2]

> **Call to Praise (29:1–2)**: *heavens*
>   "Yahweh" ×4; "glory" (29:1b, 2a)
>   three lines with similar beginnings (29:1a, 1b, 2a)
>   "strength" → God, from heavenly beings, 29:1
>
> **Cause for Praise (29:3–9b)**: *earth*
>   "Yahweh" ×10; "glory" (29:3b)
>   "voice of Yahweh" ×7
>
> **Conferral of Praise (29:9c–11)**: *heavens*
>   "Yahweh" ×4; "glory" (29:9c)
>   four lines with similar beginnings (29:10a, 10b, 11a, 11b)
>   "strength" → people, from Yahweh, 29:11a

Each of the three sections commences with references to "glory": 29:1b (also 29:2a), 29:3b, and 29:9c. In addition, the first section has three lines beginning with "ascribe to Yahweh" (29:1a, 1b, 2a), and the last section has four lines commencing with "Yahweh" (29:10a, 10b, 11a, 11b). In short, "the whole poem is a celebration of the manifestation of the deity in glory and splendor, power and majesty, symbolized by the seven claps of thunder [i.e., the seven mentions of the divine 'voice': 29:3a, 4a, 4b, 5a, 7, 8a, 9a], with each compelling the obeisance of his subjects, and exacting an appropriate acknowledgement from the world at large."[3]

---

1. And every verse in this central portion, except for 29:6, the middle verse of the section (and of the psalm), has "the voice of Yahweh."

2. Modified from Goldingay, *Psalms*, 1:413. While the location of the opening and closing sections appear other worldly, Delitzsch, *Biblical Commentary*, 1:373, has perceptively noted that "*Gloria in excelsis* is its beginning [29:1–2], and *pax in terris* its conclusion [29:11b]."

3. Freedman and Hyland, "Psalm 29," 246.

PSALM 29:1–11

Theological Focus

> The absolute supremacy of the one, true, glorious, and mighty God—who has conquered chaos in the cosmos, who controls all things in nature, and who is enthroned forever over all, subordinating all other beings to himself—deserves complete loyalty from his people, whom he then blesses with strength and peace.

Commentary

Call to Praise (29:1–2)

The exaltation of God is urged of "heavenly beings" (29:1a) and so this glorification is likely conducted in the realm of deity/heavenly temple (as also is the subsequent glorification of God in the last section—*Conferral of Praise*, 29:9c–11). Such an ascription of "glory" and "strength" to Yahweh (29:1b) is to acknowledge that these attributes belong to him and to no other god, and his majesty alone is to be worshiped.[4]

On the identity of these entities, we are less clear. "Heavenly beings" in 29:1a is literally "sons of the mighty/gods [אֵלִים, 'elim]" (the Targums have מלאכיא, ml'ky', "angels"). In the plural and with "sons of" (i.e., בְּנֵי, bne, "sons," in the construct form) as in 29:1a, it likely indicates members of the divine court, angelic beings located in the presence of God.[5] Like the biblical אֵל, 'el (as in 29:1a), the Akkadian *ilu* and the Ugaritic *'il* also indicate divinity of some sort.[6] For instance, "sons of god," *bn 'ilm*, shows up in a Ugaritic text to indicate the many progeny of El, the chief of the pantheon.[7] Thus one begins to notice a theme here at the beginning of Psalm 29 that will be developed throughout the composition: salvos launched against sacral terms and cultic persona in the pantheon of Israel's ancient Near East neighbors. "The threefold use of the imperative ... ['ascribe'] here is the syntactical throwing down the polemical gauntlet to any who would withhold from the Lord that which rightly is due to him—and only to him."[8]

Cause for Praise (29:3–9b)

The reason for the praise called for in 29:1–2 follows in 29:3–9b. This section is striking for its seven-fold repetition of "the voice of Yahweh." Of note, Baal is also enumerated seven times in a Ugaritic list.[9] And this god's "voice," too, figures prominently in poems about him and

---

4. The word הֲדָרָה, *hadarah*, "majesty" (29:2b; elsewhere הָדָר, *hadar*) has connotations of "splendor" and "glory," and is often found in the Psalter juxtaposed with these attributes of deity (see 8:5; 21:5; 45:3–4; 96:6; 104:1; 111:3; 145:5). Here in 29:2, "glory" and "majesty" occur in parallel.

5. See Ps 89:6 for the use of the same term, "sons of the mighty/gods" = "heavenly beings"; also 97:7; 103:20–22; see 148:1–3 for worship conducted by denizens of the heavenly realm.

6. Smith, *Origins of Biblical Monotheism*, 6.

7. See *KTU* 1.4 iii 14 (see Wyatt, *Religious Texts*, 96).

8. deClaissé-Walford et al., *Book of Psalms*, 284.

9. *KTU* 1.47 5–11 (see Wyatt, *Religious Texts*, 361); the corresponding Ras Shamra text 20.24 3–10 has Adad, the Akkadian god, equivalent to Hadad, the Syrian storm god, instead of Baal (see Wyatt, *Religious*

his consort, Anath; as well, there are references to "cedar," "quaking," and "lightning" and "thunder" in these compositions, all with parallels in Ps 29:3–9b:[10]

> And (he [Baal] will) peal his *thunder* in the clouds,
> Flashing his *lightnings* to the earth.
> The house of *cedar*—let him burn it.
>
> Baal op[ens] rifts in [the cloud]s,
> Ba[al gives] forth his holy *voice* [*qlh;* and קוֹל, *qol,* in Ps 29:3–9b],
> Baal discharges the ut[terance of his li]ps.
> His h[oly] *voice* [convulses] the earth ... the mountains quake,
> A-tremble are ...
> East and west, earth's high places reel.
>
> "Baal's enemies, why do you *quake*?
> Why do you *quake* ...?"
> Baal's eye seeks out for his hand
> When the yew-club [*arz;* and אֶרֶז, *'erez,* in Ps 29:5 = *cedar*] swings in his right hand ...

That Canaanite theology is in the background is not surprising; the geographical references in 29:6, 8—Lebanon, Sirion (i.e., Hermon), and Kadesh[11]—indicate northern Canaan as the scene of all the divine activity, particularly the mountains in the area. Even these symbols of might, including those substantial cedars of Lebanon (29:5[12]), are no match for divine power. Just the "voice of Yahweh" is enough to throw these strongholds into disarray! The thundering of Yahweh, his utterance of power, his voice of majesty, destroys trees (29:5), quakes the land (29:6, 8) and its large trees (29:9ab[13]), and is accompanied by forked lighting ("split flames of fire," 29:7)—all arranged chiastically for maximal impact.

29:5	Trees ("cedars," ×2)
29:6	Terrain ("Lebanon"; "Sirion")
29:7	Lightning ("flames of fire")
29:8	Terrain ("wilderness of Kadesh")
29:9ab	Trees ("trees"; "forests")

Texts, 360–61). Another text, *KTU* 1.101 3–4 (see Wyatt, *Religious Texts*, 388), has Baal, in the context of his enthronement over the flood, carrying "seven lightning-flashes ... a tree-of-lighting [in his] ri[ght hand]"—likely forked lightning implied in 29:7. Seven thunders are also audible in Rev 10:3–4, indeed with the article—"*the* seven thunders" (αἱ ἑπτὰ βρονταὶ, *hai hepta brontai*)—suggesting a specific reference thereof, perhaps an allusion to the "voice[s] of Yahweh" in Psalm 29.

10. "Poems about Baal and Anath," II AB v 79–73 (*ANET* 133); and II AB vii 27–34, 38–41 (*ANET* 135) (italics in English have been added to terms corresponding to those in Psalm 29).

11. In textual proximity with Lebanon and Hermon, this is likely Kadesh in Syria (not the one south of Canaan).

12. Also in Pss 72:16; 92:12; 104:16.

13. The *polel* of חיל, *chyl*, means "give birth," not "*cause to* give birth" (29:9a), but that does not fit the subject, "the voice of Yahweh." It is best to retain the sense of the same verb in 29:8a, 8b (though in the *hiphil*), "to quake." With "forests" in the next line, 29:9b, אלות, *'lwt* ("deer") in 29:9a is also best emended to אֵילוֹת, *'elot* ("large trees" or "oaks"; a variant of the regular plural אַיָּלִים, *ayyalim*). Thus, "the voice of Yahweh quakes the large trees."

The parallel of 29:3 (with Yahweh's control over "waters," ×2) with the conquering activity of Baal, commonly seen as a storm-god,[14] over the "sea" and "mighty waters/river," is notable:[15]

> What manner of enemy has risen against Baal,
> of foe against the Charioteer of the Clouds?
> Surely I smote the Beloved of El, *Yam* ["sea"]?
> Surely I exterminated *Nahar*, the mighty god ["or god of mighty waters/river"]?

In Canaanite mythology, these "waters" were enemies to be overcome, perhaps metaphors for the chaos and disorder of life:

> "The waters" stand for tumultuous forces that threaten to overwhelm the regular order of life, in the way that a flood can overwhelm people, land, and even cities. They can stand for such tumults as we experience them in political life ... [Pss 18:16; 46:3; 77:18–19; 124:4–5; 144:7] and personal life ... [Pss 32:6; 69:1–2, 14–15]. They can also stand for such tumults as supernatural realities ... [Pss 74:13; 93:4], the forces over which Yhwh asserted control at creation ... [Pss 33:7; 74:13].[16]

In Yahwism, however, not only has God overcome these forces of disorder, he is far more powerful than Baal, the god who defeated the "waters."

> Although the emphasis throughout ... [Ps 29:3–9b] is on the thundering voice of the Lord, the allusion throughout is to the weaker thunder of Baal. ... The praise of the Lord, by virtue of being expressed in language and imagery associated with the Canaanite weather-god, Baal, taunts the weak deity of the defeated foes, namely the Canaanites. Thus, the poet has deliberately utilized Canaanite-type language and imagery in order to emphasize the Lord's strength and victory, in contrast to the weakness of the inimical Baal.[17]

The length of this section thus emphasizes what the psalmist wishes to point out: the sovereignty of God over chaos and over all earthly domains, and even over every other god, is incontrovertible—Yahweh is Lord of all! Thus the entire section, 29:3–9b, is a theophanic description (*Cause for Praise*), surrounded on either side by an exhortation to glorify God (*Call for Praise*, 29:1–2) and the resulting exaltation of God (*Conferral of Praise*, 29:9c–11). The many elements of this section that has parallels in Baal texts make the psalm "function as a polemical statement over against Canaanite faith ... , which was a longstanding source of temptation to Israelites."[18]

---

14. See Green, *Storm-God*, 173–78. Baal-Hadad, the Syrian storm god, is depicted on the Ugaritic "Great Stele of Baal" carrying a stylized and apparently forked thunderbolt in his left hand (Schaeffer, "Les Fouilles," Plate 16).

15. *KTU* 1.3 iii 38–39 (see Wyatt, *Religious Texts*, 79 [italics added]).

16. Goldingay, *Psalms*, 1:417. The "great waters" in 29:3c suggest that this might be the Mediterranean Sea.

17. Craigie, *Psalms 1–50*, 246.

18. Goldingay, *Psalms*, 1:414.

Conferral of Praise (29:9c–10)

At 29:9c, there is a change of scene, from the quasi-violent effects of a theophany/storm on earth (29:3–9b), to the stability of the divine temple in the heavenlies. Indeed, this is a return to the domain of deity which had opened the psalm (29:1–2), and a response to that section's exhortation to ascribe glory and strength to Yahweh.

Ironically enough, even with the mention of the divine voice seven times in 29:3–9b, God never speaks in this composition. "The phrase ['voice of Yahweh'] is less about content than about an impression that is left—the impression of the Lord's strength, might, and glory."[19] Indeed, the only speech recorded in the psalm is what "everyone"[20] says in the heavenly temple (29:9c–10).[21] The verses 29:9cβ–10a and 29:10b contain elements that correspond to each other (attributes of Yahweh, prepositional phrases with ל, *l*, and identical verbs[22]), though not necessarily in parallel sequence: the Hebrew is shown):[23]

29:9cβ–10a

כְּבוֹד יְהוָה	לַמַּבּוּל	יָשַׁב
kvod yhwh	lammabbul	yashav
"The glory of Yahweh	at the flood	sits"

29:10b

יְהוָה מֶלֶךְ	לְעוֹלָם	וַיֵּשֶׁב
yhwh melek	l'olam	wayyeshev
"Yahweh, King"	"forever"	"and He sits"

---

19. deClaissé-Walford et al., *Book of Psalms*, 285.

20. Likely the "heavenly beings" in 29:1a; they are doing what was bidden them (29:1–2), after they witnessed Yahweh's dominion over all nature (29:3–9b).

21. With Goldingay, *Psalms*, 1:420, I see 29:9c as commencing the third and final section of the psalm; what "everyone" says is cited in 29:9cβ–11, beginning with "the glory [of] Yahweh." Elsewhere in the Psalter, this phrase is found in 104:31 (along with "forever," also related to a storm-theophany, 104:32), and in 138:5 (related to divine kingship over all other regents, 138:4).

22. The sequences of the two parts are not parallel in the Hebrew: the Hebrew of 29:9cβ–10a is as shown, but 29:10b (literally: "and-He-sits Yahweh [the] King forever") has been reordered in the figure to show the correspondence of its linguistic elements to those in 29:9cβ–10a.

23. In light of the parallelism, it might also be that the enthronement referred to is the instant of God's overcoming of the chaos of the waters, and that the preposition ל in לַמַּבּוּל has the sense of "from/since": "The glory of Yahweh sits [enthroned] *from* the flood," making it a notation of time, as is the corresponding prepositional phrase לְעוֹלָם, "forever," in 29:10b (Dahood, *Psalms I*, 180; also see Pss 89:9–14; 93:2–4). "The psalm asserts that there was such a moment, and that it had permanent consequences. That assertion of authority would then last 'forever.' The tumultuous waters will never be able (successfully) to reassert themselves" (Goldingay, *Psalms*, 1:420–21). Congruent to this interpretation is the fact that in the OT מַבּוּל, *mabbul*, is employed only in connection with the Genesis flood (11× in Genesis 6–11). This reading is not incongruent with my translation, "at the flood," that can be a time-stamp as well as a place-locator.

This section, too, is redolent of Canaanite elements, including mountains and waters, lightnings and thunder:[24]

> Baal sits like the base of a mountain;
> Hadd [Baal-Hadad, the Syrian storm god] se[ttles] as the *ocean*,
> in the midst of his *divine mountain,* Saphon.
>
> Seven *lightning-flashes* [ ],
> eight bundles of thunder,
> a tree-of-*lightning* [in his] ri[ght hand].
>
> [His] horn is [exal]ted;
> his head is in the snows in heaven,
> [with] the god there is abounding *water*.

And, after destroying Yam and Nahar ("sea" and "river"—the waters of chaos), Baal, too, is said to be enthroned:[25]

> Baal gathered up,
> and drank <Prince> *Yam* to the dregs;
> he exterminated Ruler *Nahar*.
>
> "For our captive is Pr[ince *Yam*],
> [for] our captive is Ruler *Nahar*!"
>
> "Yam is indeed dead!
> Baal will rul[e   ]."

Baal may have conquered chaos and become enthroned, but only Yahweh is the King of kings and the Lord of lords. And this God is a benevolent and beneficent deity, as indicated by the final verse of the psalm, 29:11, constructed with parallel elements:

> ***Yahweh,***
>   strength
>   to His people
>   He gives;
> ***Yahweh,***
>   He blesses
>   His people
>   with peace."

There is no indication that the speakers in 29:9cβ–10 had concluded their utterance in those particular verses; neither is there any sign of shift in speakers between 29:9cβ–10 and 29:11. Rather, "glory" and "strength" paired in 29:1a appear to be paired here, too: "glory" in 29:9cβ, and "strength" in 29:11a, thus keeping 29:9cβ–11 a joint unit and a single utterance

---

24. *KTU* 1.101 R 1–4, 6–7 (see Wyatt, *Religious Texts*, 388 [italics added]); part of this text was cited earlier.
25. *KTU* 1.2 iv 27–28, 30, 32 (see Wyatt, *Religious Texts*, 67–69 [italics added]).

by those heavenly beings. This also makes the *inclusio* precise: what was solicited in 29:1–2 is delivered in 29:9cβ–11.[26]

But there is one twist: the *Call to Praise* had "strength" ascribed *to* Yahweh; here in the *Conferral of Praise* it is strength *from* Yahweh that is bestowed, and that upon his people. More likely, these two aspects are identical: ascribing strength to Yahweh is equivalent to proclaiming that Yahweh invests his people with strength, for the latter implies that Yahweh possesses strength in the first place to do so. Indeed, after the depiction of divine strength over chaos in 29:3–9b, it appears that God's people would need that imparted strength from God to extend order over chaos in God's world, in partnership with God (29:11a). The consequence? Peace, a blessing from God (29:11b).

And so, in this *Conferral of Praise* we return to the opening theme (*Call to Praise*, in 29:1–2), with the theophanic storm sandwiched in between the two sections as the *Cause for Praise* (29:3–9b).[27] "The divine beings are presumably offering their recognition in light of what they have seen on earth. The impressiveness of what results on earth from Yhwh's voice resounding there makes them bestow honor on Yhwh as they were bidden."[28] In sum, Psalm 29 affirms the sovereignty and dominion of God over every other heavenly being, by demonstrating his enthronement and might over chaos and over nature, employing terms and notions oft used of Canaanite deities, and by having the members of the heavenly council offer praise to God. God's people must therefore, likewise, respond to the implicit call of this psalm to be faithful to him and to him alone, praising and exalting him in their turn.

Sermon Map

I. God's Domination
   Over chaos (29:3–4, 10)
   Over nature (29:5–9b)
   Move-to-relevance: Our lack of domination over anything

II. God's Distinction
   Deserving of glory from all beings (29:1–2, 9c–10)
   Move-to-relevance: The transcendence of the Creator

III. God's Donation
   Consequence of loyalty: blessing of strength and peace (29:11)
   Move-to-relevance: Our need for God's strength

IV. *Be Loyal Citizens of the King!*
   Developing greater loyalty to God

---

26. Goldingay, *Psalms*, 1:421.
27. deClaissé-Walford et al., *Book of Psalms*, 285.
28. Goldingay, *Psalms*, 1:420.

PSALM 30:1–12

Psalm of Reorientation

Lamenting to Rejoicing

PSALM 30 IS RECOGNIZED as being a paradigmatic song of praise for recovery, "a textbook example of a thanksgiving or testimony psalm."[1] I label it a "reorientation" psalm because it goes from one pole, lament, to the other, praise/thanksgiving, with a new normal achieved as God delivers the supplicant from his distresses, and the latter, in turn, vocalizes gratitude to deity.

Translation

30:1   I will exalt You, Yahweh, for You have lifted me up,
          and You have not let my enemies rejoice over me.
30:2   Yahweh, my God, I cried to You for help, and You healed me.
30:3   Yahweh, You brought up, from Sheol, my soul;
          You kept me alive, [apart] from those going down to the pit.
30:4   Make music to Yahweh, His devout ones,
          and give thanks to His holy memory.
30:5   For [there is] a moment in His anger,
          [but a] life[time] in His favor;
       weeping remains for the night,
          but in the morning an exclamation of joy.
30:6   Now I—I said in my prosperity,
          "I will not be shaken forever."
30:7   Yahweh, in Your favor
          You had made my mountain stand [in] strength;
       [then] You hid Your face,
          I became terrified.

---

1. Goldingay, *Psalms*, 1:424.

30:8   To You, Yahweh, I was calling,
           and to the Lord I made supplication [for grace]:
30:9   "What profit is there in my blood,
           when I go down to the hole?
           Will it give You thanks You—dust?
           Will it proclaim Your faithfulness?
30:10 Hear, Yahweh, and be gracious to me.
           Yahweh, become a helper to me."
30:11 You turned my lamenting into dancing for me;
           You undid my sackcloth and You girded me with joy,
30:12 so that [my] inner being can [now] make music to You and not be silent.
           Yahweh, my God, forever I will give You thanks.

Structure

The careful structuring of Psalm 30 is notable, bookended by commitments to praise:

> Commitment to Praise 1 (**30:1aα**): "I will exalt You"
>   Cause for Praise 1 (**30:1aβ–3**): "rejoice" (שׂמח, *smch*)
>   Call to Praise (**30:4–5**)
>   Commemoration for Praise (**30:6–10**)
>   Cause for Praise 2 (**30:11**): "joy" (שִׂמְחָה, *simchah*)
>   Commitment to Praise 2 (**30:12**): "I will give You thanks"

As with many of the thanksgivings, and even the laments, the exact situation that precipitated the original crisis is obscure, and perhaps intentionally so, in order to enable its recontextualization in times and spaces distant from the ancient Israelite poet. At any rate, the crisis—metaphorical or otherwise—is serious, with adumbrations of death in the background: "Sheol" and "grave" (30:3); "hole," i.e., grave, and "dust" (30:9); and "lamenting" and "sackcloth" (30:11).

A remarkable number of "poetic polarities" mark this composition as one of thanksgiving:[2] "heal" (רפא, *rph'*, 30:2) vs. "Sheol" (30:3a; where the רְפָאִים, *rpha'im*, occupants of the land of the dead, live: see 88:10; Isa 14:9; 26:14, 19) and "pit" (Ps 30:3b; i.e., grave); "alive" vs. "pit" (30:3b); "lifted . . . up" (30:1a) and "brought up" (30:3a) vs. "going down" (30:3b, 9b); also "lifted . . . up" vs. "over me" (30:1); "anger" vs. "favor" (30:5ab); "moment" vs. "life[time]" (30:5ab); "night" vs. "morning" (30:5cd); "weeping" vs. "exclamation of joy" (30:5cd); "prosperity" (30:6a) vs. "terrified" (30:7d); "shaken" (30:6b) vs. "stand [in] strength" (30:7b); "favor" (30:7a) vs. "hid Your face" (30:7c); "lamenting" vs. "dancing" (30:11a); "undid my sackcloth" vs. "girded me with joy" (30:11b); "make music" vs. "be silent" (30:12a). This is the life of a child of God, lived between the extremes of such

---

2. deClaissé-Walford et al., *Book of Psalms*, 290.

experiences. Indeed, the reversal motif is explicitly labeled: Yahweh "turned" (30:11a)—a divine act of grace ("supplication [for grace]" in 30:8b is חנן, *chnn*, from חֵן, *chen*, "grace"). Even the structure of the psalm shown above reflects a textual reversal: the sequence of *Commitment to Praise 1* (30:1aα) → *Cause for Praise 1* (30:1aβ–3), is turned around later with *Cause for Praise 2* (30:11) → *Commitment to Praise 2* (30:12).

Theological Focus

> The rescue of God's people from their dire circumstances—that may even have been the result of divine chastening for presumption—a dramatic reversal by the gracious and personal intervention of God that demonstrated his favor upon them, calls for long-lasting public praise and thanksgiving to the architect of their deliverance.

Commentary

Commitment to Praise 1 (30:1aα)

The psalm commences (30:1aα) and concludes (30:12) with the intent of the psalmist to praise and exalt God (both employ first-person imperfect verbs).

Cause for Praise 1 (30:1aβ–3)

The *Commitment to Praise* is followed by the *Cause for Praise*, the divine rescue effected by God for the supplicant over his enemies. "Lift up" (30:1a) translates a rare verb that is elsewhere also used of drawing up well-water (דלה, *dlh*, Exod 2:16, 19; Prov 20:5), an image appropriate for the sufferer trapped in a metaphorical deep grave ("Sheol" and "pit" in Ps 30:3, and "hole" in 30:9b[3]). Out of this hole, Yahweh "brought up" the psalmist's soul, keeping him alive (30:3). This abyss may well have been a serious disease as hinted by the use of "healed" (30:2), though this, too, may simply be an image of restoration from some other kind of lethal danger.

The downward movement of the psalmist vs. the upward movement accomplished by Yahweh was noted above, but a revisit of the antithesis (in light and dark gray below) in 30:1aβ–3 is illuminating:

30:1aβ–b	"You have lifted me up"	"enemies … over me"
30:2	"I cried to You for help and You healed me"	
30:3	"You brought up from Sheol, my soul"	"those going down to the grave"

---

3. The word בוֹר, *bor*, "pit," can also mean "cistern." "Hole" (שַׁחַת, *shachat*) is a synonym for Sheol (see 16:10). Both essentially indicate the grave, the place of death.

The centerpiece of 30:2 is the essence of this section, and indeed, of the entire psalm—the rescue (reorientation) performed by God in response to the cry of the psalmist for help.

In any case, in the first three verses, comprising the *Commitment to Praise 1* and the *Cause for Praise 1* (30:1–3), the "You" is prominent: "Yahweh" (30:1a, 2, 3a), "my God" (30:2a), and "you" seven times in pronominal and prepositional suffixes and verb forms: deity shows up eleven times. "It is the relationship between the psalmist and the cosmic God who is also a personal *you* that is the driving force of Psalm 30."[4]

Call to Praise (30:4–5)

In a pedagogical aside, the psalmist shifts his address from Yahweh to the members of his own community (30:4–5; other than these two verses, the psalm is exclusively an "I"–"You" dialogue). This section is bounded by its first Hebrew word translated "make music" (30:4a) and its last word translated "exclamation of joy" (30:5d).[5] The reason why the "devout ones" (30:4a[6]), the faithful committed people of Yahweh, must sing praise to him is outlined in 30:5 with a quartet of antonymous terms (see above). A "moment in His anger" is turned into "a life[time] in His favor" (30:5ab), apparently overnight (30:5cd): "the crying with which the person lies down to sleep in the evening is replaced in a very short time, the time between evening and morning (which to a sleeping person seems like no time at all) by the longer-lasting joy which appears in the morning of a new day."[7] In sum, God's "anger is short-lived, his love long-lasting."[8] The psalmist was kept "alive" by Yahweh (חיה, *chyh*, 30:3b) so that deity may show him a "life[time]" of favor (חַי, *chay*, 30:5b).

The mention of divine "anger" in 30:5a may reflect the psalmist's awareness that the bleak situation he was in, with enemies rejoicing and he near death, had something to do with past sins of his own (perhaps his complacency as noted in 30:6; below). But the focus here is on the fact that whatever caused the kindling of God's ire, even if that provocation were one's own iniquity, the resulting chastisement would be momentary. In other words, the rescue effected by Yahweh was not one's to earn, but entirely a matter of grace (also reflected in 30:8b, 10a).

Commemoration for Praise (30:6–10)

After the notation of divine "favor" in 30:5b, the psalmist returns to how exactly this divine "favor" (again in 30:7a) had been extended to him—a commemoration, a recollection, of how God was deserving of praise, a reflexive recounting of what had happened (30:6–10).[9] Thus, though the song could have concluded with 30:5, it goes on to repeat the story with more nuance.[10]

---

4. deClaissé-Walford et al., *Book of Psalms*, 292.

5. The "holy memory" (30:4b) is likely a circumlocution for the divine name (see 97:12; and the parallelism in 6:5). Also, the "giving thanks" elsewhere in this psalm is to "You" (30:9c, 12b—which also has "make music" in 30:12a, as does 30:4a) making it likely that that is the case with the thanksgiving in 30:4b as well.

6. These חֲסִידִים, *chasidim*, are the ones who have experienced God's חֶסֶד, *chesed*.

7. Landau, "Word-Pair," 262.

8. Goldingay, *Psalms*, 1:428.

9. This section has two first-person direct speeches of the psalmist, in 30:6b and 30:9–10.

10. Goldingay, *Psalms*, 1:429.

Apparently, it all began in a past time with the psalmist's "prosperity." Emphatically ("now I—I said," 30:6a) he confesses his earlier complacent attitude: "I will not be shaken *forever*" (30:6b), he had thought.[11] The one who ought to have been giving thanks to God "forever" (30:12b) had seemingly been thanking himself for his eternally unshakable state! Indeed, 30:7 is almost an explicit acknowledgment of this conceit: it was Yahweh, in his favor and grace, not the psalmist himself, who had made the latter's "mountain stand [in] *strength* [עֹז, *ʿoz*]" (30:7ab). This is reiterated in a subtle way in 30:10a, as the supplicant requests that Yahweh become a "helper [עֹזֵר, *ʿozer*]" to him: deity alone is the strength-/help-giver. But God does not stand for such vanity, cockiness, and presumption, especially from his own people, and he had "hidden [his] face"—disaster struck—and "I *became* [היה, *hyh*] terrified" (30:7cd). In another wordplay in 30:10a, a now-contrite psalmist appeals to Yahweh that he, God, "*become* [היה] a helper to me." One could remap the sequence of events in 30:6–10 this way: divine charity (30:7ab) → human complacency (30:6) → divine chastening (30:7cd) → human compunction (30:8–10)—he asks for grace (notice "supplication for *grace*" in 30:8b, and "be *gracious*" in 30:10a). The text is itself neatly ordered with positive and negative elements (as shown below), even if not chronologically arranged (as discussed above):

30:6	What the supplicant had said *once*	−
30:7ab	What God had done *once*	+
30:7cd	What God did *afterwards*	−
30:8–10	What the supplicant said *afterwards*	+

In 30:9–10, the supplicant attempts to motivate Yahweh, citing in direct speech what he had pled for: if he were to die—become "dust"—God would lose one of the voices in his praise choir. Therefore, would that God act to deliver him from such a termination of life.

Cause for Praise 2 (30:11)

The reason for praising is specified again with more oppositions (see above): lament → "joy" (שִׂמְחָה), and with that the psalm ends as it had begun (with "rejoice," שׂמח, in 30:1b), There at the start of the prayer it was the enemy who was going to "rejoice"; now it is the psalmist! As with the dangerous circumstance that the psalmist was in, with the divine intervention, too, we are given hardly any detail how exactly God extricated the psalmist from his plight, lending the psalm the flexibility for use in future generations distant from the provenance of the poem. In any case, God directly and personally took action, as the doffing of sackcloth and donning with joy implies: "*You* undid" and "*You* girded" (30:11b). And the wordplay in 30:11 is also deliberate: "You turned" is הָפַכְתָּ, *haphaktta*; "you undid" is פִּתַּחְתָּ, *pittachtta*.

---

11. The word שָׁלוּ, *shalu*, "prosperity," also has the sense of "ease" and "careless security" (employed of the wicked in 73:12); its cognate שַׁלְוָה, *shalwah*, in Prov 1:32 also demonstrates this idea, and it is used of the Sodomites in Ezek 16:49.

Commitment to Praise 2 (30:12)

This commitment to praise marks the formal conclusion of this psalm of reorientation with another *inclusio*: "Yahweh, my God" (30:12b, reiterating the same vocative in 30:2). The supplicant's "new awareness of the source of health and of the meaning of existence would accompany him for the remainder of his life, and so he determines that his thanksgiving to God should be not a single event, but should continue *forever*."[12] Rather than praising himself "forever" (30:6b), the saved sufferer has come to his senses, to give thanks to Yahweh "forever" (30:12b). It is likely that this praise is intended to be public, as the verb "make music" indicates: what the psalmist committed to do in 30:12a was earlier exhorted of all of God's faithful in 30:4. Yes, Yahweh deserves the praise and thanks . . . "forever"!

Sermon Map

I. Divine Charity
   The blessing and favor of God (30:7ab)
   Move-to-relevance: Our blessings

II. Human Complacency
   The denial: God's favor and exaltation of self (30:6)
   Move-to-relevance: Our presumption

III. Divine Chastening
   The correction of the presumptuous (30:7cd)
   The consequences: enemies, near death, lament (30:1–5, 9–11)
   Move-to-relevance: Our disciplining

IV. Human Compunction
   The pleas for grace (30:2, 9–10)

V. *Sing to the Savior!*
   Response of praise and thanksgiving (30:1, 4, 11–12)
   Specifics on thanksgiving for rescue and reorientation

---

12. Craigie, *Psalms 1–50*, 255. This is another reason to label this psalm as one of reorientation, where the final state is better than the original one. "Inner being," כָּבוֹד, *kavod* (30:12a) is better read as כְּבֵדִי, *kvedi*, "my liver" (see on 16:9).

PSALM 31:1–24

Psalm of Disorientation

Falling upon God's Hand

PSALM 31 INTERLACES PRAYERS for deliverance to Yahweh with assertions of trust in him, but "repetition of this kind may simply be part of the rhetoric of prayer."[1] The poem concludes with the praise of deity having heard the prayer of the supplicant and with a call to the community to remain committed to this gracious God who alone can deliver.

Translation

31:1 In You, Yahweh, I take refuge;
    let me not be shamed forever;
    in Your righteousness save me.
31:2 Incline Your ear to me,
    rescue me quickly;
be to me a rock, a stronghold,
    a house of steadfastness to deliver me.
31:3 For my cliff and my steadfastness You [are];
    because of Your name You will lead me and guide me.
31:4 You will bring me out of the net which they laid secretly for me,
    for You [are] my stronghold.
31:5 Into Your hand I commit my spirit;
    You have redeemed me, Yahweh, God of truth.
31:6 I hate those who revere worthless idols,
    but I—in Yahweh I trust.
31:7 I will jubilate and be joyous in Your lovingkindness,
    because You see my affliction;
    You know the distresses of my soul.

---

1. Goldingay, *Psalms*, 1:437.

31:8 And You do not give me over into the hand of the enemy;
    You stand my feet in a broad place.
31:9 Be gracious to me, Yahweh,
    for I am distressed;
weakened by provocation is my eye,
    my soul and my insides [too].
31:10 For it is spent in torment, my life,
    and my years in groaning;
it has stumbled because of my iniquity—my ability,
    and my bones, they have weakened.
31:11 Because of all my adversaries, I have become a reproach,
    and to my neighbors, very much [so],
and a horror to my acquaintances;
    those who see me in the street flee from me.
31:12 I am forgotten as one who is dead, out of heart;
    I have become like a broken vessel.
31:13 For I have heard the defamation of many;
    terror all around;
as they conspire together against me,
    they scheme to seize my soul.
31:14 But I—in You I trust, Yahweh;
    I said, "You [are] my God."
31:15 In Your hand are my times;
    rescue me from the hand of my enemies and from my pursuers.
31:16 Make Your face to shine upon Your servant;
    deliver me in Your lovingkindness.
31:17 Yahweh, let me not be shamed, for I call on You;
    let the wicked be shamed, let them [go] wail[ing] to Sheol.
31:18 Let false lips be silenced—
    those speaking insolently against the righteous
    with arrogance and contempt.
31:19 How great is Your goodness,
    which You have stored up for those who fear You,
which You have done for those who take refuge in You,
    before people.
31:20 You hide them in the hidden place of Your presence
    from the plots of humans;
You store them [securely] in a shelter
    from the strife of tongues.

31:21 Blessed be Yahweh,
> for He has shown the wonder of His lovingkindness to me
> in a besieged city.

31:22 But I—I said in my alarm,
> "I am cut off from before Your eyes";
> nevertheless, You heard the voice of my supplications [for grace]
> when I cried to You for help.

31:23 Love Yahweh, all you His devout ones.
> The faithful, He preserves—Yahweh—
> and fully requites the haughty doer.

31:24 Be strong and let your heart be courageous,
> all who wait on Yahweh.

Structure

With the structure of the psalm, below,[2] perhaps there was a gap of some sort between 31:20 and 31:21 that gave the supplicant explicit assurance of a divine answer to his prayer: after what has gone on before, 31:21 engages in thanksgiving and the psalm then concludes with an encouragement to God's people to be faithful to him.[3]

Prayer and Confidence (31:1–20): *Yahweh in the second person*

A	Prayer 1 (**31:1–4**)	"take refuge" (31:1a); "save" (31:2b); "rescue" (31:2b) "deliver" (31:2d); "let me not be shamed" (31:1b) "righteousness" (31:1c)
	B Confidence 1 (**31:5–8**)	"But I—in Yahweh I trust" (31:6b)
		C Lament (**31:9–13**)
	B' Confidence 2 (**31:14**)	"But I—in You I trust" (31:14a)
A'	Prayer 2 (**31:15–20**)	"take refuge" (31:19c); "save" (31:15b); "rescue" (31:15b) "deliver" (31:16b); "let me not be shamed" (31:17a) "righteous" (31:18b)

Praise and Commitment (31:21–24): *Yahweh in the third person*
Praise (**31:21–22**): "lovingkindness" (חֶסֶד, *chesed,* 31:21b)
Commitment (**31:23–24**): "devout ones" (חָסִיד, *chasid,* 31:23a)

---

2. Modified from Craigie, *Psalms 1–50*, 259. He notes that this psalm has "a high percentage of formulaic language in common with other psalms" that "might suggest that a general metaphorical interpretation is most appropriate" (Craigie, *Psalms 1–50*, 259, 261), making it possible to be employed in a variety of calamitous circumstances.

3. The second-person address to Yahweh in 31:22cd (in a section otherwise only referring to Yahweh in the third person) is perhaps because of the composer's emotional state as he reflects on what he had said in the past and how God ("You") had countered his assertion of abandonment.

Theological Focus

> When in the throes of deadly danger, the people of God prayerfully cast themselves into his hand, for he is their only refuge, and his relationship to them (extending his grace, lovingkindness, and goodness to them) and their commitment to him (faithfully seeking him and trusting him alone) give them confidence of deliverance, with adversaries getting their just deserts.

Commentary

Prayer 1 (31:1–4)

The supplicant bases his prayer on God's "righteousness" (31:1c) and "because of Your name" (31:3b)—both indicating a covenant relationship between human sufferer and divine supporter. Twice the psalmist notes "for [. . .] You . . . ," both times employing the emphatic pronoun in a verbless clause (אַתָּה [. . .] כִּי, *ki* [. . .] *'attah*, 31:3a, 4b)—for this God is his "refuge" (31:1a), "rock" (31:2c), "stronghold" (31:2c, 4b), "house of steadfastness" (i.e., an unshakable dwelling; 31:2d), "cliff," and "steadfastness" (31:3a), a piling on of synonyms that bespeak the supplicant's desire for God to deliver him.[4]

There is also an urgency to this prayer: "save me quickly" (31:2b), because the threatening nets of the enemy are laid "for me" (לִי, *li*; 31:4a); therefore, he wants God to be savior and deliverer "to me" (also לִי; 31:2c).

Confidence 1 (31:5–8)

The psalmist's confidence is explicitly declared in emphatic fashion: "but I—in Yahweh I trust" (31:6b). The carefully created lines of 31:6 underscore the point, contrasting idolaters with Yahweh-trusters, and indeed, "worthless idols" with "Yahweh" himself:[5]

> "... those who revere
> worthless idols,
> but I—
> in Yahweh
> I trust."

And why would he not trust Yahweh and rejoice in his lovingkindness (31:7a)? After all, this God, Creator of the universe has personally witnessed his affliction (31:7b) and known the distresses of his soul (31:7c). Therefore, into Yahweh's "hand" he commits himself (31:5a),

---

4. Being "shamed" (here in 31:1b, and also in 31:17a) is likely to be the consequence of enemies' accusations and attacks against the psalmist; he would *not* be shamed were deity to deliver him.

5. From Auffret, "'Tu as entendu,'" 153. In a further contrast, 31:5b has "God of *truth*," and 31:6a has "*worthless* idols."

for he knows that with God's help he will escape the enemy's "hand" (31:8a). Deliverance was nigh!

Indeed, hints of past rescues bolster the psalmist's courage as he asserts what God does not do (give him over to the "hand" of the enemy; 31:8a), and what God does do (keep his "feet" stable; 31:8b). "Distresses" (צָרָה, *tsarah*, 31:7c) implies a sense of *narrowness* (dire "straits," if you will), but God stands his feet in a *"broad* place" (מֶרְחָב, *merchav*, 31:8b). And so the supplicant cannot but "jubilate and be joyous" (31:7a) even before the divine rescue has been accomplished.

Lament (31:9–13)

At the center of the first section of the psalm (*Prayer and Confidence*, 31:1–20) is the sufferer's lament, almost entirely focused on the "I" of the supplicant: in this section there are twenty-one instances of the first person, in verbal, prepositional, and noun suffixes. The personal nouns include: "my eye," "my soul," "my insides" (31:9), "my life," "my years," "my iniquity,"[6] "my ability," "my bones" (31:10), "my adversaries," "my neighbors," "my acquaintances" (31:11), and "my soul" (31:13). All point to negative consequences for the psalmist, thus emphasizing the all-consuming and malignant nature of his adversity, no doubt taking its toll on the sufferer. No wonder the supplicant wants Yahweh to "be gracious" to him (31:9a).

That the major cause of these injurious events is external is further emphasized: both "distressed" (31:9b) and "adversaries" (31:11a) share the same root, צרר, *tsrr*. Also the assaults on the supplicant's "soul" (31:9d; and in 31:7c) are explained by the foes' attempts to seize his "soul" (31:13d)—i.e., take his life, a notion suggested also in 31:12a. What exactly the "reproach" is in 31:11a is unclear, though it certainly suggests that the illness/adversity/enmity suffered by the supplicant was rendering him noxious and abhorrent to all around him, from "adversaries" (31:11a) to "neighbors" (31:11b) to "acquaintances" (31:11c), and even to all "those who see me in the street" (31:11d). The "reproach" that the psalmist has "become" (31:11a) has caused him also to "become" (31:12b) like a "broken vessel": "the petitioner is an ancient Humpty Dumpty, a shattered pot never to be put back together again."[7] Adding fuel to the fire, there is also "defamation," "terror," "conspiring," and "scheming" that the supplicant is suffering (31:13). The situation is ruinous, indeed!

Yet there is hope, hinted in a wordplay: the psalmist had asserted that God "knows" (ידע, *yd'*, the distresses of his soul (31:7c); surely, then, God is aware of how his "acquaintances" (also from ידע) treat him (31:11c). And therefore deity will take action on behalf of his people, a trust explicitly maintained in the next section.

---

6. This appears to be a new element, seemingly out of place: "my iniquity." That does not indicate that personal sin was the causative agent of all the psalmist's distresses; rather it may simply be acknowledging the possibility that his own evildoing did play a role in the production of these disasters (albeit minor, since the issue does not crop up again in the psalm; for that reason, some read בַּעֲוֹנִי, *ba'awoni*, as בְּעָנְיִי, *b'anyi*, "my sorrow/affliction").

7. Brueggemann and Bellinger, *Psalms*, 158. Notice also the parallels: "I am forgotten [first-person perfect] as [כְּ, *k*] one who is dead, out of heart" (i.e., ready to expire; 31:12a); this is perfectly balanced by the next line: "I have become [first-person perfect] like [כְּ] a broken vessel" (31:12b).

Confidence 2 (31:14)

Adversaries may conspire together "against [עַל, *'al*]" the supplicant (31:13c), but the latter's trust is "in [עַל]" Yahweh (31:14a). This affirmation is almost identical to the earlier one in 31:6; both have the emphatic first-person pronoun: "But *I*—... I trust." The placement of these two "trust" sections around the "lament" section is, of course, significant.

Auffret perspicaciously observes that the use of prepositions in 31:13–18 is carefully organized by actions of the enemies ("–") and those of God ("+"). Despite the virulence of foes on the outside (textually outside as well: 31:13, 17–18), inside the "hand" of God (textually inside: 31:14–16; "hand" in 31:15a) is deliverance from the "hand" of enemies and from pursuers (31:15b):[8]

כְּ, "as" (31:13cα)	
עַל, "against" (31:13cβ)	–
לְ, *l*, "to" (31:13d)	
עַל, "in" (31:14a); בְּ, "in" (31:15a)	
מִן, *min*, "from" (×2; 31:15b)	+
עַל, "upon" (31:16a); בְּ, *b*, "in" (31:16b)	
לְ, "to" (31:17b)	
עַל, "against" (31:18b)	–
כְּ, "with" (31:18c)	

Thus, what is textually asserted is also textually pictured!

Prayer 2 (31:15–20)

This *Prayer 2* section parallels *Prayer 1* in 31:1–4, both seeking rescue from foes and sharing common elements: "take refuge" (31:1a, 19c); "rescue" (31:2b, 15b); "deliver" (31:2d, 16b); "let me not be shamed" (31:1b, 17a); and "righteousness/righteous" (31:1c, 18b). It was into the divine "hand" that the psalmist had committed himself (31:5a) for protection from the enemy's "hand" (31:8a); here, he recognizes that his times and days and indeed, his life, are in God's "hand" (31:15a), therefore a rescue from the "hand" of enemies and pursuers (31:15b) is assured.

The supplicant asked for God's "face" (פָּנֶה, *paneh*, 31:16a) to shine upon him (i.e., divine favor resting on him); the section ends with a confident acclamation of God keeping his people in his "presence" (also פָּנֶה, 31:20a). And, "taking refuge" "in You" (31:1b) has now turned out to be an appropriate tactic: God's goodness is heaped upon those who "take refuge in You" (31:19c). In contrast to the supplicant being "shamed" (31:1b, 17a), it is the wicked who are going to be "shamed" (31:17b)—their lot is to go "wail[ing] to Sheol."[9] Those who are characterized by "lying lips" and who are "speaking insolently" (31:18ab) end up groaning and moaning all the way into the grave (31:17b), while God's people are kept safe "from the strife

---

8. From Auffret, "'Tu as entendu,'" 160.
9. The verb יִדְּמוּ, *yiddmu*, is taken here as deriving from דמם, *dmh*, "wail."

of tongues" (31:20cd): all vocal attacks on the psalmist are repaid in kind as the attackers, now discomfited, lament their way to a hopeless end.

And this reversal is entirely due to the "goodness" of God (31:19a), "stored" for those who fear him and take refuge in him (31:19bc); and these faithful ones are also "stored" (31:20c) securely by God—his *stored* goodness in which he *stores* his people! The attackers who were "many" (רַב, *rav*, 31:13a) are countered by the goodness of God that is "great" (also רַב, 31:19a).[10] No foe is a match for God and his goodness, his lovingkindness and his loyalty to his people. And so he is certainly worthy of praise—the God who "hides" his people in the "hidden" place of his presence (31:20a).

Praise (31:21–22)

Earlier the supplicant had pled for God's "lovingkindness" to deliver him (31:16b), confident that he would subsequently rejoice in divine "lovingkindness" (31:7a). Now, in this *Praise* section, that expectation has been met, for God had demonstrated his "lovingkindness" to the psalmist (חֶסֶד, 31:21b), no doubt because the latter was one of the "devout ones" (חָסִיד, 31:23a). This was nothing but an answer to his "supplications [for grace]" (תַּחֲנוּן, *tachanun*, 31:22c), a response to his appeal to God to "be gracious" to him (חָנַן, *chnn*, 31:9a). The supplicant may have "heard" the threats and accusations of his enemies (31:13a), but here he is confident that God had "heard" his voice (31:22c) after he had implored God to "incline [his] ear" to him (31:2a). And God did!

Commitment (31:23–24)

This final charge to the community to be committed to Yahweh is structured chiastically, too:[11]

> "Love *Yahweh*,
>   *all* you His devout ones.
>   The faithful,
>   [He] preserves—
>   **Yahweh**—
>   and fully requites
>   the haughty doer.
>   Be strong and let your heart be courageous,
> *all* who wait on *Yahweh*."

The centering on Yahweh here is undoubtedly deliberate: it is he who has delivered the psalmist, and it is he who will deliver all in the divine community. The recommendation to "love Yahweh" (31:23a) is of a piece with the psalmist's prior affirmation: "I hate those who revere

---

10. The wordplay here is striking: "How great" (מַה רַב, *mah rav*) at the beginning of 31:19a corresponds sonically to "from the strife" (מֵרִיב, *meriv*) at the end of 31:20d. And both 31:20ab and 20cd are syntactically identical: second-person singular *yiqtol* verb ("You hide/store") + third-person plural suffix ("them") + בְּ (*b*)-phrase ("in . . .") + מִן (*min*)-phrase ("from . . .").

11. From Auffret, "'Tu as entendu,'" 164.

worthless idols" (31:6a)—worthless indeed, effete and ineffective for deliverance. God, on the other hand, is the gracious one, full of lovingkindness, overflowing with goodness, and faithful to his people, rescuing them from all danger.

Sermon Map

I. Trouble

    Dangerous circumstances (31:9–13)

    Move-to-relevance: Our dire situation and enemies

II. Trust

    Confidence of God's people (30:5–8, 14)

    Move-to-relevance: Our confidence

III. *Talk and Tell!*

    Prayer (30:1–4, 21–22)

    Praise (30:23–24)

    Specifics on praying and praising

PSALM 32:1–11

Psalm of Reorientation

The Blessed Confessor

PSALM 32 IS INCLUDED within the set of seven psalms traditionally labeled "penitential" (Psalms 6; 32; 38; 51; 102; 130; and 143) but there is nothing about penitence here. Rather, it is autobiographical (about concealed sins confessed and then forgiven) and pedagogical (about the advisability and advantages of seeking forgiveness of sins).[1] Goldingay is right: "How extraordinary that it declares the good fortune not of the faithful person (like Ps. 1) but of the faithless person, not of the torah-keeper but the torah-breaker"—after their faithlessness and torah-breaking have been confessed and forgiven, of course.[2]

Translation

32:1 Blessing [upon] the one pardoned of rebellion,
    whose sin is covered.
32:2 Blessing [upon] the person
    to whom Yahweh does not consider iniquity,
    and in whose spirit there is no deceit.
32:3 When I kept silent, my bones wasted away
    through my groaning all day long.
32:4 For day and night Your hand was heavy upon me;
    it was directed to my destruction [as] with the dry heat of summer.

---

1. Elements of wisdom in the psalm include: blessing (32:1–2), advice (32:6, 9), aphorism (32:10), vocabulary and style ("instruct," "teach," "counsel," in 32:8; "path" and "walk" as metaphors of conduct in 32:8a; animal comparisons in 32:9; and the equation of "righteous ones" with the "upright of heart" in 32:11bc). A number of trios also characterize the psalm—there are three words/descriptors each for: sin (in 32:1–2; and repeated in 32:5); forgiveness (32:1–2); confession (32:5); divine protection (32:7); divine instruction (32:8); and joy (32:11). See Waltke et al., *Psalms as Christian Lament*, 109.

2. Goldingay, *Psalms*, 1:454.

32:5   My sin I acknowledged to You,
           and my iniquity I did not cover;
       I said, "I will confess my rebellions to Yahweh";
           and You—You pardoned the iniquity of my sin.
32:6   Therefore, let everyone who is devout pray to You
           at a time when [He is] found.
       Surely in a flood of great waters
           they will not draw near to him.
32:7   You are a hiding place to me;
           from distress You preserve me;
           with shouts of salvation You surround me.
32:8   "I will instruct you and I will teach you in the path which you should walk;
           I will counsel [you] with My eye upon you.
32:9   Do not be like the horse, the mule,
           without understanding,
       whose advance is to be curbed with bit and bridle,
           [or] they will not approach you."
32:10 Many are the pains of the wicked,
           but he who trusts in Yahweh, lovingkindness shall surround him.
32:11 Be joyful in Yahweh
           and jubilate, righteous ones;
           and shout for joy, all [who are] upright of heart.

Structure

The psalm is finely structured, essentially the first half being negative (with mentions of sin, but no mention of the wicked or the righteous) and the second half being positive (with no mention of sin, but with mentions of the wicked and the righteous); the theme of blessedness, or the lack thereof, percolates throughout (see figure below).[3]

---

3. From Botha, "Psalm 32," 1–4; and Potgieter, "Structure and Homogeneity," 3–5.

Blessedness Affirmed (32:1–2): *To Community*
"Yahweh"; "sin"; "cover"; "rebellion"
"pardoned"; "iniquity"; "in … spirit"

−   **Unblessedness Afflicted** (32:3–4): *To Yahweh*
God's hand "upon me" (32:4a)

Unblessedness Absolved (32:5): *To Yahweh*
"Yahweh"; "sin" (×2); "cover"; "rebellions"
"pardoned"; "iniquity" (×2)

Blessedness Advocated (32:6–7): *To Yahweh*
"everyone [כָּל, *kal*]"; "devout [חָסִיד, *chasid*]"; "great [רַב, *rav*]"
"shouts"; "surround"

+   **Blessedness Advanced** (32:8–9): *From Yahweh*
God's eye "upon you" (32:8b)

Blessedness Appreciated (32:10–11): *To Community*
"all [כָּל]"; "lovingkindness [חֶסֶד]"; "many [רַב]"
"shout"; "surround"

Theological Focus

Confession of one's sins leads to the blessedness of God's forgiveness and the security of his lovingkindness, an occasion for great joy, and ensures God's continued guidance in his paths, in contrast to wicked, whose rebellious and deceitful resistance to confession leads to the distress of divine chastisement and the agonies of debilitation.

Commentary

Blessedness Affirmed (32:1–2)

The topic of the psalm is explicitly noted at its commencement and its conclusion: blessedness and joy for forgiven ones is affirmed (32:1–2 and 32:10–11[4]): אַשְׁרֵי, *'ashre*, "blessing," in 32:1a, 2a, is sonically balanced by יִשְׁרֵי, *yishre*, "upright," in 32:11c. Yes, those forgiven are reckoned upright, for "Yahweh does not consider iniquity" to them (32:2b).[5] On the other hand—looking at the negative aspect of the benedictions of 32:1–2—those covering up their rebellions, sins, and iniquities are considered "deceitful" (32:2c), later labeled "wicked" (32:10a). The three synonyms for malfeasance in 32:1–2 ("rebellion," "sin," and "iniquity"; also in 32:5) "specify the full dimension of human evil." Likewise, the three synonyms for forgiveness in 32:1–2 ("pardon," "cover," "not consider") "indicate the completeness of the divine deliverance

---

4. In the last two verses of the psalm, the forgiven and unforgiven become "righteous" and "wicked," respectively.

5. This is also emphasized in the wordplay of לֹא, *lo'* ("Yahweh does *not* consider iniquity") and לוֹ, *lo* ("*in whose* spirit there is no deceit") (32:2bc).

from evil which makes happiness possible."[6] And this blessedness of forgiveness is contrasted with the bane of unforgiven evildoers in 32:3–4 (below).

Unblessedness Afflicted (32:3–4); Unblessedness Absolved (32:5)

The unblessedness afflicted by unforgiven sin can be grievous, as admitted by the psalmist in a personal statement following the more general beatitudes of 32:1–2. He was groaning "all *day*" (32:3b) because "*day* and *night*" the hand of God was heavy upon him (32:4a), almost destroying him, with his bones "wasting away" (32:3a)—all symbolizing the sufferer's spiritual debilitation.[7] Failure to confess one's sins is certainly unhealthy, bringing upon oneself divine chastisement for what is nothing but overt rebellion. So the suffering psalmist could no longer "keep silent" (32:3a), i.e., he could not refrain from making his confession, and 32:5cd contains exactly what he said to himself: "I said, 'I will confess . . . .'"[8]

The resulting absolution of unblessedness by confession is detailed in 32:5, a verse packed with words borrowed from 32:1 ("Yahweh," "sin," "cover," "rebellions," "pardoned," "iniquity"). The act of acknowledging (אוֹדִיעֲךָ, *'odi'aka*, "I acknowledged," from ידע, *yd'*, 32:5a) is rendered equivalent to the act of confessing (אוֹדֶה, *'odeh*, "I will confess," from ידה, *ydh*, 32:5c). And, as if to underscore the importance of such confession, the various synonyms for misdeeds against God are arranged chiastically in this verse:

> "my sin"
>   "my iniquity"
>   "my rebellions"
>   "iniquity"
> "my sin"

Four of the five instances here have the first-person suffix: i.e., one is not to forget that the sins are one's own doing and are ineradicable without confession to God. Indeed, the first and last word of 32:5 is חַטָּאתִי, *chatta'ti* ("my sin")! But equally forceful is the dramatic reversal accomplished by God: "and *You*—You pardoned" (32:5d, with the emphatic added pronoun "You"). A breakthrough! "Confession is like opening the floodgate of a dam. When there is no confession, the waters pile up behind the dam, creating immense pressures on the wall, but as soon as the floodgate is opened, the waters subside and the pressures diminish."[9] The ironic use of "cover" should not be missed: in 32:1b the passive verb indicated forgiveness—an act of God; here in 32:5b the active verb indicates hiding—an act of the offender (which, of course, the psalmist is averring he did *not* engage in). What sinners need is not to hide their own sins, but *God* to hide them!

---

6. Craigie, *Psalms 1–50*, 266.

7. The word לְשַׁדִּי, *lshaddi*, in 32:4b is unclear as it stands; it is best read as לְשֻׁדִּי, *lshuddi*, "to my destruction."

8. "Keeping quiet is not a mark of OT piety. OT piety makes a noise, either in lament and prayer or in thanksgiving and praise," and, I'd add from this psalm, in confession (Goldingay, *Psalms*, 1:455).

9. Craigie, *Psalms 1–50*, 267.

Blessedness Advocated (32:6–7); Blessedness Advanced (32:8–9)

So moved and transformed is the psalmist by his own experience of confession, that he proceeds to recommend the same openness with God to the rest of his community. Doing so, by praying "to" God (אֶל, 'el, 32:6a), would result in the chaotic and turbulent waters not coming near "to" him (אֶל, 32:6d). God's people are bidden to seek him in confession "at [לְ, l] a time when [He is] found" (32:6b), in the calm before the storm hits, so that when it does, "in [לְ] a flood of great waters" (32:6c), they might be safe. Those "great" (רַב) waters will not touch the confessor, but for the wicked, who ostensibly refuse to confess, "many" (also רַב) will be their pains (32:10a). The ones who do not cover their sins before God, are the חָסִיד ("devout," 32:6a) who bank on God's חֶסֶד (chesed, "lovingkindness," 32:10b). And to them, God becomes a hiding place (32:7a). The pronoun אַתָּה, 'attah, "You," emphatically used in 32:5d to indicate divine pardoning, recurs in 32:7a: it is God and God alone who is a place of refuge, "preserving" the faithful, "surrounding" them with "shouts of salvation" (32:7bc). Thus, "commitment *to* Yhwh . . . opens one to the commitment *of* Yhwh."[10]

But it is not only the current relief from chastisement for unconfessed sin that the psalmist experiences from God. Ongoing instruction and counsel for the maintenance of blessedness are promised by God's own direct speech cited in 32:8–9.[11] "After the wrongdoing and the confessing, Yhwh effectively offers the resources to ensure that the worshipper will not fall into the same mistake again."[12] On the other hand, if they display a stubborn and rebellious resistance to confessing their sins, God's people are only being like recalcitrant and unsubmissive animals (32:9).[13]

Blessedness Appreciated (32:10–11)

The psalm concludes with a deep appreciation of the blessedness of forgiveness, in contrast to the "pains" (unblessedness) experienced by the wicked—non-confessors (32:10a). Confessors, on the other hand, will "be joyful," "jubilate," and "shout for joy" (32:11), an exhilaration experienced by "all" (כֹּל, kol) the upright and righteous who have found forgiveness (32:11bc), i.e., "everyone" (also כֹּל) who has prayed to God in confession (32:6a). No one is exempt: *all* need to confess, and *all* who confess enjoy blessedness. Earlier we found that upon confession, God "surrounded" his people with "shouts" (רֹן, ron) of salvation (32:7c); now, these same forgiven souls, "surrounded" by God's lovingkindness (32:10b), engage in "shout[ing] for joy" (from the root רנן, rnn) (32:11c). Celebration is called for!

In sum, Psalm 32 is a foundational psalm for the people of God, "illustrating powerfully the prerequisite of spiritual health, namely a self-conscious awareness of one's sinful life and the necessity of acting upon that awareness in confession before God."[14] Amen!

---

10. Goldingay, *Psalms*, 1:460 (emphases original).

11. While there is a second-person plural verb, "be," in 32:9a, the singular "you" in 32:9d makes it clear that there is no change of speaker (or singular addressee) in 32:9: the pedagogical intent of God's speech continues in this verse.

12. Goldingay, *Psalms*, 1:459.

13. I take עֶדְיוֹ, 'edyo, as a noun from עדה ['dh] I, "advance" (or even possibly from עדה III, "speed"), not from עדה II, "adorn": thus, "whose advance is to be curbed" (32:9c). See Goldingay, *Psalms*, 1:452ni. So: "They will not approach you," i.e., they will not submit to you.

14. Craigie, *Psalms 1–50*, 268.

Sermon Map

I. Unblessedness
   The unblessedness of failure to confess (32:3–4, 10a)
   Move-to-relevance: Our unconfessed sins
II. Blessedness
   The blessedness of confession (32:1–2)
   The necessity of confession for peace and security (32:6–7)
   Move-to-relevance: Our need for peace and security
   The maintenance of blessedness (32:8–9)
   Cause for celebration (32:10b–11)
III. *Be Blessed Reprieved!*
   Confession (32:5)
   Specifics on confessing: individual/corporate

PSALM 33:1–22
Psalm of Orientation

Singing of the Sovereign

PSALM 33 IS A composition about God who gets a mention in almost every line of the poem (the exceptions being 33:16–17, 19); but only in the last verse, 33:22, is he directly addressed.

Translation

33:1 Shout for joy, righteous ones, in Yahweh;
   to the upright, praise is fitting.
33:2 Give thanks to Yahweh with the lyre;
   with a ten-stringed instrument, make music to Him.
33:3 Sing to Him a new song;
   play skillfully with a shout of joy.
33:4 For upright is the word of Yahweh,
   and all His work [is] in faithfulness.
33:5 He loves righteousness and justice;
   the lovingkindness of Yahweh, it fills the earth.
33:6 By the word of Yahweh the heavens, they were made,
   and by the breath of His mouth all their host.
33:7 He gathers as a heap the waters of the sea;
   He puts in storehouses the deeps.
33:8 Let all the earth [be in] fear of Yahweh;
   let all the inhabitants of the world be in awe of Him.
33:9 For He spoke, and it was;
   He commanded, and it stood.
33:10 Yahweh, He frustrates the plan of the nations;
   He thwarts the intentions of the peoples.

33:11 The plan of Yahweh forever stands,
    the intentions of His heart from generation to generation.
33:12 Blessing [upon] the nation whose God is Yahweh,
    the people He has chosen as an inheritance for Himself.
33:13 From the heavens Yahweh watches;
    He sees all humanity;
33:14 From the foundation-place of His dwelling He looks
    at all the inhabitants of the earth,
33:15 The One who forms together their hearts
    [is] the One who understands all their works.
33:16 The king is not delivered by a great army;
    a warrior is not rescued by great strength.
33:17 False [hope] is a horse for deliverance;
    and by its great strength it does not save.
33:18 Behold, the eye of Yahweh [is] on those who fear Him,
    on those who wait on His lovingkindness,
33:19 to rescue their soul from death
    and to preserve them alive in famine.
33:20 Our soul longs for Yahweh;
    our help and our shield is He.
33:21 For our heart rejoices in Him,
    for in His holy name we trust.
33:22 May Your lovingkindness, Yahweh, be upon us,
    even as we wait on You.

Structure

A chiastic structure is visible in Psalm 33, with the *Dominion* and preeminence of Yahweh at the center:

A   *Invocation* (**33:1–5**): "lovingkindness" (33:5)

        Creation (**33:6–9**): God's "mouth" (33:6b)
   B   "heavens" (33:6a); "all" (×3; 33:6b, 8a, 8b)
        "fear" (33:8a); "all the inhabitants" (33:8b)

      C   *Dominion* (**33:10–12**): God's "heart" (33:11b)

        Redemption (**33:13–19**): God's "eye" (33:18a)
   B'   "heavens" (33:13a); "all" (×3; 33:13b, 14b, 15b)
        "fear" (33:18a); "all the inhabitants" (33:14b)

A'   *Affirmation* (**33:20–22**): "lovingkindness" (33:22)

PSALM 33:1–22

Theological Focus

The lovingkindness of God, the Creator of all things whose purposes are forever, is extended towards his people who fear him and trust him to preserve and deliver them, and who therefore rejoice greatly in their God—unlike those who do not fear God and who trust in everything but him, and whose self-directed purposes are defeated by God.

Commentary

Invocation (33:1–5)

The *Invocation* to praise God has five imperatival elements ("shout for joy," "give thanks," "make music," "sing," and "play skillfully" in 33:1–3) balanced by five attributes of God/his word/his deeds ("upright," "faithfulness," "righteousness," "justice," and "lovingkindness" in 33:4–5). It is the "righteous" and the "upright"—those committed to God (33:1a, 1b)—who are called to praise, and in turn, God's word is described as "upright"[1] and he loves "righteousness" (33:4a, 5a). What Yahweh is, his faithful ones are; what he loves, his devout must become.[2] The emphasis of the praise is clearly on sound: there are lyres, ten-stringed instruments, music, song, etc.[3] And the character of the one being praised is related tangentially to sound: "word of Yahweh" (33:4a). Of note, all the imperatives here are plurals: a communal and corporate praise of deity is being urged.

---

1. Goldingay, *Psalms*, 1:466, notes that lacking a Hebrew word for "promise," "the context may suggest that this word of Yhwh's is a declaration of intent about the future, a common meaning in the Psalms"—the "upright," true word as a pledge that can be trusted and praised (as in 56:4; 105:42; 106:24; 119:25).

2. As in other such moral descriptions of God's people in the Psalter, these do not indicate absolute moral purity; rather they are relational terms, indicating those who are committed to, rely upon, and are faithful unto God, "aware of their own frailty, finitude, and fallibleness" and thus "driven into the arms of mercy, to be totally reliant on a relationship with the Lord" (deClaissé-Walford et al., *Book of Psalms*, 313).

3. The progression in 33:1–3 is from voice (33:1) to instruments (33:2) to voice + instruments (33:3) (Seok, "In Search of the Theological and Hermeneutical Significance," 100). The "new song" of 33:3a is an "ever-new freshness of the praise of God," a renewal of praise, as God and his deeds are experienced day by day (Craigie, *Psalms 1–50*, 272). Altogether, the first three verses have two terms for praise each, for a total of six: "shout for joy," "praise," "give thanks," "make music," "sing," and "play skillfully."

Both 33:1 and 33:2 are skillfully arranged in chiastic fashion, adding poetic form to the musical intent of the words.[4]

Psalm 33:1
"shout for joy"
    "righteous ones"
        "Yahweh"
    "upright"
"praise"

Psalm 33:2
"give thanks to Yahweh"
    "with the lyre"
    "with a ten-stringed instrument"
"make music to Him"

In fact, 33:4 is also chiastic, the divine "word" and "work" being clothed in "uprightness" and "faithfulness":

Psalm 33:4
"upright"
    "word of Yahweh"
    "all His work"
"faithfulness"

In a summary that is expanded upon in subsequent verses, the *Invocation* also proceeds to give reasons for all this praise of God (33:4–5): God's upright word, faithful work, his righteousness, justice, and lovingkindness.[5]

Creation (33:6–9)

God is praiseworthy because of the might exercised in his *Creation*, accomplished by his "word," the "breath of his mouth," his "speaking," and his "commanding" (33:6a, 6b, 9a, 9b). Thus in this section the divine "mouth" is prominent, with all that proceeds from it.

God's dominion knows no equal, and it knows no limits—it is *all*-encompassing ("all" in 33:6b, 8a, 8b). Everything comes from the hand of God and all forces of chaos (symbolized by the "waters," "sea," and "deeps," 33:7) he controls, sequestering (incarcerating?) them away, precluding their wreaking havoc. The "host" of the heavens (33:6b), that God also created,

---

4. From Seok, "In Search of the Theological and Hermeneutical Significance," 90–91.

5. God's lovingkindness filling the earth (33:5) points out how deity relates to all his people in all the world: he *never* fails them or forsakes them. The connection of 33:4–5 with what follows is evident in: the repetition of "all" in 33:4b, 6b, 8a, 8b, 13b, 14b, 15b; "work[s]" in 33:4b, 15b (both מַעֲשֵׂה, ma'aseh), and "made" (עָשׂ, 'sh) in 33:6a; "word of Yahweh" in 33:4a, 6a; "earth" in 33:5b, 8a; and "lovingkindness" in 33:5b, 18b, 22a.

indicates the denizens of the spiritual realm, perhaps specifically the heavenly army of God. But *all* are merely agents of God, created to do the will of the mighty One.[6]

Therefore, the psalmist exhorts, "all the earth" and "all the inhabitants of the world" should "fear" Yahweh and "be in awe" of him (33:8). God's lovingkindness fills the "earth" (33:5b), but unless the dwellers on "earth" (33:8) reverence him, that divine lovingkindness will fail to be experienced by them. Instead, there will be consequences.

Dominion (33:10–12)

If God's "mouth" was the focus of 33:6–9, here it is God's "heart" (33:11b), i.e., the divine "plan" and "intentions" (33:11). These purposes of God directly counteract the human "plan" and "intentions" (33:10) of unbelieving peoples. The structure of 33:10–11 is carefully created as four pairs of elements:

A	"Yahweh, He frustrates	
B		the *plan* of the nations;
A'	He thwarts	
B'		the *intentions* of the peoples."
B''		"The *plan* of Yahweh
A''	forever stands,	
B'''		the *intentions* of His heart
A'''	from generation to generation."	

This deliberate, but seemingly irregular, construction of 33:10–11 precisely counterposes the "plan" and "intentions" of the peoples" (*B*, *B'*) with the "plan" and "intentions" of Yahweh (*B''*, *B'''*). The former are negated (*A*, *A'*) and the latter established (*A''*, *A'''*). These verses seem to be arguing that no matter how or where one slices the text, the truth of God's absolute dominion is incontrovertible and unassailable! Just as God spoke and the universe "stood" (עמד, *'md*, 33:9b), so also his plans "stand" forever (also עמד, 33:11a): no doubt, God's word and his breath (33:6–9) are being equated to God's plan and intentions (33:10–11).

Notice also that though God frustrates/thwarts the plan/intentions of the "nations" and "peoples" (both plural; 33:10), he blesses his chosen "nation" and "people" (both singular; 33:12): a divine partiality (or nepotism, if you will) towards his own. The latter are those who align themselves with God's "plan" and "intentions" (33:11) and it is for that reason they are blessed. How they are blessed is detailed below.

---

6. Not only does all this refer to God's *Creation*, the verbal links between Psalm 33 and the account of the exodus also point to God's redemption (expounded further in 33:13–19): "lovingkindness" (Ps 33:5b, 18b, 22a; Exod 15:13); "breath," "heap," "sea," and "deeps" (Ps 33:6–7; Exod 15:8); "fear" and "inhabitants" (Ps 33:8; Exod 15:11, 14–15); "inheritance" (Ps 33:12b; Exod 15:17); "place [. . .] of His/Your dwelling" (Ps 33:14a; Exod 15:17); "army" and "horse" (Ps 33:16–17; Exod 15:1, 4, 19, 21); and "name" (Ps 33:21b; Exod 15:3). See Botha and Potgieter, "'Word of Yahweh,'" 5–6.

Redemption (33:13–19)

Whereas 33:6–9 was symbolic of God's "mouth" and 33:10–12 of his "heart," here in 33:13–19 it is the divine "eye" (33:18a) that is prominent: God "watches," "sees," and "looks" (33:13–14a; and he "understands," 33:15b). All that to describe divine omniscience: the Creator of hearts (33:15a), who sees "*all* humanity" (33:13b), "understands *all* [the] works" (33:15b) of "*all* the inhabitants of the earth" (33:14b).[7] This seeing by deity is given prominence in the structure of 33:14:[8]

> "From the foundation-place
> of His *dwelling* [from ישב, *yshv*]
> **He looks**
> at all the *inhabitants* [from ישב]
> of the earth."

The divine dweller of the heavens sees the human dwellers of the earth—all of them, and all their deeds (33:14–15). After all, he whose "heart"-intentions are immutable and forever (33:11b) is the one who formed their "hearts" (33:15a).[9]

For his own people, however, God reserves a special gaze: All the inhabitants of the earth are exhorted to "fear" Yahweh (ירא, *yr*', 33:8a), for he is the one who "sees" all humanity (ראה, *r'h*, 33:13b), and so his eye, in a special and benevolent way, is upon those who "fear" him (ירא, 33:18a), his attention driven by his lovingkindness towards those who wait on him (33:18). And thus deity rescues and delivers his people from all their distresses—redemption!

We see "king," "army," "warrior," and "horse"—all motifs of power (33:16–17a). These four are balanced by four words of liberation: "deliver," "rescue," "deliverance," and "save"—all expected outcomes of trust in (human) powers that be (33:16–17). Some, ostensibly the non-God-fearers, put their hope in these—"*great* armies," the warrior's "*great* strength," and the "*great* strength" of the horse (33:16a, 16b, 17b). But alas, what is "great" in the eyes of mankind is of no avail: their false and deceptive number, might, and prestige "do not save" (33:17). Only God can, and he *will* save his people, "those who fear him" (33:18–19)![10]

---

7. This trio of "all" balances the three instances of "all" in the corresponding *Creation* section, in 33:6b, 8a, 8b. Such a repetition of "all" is further emphasized in the repeat of אֶל כָּל, *'el kal*: God's "looking *at all* [אֶל כָּל] the inhabitants" (33:14) is equated to his "understanding [*of*] *all* [אֶל כָּל] their doings" (33:15b).

8. Indeed, 33:13 and 33:14 are parallel: each has the location of Yahweh, mentions of his sight and of the object of his vision.

9. As was noted, the heavenly worker ("work," מַעֲשֶׂה, 33:4b) and maker ("made," also עשה, 33:6a) understands all the "works" (מַעֲשֶׂה, 33:15b) of humanity.

10. Human contrivances and appurtenances will not "rescue" one (33:16b); but God—he "rescues" the souls of his people from death and preserves their lives in famine (33:19). Needless to say, "the deliverance is not only *from* the terminal disasters which face a living person, but *into* a fullness of life in relationship with God" (Craigie, *Psalms 1–50*, 275 [italics added]).

Affirmation (33:20–22)

This section, containing the only first-person plurals in this psalm, concludes the song of praise with an *Affirmation* of "waiting" upon God (33:22b), for whom his people "long," and upon whom they "trust," for he is their "help" and their "shield" (33:20–21).

> To hope, to trust, and to wait, in the Old Testament, are not empty, passive activities—at least not if one means that there is not specific content or urgency to them. To wait is not just to do nothing. To hope is not merely to close one's eyes and accept what comes next. They are aggressive verbs in the theological sense that to hope in the Lord's *hesed* ["lovingkindness"] is actively to place one's identity and future in God's hands. To wait on the Lord is to look confidently to God for deliverance and to expect that deliverance.[11]

The intentions of God's "heart" stands forever (33:11b), and so the "heart" of God's faithful rejoices (33:21a), confident as they are in God's benevolence, his "lovingkindness" towards them (33:22a). "Though the themes of God's creative role and might are central to the psalm's substance, it is perhaps his *lovingkindness* that dominates the whole; it permeates the created earth . . . [33:5b], it is in the Lord's deliverance of his people . . . [33:18], and it is integral to the concluding prayer . . . [33:22]."[12] In a sense, then, the psalm begins and ends with God's "lovingkindness." That's all we hope for, and that's all we need!

Sermon Map

I. God's Mouth
   God and his word: upright, faithful, righteous, just, loving (33:4–5)
   Power of God's word in creation (33:6–9)
   Move-to-relevance: Our disregard of the Creator

II. God's Heart
   God and his purposes: forever, unwavering (33:10–12)
   God's blessing of his people (33:12–15)
   Move-to-relevance: Our misunderstanding of his loving purposes

III. God's Eye
   God and his omniscience (33:13–15)
   God's gaze upon his people (33:18–19)
   Deliverance only from God (33:16–17)
   Move-to-relevance: The true source of deliverance

IV. *Joyfully and Hopefully Praise!*
   Joy and hope (33:1–3, 20–22)
   Specifics on praising and waiting

---

11. deClaissé-Walford et al., *Book of Psalms*, 318.
12. Craigie, *Psalms 1–50*, 275.

PSALM 34:1–22

Psalm of Disorientation

God-Fearers Praising God

PSALM 34, ANOTHER ACROSTIC,[1] has no explicit thanksgiving; neither is any line of the composition addressed to God, though "Yahweh" is the most frequently occurring word in the poem (sixteen times in twenty-two verses). The psalm focuses mostly on "generalizations about Yhwh and on driving home implications for listeners"—more תּוֹרָה (*torah*, instruction) than תּוֹדָה (*todah*, thanksgiving).[2]

Translation

34:1	[א ALEPH]	I will bless Yahweh at all times;
		continually His praise [will be] in my mouth.
34:2	[ב BETH]	In Yahweh my soul boasts;
		may the humble hear and may they rejoice.
34:3	[ג GIMEL]	Magnify Yahweh with me,
		and let us exalt His name together.
34:4	[ד DALETH]	I sought Yahweh, and He answered me,
		and from all my terrors He rescued me.
34:5	[ה HE]	They look to Him and are radiant,
		and their faces are not ashamed.
34:6	[ז ZAYIN]	This afflicted one cried, and Yahweh heard,
		and from all his distresses He delivered him.
34:7	[ח CHETH]	The angel of Yahweh encamps around those who fear Him,
		and saves them.
34:8	[ט TETH]	Taste and see that Yahweh is good;
		blessing [upon] the one who takes refuge in Him.

---

1. This psalm is an incomplete acrostic, lacking the ו *Waw* segment; it also adds a second פ *Pe* segment at the end.
2. From Goldingay, *Psalms*, 1:477.

34:9	[י YODH]	Fear Yahweh, you His holy ones;
		for there is no lack to those who fear Him.
34:10	[כ KAPH]	The young lions want and hunger;
		but they who seek Yahweh shall not lack any good thing.
34:11	[ל LAMED]	Come, children, hear me;
		the fear of Yahweh I will teach you.
34:12	[מ MEM]	Who is the one who desires life
		and loves [many] days to see good?
34:13	[נ NUN]	Preserve your tongue from evil,
		and your lips from speaking deceit.
34:14	[ס SAMEKH]	Depart from evil and do good;
		seek peace and pursue it.
34:15	[ע AYIN]	The eyes of Yahweh are toward the righteous,
		and His ears to their cry for help.
34:16	[פ PE]	The face of Yahweh is against those who do evil,
		to cut off their memory from the earth.
34:17	[צ TSADE]	They wail, and Yahweh hears,
		and from all their distresses He rescues them.
34:18	[ק QOPH]	Yahweh is near to the brokenhearted,
		and those crushed in spirit He delivers.
34:19	[ר RESH]	Many are the troubles of the righteous,
		but from all of them He rescues him—Yahweh.
34:20	[ש SHIN]	He keeps all his bones,
		not one of them is broken.
34:21	[ת TAW]	Evil shall slay the wicked,
		and those who hate the righteous will be guilty.
34:22	[פ PE]	Yahweh redeems the soul of His servants,
		and none of those who take refuge in Him will be guilty.

Structure

This psalm may be structured as having a section of *Praise* followed by one of *Pedagogy*:[3]

> **Praise (34:1–10)**
> *Exaltation of God* **(34:1–3)**: humble to "hear" (34:2b)
> God: Powerful to save **(34:4–10)**: afflicted "heard" by God (34:6a)
> "Yahweh" (×6); "all" (×4); "faces" (34:5b); "fear Him" (34:7a)
> "Yahweh heard, and from all his distresses delivered him" (34:6)
>
> **Pedagogy (34:11–22)**
> *Exhortation to learn of God* **(34:11–14)**: children to "hear" (34:11a)
> God: Protector of the righteous **(34:15–22)**: God "hears" (34:17a)
> "Yahweh" (×6); "all" (×4); "face" (34:16a); "fear of Yahweh" (34:11b)
> "Yahweh hears, and from all their distresses rescues them" (34:17)

Theological Focus

Those fearing the praiseworthy God, and learning to do so more and more—i.e., seeking him by pursuing good and eschewing evil—are the righteous, the servants of God, whom God, in his goodness, hears and delivers from all manner of terrors external and distresses internal, while those wicked ones seeking evil and self-sufficiency will be punished.

Commentary

Praise (34:1–10)

The call for ceaseless praise is highlighted by the center of the chiastic structure of 34:1:

> "I will bless Yahweh
> at all times;
> continually
> His praise [will be] in my mouth."

God is praiseworthy at "all" times (34:1a) because of his rescue of his people "from *all*" terrors (34:4b) and "from *all*" distresses (34:6b), and because of his provision of "all" good things (34:10 has the same Hebrew word, translated "*any* good thing"). "All" of this (!) God does for his people, the "humble" (עָנָו, 'anaw, 32:2b) and the "afflicted" (also עָנָו, 34:6a), whose pleas he

---

3. Modified from Botha, "Social Setting," 180–81.

"answered" (עָנָה, 'anah, 34:4a).⁴ And so, the humble "*hear* and rejoice" (34:2b) because God has first "heard" (34:6a). Yes, God is praiseworthy.⁵

The resulting radiance of the rescued (the "they" of 34:5a) is equivalent to their unashamed faces (34:5b): the One they trusted in has heard them and rescued them—no more the shame of appearing to be rejected by their God. The move of generalization from the singular "I" of the psalmist (34:4) to the plural "they" of the community (34:5) is also repeated in 34:6–7, with the singular "this afflicted one" shifting to the plural "those who fear Him." What God has accomplished for one, he accomplishes for all, for the entire community of his people.⁶

This psalm boldly adduces evidence for the efficacy of prayer by asserting that God answers/hears (34:4a, 6a, 17a; see below). Indeed, not only does God hear and answer, the angel of Yahweh (found in the Psalter only in Psalms 34 and 35)—perhaps the commander of Yahweh's army (as in Josh 5:14) or even a member of the Godhead⁷—forms a protective cordon around "those who *fear* Him [God]" and saves them (Ps 34:7). Therefore, the people of God are exhorted to "*fear* Yahweh" (34:9a); consequently, there is no lack to those who "*fear* Him" (34:9b).

That is not all. Notice the structuring of 34:9b, 10b:

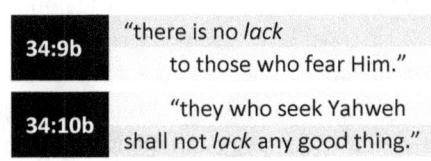

God-seekers will suffer no lack of "good"—the "goodness" of God (34:8a) is manifest to all who take refuge in him.⁸ In other words, fearing God results in seeing the goodness of God (indeed, "good" occurs in 34:8a, 10b, 12b, 14a). This is underscored by the wordplay as well: to "taste *and see* [וּרְאוּ, *ur'u*]" the goodness of Yahweh (34:8a) is to "*fear* [יְראוּ, *yr'u*]" him (34:9a—in

---

4. In more wordplays, the "praise" (תְּהִלָּה, *thillah*) of 34:1b is acoustically equated to the "boasting" (תִּתְהַלֵּל, *tithallel*) of 34:2a; likewise, "may [they] hear" (יִשְׁמְעוּ, *yishm'u*) and "may they rejoice" (יִשְׂמָחוּ, *yismachu*) are sonically parallel (34:2b).

5. The magnification and exaltation of God in 34:3 is, of course, not mankind adding to divine greatness, but an acknowledgment and announcement thereof.

6. As was mentioned, Psalm 34, like the most recently encountered acrostic, Psalm 25, lacks a ו *Waw* segment: it should have followed the ה *He* segment of 34:5. The ו *Waw* segment in the last acrostic psalm that had it, Psalm 9, bore the affirmation that "Yahweh sits forever; He has established His throne for judgment," etc. (9:7), the segment thereby restoring order into the alphabetic setup of that psalm as deity enters the scene left chaotic by the wicked and their evil (see on Psalm 9). It is quite possible that the missing ו *Waw* segments in Psalms 25 and 34 reflect the truth of real life in a real world: there is *no* obvious sign of Yahweh's reign. Other similarities between Psalms 34 and 25 include: the number of words (158 in each) (Freedman, "Patterns in Psalms 25 and 34," 133), and identical words/roots commencing several segments (מ *Mem*, ע *Ayin*, פ *Pe*, ש *Shin*, ת *Taw*, and the final פ *Pe*). Psalm 34 refers to the pleas of Psalm 25 and shares their vocabulary as it shows God answering prayer. Compare the corresponding alphabetic segments: 34:15 with 25:15; 34:16 with 25:16; 34:17 with 25:17; 34:19 with 25:19; 34:20 with 25:20; and 34:22 with 25:22. See Benun, "Evil and the Disruption of Order," 14–15.

7. See Gen 16:7–12; 22:11–12, 15–17; Josh 5:14 (where Joshua calls him "Lord"); Jdg 6:22–24.

8. "The one" in 34:8b translates גֶּבֶר, *gever*, which is particularly masculine, but the notion here is applicable to all, regardless of gender.

249

fact, "fear" begins and ends 34:9). The "young lions" of 34:10a are the most powerful of animals and the most unlikely to go hungry, being predators at the apex level. But, the psalmist points out, even these potent beasts may suffer lack, and the seekers of God never will. Young lions are self-sufficient and still fail; God-fearers are God-sufficient, and deity never fails them. In sum, the God-seeker and God-fearer, the one who goes to God for every need, will lack nothing, for divine protection and providence is always available for such a person. That is why God is worthy of all praise, all the time!

Pedagogy (34:11–22)

After the accounting of the praiseworthiness of this great God, the psalmist has some recommendations for members of his community. This "pedagogy" section begins with the ל *Lamed* segment of the acrostic, 34:11; the colon יִרְאַת יְהוָה אֲלַמֶּדְכֶם, *yir'at yhwh 'alammedkem* ("the fear of Yahweh I will teach you," 34:11b) forms the center of the psalm, with 77 words preceding (in 34:1–11a) and 77 following (in 34:12–23).[9] Strikingly, this ל *Lamed* segment verse actually contains the verbal stem למד, *lmd* (highlighted above) that spells out the name of the letter, *Lamed*, that means "to teach."[10] The goal of the psalm—to teach the fear of God[11]—is thus verbally painted into the middle of the composition (and in its overall structure—see below).

"Children" (בָּנִים, *banim*, or "sons"), perhaps the psalmist's pupils, are urged to "hear" (34:11a) about fearing the God who, in turn, "hears" his people (34:6a, 17a). What exactly this fear entails is explicated in the following verses, and made visible in the layout of the contrasting terms "good" and "evil" in 34:12–14:

34:12b	"good"	
34:13a		"evil"
34:14aα		"evil"
34:14aβ	"good"	

If one desires to "see good" all one's days (34:12b), and to "see" that Yahweh is "good" (34:8a), and not lack any "good" (34:10b), one must pursue "good" and eschew evil (34:14a). The experience of God's people (their not lacking any good) is closely tied to the character of their God (who is intrinsically good) and their own resulting behavior (their pursuit of good).[12] And that experience of unmitigated good is equated to a long life of peace and security (34:12, 14b).

One must not forget that the psalm is a poem, and a rhetorically artistic one at that; it does not provide a list of *x* number of things to engage in, so as to produce *y* quanta of results,

---

9. Maloney, "Word Fitly Spoken," 130.

10. This is not unique for this psalm: the כ *Kaph* segment begins with כְּפִירִים, *kphirim*, the first two consonants of which spell כפ, *kp* (34:10a); the מ *Mem* segment contains יָמִים, *yamim*, "days," that has a duplication of that consonant (34:12b); and the ע *Ayin* segment has the letter spelled out, עַיִן, *'ayin*, "eye" (34:15a) (Ceresko, "ABCs of Wisdom," 100).

11. We have already encountered the concept of "fear" of God in 34:7a, 9a, 9b.

12. Goldingay, *Psalms*, 1:480, likewise, notes the link between the theological, behavioral, and experiential.

and thus to enjoy *z* units of goodness.[13] Rather, the verses here, with their quasi-synonymous imperatives, seek to overwhelm the reader (the pupil?) with their thrust. In that regard, note three neat trios organized by syntactical and conceptual function, in 34:12–14:

34:12	Interrogative elements	"desires life" "loves [many] days" "to see good"
34:13–14aα	Negative elements	"preserve your tongue from evil" "[preserve] lips from speaking deceit" "depart from evil"
34:14aβ–b	Positive elements	"do good" "seek peace" "pursue [peace]"

Stated another way, God is against those who "do" evil (34:16a;[14] in contrast to those who "do" good, 34:14a) and the consequence of their mischief will be dire: even their memory will be cut off from the earth (34:16b). And their "evil" will return upon their own heads: "*evil* shall slay the wicked" (34:21a).

In short, "the righteous are blessed and protected; there is no place where they are beyond divine vision and there is no crisis so distant that God cannot hear their cry for help [34:15]. The positive metaphor of the all-seeing eye [and all-hearing ear] of God is converted in . . . [34:16] to the negative imagery of a divinely angry countenance [face], set firmly against the perpetrators of evil."[15] The contrast between the righteous and the evil is heightened in the last few verses of the psalm:[16]

34:15	"righteous"
34:16	"those who do evil"
34:17–20	"righteous" (34:19a)
34:21	"wicked"
34:22	"servants"

The culminating and unexpected label, "servants"—"*His* servants"—emphasizes the intimate alliance between God and his people (and also equates them with the "righteous"). They are the ones who are "heard" by God (34:6a, 17a), and they are the ones who are "rescued"/"delivered"

---

13. Neither is this text (and the many like this in the Psalter) intended to create the impression of a contractual form of works leading to blessing. Such passages simply point to the responsibility towards God of those who are in relationship to God to live righteously: a God-glorifying, Spirit-driven, merit-excluding, grace-accepting, faith-exercising obedience of the one who is already a child of God growing in Christlikeness. See Kuruvilla, *Privilege the Text!*, 189–209, 252–68.

14. That these offenders are perpetrating their "evil" (רָעָה, *ra'ah*; 34:16a) against the people of God is suggested by 34:19a that describes the "troubles" (also רָעָה) of the righteous, and by 34:21b that points out the hatred of the latter by the former.

15. Craigie, *Psalms 1–50*, 281.

16. From Hanson, "Alphabetic Acrostics," 80. From the context, the "they" in 34:17 refers to the righteous, carried over from 34:15.

by him "from all" (34:4b, 6b, 17b, 19b) their "terrors," "distresses," and "troubles."[17] Blanket deliverance for the "brokenhearted, and those crushed in spirit" (34:18) is nigh![18] Another structural treat is poetically spread for us in 34:19–20 to fortify this notion:[19]

> "Many are the troubles ...,
> but from *all* of them
> [He] rescues him—
> **Yahweh.**
> He keeps
> *all* his bones,
> not one of them ...."

The emphasis on God being the absolute protector and preserver of his people is unmistakable! No wonder the "soul" of the psalmist could boast in this God (34:2a), for this is a deity who redeems the "soul" of his servants (34:22a).[20] Nonetheless, Craigie's caveat is appropriate:

> God's presence is experienced *within* these crisis situations [whence the righteous cry]; there is no divine guarantee that the righteous will escape the crises and trials of modern existence. . . . The wisdom theology offers no easy alternatives with respect to life's hardships; there may be protection from evil or deliverance in evil, but the only thing common to the lives of the righteous is the continuation of the divine oversight and care. . . . The psalm, if fully grasped, dispels the naiveté of that faith which does not contain within it the strength to stand against the onslaught of evil.[21]

There is also a striking refrain in 34:4, 6, 17, comprising desperate plea + deity's response + dire situation + divine deliverance (going down the columns):[22]

Psalm 34:4	Psalm 34:6	Psalm 34:17
First-Person Singular	*Third-Person Singular*	*Third-Person Plural*
"I sought Yahweh,	"This afflicted one cried,	"They wail,
and He answered me,	and Yahweh heard,	and Yahweh hears,
and from all my terrors	and from all his distresses	and from all their distresses
He rescued me."	He delivered him."	He rescues them."

17. See also the repetition of "all" (כֹּל, *kol*) in this "pedagogy" section: rescue of the righteous from "all" distresses and troubles (34:17b, 19b), with "all" their bones intact (34:20a), and with "none" of those refuge-seekers punished (לֹא ... כֹּל, *lo'... kol*; 34:22b); this balances the four instances of "all" in the first "praise" section, as was noted earlier.

18. The God who is near to the "*broken*hearted" (שׁבר, *shbr*; 34:18a) will prevent their bones being "broken" (also שׁבר; 34:20). Thus we see a healing God who restores the "heart" (34:18a), "spirit" (34:18b), "bones" (34:20a), and the "soul" (34:22a) of his people, his servants.

19. From Auffret, "Allez, fils, entendez-moi!," 15.

20. Also note the wordplay in these verses: "may they rejoice" in 34:2b is יִשְׂמְחוּ, *yismachu*; and "[they] will be guilty" in 34:21b, 22b is יֶאְשְׁמוּ/יֶאְשָׁמוּ, *ye'shamu/ye'shmu*. The ones rejoicing in Yahweh will be ones redeemed by Yahweh—no guilt for them!

21. Craigie, *Psalms 1–50*, 1:281.

22. Modified from Benun, "Evil and the Disruption of Order," 14–15.

The thrice-iterated refrain asserts over, and over, and over that God answers his people's pleas for help—from *all* his people (the progression from first-person singular, to third-person singular, finally to third-person plural makes that comprehensiveness literarily manifest). The God who has answered prayers in the past will do so in the present, and again in the future. And that is exactly what the ק *Qoph* segment establishes in 34:18: "Yahweh is near to the brokenhearted, and those crushed in spirit He delivers."[23]

As with Psalm 25, the final verse is a פ *Pe* segment (25:22; 34:22), a reduplication of the letter putting it outside the acrostic pattern.[24] And so, in both psalms, the first word of the opening א *Aleph* segment, the first word of the middle ל *Lamed* segment, and that of the closing פ *Pe* segment, respectively commencing with א, ל, and פ (*a*, *l*, and *p*), hint at the verb אלף, *alp*, "learn"—the thrust of this psalm: *learn* the fear of God (34:11)![25]

Sermon Map

I. Cause for Continual Praise: Answered Prayer
    Answered prayer for deliverance (34:1–7; 15–22)
    Move-to-relevance: Our distresses and need for deliverance

II. Condition for Answered Prayer: Fearing God
    Fearing God (34:11, 13–14)
    Move-to-relevance: Maintaining a relationship to God

III. Consequence of Fearing God: Experiencing Goodness
    Experiencing God's goodness (34:8–10, 12)
    Move-to-relevance: Our self-sufficiency for our own "good"

IV. *Fear God, Feel Good!*
    Specifics on fearing God

---

23. Such an assurance (in the "person" of the ק *Qoph* segment) is lacking in Psalm 25, otherwise quite similar to Psalm 34. The absence of the ק *Qoph* segment in Psalm 25 "may poetically represent the lack of past evidence for God's intervention." Not so in Psalm 34 that makes a firm declaration that God has and will continue to answer the prayers of his people in distress. In all likelihood, this is what is being dramatically asserted, both verbally and literarily, by the reappearance of the ק *Qoph* segment in 34:18. See Benun, "Evil and the Disruption of Order," 15. Adding to the poesy is the chiasm in each of 34:18 and 34:20: "Yahweh is near / to the brokenhearted, // and those crushed in spirit / He delivers"; and "He keeps / all his bones, // not one of them / is broken," respectively.

24. The פ-word that commences both final verses in these two psalms is derived from the same root, פדה, *pdh* ("redeem").

25. Interestingly, if the *matres lectionis* (consonants functioning as vowels) are removed from 34:1, we are left with twenty-three consonants in that verse, the first an א, the middle a ל, and the last a פ, paralleling the overall layout of the psalm and reinforcing the אלף theme (Ceresko, "ABCs of Wisdom," 100–101).

PSALM 35:1–28

Psalm of Disorientation

God Fighting for His People, Against Their Enemies

In Psalm 35, the psalmist is under attack by adversaries, and he struggles to arrive at a point where he can praise God. But he finally does. And that in three rounds of this composition, each one with plaints and pleas and praises.

Translation

35:1 Contend, Yahweh, with those who contend with me;
    fight with those who fight me.
35:2 Take hold of scutum and shield
    and arise for my help.
35:3 And draw the spear and the hatchet to meet those who pursue me;
    say to my soul, "I am your deliverance."
35:4 May they be ashamed and may they be disgraced who seek my soul;
    may they be turned back
    and may they be humiliated who devise my trouble.
35:5 May they be like chaff before the wind,
    with the angel of Yahweh thrusting [them away].
35:6 May their way be dark and slippery,
    with the angel of Yahweh pursuing them.
35:7 For without cause they hid the hole of their net for me;
    without cause they dug [it] for my soul.
35:8 May devastation come upon him without his knowing,
    and may the net which he hid capture him;
    into that devastation—may he fall into it.
35:9 And my soul will jubilate in Yahweh;
    it will exult in His deliverance.

35:10 All my bones they will say, "Yahweh, who is like You,
    the rescuer of the afflicted from one who is stronger than him,
    and the afflicted and the needy from the one who robs him?"
35:11 Violent witnesses arise;
    things that I do not know they ask me.
35:12 They repay me evil for good—
    [like] bereavement [of children] to my soul.
35:13 But I—when they were sick,
    my clothing was sackcloth;
  I afflicted with fasting my soul
    when my prayer returned to my bosom.
35:14 Like [mourning for] a friend, like [mourning for] a brother, I went about;
    like one mourning for a mother, gloomy, I was [brought] low.
35:15 But at my stumbling they rejoiced and they gathered together;
    they gathered together against me,
  smiters I did not know—
    they tore at me unceasingly.
35:16 Like profane twisted mockers,
    [they] gnashed at me with their teeth.
35:17 Lord, how long will You look on?
    Restore my soul from their ravages,
    my only [soul] from the lions.
35:18 I will give You thanks in the great assembly;
    among a vast throng I will praise You.
35:19 Let them not rejoice over me falsely—my enemies;
    [or] those who hate me without cause wink the eye.
35:20 For they do not speak peace,
    but against the quiet in the land
    deceitful words they devise.
35:21 They opened wide their mouth against me;
    they said, "Aha, aha, our eyes have seen."
35:22 You have seen, Yahweh, do not be silent;
    my Lord, do not be far from me.
35:23 Stir up Yourself, and wake up to my justice,
    my God and my Lord, and to my cause.
35:24 Judge me, according to Your righteousness, Yahweh my God,
    and let them not rejoice over me.
35:25 Let them not say in their heart, "Aha, our desire."
    Let them not say, "We have swallowed him."

35:26 May they be shamed and may they be humiliated all together—
   those who rejoice [at] my trouble;
 may they be clothed with shame and ignominy—
   those who magnify [themselves] against me.
35:27 May they shout for joy and may they rejoice—
   those who take pleasure [in] my vindication;
 and may they continually say, "May Yahweh be magnified,
   the One who takes pleasure in the peace of His servant."
35:28 And my tongue, it will declare Your righteousness,
   [and] all day Your praise.

Structure

The structure of Psalm 35 is based on three rounds of plaints, pleas, and praises:[1]

Round 1: **Psalm 35:1–10**
 Petitionary Plaints (**35:1–3**)
 Imprecatory Pleas (**35:4–8**): "may they be shamed" (35:4a) "humiliated" (35:4c); "my trouble" (35:4c)
  "may they ..." (35:4aα, 4aβ, 4b, 4c, 5a, 6a, 8a, 8b, 8c)
 Anticipatory Praises (**35:9–10**)

Round 2: **Psalm 35:11–18**
 Petitionary Plaints (**35:11–17**)
 Anticipatory Praises (**35:18**)

Round 3: **Psalm 35:19–28**
 Petitionary Plaints (**35:19–24**)
 Imprecatory Pleas (**35:25–26**): "may they be shamed" (35:26a) "humiliated" (35:26a); "my trouble" (35:26b)
  "let them/may they ..." (35:25a, 25b, 26aα, 26aβ, 26c)
 Anticipatory Praises (**35:27–28**)

The predominant attack is personal, directed directly against the supplicant, with the martial elements in *Round 1* underscoring the intensity of the assault.[2] The legal vocabulary in the petitionary plaints in every round—"contend" (ריב, *ryb* [×2], 35:1a), "witnesses" (35:11),

---

1. There is no reason to suspect that each of the three rounds details a different situation.
2. That the language in 35:2a, 3a is hyperbolic seems obvious: even though the plea is unto God, a human warrior would not be able to take up both shield (small torso guard employed by the cavalry) and scutum (larger whole-body protector used by the infantry), or both spear and hatchet, at the same time. With the mention of defensive (35:2) and offensive (35:3) weaponry, the psalmist asks for nothing less than God's complete, total, exhaustive, comprehensive protection from the distresses tormenting him!

"justice" (35:23a) and "cause" (also רִיב, 35:23b)—show the human plaintiff presenting his "case" to the divine adjudicator.

Theological Focus

> The dire situation of distress experienced by God's people, caused by opponents intent on destroying them—despite the righteous solicitude of the former for the latter in the past, repaid by evil in the present—prompts the faithful to confidently request God's destruction of these now-rejoicing opponents on the basis of his righteousness, resulting in the people of God being vindicated and rejoicing in their deliverance and praising God.

Commentary

Round 1 (35:1–10)

This round sets the stage for the rest of the psalm with some clear demarcations: the petitionary plaints (35:1–3) are directed to God in the second person; the imprecatory pleas (35:4–8) are about the enemies in the third person; and the anticipatory praises (35:9–10) are essentially first-person oriented (indirectly by means of "my soul" and "my bones").

The situation of the psalmist is dire: the intensity of the personal attack of virulent foes against him is emphasized by the multiple mentions of "my soul" in this *Round 1* (34:3b, 4a, 7b, 9a) and in the rest of the psalm (35:12b, 13c, 17b). Notice how a verbal picture is painted in 35:7–8:

> "hid" (35:7aα)
>   "net" (35:7aβ)
>   "for me" (35:7aγ)
>   "for my soul" (35:7b)
>   **"devastation … without his knowing" (35:8a)**
>   "net" (35:8bα)
> "hid" (35:8bβ)

Essentially, "me" and "my soul" (in the center) are trapped in the "net" which the enemy "hid" (both located on either side of "me" and "my soul"). And all of these assaults are "without cause," afflicting the innocent supplicant (35:7a, 7b; also 35:19b). But the twist in this "story" is that "devastation comes upon him [the *enemy*] without his knowing": in the placement of that colon (35:8a) within the chiasm (within the hidden net?) we discover that after this dramatic reversal it is *he*, the opponent, who has been trapped in his own concealed threat ("net"): "may the net which he hid capture him; into that devastation—may he fall into it" (35:8bc). In the literary telling, he already has; the tables have been overturned, textually, pictorially!

In the overall structure of 35:1–10, this rescue requested from God is once again emphasized. The imprecatory pleas (35:4–8; pertaining to the foes: "may they . . .") are centrally arranged, with identical verbiage, all pertaining to God, set on either side of those denunciations:

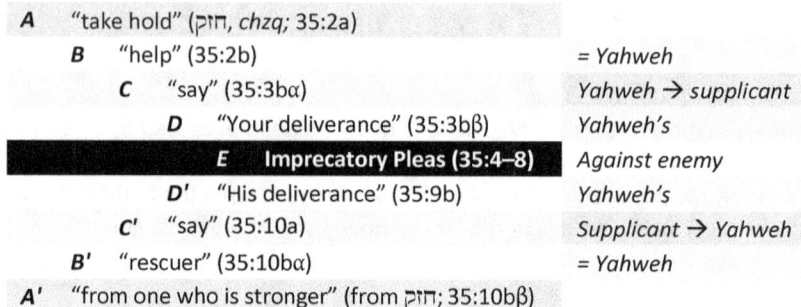

Simply put, the might of Yahweh and his deliverance of the faithful, testified to in 35:3b, 10a, hems in the offending foes being imprecated against. They, in contrast, are going to be shamed, disgraced, repulsed, humiliated (35:4), dispersed, expelled (35:5), tripped, pursued (35:6), devastated, ensnared, and toppled (35:8).³ A comprehensive collapse and comeuppance, indeed, for those cruel and callous ones causing calamities for the righteous (35:4b)! Just deserts are also visible in the wordplay: they will be "humiliated" (חפר, *chpr*, 35:4c, 26a) who "dug" (also חפר, 35:7b) a hole to entrap the supplicant. And those who "pursued" the supplicant (35:3a) will now be "pursued" by none other than the angel of Yahweh (35:6b).⁴ There is no discrepancy between this external agent seeking to punish evildoers, and the latter falling into pits and nets of their own design. No doubt the causative agent, proximal or distal, of the overthrow of malefactors is God, one way or the other, directly or indirectly.

And so the psalmist can expect to rejoice (35:9–10): "my soul" (35:3b, 4a, 7b) that was being blitzkrieged and battered by hostile forces is now "my soul" (35:9a) that will be blissful in God and will boast in his deliverance (35:9); indeed, the very depths of his being—"all my bones" (35:10a)—will praise God!

Round 2 (35:11–18)

In *Round 2*, the imprecatory pleas are absent. Instead, we have an extended section of petitionary plaints (35:11–17)—laments—followed by anticipatory praises (35:18).

We see again why the supplicant bid God to "arise" to help him (35:2b): "violent witnesses" were themselves "arising" (35:11a). What exactly their witnessing was about is unclear; false accusations are likely to be in view. Neither do we know how these attacks were violent, though a link to the "smiters" in 35:15c is possible: both in 35:11b and in 35:15c

---

3. Even though "one who is stronger" (35:10b) refers to the enemy, it is the *defeated* enemy who is in view here, conquered by the One who is even stronger than this evil strongman.

4. This personage, likely the commandant of God's army, or a member of the Godhead himself, shows up twice in this psalm (35:5, 6) and only one other time in the Psalter (in 34:7).

we have "I do/did not know."[5] The grotesque description of the mockers in 35:16,[6] gnashing their dentition at the psalmist, and their equation with ravaging "lions" (35:17bc), only make the picture more dreadful.

The psalmist makes protestations of innocence, that his good deeds are now being repaid by evil (35:13–14): he had mourned and fasted and prayed for his foes when they were ill, continuing in these exertions even when his intercessions were unanswered ("returned to my bosom," 35:13). In the days of his ascetic distress on their behalf, he was like a bereaved person who had lost a sibling or a parent (35:14). The one willing to make even repeated prayers (i.e., those that "returned [שׁוּב, shwv]") for the welfare of his foes (35:13d) is now beseeching God to "restore [also שׁוּב]" his soul from the harassment of the ones he had pled for (35:17b). He who had once "afflicted" himself on their behalf (35:13c) is now being "afflicted" by those ingrates (35:10b, 10c). Thus, all he gets in return now for his benevolence and altruism towards them is malevolence and abuse, rendering him like one bereaved of a child (35:12c).[7] These claims to unrequited righteousness in 35:13–14 are of no avail: there seems to be no hope, for he is hemmed in, literally and literarily, by the treacheries of 35:11–12 and 35:15–16!

> False accusations (35:11)
>   Foul deeds (35:12)
>   **Faithful righteousness** (35:13–14)
>   Foul deeds (35:15)
> False accusations (35:16)

Notice the repeated first-person suffixed pronoun, עָלַי, 'alay, "against/at me," in 35:15b, 16b, and later in 35:21a, 26d—the ganging up of these adversaries in opposition to him ("gathered together," 35:15a, 15b). And once again, the repetition of "my soul" in 35:12b, 13c, 17b adds to the pathos, as these wicked ones "rejoice" in triumph (35:15a, 19a).

Hounded by these provocations and aggressions, the sufferer calls upon God for rescue in 35:17 and, quite remarkably, moves forthwith into an anticipatory praise in 35:18.[8] The confidence of the supplicant is palpable!

---

5. In any case, the vagueness of the historical situation that prompted the writing of the psalm lends this text a transtemporal quality, enabling it to be reutilized in many others' lives, in many other places, at many other times.

6. I follow Goldingay, *Psalms*, 1:488n3, on 35:16a, with regard to מָעוֹג, ma'og; he sees this word derived "from a second root 'ûg [עוג], meaning 'be bent' (. . . but I take the genitive as descriptive rather than objective)." Thus: "*twisted* mockers."

7. The verb שׁכל, shkl, in the *qal* means "being bereaved of children": Gen 27:45; 42:36; 43:14; 1 Sam 15:33. Strikingly then, we have in Ps 35:12b a mother mourning for the loss of children, and in 35:14b a child mourning the loss of a mother! Also notice the wordplay: "they ask me" in 35:11b is יִשְׁאָלוּנִי, yish'aluni; "they repay me" in 35:12a is יְשַׁלְּמוּנִי, yshallmuni: i.e., the vocal challenges of those "violent witnesses" (35:11a) was akin to repayment to psalmist for the good he had done for them.

8. This verse and the next (35:18, 19) are each organized chiastically: "I will give You thanks / in the great assembly; // among a vast throng / I will praise You"; and "Let them not rejoice over me falsely / —my enemies; // [or] those who hate me without cause / wink the eye."

Round 3 (35:19–28)

The final round of Psalm 35 is similar to the first round, with plaints, pleas, and praises. The imprecatory pleas in *Round 3* (35:25–26) closely parallel those in *Round 1* (35:4–8), with several terms shared (see structure of the psalm above).

This round is also characterized by the most direct addresses to deity employing the vocative (six of the nine such instances in the psalm): "Yahweh" in 35:22a, 24a (also in 35:1a, 10a); "Lord" in 35:22b, 23b (also in 35:17a), and "God" in 35:23b, 24a. Clearly, a finale is expected in *Round 3* and the intensity of the prayer-poem is reaching a crescendo. God is being asked to act in congruence to his "righteousness" (צֶדֶק, *tsedeq*, 35:24a) so that the psalmist's "vindication" is realized (also צֶדֶק, 35:27b); deity is then ultimately praised for his "righteousness" (צֶדֶק, 35:28a). That is in line with a second collection of "let them/may they ..." in 35:25a, 25b, 26aα, 26aβ, 26c, 27a, 27c: when God acts in his righteousness towards the righteous, the unrighteous are thoroughly discomfited.

These foes are "winking the *eye*" (35:19b)—likely a gesture of deceit and characteristic of the wicked, the perverted, and the evildoer (Prov 6:12–13; 10:9–10). Their eyes may have been blinking in derision, but their "eyes" had also triumphantly "seen [רָאָה, *r'h*]" the defeat of their prey (Ps 35:21b). That, however, would be no cause for worry for the God-fearer, for deity who had been beseeched to "look [רָאָה]" at the psalmist's plight (35:17a) is now explicitly noted to have "seen [רָאָה]" (35:22a). When God sees, God acts, and the rest is history!

These violent offenders do not speak "peace" (35:20a), but God—he is the one "who takes pleasure in the *peace* of his servant" (35:27d). In a similar contrast, the "speaking" (דבר, *dbr*) and "words" (דָּבָר, *davar*) of these evildoers is noted in 35:20a, 20c, as *not* extending "peace." They "say" contemptuous things (35:21b, 25a, 25b[9]), but in the end it will be God's people who have the final "say" (35:27c). And what they say paints a poignant reversal: "those who take pleasure" in the psalmist's victory (35:27b; i.e., members of God's community) will magnify Yahweh "the One who takes pleasure" in the *shalom* of his servant (35:27d). And the fate of those enemies is finalized: "May they be shamed" (35:26a; and 35:4a), and "may they be clothed with shame" (35:26c). The shaming of the evildoers *is* going to happen!

The section of petitionary plaints (35:19–24) has an *inclusio*, "Let not my enemies/let them not rejoice over me" (35:19a, 24b). Earlier, in *Round 2*, these foes were described as "rejoicing" (35:15a). Now, the sufferer is convinced that the situation is going to be reversed: it would be the community of the psalmist who would be rejoicing (35:27a), not the cabal of his enemies. This overthrow is depicted with precise symmetry in the text:[10]

	35:26ab (Enemies)	35:27ab (God's People)
Jussive	"May they be shamed	"May they shout for joy
Conjunction + Jussive	and may they be humiliated ...—	and may they rejoice—
Substantive Adjective	those who rejoice	those who take pleasure
Noun + first-person suffix	[at] my trouble."	[in] my vindication."

---

9. The evil ones' "Aha, our desire" (35:25a) may be paraphrased: "We've got what we wanted—him!" And they proceed to devour the afflicted soul (35:25b).

10. All the four jussives (both pairs) are *qal* imperfect verbs.

And the consequence? Instead of the malefactors "magnifying" themselves against the righteous (35:26d), it would be the righteous "magnifying" Yahweh (35:27c), declaring his righteousness and his praise all day (35:28)! O, magnify the Lord!

Sermon Map

I. Righteousness of God's People
   Solicitude for others (35:13–14)
   Move-to-relevance: Our care for others

II. Repayment to God's People
   Reciprocation with evil (35:11–12, 15–16, 20–21)
   Move-to-relevance: Our righteousness recompensed with evil

III. Reparation for God's People
   Requesting just treatment (35:1–8, 17, 19, 22–26)
   Move-to-relevance: God requites in his righteousness

IV. *Request and Rejoice!*
   Invoking God to make restitution (35:9–10, 18, 27–28)
   Specifics on praying with celebration

PSALM 36:1–12

Psalm of Orientation

The Overthrow of the Wicked

WHILE IT READS MOSTLY as a psalm of orientation, there are elements of disorientation, too, in Psalm 36: complaint about foes, trust in God, and petition for help.

Translation

36:1   The utterance of rebellion of the wicked is in the midst of my heart;
       there is no terror of God before his eyes.

36:2   For it flatters him [too much] in his eyes,
       to discover his iniquity [and] to hate [it].

36:3   The words of his mouth are harm and deceit;
       he has ceased to be wise [and] to do good.

36:4   Harm he devises upon his bed;
       he sets himself upon a path that is not good;
       evil he does not reject.

36:5   Yahweh, to the heavens [extends] Your lovingkindness;
       Your faithfulness unto the skies.

36:6   Your righteousness [is] like the highest mountains;
       Your judgments, [like] the great deep;
       human and animal You deliver, Yahweh.

36:7   How precious [is] Your lovingkindness, God.
       And humans take refuge in the shadow of Your wings.

36:8   They drink their fill from the richness of Your house;
       and [from] the river of Your luxuries You make them saturated.

36:9   For with You is the fountain of life;
       in Your light we see light.

36:10 Extend Your lovingkindness to those who know You,
and Your righteousness to the upright of heart.
36:11 Let it not come upon me, the foot of haughtiness,
and the hand of the wicked, let it not drive me away.
36:12 There the doers of harm have fallen;
they have been overturned and are not able to rise.

Structure

Where one may have expected a lament of distress caused by enemies, one sees 36:1–4 reading more like the disposition of those adversaries; rather than an assertion of confidence in God, we see 36:5–9 looking more like a doxology; and instead of a closing petition for aid against evildoers, 36:10–12 looks more like the deliverance of the righteous. This, it seems, is what happens in God's world; hence my label of this psalm as one of orientation.

> **Disposition of Evildoers (36:1–4)**
> 3 negative particles (36:1b, 4b, 4c)
> "wicked" (36:1a); "harm" (36:3a, 4a); "heart" (36:1a)
> Motifs: lying on bed, walking (36:4ab)
>
> **Doxology for God (36:5–9)**
> *God's character in general (36:5–6)*
> Starts with "lovingkindness" (36:5)
> *God's lovingkindness in specific (36:7–9)*
> Starts with "lovingkindness" (36:7)
>
> **Deliverance of Righteous (36:10–12)**
> 3 negative particles (36:11a, 11b, 12b)
> "wicked" (36:11b); "harm" (36:12a); "heart" (36:10b)
> Motifs: walking, falling (36:11–12)

Botha observes that the Hebrew prepositions create a poetic arena, especially in the first two sections (36:1–9). The space dealing with the wicked is constrained and limited: "*before* his eyes," 36:1b; "*in* his eyes," 36:2a; "*upon* his bed," 36:4a; "*upon* a path," 36:4b. On the other hand, the space dealing with God is extended and unlimited: "*to* the heavens," 36:5a; "*unto* the skies," 36:5b; "*like* the highest mountains," 36:6a; "[*like*] the great deep," 36:6b. Not surprisingly, the prepositional spaces dealing with the righteous, who are allied with God, relate to the aegis and care of God: "*in* the shadow of Your wings," 36:7a; "*from* the richness of your house," 36:8a; "[*from*] the river of Your luxuries," 36:8b; "*with* You," 36:9a; and "*in* Your light," 36:9b.[1] We know how this is going to end!

Notice also how the future of the righteous is adumbrated in the layout of key terms: the humans (ostensibly the faithful; 36:6c, 7b–9) are protected on either side (and on the

---
1. Botha, "Textual Strategy," 514.

inside) by God and his character—particularly his lovingkindness of which they are beneficiaries—barricading them from the wickedness and iniquity that threaten them from without (36:1–4, 11–12):[2]

36:1–4	"wicked," "harm"	Evildoers
36:5–6b	"lovingkindness," "righteousness"	God
36:6c	"human"	Righteous
36:7a	"lovingkindness"	God
36:7b–9	"humans"	Righteous
36:10	"lovingkindness," "righteousness"	God
36:11–12	"wicked," "harm"	Evildoers

Theological Focus

The wicked—utterly iniquitous and oppressing the righteous, and seeing no necessity for fearing God, consumed as they are by themselves—are restrained by God's lovingkindness which, extending to the righteous, preserves and bountifully blesses them, enabling them to witness the overthrow of the wicked by God.

Commentary

Description of Evildoers (36:1–4)

The character of the wicked is showcased by their thoughts and words right at the commencement of the psalm: "rebellion," "wicked" (36:1a); "no terror of God" (36:1b); "flattered" (36:2a); not "hating" iniquity (36:2b); "words of . . . harm and deceit" (36:3a); not "wise," not "doing good" (36:3b); devising "harm" (36:4a; "harm" also occurs in 36:12a); going down a "path that is not good" (36:4b); and not rejecting "evil" (36:4c). Three negative particles emphasize the vileness of these foes: "*no* terror of God" (36:1b); "a path that is *not* good" (36:4b); and "evil he does *not* reject" (36:4c).[3] Altogether iniquity pervades the first four verses.

In addition, body parts of these malefactors are mentioned: "eyes" (36:1b, 2a) and "mouth" (36:3a)—they see evil and speak evil. Incidentally, two prepositional phrases follow "eyes" in 36:2a: "*to* discover his iniquity" and "*to* hate [it]" (36:2b). Similarly, two prepositional phrases follow "mouth" in 36:3a: "*to* be wise" and "*to* do good" (36:3b; negated, of course). These organs and the parallel prepositional usage point to evildoers as seeing only themselves in their own eyes and spouting whatever they want from their mouths. In fact they are so taken by themselves ("flattered," 36:2a), they are blinded to their own iniquity and fail to hate such wickedness (36:2b). And, not surprisingly, there is "no terror of God before [their] eyes" (36:1b). Oblivious, or perhaps indifferent, about their own immorality, these iniquitous ones

---

2. Modified from Auffret, "'Yahvé, Qu('elle nous est) chère,'" 70.
3. "Good" occurs twice (36:3b, 4b), only to be negated both times.

are "the incarnation of the temptation to live life by setting up the self as the autonomous standard, to live life according to 'what seems good to me.'"[4]

So, from concocting iniquity "*upon* [their] bed" they sally forth "*upon* a path that is not good" (36:4ab). What they contrived lying down, they are now perpetrating as they go about upright.[5] And all of this evil directly affects the righteous "in the midst of my *heart*" (36:1a)—a punch to the gut, hard and deep, sore and painful, hurtful and grievous.

Doxology for God (36:5–9)

For the first time in the psalm, "Yahweh" shows up, and does so suddenly, as he is addressed in the vocative (36:5a). One might have expected a description of the righteous to follow the description of evildoers, but, no, it is God who is described, praised, and blessed: *Doxology for God*. The logic, however, is impeccable: "Here are the wicked [36:1–4], and here You are, O God . . . [36:5–9]. Therefore, . . ." and then comes a request for the deliverance of God's people (and the disposition of the wicked; 36:10–12).

This doxology of 36:5–9 serves as a stark contrast to the evil of the iniquitous. The God being praised is the God the immoral have dismissed: they have rejected God's lovingkindness and largesse, generously extended to "human and animal" (36:6c), they have repelled his protective wings, and they have refused the goodness of his house (36:7b, 8[6]). What a contrast: "a rebellious, faithless, slippery, harmful, deceptive evildoer" vs. a God "characterized by commitment, truthfulness, faithfulness, authority, and deliverance."[7] No fountain of life or light for them (36:9)!

God's character is described in general in 36:5–6: his "lovingkindness," "faithfulness," "righteousness," and "judgments" compared, respectively, to the awe-evoking vastness of the heavens, skies, mountains,[8] and oceans. Then comes God's character again, focusing on his "lovingkindness," in 36:7–9. Thus both subsections begin with "lovingkindness" (36:5a, 7a). While the first subsection attends to the majesty and magnificence of creation to stage those divine attributes,[9] the second converges to a specific locus, the precincts of the temple (36:8), from whence cometh divine lovingkindness to God's covenanted people.[10] Unlike

---

4. Jacobson, "Psalm 36:5–11," 64.

5. The individual wicked person is, no doubt, symbolic of a crowd of equally nefarious ones, hence my use of plurals here.

6. The "river of Your luxuries" and "fountain of life" have resonances with Ps 46:4; Ezek 47:1–12; Rev 22:1–3—the bounty of God's blessings in the eschaton and, to some extent, even in the here and now. "Luxuries" is עֶדֶן, *'eden*, which also is "Eden," thus also linking Ps 36:8b and the "saturation" of God's people by the "river of luxuries" with the actual rivers that flowed from that Garden, the holy of holies in the creation temple (Gen 2:10–14): Eden, after all, is the locus of God-breathed life, salutary for every divine purpose and for all human fulfillment. Goldingay, *Psalms*, 1:510–11, noting that "richness" also indicates "fat" (Ps 36:8a), observes that this "drinking of fat" is a striking idiom for the magnificence of the divine feast.

7. Goldingay, *Psalms*, 1:509.

8. "Highest mountains" in 36:7a is הַרְרֵי־אֵל, *harre-'el*, with אֵל, the name of God, being employed adjectivally as a superlative.

9. Also, of note, 36:5a, 5b, 6a, 6b are each constructed in parallel fashion: divine attribute (+ second-person masculine suffix) likened to an element of creation.

10. That the temple, especially the eschatological edifice, has resonances with Eden and creation is not surprising; see Kuruvilla, *Genesis*, 39–51.

the wicked who do not see God, but only themselves in their "eyes" (36:1b, 2a), God's people "see" God in theirs—divine light (36:9b).

Deliverance of Righteous (36:10–12)

It is now time, the poet reckons, for the deliverance of the righteous (and a final disposition of the wicked, stated in terms of the blessing that such punitive action becomes for God's people). And the appeal to God to take action in this regard grounds itself on the "lovingkindness" vaunted earlier in the doxology for God (36:10aα; reflecting 36:5a, 7–9)—may it be extended to "those who know You" (36:10aβ), and divine righteousness to "the upright of heart" (36:10b).[11] Whereas the vile and rebellious utterances of the wicked had hit the "heart" of the righteous (36:1a), that blow has been replaced by the blessing of divine righteousness extended to the "upright of *heart*" (36:10b). The three negative particles in this conclusion of the psalm (in 36:11a, 11b, 12b) pertain to the righteous,[12] and reflect the three in the commencement of the prayer (in 36:1b, 4b, 4c) that pertained to the wicked.

36:1b	"no [אֵין, *'en*] terror"	"not [אַל, *'al*] come"	**36:11a**
36:4b	"not [לֹא, *lo'*] good"	"not [אַל] drive me away"	**36:11b**
36:4c	"does not [לֹא] reject"	"not [לֹא] able to rise"	**36:12b**

The downfall of the wicked is under way—a signal of the deliverance of the righteous. Those who were headed down "a path that is not good" (36:4b) are now "fallen"—"overturned and . . . not able to rise" (36:12). Even the reference to these evildoers' "foot" (36:11) is a take on the motif of their haughty and oppressive march that tramples underfoot the people of God.[13] The posture of these malfeasants shows up in an organized fashion throughout the psalm, from lying flat to fallen flat:

36:4a	"bed"
36:4b	"path"
36:11a	"foot"
36:12	"fallen," "not able to rise"

"*There* the doers of iniquity have fallen" (36:12a)—there is a stunning finality in the use of the adverb of position, "there."

In sum, this final section, 36:10–12, points to the deliverance of the righteous from the lethal assaults of the wicked. God is urged to act against the wicked, on behalf of the righteous,

---

11. This may sound like the typical plea of a psalm of disorientation, but there is no indication that the psalmist or his cohort are currently being afflicted by any distress (though that may be implied).

12. The last in 36:12b, directly relate to the unrighteous, but their "*not* being able to rise" is indirectly a blessing for the righteous.

13. And perhaps the righteous were being "driven away" from the temple, thrust away by the wicked's "hand" (36:11b)?

PSALM 36:1-12

and he does. This is how life is, in the lovingkindness of God, how life ought to be for the righteous in this less-than-ideal world—thus, this is a psalm of orientation. Therefore, the composition attempts to convince God's people to live (and luxuriate!) in his lovingkindness and not in lawlessness that can only end in lament.

Sermon Map

I. Lawlessness of Evildoers
    Character of the wicked; oppression of the righteous (36:1–4)
    Move-to-relevance: Evildoers in our lives

II. Lovingkindness of God
    Character of God; blessing of the righteous
    Move-to-relevance: God's manifest blessings

III. Liberation of Righteous
    Call to God; overthrow of the evildoers (36:10–12)
    Move-to-relevance: God's preservation of us

IV. *Live in Lovingkindness, not in Lawlessness!*
    Specifics on choosing the right side

PSALM 37:1–40

Psalm of Orientation

Hope of the Righteous Against the Wicked

PSALM 37 COMPRISES FORTY verses that would be quite at home in the book of Proverbs. There is recommendation and reason (37:1–2, 8–9, 27–28), advice and consequences (37:3–6), contrasts between the behavior of the righteous and that of the wicked (37:9, 10–11, 17, 21, 22, 37–38), a "better is . . . than . . ." aphorism (37:16), appeals based on the psalmist's experience (37:25, 35–36), and even the term "wisdom" itself occurring for the first time in the Psalter (חָכְמָה, *chakmah*; 37:30a).[1] No sequential development of thought running through the psalm is discernible; it appears to be an anthology of wisdom sayings, "an instructional poem."[2] However, it is an acrostic that, at the very least, points to how divine order in the world ought to be manifest, particularly in light of the prominence of distinctions between the wicked who prosper and the righteous who don't, and the recompense each receives.[3] "The main themes are that one should have patience and trust in God always keeping in mind that the wicked—even if they are now rife and successful—will perish, and the righteous—who are now few and threatened—will prevail and inherit the land."[4]

Translation

37:1 [א ALEPH]   Do not let your anger burn because of evil ones;
                 do not envy wrongdoers.

---

1. See Goldingay, *Psalms*, 1:517.

2. Craigie, *Psalms 1–50*, 296 (italics removed).

3. Goldingay, *Psalms*, 1:518. Antitheses between the righteous inheriting land and the wicked being cut off therefrom are found in 37:9, 10–11, 18–20, 22, 28–29, 34, 37–38. The fate of the latter (or of their implements) is particularly graphic and final: they are "cut off" (37:9a, 22b, 28c [even their descendants], 34c, 38b); "broken" (37:15b, 17a); and "destroyed" (37:38a).

4. Benun, "Evil and the Disruption of Order," 15. In the current dispensation, "land" may be considered as the divine kingdom, or the microcosm thereof that a righteous person of God inhabits and is a citizen of (or one that a community of God's people occupy and are natives of), awaiting the divine macrocosm that is to come. As noted below, "abiding" in the land is to live with God (37:3b, 27b, 29b); "possessing" it earmarks the blessing/rewards from God for so abiding (37:9b, 11a, 22a, 29a, 34b).

37:2		For like grass they will quickly shrivel,
		and like the green herb they wither.
37:3	[ב BETH]	Trust in Yahweh and do good;
		abide in the land and cultivate faithfulness.
37:4		So take delight in Yahweh;
		and He will give you the requests of your heart.
37:5	[ג GIMEL]	Commit to Yahweh your path;
		and trust in Him, and He will do [it].
37:6		He will bring forth like light your vindication
		and your justice like the noonday.
37:7	[ד DALETH]	Be still before Yahweh and wait patiently on Him;
		do not let your anger burn
		because of the one who prospers in his path,
		because of the person who carries out nefarious schemes.
37:8	[ה HE]	Forsake anger and abandon wrath;
		do not let your anger burn; [it leads] only to evildoing.
37:9		For evil ones will be cut off, but those hoping in Yahweh,
		they—they will possess the land.
37:10	[ו WAW]	So yet a little while and there will be no wicked person;
		and you will look carefully for his place and he will not be there.
37:11		But the afflicted will possess the land
		and they will take delight in abundant prosperity.
37:12	[ז ZAYIN]	The wicked schemes against the righteous,
		and gnashes at him with his teeth.
37:13		The Lord laughs at him,
		for He sees that his day is coming.
37:14	[ח CHETH]	The sword they have drawn—the wicked—
		and they have bent their bow,
		to bring down the afflicted and the needy,
		to slaughter those [who are] upright in [their] path.
37:15		Their sword will enter their [own] heart,
		and their bows will be broken.
37:16	[ט TETH]	Better is the little of the righteous
		than the wealth of many wicked.
37:17		For the arms of the wicked will be broken,
		but the righteous are supported [by] Yahweh.
37:18	[י YODH]	Yahweh knows the days of the blameless,
		and their inheritance will be forever.
37:19		They will not be ashamed in the time of evil,
		and in the days of famine they will be satiated.

37:20 [כ KAPH]	But the wicked will perish, and the enemies of Yahweh—	
	like valuable pastures they are consumed; in smoke they are consumed.	
37:21 [ל LAMED]	The wicked borrows and does not repay,	
	but the righteous is gracious and gives.	
37:22	For those blessed by Him will possess the land,	
	but those cursed by Him will be cut off.	
37:23 [מ MEM]	By Yahweh one's steps are established,	
	and in His path he delights.	
37:24	Though he fall, he will not be thrown down,	
	for Yahweh supports his hand.	
37:25 [נ NUN]	I was young, [now] also old,	
	but I have not seen the righteous forsaken,	
	or his descendants seeking bread.	
37:26	Every day he is gracious and lends,	
	and his descendants are a blessing.	
37:27 [ס SAMEKH]	Turn aside from evil and do good,	
	and abide forever.	
37:28	For Yahweh, He loves justice and does not forsake His devout;	
	they are kept unto forever,	
	but the descendants of the wicked will be cut off.	
37:29	The righteous will possess the land	
	and abide in it always.	
37:30 [פ PE]	The mouth of the righteous utters wisdom,	
	and his tongue speaks justice.	
37:31	The law of his God is in his heart;	
	his footsteps do not slip.	
37:32 [צ TSADE]	The wicked spies upon the righteous,	
	and seeks to kill him.	
37:33	Yahweh, He will not abandon him into his hand	
	and He will not let him be condemned when he is judged.	
37:34 [ק QOPH]	Hope in Yahweh and keep His path,	
	and He will exalt you to possess the land;	
	when the wicked are cut off, you will see [it].	
37:35 [ר RESH]	I have seen a wicked one, violent,	
	displayed like a flourishing native [tree].	
37:36	Then he passed away, and behold, he was no more;	
	I sought him, but he could not be found.	
37:37 [ש SHIN]	Watch the blameless one, and see the upright;	
	for [there will be] posterity to the person of peace.	

37:38	But rebels will be altogether destroyed; the posterity of the wicked will be cut off.
37:39 [ת TAW]	But the deliverance of the righteous is from Yahweh, their stronghold in time of distress.
37:40	Yahweh helps them and saves them; He saves them from the wicked and delivers them, for they take refuge in Him.

Structure

While the divisions shown below are not entirely waterproof (as expected for a wisdom-like composition), one might structure the psalm in this fashion:

37:1–11	**Exhortation 1:** "do good [טוֹב, *tov*]" (37:3a); "abide" (37:3b) "possess the land" (37:9b, 11a); "cut off" (37:9a) "and he will not be there" (וְאֵינֶנּוּ, *w'enennu*, 37:10b) "hoping in Yahweh" (37:9a)
37:12–15	**On the Wicked**
37:16–22	**Wicked *vs.* Righteous:** "better [טוֹב]" (37:16a) "possess the land" (37:22a); "cut off" (37:22b)
37:23–26	**On the Righteous**
37:27–40	**Exhortation 2:** "do good [טוֹב]" (37:27a); "abide" (37:27b, 29b) "possess the land" (37:29a, 34b); "cut off" (37:28c, 34c, 38b) "he was no more" (אֵינֶנּוּ, *'enennu*, 37:36a) "hope in Yahweh" (37:34a)

Theological Focus

The people of God, in the face of oppression by the wicked who flourish and prosper temporarily, trust in God, persist in doing good, and walking in God's way guided by him and delighting in him, they thereby delight him—resulting in the wicked being defeated soundly and soon, disqualified from rewards, and displaced altogether by a just God who, in contrast, rewards the faithful under his care, blessing them eternally.

Commentary

On the Acrostic of Psalm 37

Psalm 37 is another incomplete acrostic like Psalms 9–10, 25, and 34: here, the ע *Ayin* segment is lacking. Also, most segments have a primary and a secondary verse (as in Psalms 9–10), except for the ד *Daleth*, כ *Kaph*, and ק *Qoph* segments that have only primary verses (37:7, 20, 34): ד and ק form, respectively, the fourth letter from the beginning and the fourth from the end; כ, the eleventh letter, becomes, in the absence of ע, the center of the remaining twenty-one letters.[5] In addition, there is an added, anomalous verse (37:29; a tertiary verse) after the primary and secondary verses of the ס *Samekh* segment (37:27–28). Benun notes the intricate patterning of the psalm that clearly is by design:[6]

	Letter Segments	Verses per Segment	Words per Section	
A	א, ב, ג ', b, g	2	42	
B	ד d	1	11	**10 letters**
C	ה, ו, ז, ח, ט, י h, w, z, ch, t, y	2	88 (46+42)	
D	כ k	1	10	**1 letter**
C'	ל, מ, נ, ס, פ, צ l, m, n, s, p, ts	2	88 (42+46)	
B'	ק q	1	11	**10 letters**
A'	ר, ש, ת r, sh, t	2	41	

The number of verses/segment alternates between two verses/segment and one verse/segment for each of the seven groups, A through A' (see Verses per Segment above.) And the word count in corresponding groups of letter segments is almost identical (see Words per Section, above), with one important exception: group C' (comprising the ל, מ, נ, ס, פ, and צ segments) actually contains 94 words, but if the six words of that anomalous verse in 37:29 (where the missing ע *Ayin* segment should have been—the now-tertiary verse of the ס *Samekh* segment) are discounted, one gets a total of 88 that matches the words in the corresponding group C (comprising the ה, ו, ז, ח, ט, and י segments). This seems to indicate that 37:29 is "simply out of place."[7] As if that weren't enough, the primary verses of each of the six segments in group C have a total of 46 words; the secondary verses have 42. Remarkably, it is the inverse with the corresponding group: the primary verses of the six segments in group C' have 42 words; the secondary verses, 46 (again excluding 37:29 in this calculus). In sum,

---

5. Benun, "Evil and the Disruption of Order," 27n50. Much of the detail for the explanation of the acrostic is taken from Benun's magisterial essay.

6. Modified from Benun, "Evil and the Disruption of Order," 16.

7. Benun, "Evil and the Disruption of Order," 17.

37:29 appears to have been a deliberate insertion, a toppling of the pattern, an upsetting of the routine, so to speak. For what purpose?

Interestingly, that out-of-place verse begins not with a ע word as one would have expected if it were a ע Ayin segment (that has seemingly disappeared), but with צַדִּיקִים, tsaddiqim ("the righteous"). In fact, 37:30 begins with a compound word also containing צַדִּיק, tsaddiq: פִּי־צַדִּיק, pi-tsaddiq ("mouth of *the righteous*"). Putting these observations together, one might postulate a loose syllogism:

If:
    not-ע = צדיק (*tsdyq*, "righteous"),
then:
    ע = not-צדיק ("not righteous");
therefore:
    ע = רשע (*rshʻ*, "wicked")!

And thus, where "wicked," רשע (= ע) is missing, we find, instead, צדיק, in 37:29: the righteous are where the wicked are not! Adding to the intrigue, רשע occurs fourteen (= 7 × 2) times in Psalm 37, more than twice the number in any other psalm, and the letter ע (= "wicked," רשע, by our syllogism) is found 70 times (= 7 × 10) in Psalm 37—both multiples of 7, a significant biblical number.[8]

All of this makes 37:10 (preceding the anomalous verse, 37:29) and 37:35–36 (following it) become revealing statements not just about the fate of the wicked in life, but also about the ultimate fate of the "wicked," רשע, represented by the ע Ayin segment gone AWOL in the psalm at 37:29.

---

8. Benun, "Evil and the Disruption of Order," 20.

My glosses of these two texts, preceding and following 37:29, are in italics and shaded below (bear with me in this hermeneutical experiment; I promise it will go somewhere!):[9]

> **Psalm 37:10**
> "So yet a little while
> *[in a few verses hence]*
> and there will be no wicked person [רשע]
> *[no ע Ayin segment]*;
> and you will look carefully for his place
> *[wondering where ע has gone, at 37:29]*
> and he [רשע] will not be there"
> *[the ע Ayin segment will be missing]*.
>
> **Psalm 37:35–36**
> "I have seen a wicked one [רשע] ...
> *[רשע: 7 × 2 times in Psalm 37]*,
> displayed like flourishing native [tree]
> *[ע: 7 × 10 times in Psalm 37]*.
> Then he [רשע] passed away, and behold, he was no more
> *[both from real life, and from the text at 37:29]*;
> I sought him [רשע]
> *[in Psalm 37, expecting to find him at 37:29]*,
> but he [רשע] could not be found"
> *[the ע Ayin segment was gone]*!

To state the obvious, the disappearance of the ע *Ayin* segment at 37:29 occurs immediately after the last word of 37:28. But the last word there is נִכְרָת, *nikrat*, "[they] will be cut off," referring to the descendants of the "wicked," רשע. Indeed, they are "cut off" in more ways than one. Thereby, both text and thrust of text congruently and comprehensively attest to a future where the רשע (= ע) will be no more, thus encouraging the righteous not to be aggrieved by the evanescent prosperity of those vile ones or to envy them: the fate of the wicked has been sealed![10] In sum, the anomalous ע verse, 37:29, bears the prominent message of the psalm: "The righteous will possess the land and abide in it always [but the wicked will vanish]"—a

---

9. Modified from Benun, "Evil and the Disruption of Order," 21.

10. Why are these the particular verses, 37:10 and 37:35–36, the ones that cleverly simulate (paint?) textual content in literary form? The first, 37:10, is seven words long, begins at the seventieth word of the psalm, and ends at its seventy-seventh. The second, 37:35, is striking in that every one of its six words contains either a ר or a ע or both: the combination, רָע, of course, means "evil." Besides, both these key verses are preceded by verses that, in each case, remind readers that "evil ones" (from רעע, *r*ʿʿ; 37:9a) and the "wicked" (רשע, *rshʿ*; 39:34c) will be "cut off" and "you will see [it]." These verses also contain the verb קוה, *qwh*, "to hope" (37:9a, 34a), both instances indicating the response of the righteous towards Yahweh: they hope for the "cutting off" of these nefarious enemies and—*voila!*—the wicked (represented by both רשע and the ע *Ayin* segment) disappear (or soon will), as the following verses, 37:10 and 37:35–36, explicitly attest (see Benun, "Evil and the Disruption of Order," 21). Perhaps 37:16 is equally self-reflective: "Better is the little of the righteous [צדיק occurs only nine times in the psalm—a 'little'] than the wealth of many wicked [רשע occurs fourteen times—the 'many']." These artistic literary devices add considerably to *how* it means, i.e., to the text's force, thrust, and impact (pericopal theology), and therefore it contributes significantly to *what* it means. These filigrees of nuanced writing are ingenious rhetorical stratagems that clue us to authorial *doing* in the psalm. See Benun, "Evil and the Disruption of Order," 21, 28n59, 28n60.

notion repeated also in 37:9b, 11a, 22a, 34b (also see paraphrases in 37:3b, 18b, 27b).[11] The discussion about the acrostic and its import leads naturally to the recommendation of this psalm for its readers and users, in its two exhortation sections, at the beginning (37:1–11; *Exhortation 1*) and the end of this remarkably intricate composition (37:27–40; *Exhortation 2*). Now on to the various parts of the composition....

Exhortation 1 (37:1–11)

At the outset there is a hint that evildoers are flourishing and that the righteous are both angry (at God for his inaction? at the unfairness of it all?[12]) and envious (of those wicked) (37:1). However, the prosperity of malefactors will be short-lived (37:2). Rather than be angry, then, the people of God are called to trust him (37:3a, 5b), do good, abide, and be faithful (37:3). Both here in 37:3b and in 37:27b, "abide" is an imperative—"a challenge to the hearer, a goal to be achieved, or a task to be involved in as part of the exhortation to trust and obey" God.[13] But "*possessing* the land" (as opposed to *abiding* in it) is a consequence of blessing from the hand of God, the result of his people "abiding" in the land. It seems, therefore, that "abiding" is to live faithfully in God's way, by divine demand, with the abundant "possession" being equivalent to the rewards that God gives for that faithfulness.[14]

Such faithful living ("trusting" and "doing"; 37:3a) and enjoying the consequences (of divine blessings, both now and in the future) is what it means to delight "in Yahweh" (עַל־יְהוָה, *'al-yhwh*; 37:4a), to "be still" before him (37:7a), and to "wait" on him (37:7a[15]). The consequence of such commitment "to Yahweh" (also עַל־יְהוָה; 37:5a) is that their desires will be met (37:4b), and God will act on their behalf ("do," 37:5b), ostensibly against evildoers troubling them. "Wrong*doers*" may abound (from עשה, *'sh*; 37:1b), but the righteous are called to "*do* good" (עשה; 37:3a; also 37:27a); then, God will, in turn, "do" (also עשה; 37:5b). Thus, "trust ... and do ..." (37:3a) becomes "trust ... and He will do ..." (37:5b). And soon "there will be no wicked person, ... he will not be there" (37:10). So, despite the temporary turbulences caused by these malefactors along the way, the righteous resolutely yield their "path" to God (37:5a), rather than look at the wicked prospering in *their* "path" (37:7c). One day God will vindicate his people with justice (37:6) and then these God-"delighters" (37:4a) will, in turn, "take delight" in bountiful prosperity at the hand of God (37:11b). God is the sure and *only* hope!

On the Wicked (37:12–15)

While this section focuses on the wicked, the word (רשע) is liberally peppered all over this psalm, in this section and elsewhere.[16] They come in singular and plural sizes,[17] reflecting

---

11. Interestingly, with regard to the land, "possessing" it or being "cut off" from it are used together in 37:9, 22, 28–29, 34; only in 37:11 is the former used alone; only in 37:38 is the latter used alone.

12. "Burning anger" shows up in 37:1a, 8b; and "anger" in 37:7b, 8a.

13. Vander Hart, "Possessing the Land," 139–40.

14. Notice the emphatic pronoun in 37:9b, stressing the certainty of land possession: "they—they will possess."

15. On 37:7, I follow Goldingay, *Psalms*, 1:514nd, who reads הִתְחוֹלֵל, *hitcholel*, as deriving from חִיל [*chil*] II, a form of יָחַל, *yachal*, "wait." A synonym, קוה, that also means "hope" (or "wait") is found in 37:9a, 34b.

16. See 37:10a, 12a, 14a, 16b, 17a, 20a, 21a, 28c, 32a, 34c, 35a, 38b, 40b. Then there is "be condemned," also רשע, in 37:33b.

17. As also do the "righteous": 37:12a, 16a, 17b, 21b, 25a, 29a, 30a, 32a, 39a (and there is also "blameless

the fact that "there are often singular and plural threats in our world."[18] And these oppressors were "bringing down" the "upright in [their] path" (37:14b): upright walkers were becoming face-down "fallers."

Scheming against the righteous, the wicked gnash at them with their teeth—a gesture of anger (37:12), but then it is God who laughs at them, likely showing *his* teeth (37:13a). Deity, unlike fretting humans, sees ahead. And the day of the reckoning of the wicked was "coming" (בא, *bw'*; 37:13b); it would be these evil ones' own swords (37:14) that would "enter" their hearts (also בוא; 37:15a). They might bend the "bow" (37:14b), but once again those same vain implements, their "bows," would be "broken" by God (37:15b)—and not only their bows, but the arms of the wicked, too ("broken," in 37:17a). Craigie calls this the "'boomerang principle' of evil," propelled by God, no doubt, as the passives in 37:15b, 17a indicate.[19]

Wicked vs. Righteous (37:16–22)

The contrast between the wicked and righteous is not restricted to this section, but here we do see it more sharply, most pronounced in the first verse of the section, 37:16. The ones urged to do "good" (טוב; 37:3a) are now blessed with "better" (also טוב; 37:16a).[20]

37:16a	"better"	"little"	"righteous"
37:16b	"wealth"	"many"	"wicked"

Goldingay suggests that the "breaking" of the arms of the wicked (37:17a) may ironically depict their limbs succumbing under the weight of the wealth they are carrying! On the other hand, the righteous are "supported [by] Yahweh" (37:17b).[21] The Lord who laughs because the "day" of the wicked is coming (37:13b) also intimately knows the "days" of the righteous (37:18a) and their imminent blessing; others might suffer in the "day" of famine, but God's people will be satiated (37:19b) and, indeed, their blessing will last forever (37:18b)! The wicked don't stand a chance, "consumed" as they are (×2; 37:20b). Their prosperity is transient and evanescent. As was noted, the כ *Kaph* segment is the central one in this acrostic psalm, and its second line, 37:20b, forms the central line of the psalm, resounding with כs: בִּיקַר כָּרִים כָּלוּ בֶעָשָׁן כָּלוּ, *kiqar karim kalu ve'ashan kalu*; the first occurrence of כלה, *klh* ("consume") in this verse is also the central word of the psalm—the 149th out of a total of 297 words.[22] Thus a core theme of this composition is underlined in 37:20: the wicked are done for!

In fact, even while they live, they are trapped: in financial crises, they borrow but are unable to repay—they are in great need—unlike the righteous who have plenty and are gracious, so much so they can even lend (37:21; see 37:26a). All that to say, it is the righteous who are

---

one" in 37:37a, and the "upright," in 37:14b, 37a).

18. deClaissé-Walford et al., *Book of Psalms*, 353.

19. Craigie, *Psalms 1–50*, 298. Or a righteous divine spanner cast into wicked human machinations.

20. One day, however, the "wealth of the *many* wicked" (רב, *rav*, 37:16b) will meet its match (and be exceeded by) the "*abundant* prosperity" (רב, *rov*, 37:11b) of the righteous.

21. "If Yhwh is upholding you, a little is enough. If Yhwh is not doing so, even abundance will not be enough" (Goldingay, *Psalms*, 1:525).

22. Benun, "Evil and the Disruption of Order," 27n50.

blessed—they will get their rewards; the wicked will be left bereft (37:22). So there is no need to fret over the transient economic boom of the wicked; they will soon go bust—permanently!

On the Righteous (37:23–26)

When the steps of the righteous ones[23] are established by God, God delights in the "path" that they step out on (37:23).[24] And that means being blessed, flourished, and prospered. Though falls are not precluded as this way is followed, the righteous are never thrown down, because there is One who holds their "hand" (37:24), giving them "support" (37:17b, 24b), and keeping them from the "hand" of the wicked (37:33a). In contrast, as has been seen already, the "arms" of evildoers are broken (37:17a).

Then follows an aside, a testimony from one who is apparently aging: never has the psalmist witnessed the righteous or their descendants "forsaken" or in need (37:25b). If God's people "forsake" evil ways (37:8a), then he never "forsakes" them (37:28a) or "abandons" them (37:33a; all translate עזב, 'zv)—his blessing is assured. And, with their grace and generosity, the righteous, and even their descendants, are so blessed that they, in turn, can become a blessing to others (37:26; also 37:21)!

Exhortation 2 (37:27–40)

This extended exhortation closes out the psalm. Once again, the people of God are urged to "do good" and "abide" in the land (37:3, 27; also 37:29). That this dwelling is long-lasting is emphasized by "forever" in 37:27b, 28b (also in 37:18b), and "always" in 37:29b. The one who hopes in God and "keeps" his path (שמר, shmr; 37:34a[25]) is the one who will be "kept" forever by God (שמר; 37:28b), exalted to possess the land (37:34b). Indeed, the readers of the psalm are urged to "watch" the blameless and upright ones (also שמר; 37:37a); emulating the righteousness of the latter, the former, too, will be blessed with posterity (37:37b). The motif of lineage is emphasized by the repetition of "descendants"—of the righteous—in 37:25c, 26b. On the other hand are the "descendants" of the wicked (37:28b): they, like their progenitors will be "cut off."[26]

God is a God of fairness and he sees the affliction of his people; their vindication is forthcoming in his "justice" (37:6b), for he "loves *justice*" (37:28a), and presumably also do those who speak "justice" (37:30b), so deity will not let these faithful be condemned by evildoers' "judgment" (37:33b; all employing the root שפט, shpt). The righteous may "see" the wicked flourishing (37:35a), but the time is coming when they will "see" them cut off (37:34c[27]). If that is their fate, why look at them at all? Instead, God's people are urged to

---

23. The Hebrew word translated "one" specifically indicates a male; of course, it intends a generic human.

24. Though their steps are divinely established, there is human responsibility involved in treading a "path" (37:34a), whether one is righteous (37:5a) or wicked (37:7c). "Delight" in 37:23b and "take delight" in 37:4a, 11b translate two different Hebrew verbs.

25. For those who keep God's law their "footsteps" will not slip (37:31a; also see 37:23a using another word, "steps") and thereby they are enabled to continue on the divine "path" (37:34a). All are metaphors of a walk with God, a life lived in his presence.

26. With a clever wordplay, the contrast with the wicked is brought to the fore: not "kept" (37:24a), they will be "destroyed" (both from שמר, 37:38a).

27. The last word of 37:34 (תִּרְאֶה, tir'eh, "you will see") and the first word of 37:35 (רָאִיתִי, ra'iti, "I have

"see" the blameless and the upright (37:37a) and to follow their example. There is an alternation between the first and third person in 37:35–36, surrounded by two imperatives (second person) at the beginning and end of the sequence (37:34, 37), stressing the importance of being like the righteous and not like the wicked:

37:34	"wait," "keep [שמר]"	**Second person**
37:35	"I have seen"	First person
37:36a	"he passed away" "he was no more"	Third person
37:36bα	"I sought him"	First person
37:36bβ	"he could not be found"	Third person
37:37	"watch [שמר]," "see"	**Second person**

"This alternating pattern functions to highlight the divine reversal experienced by the wicked, powerful person—from riches to rags, so to speak (or from powerful existence to non-existence)—and witnessed by the poem's speaker."[28] The consequence for those heeding these words, for those persons of peace, is posterity (37:37b). The "upright" who were once going to be slaughtered (37:14d) will be the "upright" who see their descendants (37:37a). "In the short run, the wicked seem to prosper, whereas the righteous very often seem to suffer at their hands. But it is the longer run that counts, and in the long run the only true satisfaction is to be found in the righteousness which is the hallmark of the one who lives in relationship with the living God."[29] And so deliverance and salvation (the roots of each occur twice in 37:39–40) have been accomplished for these who take refuge in God, and will be accomplished for the righteous in the future, too—always!

Sermon Map

I. Evildoers Boom
   Flourishing of the wicked (37:7cd, 12, 4, 32, 35)
   Move-to-relevance: Prospering wicked around us

II. Faithful Burn
   Reaction to the flourishing wicked (37:1, 7b, 8)
   Move-to-relevance: Our reaction to the prospering wicked

III. God Busts and God Blesses
   Evildoers ruined (37:2, 9a, 10, 13, 15, 17a, 20–21a, 22b, 36, 38)
   Faithful rescued (37:6, 17b, 23–24, 28, 33, 37, 39–40)
   Faithful rewarded (37:9b, 11, 18–19, 21b, 22a, 25–26, 29)
   Move-to-relevance: God's preservation of us

IV. *Don't Worry, Do Wait!*
   Trusting God faithfully (37:3–5, 7a, 16, 27, 30–31, 34)
   Specifics on trusting and waiting

---

seen") are derived from the same root, ראה, *r'h*).

28. Maloney, "Word Fitly Spoken," 166.
29. Craigie, *Psalms 1–50*, 299–300.

PSALM 38:1–22

Psalm of Disorientation

Sin and Suffering

THIS IS ONE OF seven psalms traditionally considered penitential (Psalms 6; 32; 38; 51; 102; 130; and 143). The awareness of personal guilt is prominent in Psalm 38, with the wrath of God raising the specter of punishment. Nevertheless, in this psalm there is also the agony of external attacks. Perhaps these are indirectly linked to the sin of the pleader—God's discipline manifest in and through adversaries' assaults.[1]

Translation

38:1 Yahweh, do not in Your wrath rebuke me,
    or in Your fury chastise me.
38:2 For Your arrows, they have gone down into me,
    and it has gone down upon me—Your hand.
38:3 There is no soundness in my flesh because of Your rage;
    there is no health in my bones because of my sin.
38:4 For my iniquities have gone over my head;
    like a heavy weight they weigh too much for me.
38:5 My wounds stink, they putrefy,
    because of my folly.
38:6 I am bent over, I am brought low utterly;
    all day going about, I am darkened.
38:7 For my loins, they are filled with burning,
    and there is no soundness in my flesh.
38:8 I am prostrated and crushed utterly;
    I wail from the groaning of my heart.

---

1. In any case, as with other psalms, the specificity of sin, sickness, and situation is hard to pin down, rendering the psalm employable in a variety of circumstances. In fact, it is nigh impossible for one individual to suffer *all* of the described physical symptoms simultaneously (see below).

38:9 Lord, before You is all my desire;
>   and my sighing is not hidden from You.
38:10 My heart palpitates, my strength forsakes me;
>   and the light of my eyes, even that is not in me.
38:11 My loved ones and my friends stand aloof from before my plague;
>   and my relatives stand afar.
38:12 Those who pursue my life lay snares;
>   and those who seek my evil speak of ruin,
>   and [of] betrayal they mutter all day.
38:13 But I—like one deaf, I do not hear,
>   and like one mute who does not open his mouth.
38:14 And I have become like a person who does not hear,
>   and in whose mouth are no arguments.
38:15 For on You, Yahweh, I wait;
>   You yourself will answer, Lord, my God.
38:16 For I said, "May they not rejoice over me;
>   when my foot staggers, they exalt themselves against me."
38:17 For I am about to stumble,
>   and my pain is continually before me.
38:18 For my iniquity I confess;
>   I am anxious because of my sin.
38:19 But my enemies are vigorous, powerful;
>   and many are those who hate me falsely.
38:20 And those who repay evil against good,
>   they bear enmity against me, for I pursue good.
38:21 Do not forsake me, Yahweh;
>   my God, do not be far from me.
38:22 Hasten to my aid,
>   Lord, my deliverance.

Structure

The psalm may be structured thus, beginning and ending with pleas that envelop a central plaint:[2]

Plea 1 (38:1)
    "Yahweh" (38:1a); "not" (אַל, *'al*; 38:1a)

Plaint (38:2–20)
    Ailments and Sin (38:2–10)
        Lament and Confession (38:2–5; confession: 38:3b, 4, 5b)
        Lament and Trust (38:6–10; trust: 38:9)
            "health" (שָׁלוֹם, *shalom*; 38:3b); "bones" (עֶצֶם, *'etsem*; 38:3b)
            "like" (38:4b); "because of my sin" (38:3b)
            "my iniquities" (38:4a); "all day" (38:6b)

    Attacks and Sin (38:11–20)
        Lament and Trust (38:11–16; trust: 38:15)
        Lament and Confession (38:17–20; confession: 38:18)
            "repay" (שׁלם, *shlm*; 38:20a); "vigorous" (עצם, *'tsm*; 38:19a)
            "like" (38:13, 14a); "because of my sin" (38:18b)
            "my iniquities" (38:18a); "all day" (38:12c)

Plea 2 (38:21–22)
    "Yahweh" (38:21a); "not" (אַל, 38:21a, 21b)

Theological Focus

The consequences of sin can be internally tormenting, physically debilitating, and chastisement for sin at the hand of a displeased God raises the potential of external troubles as well—assaults from foes and abandonment by friends—but confession of sin, with an abiding trust in God, results in deliverance.

Commentary

Plea 1 (38:1)

The psalm begins and ends with pleas, each calling upon Yahweh in the vocative (38:1a, 21a; also "God," in 38:21b; and "Lord" in 38:22b). It is curious that the only direct references to deity—employing "Yahweh," "Lord," or "God"—are all in the vocative. Besides these, "Yahweh" in the vocative occurs in 38:15a, and never in the actual plaint (38:15 is a word of trust within a lament); likewise, "Lord" in 38:9a, 15a (both are statements of trust within the plaint); as well, "God" in 38:15b. Perhaps this exclusive use of the vocative pertaining to deity, though not in the laments proper where the poet bemoans his internal and external plights, is an acknowledgment that he was deserving of those ailments and attacks.

---

2. Modified from Goldingay, *Psalms*, 1:538; and Auffret, "'Toi, tu répondras,'" 309.

The way in which the parallel clauses in 38:1a and 38:1b are structured, with the prepositional phrases fronting them ("in Your wrath . . ."; "in Your fury . . ."), emphasizes the anger of deity and the psalmist's tacitly granting its validity. It might even suggest that "rebuke" and "chastisement" are appropriate, but only in God's restricted ire, not in his unconstrained "wrath" or "fury" (i.e., "God, discipline me, but not *in anger!*"). In this, the opening plea differs from the corresponding closing one (38:21–22): there the sufferer wants divine presence, divine aid, and divine deliverance (i.e., "God, discipline me not *at all!*").

Plaint: Ailments and Sin (38:2–10)

Both God's arrows and God's hand have "gone down" into/upon him (38:2a, 2b). The verse, 38:2, is chiastically structured:

> "For Your arrows,
>   they have gone down into me,
>   and it has gone down upon me—
> Your hand."

This gives the sense that God's arms (in both senses of the word!) are compressing the sufferer in the middle, and coming down upon him—straits painful, indeed.

The reason for this is clear in the parallel phrases: "because of Your rage" (38:3a), which in turn was "because of my sin" (38:3b) and "because of my folly" (38:5b): the supplicant is clearly aware of his own culpability. The consequence of divine discipline is unsoundness of flesh (38:3a) and ill-health of bones (38:3b). The "weight" of his "iniquities" is unbearable (38:4), rendering the afflicted one "brought low utterly" and "darkened" (38:6). In 38:6a, two verbs are followed by an adverbial clause; in 38:6b, an adverbial clause is followed by two verbs (below). The central adverbs emphasize the desperate and longstanding predicament the psalmist is in:

Verb	"I am bent over,
Verb	I am brought low
Adverb	utterly;
Adverb	all day
Verb	going about,
Verb	I am darkened."

While 38:6 does not address sin, there is clearly a sense that "suppliant's bentness of body issues from bentness of life"—*homo incurvatus in se*.[3] At any rate, the description of his physical indisposition is graphic: stinking and putrefying wounds (38:5a), burning loins (38:7a), and total prostration—"crushed utterly" (38:8a). The repeat of "utterly" (38:6a, 8a) points to the intensity of the affliction. All the psalmist can do is "wail from the groaning of my heart" (38:8b); that organ, his "heart," is palpitating, his strength is dissipating, and the

---

3. Goldingay, *Psalms*, 1:542.

light of his eyes—perhaps a sign of life—is vanishing (38:10; corresponding to the darkness the supplicant was in, 38:6b).

> It is tempting, but probably misleading, to try to diagnose the nature of the complaint from the poetic description of it which is provided. At first sight, it appears that the patient has almost every disease in the book; the opening description of unhealthy "flesh" and "bones" is a blanket description, the "flesh" specifying dermatological or surface complaints, the "bones" covering all internal complaints. The specific complaints are staggering in their proportions: open wounds, burning loins (ulcers?), numbness, congestion, a "growling heart," palpitations, and trouble with the eyes.... By the same token, the breadth of description makes this psalm more appropriate for general usage as a prayer.[4]

In the midst of this lugubrious lament there is a note of trust in 38:9, introduced with a vocative, "Lord": all he wants, his desire, his need, is before God who sees; and his suffering, God knows. Would that God withdraw his hand!

Plaint: Attacks and Sin (38:11–20)

Thus far, it has all been about God and the sufferer (and therefore the earlier section dealt with *Ailments and Sin*). In this section, we see more characters emerging, mostly enemies (and so *Attacks and Sin*) and some friends. Sin is still involved (38:18). It is bad enough to suffer the consequences of sin; it is worse when you have foes taking advantage of the crisis (of divine discipline for sinning) and laying traps for you, seeking your evil, and plotting your ruin (38:12). But when associates "stand aloof" and kinfolk "stand afar" (both using עמד, *'md*; 38:11), the situation is dire. The irony is pungent: "Our friends and neighbors are the people who are supposed to be near us—they *are* near us, by virtue of being members of our family and community. But these near ones stand far off!"[5] Alienation from God has now become alienation from one's fellows!

In any case, the sufferer is struck deaf and dumb—both "hear" and "mouth" each occur twice in 38:13–14.[6] There is no more he can hear, there is no more his mouth can say. He can only wait upon God who, he hopes, will answer (38:15). Though the sufferer has become mute, he is sure that God will take it upon himself to answer the invective of adversaries.[7] This note of trust here in this section also addresses deity in vocatives, "Yahweh," "Lord," and "my God" (38:15; as did the utterance of trust in the previous section, 38:9: "Lord").

But the enemies are rejoicing at their triumph over the sufferer; he falls, they crow (38:16). The psalmist is now at breaking point, made clear in a linguistic paradox: "I am *about to* [כון, *kwn*, also 'made firm'] stumble" (38:17), i.e., he is "fixin' to fall apart."[8] But even here, he is acutely conscious of the potential role "my iniquity" and "my sin" may have

---

4. Craigie, *Psalms 1–50*, 303–4.
5. Goldingay, *Psalms*, 1:546.
6. Note the emphatic first-person pronoun in 38:13: "But I—... I do not hear." And both 38:13 and 38:14 begin with the conjunction ו translated "but/and," suggesting the psalmist's total helplessness.
7. Was this enemies' slander or false accusations? In any case, there is irony again: What request from a *dumb* person was God going to hear in order to answer? And, in turn, what answer from God would a *deaf* person manage to hear? But the scrambled ideas of 38:15 are excusable, arising as they do from the depth of the psalmist's anguish and torment.
8. As they say in this part of the world (where I was, while writing on Psalm 38).

played in this whole harrowing affair, so he confesses (38:18), and even claims to have been doing "good" (and getting repaid with evil) and "pursuing good" (and therefore being the target of enmity) (38:20). His foes, thus, are both "*against* good" and "*against* me" (38:20), the one doing good. The pleader's "health" (שָׁלוֹם) was gone and his bones (עֶצֶם) were shot (38:3b); the good he has done is "repaid" (שׁלם; 38:20a) with evil by enemies who are "powerful" (עצם; 38:19a). These wordplays firmly link divine chastisement with adversarial assaults: ailments and sin are tied to attacks and sin.

Plea 2 (38:21–22)

The psalm concludes with a plea that has echoes of the opening plea in 38:1a, including the use of the vocative, "Yahweh" (38:21a; it also has the vocatives, "my God," in 38:21b, and "Lord," in 38:22b). The poet's strength had "forsaken" him (38:10a), but he pleads that God would not "forsake" him (38:21a) or be "far" from him (רחק, *rchq*; 38:21b) as were his relatives ("afar," also from רחק; 38:11b). "The two parallel negatived verbs ['forsake' and 'be afar'] have similar meaning, but the first rather suggests, 'Do not go away,' and the second, 'Do not stay away.'"[9] After all, he has confessed his sin (explicitly in 38:3–5, 18; implicitly throughout the psalm), and he was hoping and waiting upon God (38:9, 15). Shouldn't God act on his behalf? And with four brief aching words, two in each line of 38:22, the psalm concludes: "Hasten to-my-aid, Lord, my-deliverance!"[10]

In sum, "the expression of penitence does come intermingled with other elements in the psalm and is not central to it, but the psalm's chief theological significance lies in its distinctive linking of sin and suffering."[11] This is also validated in that the psalm does not achieve resolution but ends with a plea. Sin has its consequences, but confession is the route to getting right with God.

Sermon Map

I. Rottenness
   Sin (38:3b–4, 18)
   Move-to-relevance: Our rebellion against God
II. Recompense
   Sin's consequence: Ailments (38:3a, 5–8, 10, 17)
   Sin's consequence: Attacks (38:12, 16, 19–20)
   Sin's consequence: Abandonment (38:11)
   Move-to-relevance: God's discipline in our lives
III. Repentance
   Sin's confession (38:1–2, 9, 13–15, 18, 21–22)
   Move-to-relevance: The necessity of confession
IV. *Confession and Confidence!*
   Specifics on confessing and hoping in God

---

9. Goldingay, *Psalms*, 1:550.

10. The vagueness of the request should not be surprising in a psalm intended to be applied in places and in lives distant from the original setting of the text.

11. Goldingay, *Psalms*, 1:550.

PSALM 39:1–13

Psalm of Disorientation

God's Discipline and the Brevity of Life

PSALM 39 CONTINUES THE theme of chastisement for iniquity at the hand of deity from Psalm 38, though the focus in this poem is considerably different. Unlike in the previous psalm there is no significant reference to physical debilitation or deterioration; rather, the brevity of life is the prominent concern here. Also, though enemies are mentioned, their attacks are not as major an issue in Psalm 39 as they were in Psalm 38.

Translation

39:1 I said, "I will guard my paths—
   from sinning with my tongue
   I will guard my mouth with a muzzle—
   while the wicked is before me."
39:2 I was mute, silent;
   I kept quiet more than it was good,
   and my sorrow was stirred up.
39:3 My heart was hot in my inner parts;
   while I pondered, fire burned;
   I spoke with my tongue:
39:4 "Make me know, Yahweh, my end
   and the extent of my days, what it is;
   let me know how fleeting I [am].
39:5 Behold, You have set my days [as] handbreadths,
   and my duration as nothing before You;
   surely every human, [though] standing firm, is all a breath."
39:6 Surely a person goes about as a shadow;
   surely [for] a breath they make an uproar;
   He heaps up [riches] and does not know who will gather them.

39:7 And now, in what do I hope, Lord?
>   My waiting, it is upon You.
39:8 From all my rebellions rescue me;
>   do not make me a reproach of the foolish.
39:9 I am mute, I do not open my mouth,
>   because You—You have acted.
39:10 Turn aside from upon me Your assault;
>   because of the hostility of Your hand I—I perish.
39:11 With rebukes for iniquity You chastise a person;
>   and You consume as a moth what is dear to him;
>   surely every human is a breath.
39:12 Hear my prayer, Yahweh, and [to] my cry for help give ear;
>   to my tears do not be unresponsive;
> for a sojourner I am with You,
>   an alien like all my fathers.
39:13 Look away from me, that I may smile,
>   before I go and I am no more.

Structure

The structure of the psalm is straightforward: it has *Reflection* and *Request* sections, with a central verse (39:7), *Reliance*, dividing the psalm in the middle:

Reflection (39:1–6): "Yahweh" (39:4a)
"mouth" (39:1c); "mute" (39:2a); "breath" (39:5c, 6b)
"surely" (39:5c, 6a, 6b); "every human" (39:5c); "go" (39:6a); "person" (39:6a)

Reliance (39:7): *"And now, in what do I hope, Lord? My waiting, it is upon You."*

Request (39:8–13): "Yahweh" (39:12a)
"mouth" (39:9a); "mute" (39:9a); "breath" (39:11c)
"surely" (39:11c); "every human" (39:11c); "go" (39:13b); "person" (39:11a)

Each of the three parts contains an address to deity using the vocative: "Yahweh" (39:4a, 12a) and "Lord" (39:7a). These are the only explicit names for God in the psalm. The *Reflection* and *Request* sections are not entirely disparate—there are several verbal links (see above), and the theme of life's transience resonates in both (39:4–6 and 39:11bc, 13b).

PSALM 39:1-13

Theological Focus

The brevity of life, measured in handbreadths, may be the result of divine chastisement for one's own sins (perhaps complicated by assaults from enemies without, or by afflictions of diseases within), and the appropriate response to this agonizing transience is to wait and hope in God with a repentant heart, remaining with him even when all else looks bleak.

Commentary

Reflection (39:1–6)

The only mention of the ungodly in the psalm is in 39:1d ("wicked") and 39:8b ("foolish"; likely kin to each another). It is unclear why the psalmist wanted to control his tongue and mouth "while the wicked is before me" (39:1d). Perhaps a voicing of angst about the transitory nature of this existence (in 39:4–6) would provoke derision and contempt from those "wicked" (and reproaches from those "foolish"): "Look at you! Your God is either uncaring or impotent or both." In any case, the issue was "burning" at the front of the speaker's mind (39:3b), and despite his attempts at silence, he finally gives vent to speech (39:3c): he goes from not "sinning with my tongue" (39:1b) to "speaking with my tongue" (39:3c). And what he says to God follows, in 39:4–5.[1]

For whatever reason,[2] he is moved to meditate upon the shortness of his days and the proximity and inevitability of death. Since God was the one who had determined the brevity of his life, 39:5a reads like an accusation: "Behold, You have set my days [as] handbreadths."[3] Yes, the wicked are "before" the psalmist (39:1d), apparently causing him all kinds of consternation, but "before" God the sufferer's life and times are completely negligible (39:5b), seemingly the infliction by an uncaring deity.

All that to say, although the explicit question is regarding the length of the psalmist's days—"what" their extent is and "how" fleeting he himself is (39:4bc), it is implicitly also a "why" question, seeking answers as to the purpose of this short and seemingly futile life, filled with divine rebuke (and external repression, as will be clear from *Request* section, 39:8–13).

---

1. It is best to consider the psalmist's direct speech as ending with 39:5, for 39:6 commences a more reflective, wisdom-like utterance that talks of humans in the third person, as opposed to the first-person considerations of the preceding verses.

2. Perhaps it had to do with a consciousness of personal sin and the resulting divine displeasure and discipline (39:9–11), that was manifesting in internal visceral affliction and/or external adversarial assaults—all permitted by God. But the psalm is silent about the details.

3. A "handbreath" (39:5a), about the width of four fingers (1 Kgs 7:26; Jer 52:21), is "one of the smallest measures in the Hebrew system of measuring" (Craigie, *Psalms 1–50*, 309).

The piercing nature of the interrogation is emphasized in the structure of 39:4–5:[4]

A	"Yahweh"
B	"end"
C	"extent"
D	"my days"
E	"what"
E'	"how"
D'	"my days"
C'	"duration"
B'	"nothing"
A'	"before You"

The multiple instances of "surely," in 39:5c, 6a, 6b (and later in 39:11c)—"more than in any chapter of the OT"[5]—underscore the grievous conviction of the supplicant.[6] Life is but a "shadow" and a "breath" (39:5c, 6a, 6b; also 39:11c). All of life's uproar and fracas, all of its turmoil and tumult, all the hullabaloo and shivaree—all are for naught. "Every human" (39:5c, 11c) is here today and gone tomorrow. The psalmist wanted to "know" the extent of his days and to "know" the evanescence of his life (39:4a, 4c), but such knowledge was impossible to attain: one could not even "know" to whom all that one has amassed in life would go, upon one's death (39:6c). No wonder "surely [. . .] a breath" echoes three times in the psalm (39:5c, 6b, 11c). So what is one to do?

Reliance (39:7)

Bogged in that predicament, we come to the central verse of the psalm, 39:7, conspicuously beginning with "and now . . . ." Strikingly, the only two words in this verse that are repeated elsewhere in the psalm are "what" (מַה, *mah*) and "it [is]" (הִיא, *hi'*)—occurring together in 39:4: מַה־הִיא, *mah-hi'*, the only such conjoining in the Psalter.[7] But in 39:7, מַה and הִיא are separated: מַה־קִוִּיתִי אֲדֹנָי תּוֹחַלְתִּי לְךָ הִיא (*mah-qiwwiti 'adonai tochaltti lka hi'*). The interposed words between מַה and הִיא in this verse look like this (in the Hebrew word order): "In-what-do-I-hope, Lord, my-waiting upon-You it-is."[8] Thus 39:7, particularly the insertion between מַה and הִיא, resolves the psalmist's question in 39:4 about his lifespan, "what it is," מַה־הִיא. "What it is" is not that psalmist will enjoy *x* number of days and *y* number of years. Rather, life, no matter how long or how short, is to be considered a continual *hoping* upon the Lord, a *waiting* for him. In other words, "one needs a paradigm shift, focusing on 'Who?' instead of 'What?' [or "Why" or "How?" or even "When?"].' . . . Instead of looking for *something*, the

---

4. From Auffret, "'Car toi, tu as agi,'" 124.

5. Goldingay, *Psalms*, 1:555.

6. Likewise, the repeats of "every/all" (כֹּל, *kol*) in 39:5c (×2), 11c, further emphasizing the universal human predicament of life's transience.

7. And there is only one other instance of מַה־הִיא in the OT, in Zech 5:6.

8. The second-person suffixed form of the preposition, לְךָ, *lka*, "upon You," occurs only in 39:7b in this psalm.

suppliant hopes in *someone*."⁹ The brevity of days is not to prompt a hedonic enjoyment of life while it lasts; it is not to be endured as a temporary turbulence before one escapes the here-and-now; and it is not an abject, miserable suffering of all that is wrong in the world. Rather, "in Psalm 39, man's brevity leads him to God and nothing but God."¹⁰ He alone is the hope; upon him alone we must wait!

Request (39:8–13)

This attestation in 39:7 apparently convinced the psalmist to turn his attention from the brevity of his life to seeking the benevolence of God.

> When he got right down to his most fundamental aspirations in life, the psalmist's hopes and desires focused upon God himself. And the realization that his ultimate focus in life was God created a new issue for the psalmist; it was no longer his enemies who were a primary source of external vexation, but an awareness of his own transgressions which became a primary source of internal vexation. If life was so transitory, and if God was its principal goal and meaning, then it was vital that transgressions (or sin) be dealt with, lest they destroy the potential and meaning of existence.¹¹

While in this psalm there is no explicit confession of, or penitence for, sin, the sufferer is undoubtedly repentant. He certainly wants to avoid any future "rebellions," as he seeks divine "rescue" from them (39:8a), lest God's chastisement continue, and his opponents ("the foolish," from the same tribe as the "wicked" in 39:1d) ridicule him for his trust in a God who is apparently unwilling to deliver his own (39:8b). In any case, the psalmist is again rendered "mute," his "mouth" shut (39:9a). Earlier he was "mute" and his "mouth" closed (39:1c, 2a) as he worried about the brevity of his life; now he is silenced because he has no excuse for his sin—God is justified in treating him thus: "You—You have acted" (39:9b). The repeated pronoun emphasizes that it is none other than deity who is behind his woes, and that he was deserving of God's reprisals. "You—You have acted" (39:9b) and as a result "I—I perish" (39:10b).

The sufferer, therefore, has only one option, to plead for the mercy of God (39:10¹²). "You did this, and *I* am perishing; only You can change my situation, I am helpless. So please would You remove Your hand of punishment from upon me?"

In 39:11, there is a bringing together of the motifs of this psalm: God's discipline and life's brevity. It becomes clear that whatever the proximal cause of the latter (attack from enemies? affliction from disease?) the ultimate cause was the former, rendering "every human ... a breath" (39:11c; also in 39:5c). Therefore the poet's plea intensifies: God is implored to hear his prayer, to give ear to his cry, and to be responsive (literally, to "not be deaf") to his tears (39:12ab). For, the supplicant confesses, he is only "a sojourner ... with You" (39:12c). There is a paradox in that assertion: "sojourner" (and "alien," in 39:12d) suggests he has no

---

9. Goldingay, *Psalms*, 1:559 (italics original).
10. Beuken, "Psalm 39," 4.
11. Craigie, *Psalms 1–50*, 309–10.
12. The verse is chiastic: "Turn aside / from upon *me* / *Your* assault; // because of the hostility of *Your* hand / *I*—/ I perish." That is to say, "If you don't turn aside, God, I perish!"

kin, but he *does* have God—"I am with You" (39:12c).¹³ One is to hope in and wait for God despite the transient nature of life and the adversities of the world that render the supplicant a sad "sojourner" and an abject "alien."

That being said, the psalmist would still prefer to have God turn his look of anger away from him, and thus give him back his smile (that he had lost to "tears," 39:12b), lest he die from the severity of divine discipline (39:13).¹⁴ And with that final plea we have an unusual ending for a lament psalm: there is no praise for rescue, no confidence of recovery, no sign that rehabilitation is nigh. The poem simply ends! What happened afterwards? "The inclusion of these . . . unrelieved psalms in the Psalter is vivid testimony to ancient Israel's willingness to retain a record of unresolved anguish."¹⁵ And that is appropriate, for in real life, too, answers to tough questions and solutions to painful problems are rarely forthcoming from God. But one can always "hope" in, and "wait" upon, the Lord (39:7) with a repentant spirit. And one should, no matter what!

Sermon Map

I. Chastisement for Sin
   The potential pain of divine discipline (39:8–13)
   Move-to-relevance: Divine discipline in our lives
II. Consequence of Sin
   The potential effect of divine discipline: brevity of life (39:1–6)
   Move-to-relevance: Attacks from without, afflictions from within
III. Confidence in God
   Waiting and hope in God with a repentant heart (39:7)
   Move-to-relevance: God our only hope
IV. *Cling to God!*
   Specifics on waiting and hoping in God with repentance in this short life

---

13. The patriarch Abraham, too, was an "alien" and a "sojourner," but certainly not abandoned by God (Gen 23:4).

14. The psalmist's "I am no more" (וְאֵינֶנִּי, *wĕnenni*; 39:13b) suggesting death, does not indicate annihilation; the same phrase was used of the patriarch Enoch (Gen 5:24).

15. Johnston, "Psalms of Distress," 80.

PSALM 40:1–17

Psalm of Disorientation

Distress, Duty, and Deliverance

THIS PSALM OF DISORIENTATION takes a reverse approach, with praise preceding petition.[1] After the first four verses (40:1–4) that talk *about* Yahweh in the third person, the rest of the psalm is directed *to* him, in the second person.

Translation

40:1 I hoped patiently in Yahweh;
    and He inclined to me
    and He heard my cry for help.

40:2 He brought me up from of the pit of destruction,
    out from the miry clay,
and He stood my feet upon a cliff;
    He stabilized my steps.

40:3 And He put in my mouth a new song,
    praise to our God;
many will see and fear
    and trust in Yahweh.

40:4 Blessing [upon] the one who has made Yahweh his trust,
    and has not turned [his] face to the proud
    and those who are entangled in falsehood.

40:5 Many things You have done,
    You, Yahweh my God—
Your wonders and Your intentions toward us;
    there is none to compare with You.
Were I to report and speak [of them],
    they would be too numerous to count.

---

1. Also of note, 40:13–17 is replicated with minor changes as Psalm 70.

40:6	Sacrifice and meal-offering You have not desired
	(ears You have dug out for me);
	whole-offering and sin-offering You have not required.
40:7	Then I said, "Behold, I have come—
	in the scroll of the book it has been written pertaining to me.
40:8	To do what is acceptable to You, my God, I have desired;
	Your law [is] in the midst of my innards.
40:9	I proclaimed righteousness in the great congregation;
	behold, my lips I have not restrained;
	Yahweh, You—You know.
40:10	Your righteousness I have not hidden in the midst of my heart;
	[of] Your faithfulness and Your deliverance I have said;
	I have not concealed Your lovingkindness and Your truth
	before the great congregation."
40:11	You, Yahweh, do not restrain Your compassion from me;
	Your lovingkindness and Your truth,
	they continually preserve me.
40:12	For evils beyond count have surrounded me;
	my iniquities have overtaken me, and I am not able to see—
	more numerous than the hairs of my head—
	and my heart has forsaken me.
40:13	Be pleased, Yahweh, to rescue me;
	Yahweh, to my help, hurry.
40:14	May they be ashamed and humiliated altogether—
	those seeking my soul to snatch it away;
	may they be driven back and disgraced,
	those desiring evil for me.
40:15	May they be desolated according to their shame—
	those saying to me, "Aha, aha."
40:16	May they exult and rejoice in You—
	all those who seek You;
	may they say continually, "May Yahweh be magnified"—
	those loving Your deliverance.
40:17	But I am afflicted and needy,
	may the Lord consider me.
	My help and my savior You are;
	my God, do not delay.

Structure

The praise appears to be for past deliverance; the petition for future deliverance:

> **Praise:** *For Past Deliverance (40:1–10)*
>   Deliverance of a trustworthy God (40:1–4): *about Yahweh*
>   Desire of a righteous God (40:5–10): *to Yahweh*
>
> **Petition:** *For Future Deliverance (40:11–17)*
>   Deliverance for self (40:11–13)
>   Defeat for foes (40:14–15): *what they say (40:15b)*
>   Delight for friends (40:16): *what they say (40:16c)*
>   Deliverance for self (40:17)

Theological Focus

> Praise for past deliverance from dire distress and near destruction, wondrously accomplished by God, enhances the trust of the rescued and of the community hearing the testimony to divine aid rendered, and moves God's people to greater obedience and commitment to God, rendering them confident in their petitions for future deliverance.

Commentary

Praise: For Past Deliverance (40:1–10)

The psalm commences by recounting (to the community?) a deliverance of the psalmist effected by God in the past (40:1–4). His patient hoping[2] and cry for help in distress resulted in God's turning to him (40:1): he was rescued from the "pit of destruction" and the "miry clay" (unfirm, unsteady, unreliable) and established on a "cliff" with "stabilized . . . footsteps" (firm, fast, fixed; 40:2cd). This was not just a lifting from below ground level up to ground level; rather, the rescue by God figuratively raised the sufferer *above* ground level, on to a cliff![3] And all this is depicted somewhat chiastically, with the firm foundation in the center, pertaining to lower limbs.[4]

---

2. The construction in 40:1a has a verb + its infinitive absolute ("in hoping, I hoped" or, as translated here, "I hoped patiently").

3. We are unable to specify what that current distress was; that is, no doubt, intentional: analogies to the dire situations of God's people anywhere and at any time are permissible by this non-specification.

4. Modified from Auffret, "J'ai proclamé la justice," 390.

40:1a	"I hoped patiently for *Yahweh*"
40:1c	"He *heard*"
40:2ab	"He brought me up from the pit ... from the miry clay"
40:2c	"He stood *my feet*"
40:2d	"He stabilized *my steps*"
40:3ab	"He put ... a new song, praise"
40:4c	"many will *see*"
40:4d	"trust in *Yahweh*"

This blessed individual was brought closer to God through his detrimental experience, in the midst of which he sought succor from Yahweh rather than soliciting support from the "proud" (evildoers) and those "entangled in falsehood," i.e., those falling prey to false gods or false prophets (40:4).[5]

In sum, grand deliverance had been accomplished by God and a new song of praise was being sung, publicly acclaiming deity and leading the community to "see and fear" (יִרְאוּ . . . וְיִירָאוּ, *yi'ru . . . wyira'u*; 40:3). One might have expected that they would "*hear* and fear"—how would the psalmist's "new song" be "seen"? But the phrase employed attests to the critical importance of the recounting of God's mighty deliverance in public. Others don't just hear of it; they actually *see* it as a vivid, albeit vicarious, reality. Indeed, "many" of God's people (רַבִּים, *rabbim*; 40:3c) would see and fear after hearing of God's "many" deeds (רַבִּים, 40:5a) in the "great" congregation (also רַבִּים, 40:9a, 10d). The hearing by the community from the blessed person who had made God his "trust" (40:4a[6]) would enhance its own "trust" in God (40:3d).

While the trust-building effects of the psalmist's public declaration of God's deliverance is creditable (40:3cd, 5ef), God's "desire" and "requirement" for the one(s) he delivers are more fundamental and not to be confused with cultic and communal activities, important though they may be (40:6a, 6c). So what exactly does God desire/require? God had "done" wonderful things for the supplicant (40:5a). Now what should the latter "do" in turn for the former (40:8a)? How are the delivered to respond to the divine deliverer?

That response is poignant, given as a direct speech of the psalmist to his God[7] and commencing with the pointed "behold, I have come" (40:7a). This is a surrender to the "desire" of God, to "do" his will (40:6a, 8a).[8] Admitting that what has been written in the

---

5. As in Amos 2:4; or Ezek 13:6–9; Hab 2:3.

6. "The one" in 40:4a is specifically "man," גֶּבֶר, *gever*, but intended generically.

7. I take the psalmist's direct speech to extend from 40:7aβ through 40:10; the whole citation considers the various attributes of God. Besides, 40:11 displays a change of tone as the supplicant begins his petition.

8. This is the only instance in the OT of "ears You have dug out for me" (40:6b; Heb 10:5 makes it "a body you have prepared for me," applying the notions of these verses to Christ). Seeing its interpolation between four kinds of temple offerings ("sacrifice," "meal-offering," "whole-offering," and "sin offering"), each pair attested negatively as something "You have *not* desired" (Ps 40:6a) or "You have *not* required" (40:6c), it is likely that the parenthetical phrase in 40:6b refers to what God, instead, *does* desire or require. In all possibility, the idiom then means that God wanted his people to listen, so much so, he hollowed out ears for them: "Listen to me, will you!" That the sacral activities not "desired" by God (40:6a) are contrasted with what was "desired" by the psalmist (40:8a) suggests that the ear-digging enterprise of deity actually did succeed: the psalmist did desire what God desired! All of this is not to say that God does not care for sacrifices, part of the ritual law that he himself had commanded. If obedience/morality was God's desire, this would undoubtedly require obedience to the OT ritual law as well. "In Jesus's dialogue with a scribe in Mark 12:28–34, he declared that keeping the foremost commandments (the moral aspect of the Mosaic Law) was 'greater' than

law ("the scroll of the book") is "pertaining to me"—i.e., "is prescribed for/concerning me" (40:7b[9])—the psalmist synchronizes his "desire" with God's "desire": "To do what is acceptable to You, my God, I have desired" (40:8a), for divine "law" is "in the midst of my innards" (40:8b). This verse, 40:8, is the central one of Psalm 40, forming an appropriate response to past deliverance, and also the appropriate ground for expecting future deliverance. Thus, 40:7b–8 creates a structure emphasizing this key verse:[10]

> "in the scroll of the book it has been written pertaining to me.
>   To do what is acceptable
>   to You,
>   my God,
>   I have desired;
>   Your law [is] in the midst of my innards."

What God had written in his law (40:7b), the supplicant has internalized and etched on his "innards" (40:8b): to do what was pleasing to God (40:7a), to live righteously.

And this "righteousness" of God that is to be "proclaimed" and "not hidden" (40:9a, 10a; i.e., the righteous requirements God makes of his people) the psalmist would therefore declare publicly, just as he previously had done after his past deliverance (40:3).[11] Indeed, he asserts that what was "*in the midst* of my innards," within the core of his being, i.e., divine law (40:8b), he will not hide "*in the midst* of my heart" (40:10a). What was emblazoned on the privacy of his heart would be expressed in the public acclamation of his saying. And just as he "said" to God in private (40:7a) that he would be willing to obey divine desire, he would also "say" in public (40:10b), testifying to the magnificence of divine righteousness, faithfulness, deliverance, lovingkindness, and truth (40:9a, 10). How can one not want to obey a deity who is righteous, faithful, delivering, abundant in lovingkindness, and true? And how can one not proclaim the greatness of this God in the presence of God's people? The importance of this corporate acknowledgment (and implicit exhortation to the community to obey) is underscored in the reuse of "behold." The supplicant had declared his willingness to obey God ("*behold*, I have come," 40:7a); now he asserts his resolve to be a witness ("*behold*, my lips I have not restrained," 40:9b).[12]

---

all the offerings and sacrifices (the ritual aspect of the Mosaic Law). Not that one can be neglected for the other (for even the ritual law has moral overtones, coming as it does from a moral Lawgiver), but there are differences in degrees of importance between them" (Kuruvilla, *1 and 2 Timothy, Titus*, 208). Goldingay (*Psalms*, 1:573) is right: "Since the OT generally assumes that Yhwh did want these offerings, it seems likely that the contrast between what Yhwh wanted and did not want is expected hyperbolically: the psalm means, 'Yhwh was less concerned for that [ritual law] than for this [overall moral conformity to divine law].'"

9. If a king is uttering these words, the inscribed words "in the scroll of the book" might well refer to Deut 17:14–20.

10. From Auffret, "J'ai proclamé la justice," 395. Indeed, if the preposition, עָלַי, *'alay* (40:7b) functions as it does in 42:5b, 6a, 11b—clearly "*within me*" there—the parallelism between "in the scroll of the book it has been written *within me*" (i.e., what is inscribed in a book has been internalized by the supplicant; 40:7b) and "Your law [is] in the midst of my innards" (40:8b) is perfectly symmetrical.

11. This testimony to divine righteousness would include declaiming "Your faithfulness and Your deliverance" (40:10b) and "Your lovingkindness and Your truth" (40:10c), all being considered here as equivalent, as is evident in the parallelism of 40:10a, 10b, 10c.

12. "To withhold praise does not damage God, but it does damage God's mission, in the sense that to

With 40:8b, the supplicant begins the transition to his petition for future deliverance, claiming that his own desire to do God's desire was something Yahweh was aware of: "You—You know" (40:9c); he proceeds to make the case that not only was he keen to obey divine demand, exalting divine righteousness, he would ensure others would, too (40:10).

Petition: For Future Deliverance (40:11–17)

Having not concealed "Your lovingkindness and Your truth" from his community (40:10c), the psalmist wants a reciprocation from God, an extension of "Your lovingkindness and Your truth" to him in his current crisis (40:11b). His "heart," once filled with the law of God and overflowing with the righteousness of God (40:8b, 10a) is the same "heart" that is now abandoning the supplicant (40:12d)—so dire is his present situation. Therefore he pleads for God not to "restrain" his compassion from him (40:11a), a reminder to deity that he, the sufferer, had not been "restrained" in his praise of God (40:9b) for his past deliverance. The psalmist's yearning was to do what was "acceptable" to God (noun: רָצוֹן, ratson; 40:8a); so now he calls upon God to "be pleased" to help him (the related verb: רצה, rtsh; 40:13a). Since "Yahweh, You—You know" the faithfulness of the psalmist (40:9c, with the emphatic use of the pronoun אַתָּה, 'attah), he addresses God similarly, "You, Yahweh, do not restrain . . ." (also using אַתָּה; 40:11a), beseeching him not to withhold his deliverance.

What exactly this experience of malaise was, is unclear. Personal sin (40:12b), physical affliction (40:12d), and persecuting enemies (40:14–15[13]) all seem to be playing a role, with the psalmist beset by distresses galore. Once it was God's wonders and intentions that were "too numerous to count" (עָצְמוּ מִסַּפֵּר, 'atsmu missapper; 40:5f); now it is the foes' evil and the supplicant's own iniquities that have reached the same magnitude of innumerability (מִסְפָּר . . . עָצְמוּ, mispar . . . 'atsmu, "beyond count . . . more numerous," 40:12a, 12c). So he makes a passionate plea for help (40:13) and for that aid to come quickly.

The five pairs of lines in the following three verses, 40:14–16, are constructed in parallel, each pair having the predicate in the first line (40:14a, 14c, 15a, 16a, 16c) and the subject in the second (40:14b, 14d, 15b, 16b, 16d). But these verses deal with two sets of people, foes in 40:14–15 (and what they say, 40:15b; these are those who "seek" the supplicant's life, 40:14b) and friends in 40:16 (and what they say, 40:16c; these are those who "seek" God, 40:16b). Thus we see in this psalm God's "desire" (40:6a), the psalmist's "desire" (40:8a), and the enemies' "desire" (40:14d). The last, of course, is diametrically opposed to the first two that are congruent and in sync.

The psalm concludes with a return to a petition for self (40:17). The sufferer wants a repeat performance of divine wonders and "intentions" (noun: מַחֲשָׁבָה, machashavah; 40:5c) from past deliverance, as he entreats God to "consider" him (the related verb: חשׁב, chshv; 40:17b) in future deliverance. The past "deliverance" that he had publicly confessed to (40:10b), he now wants reproduced (40:16abc) among those who love God's "deliverance" (40:16d). So he reiterates his need for "help" yet again (40:17c; "help" also in 40:13b). The psalmist had commenced the composition with a recollection of his having "hoped patiently" for God's past deliverance (40:1a), but "now the immediacy of the crisis propels him to the prayer: ['My God,

---

withhold praise is to withhold saving knowledge from the neighbor who needs it"—God's righteousness, faithfulness, deliverance, lovingkindness, and truth (deClaissé-Walford et al., *Book of Psalms* 379).

13. The "evil" of 40:12a appears to be aggravated by enemies who seek the psalmist's "evil" (40:14d).

do not delay')"—would that God not tarry (40:17d).[14] Though we are left with an unresolved petition at the end of this poem, the praise section (40:1–10) leaves no doubt in either the mind of the psalmist or in those of the psalm's readers that God would, in fact, deliver.

Sermon Map

I. Praise for Past Deliverance
    The rescue (40:1–2)
    The rejoicing (40:3ab, 5)
    The reassurance (40:3cd, 4)
    Move-to-relevance: Past deliverance enhancing our trust

II. Priority of the People Delivered
    Committed obedience to God (40:6–10)
    Move-to-relevance: Trust enhancing our commitment to obey

III. Petition for Future Deliverance
    Evils abounding (40:12, 14–15)
    Confident pleading (40:11, 16–17)
    Move-to-relevance: God our only hope

IV. *Desire the Desire of the Deliverer!*
    Specifics on committing to God confidently

---

14. Craigie, *Psalms 1–50*, 317.

PSALM 41:1–13

Psalm of Disorientation

Caring for Others; Cared for by God

THIS IS THE FINAL psalm in Book I of the Psalter (Psalms 1–41), and as with the concluding psalms of Books II–IV, this one also contains a beatitude (a "horizontal" blessing of humans: 41:1–2; and see 72:17; 89:15; 106:3) and a benediction (a "vertical" blessing of deity: 41:13; and see 72:18–19; 89:52; 106:48).[1]

Translation

41:1	Blessing [upon] the one who considers the insignificant;
	on the day of evil Yahweh liberates him.
41:2	Yahweh—He keeps him and preserves him alive,
	and he shall have blessing in the land.
	And do not give him over to the desire of his enemies.
41:3	Yahweh sustains him upon his couch of illness;
	all his [sick] bed You transform in his illness.
41:4	I—I said, "Yahweh, be gracious to me;
	heal my soul, for I have sinned against You."
41:5	My enemies, they say evil of me:
	"When will he die, and his name perish?"
41:6	And if he comes to see [me],
	he speaks emptiness;
	his heart gathers harm for itself;
	he goes outside; he speaks [of it].
41:7	Against me they whisper together, all who hate me;
	against me they devise evil to me:

---

1. See Barbiero, "Psalm 41:14," 321.

41:8   "A plague of Belial is poured out on him,
          and he who lies down, will not again rise up."
41:9   Even my friend, in whom I trusted—
          the one who ate my bread—
          has magnified his heel against me.
41:10 But You, Yahweh, be gracious to me and raise me up,
          that I may repay them.
41:11 By this I know that You take pleasure in me,
          for my enemy does not shout in triumph against me.
41:12 And I—in my integrity You uphold me,
          and You stand me in Your presence forever.
41:13 Blessed is Yahweh, God of Israel,
          From forever and always to forever. Amen and amen.

Structure

The poem may be structured with two sections of the psalmist's confidence in divine preservation (41:1–3, 11–13) sandwiching an inner section of concern for his perishing. The entire psalm can be seen as chiastic:

Confidence of Preservation 1 (41:1–3)
- **A**   Beatitude (**41:1a**)
  - **B**   Yahweh's preservation 1 (**41:1b–3**): "enemies" (41:2c)

Concern for Perishing (41:4–10)
- **C**   Prayer for grace 1 (**41:4**): against sin
  "Yahweh, be gracious to me"
  - Lament (**41:5–9**): "enemies" (41:5a)
    - **D**   Enemies' quote (41:5b); treachery (41:6)
       Enemies' quote (41:8); treachery (41:9)
- **C'** Prayer for grace 2 (**41:10**): against enemies
  "Yahweh, be gracious to me"

Confidence of Preservation 2 (41:11–13)
  - **B'** Yahweh's preservation 2 (**41:11–12**): "enemy" (41:11b)
- **A'** Benediction (**41:13**)

In terms of the "storying" of the psalm, one might wonder how confidence in God's preservation can interweave with concern for perishing, but that ought not to be surprising. The first section of *Confidence of Preservation 1* (41:1–3) is likely to be reflecting on a past experience; the *Concern for Perishing* (41:4–10) may be dealing with a present crisis; and the last section, *Confidence of Preservation 2*, could be gazing to the future, anticipating divine deliverance from the current predicament (41:11–13). But these speculative timestamps are not watertight.

In this psalm, there is a seeming conflation and a sense of simultaneity of all the causes of the psalmist's distress that cross textual boundaries: physical illness (41:3, 8), personal sin (41:4, 10, 12), and persecuting enemies (41:2, 5–7, 9, 11) are all equally and immediately implicated.

Theological Focus

> Having confessed their sins—and having cared for the weak and helpless—the people of God are confident of his gracious preservation of them when they suffer—even when persecuted by friends turned traitors—and are assured of divine presence with them forever.

Commentary

Confidence of Preservation 1 (41:1–3)

The beatitude introducing the psalm sets the stage: the one who has aided the weak and helpless (the "insignificant" gets blessing) (41:1a). That blessing is detailed as divine preservation: liberation from evil by Yahweh (41:1b[2]), longevity (41:2a), fruitfulness (41:2b), protection from enemies (41:2c), and healing (41:3). And all because this one cares for the "insignificant" (41:1a). This is therefore an important spiritual issue, the concern of God's people for the weak, poor, and disenfranchised. An implicit threat underlies these statements: one may *not* enjoy divine blessing if one does not so care for the "insignificant."

Concern for Perishing (41:4–10)

The potential threats faced by the psalmist included evil from enemies and illness of body (41:1–3). But then in 41:4, we are introduced to another causative agent of the supplicant's distress, besides the adversaries and ailments mentioned earlier: the psalmist's own sin. The immediacy of this concern for perishing is introduced with a direct quote to Yahweh in 41:4 (with an emphatic redundant pronoun: "I—I said . . ."). This threat appears to be divine chastisement for the psalmist's sin. And that is followed by yet another quote, this time of the enemies, ostensibly speaking to one another (41:5), wishing evil and even death upon this already despairing soul.

The intermingling of all of these nightmares is suggested by the many wordplays. Both "desire" (of enemies) in 41:2c and "soul" (= life, now beset with suffering from illness and sin) in 41:4b are translations of נֶפֶשׁ, *nephesh*. Also: "*all* his [sick] bed" in 41:3b (i.e., his illness) is equated with "*all* who hate me" in 41:7a (i.e., his enemies). Besides, the "[sick] bed" (מִשְׁכָּב, *mishkav*) of disease in 41:3b is likewise hinted at later in 41:8, in the words of enemies who want him to "lie down" permanently (שׁכב, *shkv*, in 41:8b). And while the psalmist "says" to God words of appeal (41:4a), the enemies are also "saying" something—evil against the sufferer (41:5a). As if that weren't enough, later we find that the enemies' "speaking" in 41:6b, 6d

---

2. This "evil" is likely to have been perpetrated by the psalmist's enemies, as "evil" in 41:5a, 7b indicates.

is דבר, *dbr*; and "plague" in 41:8a is דָּבָר, *dvar* (and that in another direct quote of the enemies).³ Such an entwining of causes creating an abundance of distress is also observed in earlier psalms (Psalms 38–40). In any case, this piling on of producers of pain and plight prompts the psalmist to plead for pity (41:4a): "Yahweh, be gracious to me!"⁴

Then begins an extended lament (41:5–9) comprising two parallel sections, 41:5–6 and 41:7–9: each has mention of adversaries ("enemies" and "all who hate me"; 41:5a, 7), a direct quote from them (41:5b, 8), and a description of treachery on the part of those who were friends of the sufferer (41:6, 9).⁵ In each parallel portion there is a narrowing from a plurality of foes ("enemies" and "all who hate me," 41:5a, 7a) to a singularity of troublemakers ("he" and "my friend"; 41:6, 9a). All that to say, "evil" predominates in this section. The enemies utter "evil of me" (רַע לִי, *ra' li*; 41:5a) and those haters intend "evil to me" (רָעָה לִי, *ra'ah li*; 41:7b). Undoubtedly, these adversaries who are not "considering the insignificant"—with the psalmist tacitly putting himself in that category—will miss out on blessedness from God (41:1a). Indeed, they will be punished, as we find out later in 41:10–11. Such malefactors only wish the sufferer death and an eradication of his posterity (41:5b, 8), but God, on the other hand, is the one who "preserves him alive" (41:2a).

These evildoers, pretending to be friends, speak platitudes in the presence of the psalmist, but once outside, their speech turns to hatred (41:6–7⁶), calling down upon him "a pestilence of Belial" with hopes that the stricken one will never rise again (41:8)—their desire for his sickbed to become his deathbed.⁷ All of these vile ones are "against me"—the prepositional phrase is repeated four times in the psalm: speaking "against me" (41:7a), intending evil "against me" (41:7b), deploying his heel "against me" (41:9c), and crowing in triumph "against me" (41:11b). These wicked ones are synonymously labeled "my friend, in whom I trusted," and "the one who ate my bread" (i.e., those in fellowship with the psalmist who turned traitors; 41:9ab).⁸ "Friend" in 41:9a is אִישׁ שָׁלוֹם, *'ish shalom*, "person of peace," who acts like anything but! That the evil in this lament is being perpetrated by so-called friends makes it all the more reprehensible (and grievous). But the psalmist is confident that God's grace will enable him to "repay" them (שׁלם, *shlm*; 41:10b)—just deserts! They hoped the supplicant, their prey, would never "rise" again (קוּם, *qwm*; 41:8b), but a gracious God would "raise" him up (קוּם, 41:10a). This is clearly not a rising on one's own strength: it would be God "upholding" him and "standing" him (41:12)—the grace of God. The repayment being made by the sufferer (41:10b) is not antithetical to the usual OT understanding that it is God who repays evil upon evildoers. Just as the "raising" and "upholding" and "standing"

---

3. Likely derived from דֶּבֶר, *dever*, "plague," as also in 78:50; 91:3, 6.

4. It might well be that, since 41:4 specifically mentions personal sin, that was the primary cause of all the psalmist's sorrows, with other afflictions aggravating this core problem. "Indeed, paradoxically, the fact of being a moral failure becomes a reason why Yhwh should be gracious and heal: after all, if there were no failure, there would be no need for grace" (Goldingay, *Psalms*, 1:584). That is, as the apostle Paul declared, not to encourage sin to abound so that grace may also abound.

5. And notice that, in the structure of the psalm, the lament section (41:5–9) is framed by identical pleas for God's grace (41:4, 10).

6. Goldingay, *Psalms*, 1:585, suggests that the word for "whisper," לחשׁ, *lchsh* (41:7a), is "an onomatopoeic word suggesting hissing and originally referring to snake charming. . . . The unity of their incantations seems to add to their power and make them all the more frightening."

7. Goldingay, *Psalms*, 1:585. "Belial" (41:8a) is a name for Satan: Nah 1:15; and in the NT, in 2 Cor 6:15 (with Βελιάρ, *Beliar*, a variant of Βελιάλ, *Belial*).

8. Likely these "frenemies" were members of the psalmist's community.

(41:10a, 12) is the work of God by the grace of God, so too, the recompense upon enemies is God's doing, no matter what agency God employs to accomplish his purpose.

Confidence of Preservation 2 (41:11–13)

There is the possibility of a time gap between 41:10 (plea for grace) and 41:11 (confidence in God's grace: "by this I know . . ."). In the intervening period was there an oracle in the temple or an affirmation by the priest—some concrete evidence of reversal? At any rate, the psalmist has turned the corner; he, looking to the future, is now once again confident of God's pleasure in him and that his foes will not triumph (41:11b).[9] Enemies might hate him (41:7a), wish his death (41:5b), and consider him as good as gone (41:8), but if one enjoys divine pleasure (41:11a)—linked in this psalm with caring for the insignificant (41:1)—what more can one ask for? And this God, who has deigned to be "gracious" to his suffering people as he answers their prayers (41:4a, 10a), secures the sufferer in divine "presence," not just during the days of crisis, but *forever* (41:12b)! At this point in the psalm, even the sin of the psalmist is forgotten, as he exclaims that this God would "uphold" him in his "integrity" (41:12a). Not that that integrity is intrinsic to the supplicant, but that, in yet another exhibition of grace, God would support and sustain and succor him in probity—upholding him in uprightness!

And thus the psalm (and Book I of the Psalter) concludes, with a benediction (41:13) upon this God of amazing grace. He is worthy to be blessed now and forever—"Amen and amen!"

Sermon Map

I. Care for the Weak
   God's people care for the helpless (41:1aβ)
   Move-to-relevance: Our care for the weak

II. Concern for Their Sins
   God's people have a repentant heart (41:4)
   Move-to-relevance: Grief over sin

III. Consequence of Care and Concern
   In times of affliction and persecution . . . (41:1bα, 2c, 5–9, 11a)
   . . . God cares and is concerned for them (41:1aα, 1bβ–2, 3, 10–13)
   Move-to-relevance: God cares for the carers

IV. *Care, to Be Cared For!*
   Specifics on caring for others, and being concerned about one's sins

---

9. Earlier it was likely his gaze backwards into the past that gave him the *Confidence of Preservation 1* (41:1–3).

PSALMS 42:1—43:5

Psalms of Disorientation

Depression to Deliverance

BECAUSE OF THE STRUCTURING of the stanzas of Psalms 42 and 43, it is best to consider them together, as a single unit. Psalm 42 has two stanzas (42:1–5, 6–11) and Psalm 43 one (43:1–5): each stanza concludes with a similar refrain (42:5, 11; 43:5).[1]

Translation

42:1   As the deer pants for the streams of water,
       so my soul pants for You, God.
42:2   My soul thirsts for God, for the living God.
       When shall I come and appear before the presence of God?
42:3   My tears have been to me food day and night,
       while [they] say to me all day,
     "Where is your God?"
42:4   These things I remember,
       and I will pour my soul out upon myself:
    that I [used to] go along with the throng,
       processing [with] them unto the house of God,
    with the sound of an exclamation of joy and thanksgiving,
       a crowd celebrating a festival.
42:5   Why are you depressed, my soul,
       and [why] are you disturbed within me?
    Wait on God, for I shall again give Him thanks
       [for] the deliverance [that comes] from His presence.

---

1. Besides, Psalm 43 lacks a superscription, one of only two psalms in Book II of the Psalter without a heading (the other is Psalm 71).

42:6 My God, within me my soul is depressed;
> therefore I remember You from the land of Jordan
> and the Hermons, from Mount Mizar.

42:7 Deep calls to deep at the sound of Your waterfalls;
> all Your breakers and Your waves have swept over me.

42:8 By day Yahweh will command His lovingkindness;
> and by night His song will be with me.
> A prayer to the God of my life:

42:9 I will say to God my rock,
> "Why have You forgotten me?
> Why do I go about being dark
> because of the oppression of the enemy?"

42:10 [As] with a shattering of my bones,
> my adversaries reproach me,
> while they say to me all day,
> "Where is your God?"

42:11 Why are you depressed, my soul,
> and why are you disturbed within me?
> Wait on God, for I shall again give Him thanks Him—
> the deliverance of my face, and my God.

43:1 Vindicate me, God,
> and plead my case;
> from a nation without [any] devout,
> from the deceitful person and the wicked save me.

43:2 For You are the God of my strength:
> Why have You rejected me?
> Why do I go about being dark
> because of the oppression of the enemy?

43:3 Send out Your light and Your truth,
> let them lead me;
> let them bring me to Your holy mountain
> and to Your abodes.

43:4 Then I will go to the altar of God,
> to the God of my joyous jubilation;
> and I will give You thanks You upon the lyre, God, my God.

43:5 Why are you depressed, my soul,
> and why are you disturbed within me?
> Wait on God, for I shall again give You thanks Him—
> the deliverance of my face, and my God.

PSALMS 42:1—43:5

Structure

Psalms 42–43 can be structured as three stanzas, following the boundaries made up by major refrains in 42:5, 11, and 43:5 (the only exhortations to hope in this joint composition):[2]

> **STANZA 1: Pining for the Past (42:1–5)**
>
> *Cult: house of God, crowd, celebration, festival:*
> "When shall I come [בוא, *bw'*]?" (42:2b)
>   Enemies unnamed, but quoted (42:3c)
>   **A** Minor Refrain (42:3bc): *Questioning direct speech* (enemies)
>   **Major Refrain (42:5):** Hope; *Questioning speech* (psalmist)
>
> **STANZA 2: Problem of the Present (42:6–11)**
>
> *Calamity: land, mountains, God's waters, foes*
>   Enemies named (42:9d, 10b), and quoted (42:10d)
>   **B** Minor Refrain (42:9): *Questioning direct speech* (psalmist)
>   **A'** Minor Refrain (42:10cd): *Questioning direct speech* (enemies)
>   **Major Refrain (42:11):** Hope; *Questioning speech* (psalmist)
>
> **STANZA 3: Plea for the Future (43:1–5)**
>
> *Cult: holy mountain, dwellings, altar, praise:*
> "Then I will go [אבוא]" (43:4a)
>   Enemies named (43:1b, 1c, 2d), but not quoted
>   **B'** Minor Refrain (43:2): *Questioning speech* (psalmist)
>   **Major Refrain (43:5):** Hope; *Questioning speech* (psalmist)

All the refrains, major (42:5, 11; 43:5) and minor (42:3, 9, 10; 43:2), are questioning speech, either by the enemies to the psalmist, or by the psalmist to God.[3] The psalmist never questions the enemies, and the enemies, of course, have no intercourse with God.

"My soul" occurs four times in the first stanza (42:1b, 2a, 4b, 5a), two times in the second (42:6a, 11a) and once in the third (43:5a), the progressive reduction of self-references reflecting a movement from the plight felt by this suffering soul to a sense of confidence in God. Equally in sync with that hopeful and positive trajectory, the first stanza does not name enemies, but quotes them; the second both names and quotes them; and the third only names them.[4]

---

2. Modified from Craigie, *Psalms 1–50*, 325; and Alonso Schökel, "Poetic Structure," 10. The sections—*Pining*, *Problem*, and *Plea*—are not watertight; they are simply named for the predominant theme they display.

3. There is also the psalmist's question to God in 42:2b, but that is more a rhetorical one indicating the intensity of his yearning to be in God's presence (as the parallelism with 42:2a indicates). All the major refrains are identical, the only variant being 42:5: it does not have "why" (מָה, *mah*, as do 42:11b; 43:5b); it has "His presence [פָּנָיו, *panayw*]" (instead of "my face [פָּנַי, *panay*]" as do 42:11d; 43:5d); it has "deliverance" written in plene (יְשׁוּעוֹת, not יְשֻׁעֹת [both are transliterated *yshu'ot*, but without the ו, *w*, in the second] as do 42:11d; 43:5d); and it has no second mention of "God" at the end of the refrain (as do 42:11d; 43:5d). The minor refrains have greater variation, but A and A' are similar (42:3, 10; see above), as also are B and B' (42:9; 43:2).

4. See Raabe, *Psalm Structures*, 29–50.

Likewise, discounting the major refrains (42:5, 11; 43:5), we have the following patterns of the depiction of deity in the psalm:

	Depiction of God	Frequency	Titles for God
42:1–4	Second person (42:1) Third person (42:2–4)	One verse	One (42:2a)
42:6–10	Second person (42:6–7) Third person (42:8–10)	Two verses	Two (42:8c, 9a)
43:1–4	Second person (43:1–3) Third person (42:4ab) Second person (43:4c)	Three verses Third of a verse	Three (43:2a, 4b, 4c)

The first section has only one verse with God in the second person; the second section has two in the second person; the third has more than three in the second person, an increase of references to deity that is in tandem with the decrease of references to self noted earlier. Also of note, deity is labeled as God or as Yahweh twenty-two times in Psalms 42–43, but his titles are gradually more enlightening (one title in stanza one; two in stanza two; and three in stanza three, again reflecting the growing hope and confidence of the one praying): "the living God" (42:2a); "God of my life" (42:8c); "God my rock" (42:9a); "God of my strength" (43:2a); "God of my joyous jubilation" (43:4b); and "God, my God" (43:4c). It becomes straightforward, now, to comprehend the "storying" of this composition.

Theological Focus

> In circumstances of depression and despair (perhaps the result of divine discipline), accentuated by the derision of enemies, God's people, remembering their deity, grow in hope that he has not forgotten them, trusting that his lovingkindness will be extended towards his faithful, and that God will hear their yearning and return them to his presence.

Commentary

Pining for the Past (42:1–5)

The first stanza (42:1–5) yearns for the past with nostalgia and longing. The psalmist wants the water of life (i.e., the living God and his presence; 42:1–2) but ends up with waters of sorrow ("tears," 42:3), so much so he "pours out" his soul (42:4b), as he "remembers" and pines for what once was (42:4a): enjoying the presence of God, processing with his community to the temple, and joyously celebrating a festival therein (42:2, 4c–f). But now he is faced with a taunt from his enemies:[5] "Where is your God?" (minor refrain A, 42:3bc). This lampooning of the psalmist's faith was happening "all *day*" (42:3b); no wonder his sustenance "*day* and night"

---

5. The infinitive verb translated "say" does not specify a subject: "they" is added for clarity.

was his tears (42:3a). And then the first major refrain in 42:5 underscores the intensity of the sufferer's plight and his pain. The psalmist is "disturbed" (המה, *hmh*; 42:5b); the word is likely related to the "crowd" mentioned earlier (הָמוֹן, *hamon*; 42:4f)—"an unhappy inner turmoil has replaced the celebratory communal turmoiling crowd."[6] Perhaps this is why 42:1–4 has only one verse that speaks of God in the second person, and why the focus on self is most prominent in this first stanza. The major refrain concludes the stanza with an exhortation to wait and an expectation of praise, all anticipating divine deliverance coming from the "presence" of God (42:5d), the same "presence" the supplicant had once enjoyed (42:2b).[7] In sum, the loudest note sounded in this first major refrain is one of depression and disturbance.

Problem of the Present (42:6–11)

The despair of the psalmist intensifies in the second stanza of the composition. Nothing seems to have changed from the first stanza, but things have actually become worse, as indicated by the reuse of "depressed" in 42:6a (from 42:5a): the *Problem of the Present*. The waters of life that the sufferer desired (42:1–2) had turned into the waters of grief (42:3); but here they have become the waters of trauma (42:7).[8] And, what's worse, it is God himself who is commanding the disposition of these fluids: "*Your* waterfalls," "all *Your* breakers," "*Your* waves" (42:7).[9] God, the giver of life ("the living God," 42:2a; and "God of my life," 42:8c), has apparently become complicit in the psalmist's near-death.[10] What exactly is going on here is not certain; it might be metaphorically describing divine discipline.

Once the psalmist used to "go along" (עבר, '*vr*; 42:4c) with a throng celebrating God; now it is God's own waters that have "swept" (also עבר, 42:7b) over him. Once it was the "sound" (42:4e) of festivities buoying the supplicant; now it is the "sound" (42:7a) of the turbulent waters threatening to bury him. The supplicant's depression is further expressed in the use of the first-person suffixed preposition, עָלַי, '*alay*: "within me" his soul is depressed (42:6a); and that soul is disturbed "within me" (42:11b; and the same phrase in 42:5b); all because God's dangerous waters have swept "over me" (also עָלָי; 42:7b).

He tries to "remember" again (42:6b, as in 42:4a), this time focusing on God rather than his compatriots and their cultic celebrations: "I remember *You*" (42:6b). The use of the geographical markers in 42:6bc, "land of Jordan," "Hermons" (indicating, collectively, the mountain summits in northeastern Israel), and "Mount Mizar" (uncertain location), are intended to depict the psalmist's distance from the temple in Jerusalem. Yet, even from afar, the sufferer claims that he seeks to remember God (42:6a). These ranges may have raised in his mind the imagery of chaotic waters—perhaps the "waterfalls" of the River Jordan arising in those mountains, and the seas west of these peaks with their "breakers" and "waves" (42:7). All that to say, fear and anxiety loom large!

---

6. Goldingay, *Psalms*, 2:26.

7. "Presence" is literally "face" in both instances.

8. "The supplicant longs for refreshing water, weeps watery tears, and drowns in death's waters" (Goldingay, *Psalms*, 2:28).

9. The metaphor of fluids thus saturates the first two stanzas: "streams," "water" (42:1a); "thirsts" (42:2b); "tears" (42:3a); "pour" (42:4b); "deep" (×2; 42:7aα); "waterfalls" (42:7aβ); "breakers" (42:7bα); "waves" (42:7bβ).

10. Alonso Schökel, "Poetic Structure," 7.

This attempt to "remember" God (42:6b) is a critical move when, for all appearances, God has "forgotten" him, all is dark, and the enemy's oppression has escalated (42:9, the minor refrain *B*), almost shattering his bones, their words contemptuous—"Where is your God" (the minor refrain *A'* of 42:10cd; as also in 42:3bc). Yes, the wicked had been "saying" things pejorative and derogatory (42:3b), but it appears that the psalmist was now implicitly agreeing with that negative assessment, for he too "says"—to God: "Why have You forgotten me?" (42:9ab). Indeed, just as these adversaries were continuing their derisive chant "all" day (42:10c), so also "all" of God's breakers and waves (42:7b) were putting the supplicant in lethal jeopardy. It appears that his enemies were right all along!

But the psalmist clings to a vestige of hope that Yahweh's lovingkindness and his song would be with him "by day" and "by night" (42:8ab). There is a confidence here, howbeit drowned in roiling waters, that the tears that were his food "day and night" (42:3) are going to be replaced by something far, far better. Perhaps not accidentally, 42:8, in which this hope is expressed, contains the only use of "Yahweh" in Psalms 42–43. The lovingkindness the sufferer is waiting for comes from a God covenantally obliged to his people. And so he prays to the "God of my life" and to the "God my rock" (42:8c–9). Psalm 42:9 is poignantly constructed, opposing "God, my rock" with "the oppression of the enemy," together hedging the pitiable psalmist with his plaintive whys in the middle:[11]

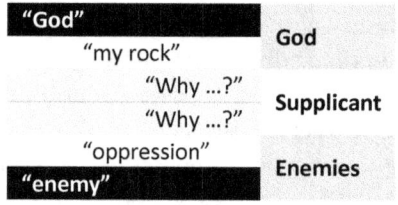

Subsequently, another major refrain (42:11) closes out the stanza and the psalm, this time more anguished than the one in 42:5.[12] Thus the psalm remains unresolved, awaiting the third stanza of the composition that Psalm 43 comprises.

Plea for the Future (43:1–5)

The composition concludes with this third stanza that contains no hydraulic motif; rather there is "Your light and Your truth" by which the psalmist expects to be "led" back to the presence of God (43:3ab). Unlike 42:1–5 where enemies were unnamed, but quoted, and unlike 42:6–11 where they were both named and quoted, here in 43:1–5, they are only named; they remain mute. Things are certainly looking better! And as if to validate that, this third stanza begins with God in the second person (43:1–3), moves to God in the third

---

11. From Auffret, "'Vers la montagne,'" 24.

12. This is inferred from the context, even though verbally, all the refrains are virtually identical. "In line with the dynamics of the poem, the refrain at the end of the first . . . [stanza] is a voice which is timid and stifled; the second time it is one of affirmation and reproach, and the third it amounts to a shout of triumph. Without any verbal alteration, the refrain undergoes a change of tone, and this should be evident when the psalm is recited" (Alonso Schökel, "Poetic Structure," 11). However, the addition of "my God" in 42:11d and 43:5d (absent in 42:5d) does suggest an upward movement at least from the first to the second stanza.

person (43:4ab), and—again unlike previous stanzas—returns to God in the second person (43:4c). So we have in Psalm 43—after the psalmist's pining for the past and his problem of the present in Psalm 42—a plea for the future that is brimming with far more hope and confidence than was seen in the preceding text.[13]

Earlier the psalmist had been confident of Yahweh's "lovingkindness" (חֶסֶד, *chesed*; 42:8a) being with him. Here we see the reason: he implies he is one of the "devout" (חָסִיד, *chasid*, apparently one of the last of this species; 43:1c). So there is an explicit plea that he would be vindicated as God pleads his case and saves him from an undevoted group of people, the deceitful and the wicked (43:1d).[14] Once again we have a minor refrain, B' (43:2) that bemoans the darkness the poet is in.[15] No wonder he asks for divine light (43:3a), by which he may return to the place he had pined for earlier in 42:1–2, 4cd—"Your holy mountain" and "Your abodes," i.e., the presence of God (43:3cd). In 42:2b, he had asked, "When shall I come [בוא] . . . ?" Here he affirms in 43:4a, "Then I will go [בוא] . . ."—when God has delivered him.[16] And as he reentered fellowship with deity he would engage in praise again, at God's altar (43:4a). Notice the progression from relative distance from God to close proximity with God: "Your holy mountain" (43:3c) → "Your abodes" (43:3d) → "altar of God" (43:4a). How can he then not be reveling in "joyous jubilation," thanking "God, my God" (43:4bc)?

It may be surprising to see that the composition and this stanza ends with the major refrain in 43:5 with its mention of depression. But here this reiteration is hued by far more hope than in the prior instances (43:5, 11). "The situation creating sorrow still exists, but as the question is asked again, 'why are you downcast [depressed]?', the response can now be given with the conviction that God has heard and answered his prayer."[17] There is no reason for sorrow or grief. While there is no indication that God has heard the psalmist's plea yet, the supplicant continues to be powered by hope: "Wait in God, for I shall again praise Him"—the deliverer, the God of his people (43:5cd).

Sermon Map

I. Hopelessness
    Discipline (42:7)
    Desire for divine presence (42:1–2, 4)
    Dejection (42:3, 5ab, 6a, 9c–11b; 43:2cd, 5ab)
    Move-to-relevance: Our days of discipline leading to depression
II. Hopefulness
    Determined remembrance of God (42:6bc)
    Confident prayer (42:5cd, 8–9b, 11cd; 43:1–2b; 3–4, 5cd)
    Move-to-relevance: Developing confidence by remembering God
III. *Remember and Recover!*
    Specifics on remembering God in confident prayer

---

13. The resolution of deliverance is still awaited at the end of this psalm, but there is a keen anticipation of this rescue and the praise of God that will ensue as a result.

14. These are likely foes that aggravated an already depressing situation (of divine discipline?); they are unlikely to have caused the anguish in the first place.

15. Also mentioned in the minor refrain B (42:9cd).

16. "Let them *bring* me to Your holy mountain" also employs בוא (43:3c).

17. Craigie, *Psalms 1–50*, 329.

PSALM 44:1–26

Psalm of Disorientation

Hanging on to Lovingkindness

PSALM 44 IS THE first of eleven "community laments" (Psalms 44; 60; 74; 79; 80; 83; 85; 90; 94; 123; and 137). Corporate though it is, in Psalm 44 there is an oscillation between the "I" of the psalmist (44:4–8, 15; a leader or liturgist? a literary convention of using the singular in lieu of the plural for the group?) and the explicit "we" of the community (44:1–3, 9–14, 17–26).[1] In any case, the psalm seems to be set in the backdrop of a military defeat suffered by God's people at the hands of the enemy (44:9–16).

Translation

44:1   God, with our ears, we have heard,
          our fathers related to us,
       the doing [that] You did in their days,
          in days bygone.
44:2   You—[with] Your hand You took possession of the nations;
          then You planted them;
       You brought trouble to the peoples,
          then You spread them out.
44:3   For not with their sword did they take possession of the land,
          and their arm did not deliver them,
       but Your right hand and Your arm and the light of Your face,
          for You were pleased with them.
44:4   You are my King, God;
          command deliverances for Jacob.

---

1. Such alternations are found both in the psalms (66:1–12, 13–20; 74:1–2, 9, 12; 123:1, 2–4; 137:1–4, 5–6; 144:1–2, 9–11, 12–15) and elsewhere in the OT. Indeed 129:1–3 explicitly asks Israel to refer to itself in the singular. Here, enemies show up in the plural (44:2–3, 7, 10b–11, 13–14), but also in the singular (44:10a, 16).

44:5 Through You, our adversaries we will knock down;
> through Your name, we will trample those who rise against us.

44:6 For not in my bow do I trust,
> and my sword does not deliver me.

44:7 But You deliver us from our adversaries,
> and those who hate us You shame.

44:8 To God we [make] praise all day,
> and to Your name forever we will give thanks.

44:9 Yet You rejected and disgraced us,
> and You did not go out among our armies.

44:10 You caused us to turn back from the adversary;
> and those who hate us plundered [us] for themselves.

44:11 You gave us as sheep to be eaten,
> and among the nations You scattered us.

44:12 You sold Your people for no value,
> and You did not increase their market price.

44:13 You made us a reproach to our neighbors,
> derision and ridicule to those around us.

44:14 You made us a byword among the nations,
> a [reason for] head-shaking among the peoples.

44:15 All day my disgrace is before me,
> and shame has covered my face

44:16 at the voice of the one who reproaches and reviles,
> at the face of the enemy and the vindictive.

44:17 All this has come upon us, but we have not forgotten You,
> and we have not dealt falsely with Your covenant.

44:18 Our heart has not shrunk back,
> nor our steps from Your way.

44:19 Yet You have crushed us in a place of jackals,
> and covered us over with the death-shadow.

44:20 If we had forgotten the name of our God
> or stretched out our hands to a strange god,

44:21 would not God find this out?
> For He knows the secrets of the heart.

44:22 Yet because of You we are killed all day;
> we are considered as sheep for slaughter.

44:23 Arouse Yourself, why do You sleep, Lord?
> Awake, do not reject perpetually.

44:24 Why do You hide Your face,
> [and] forget our affliction and our oppression?

44:25 For it has sunk down into the dust, our soul;
    it clings to the earth, our belly.
44:26 Rise up [as] a help for us,
    and redeem us for the sake of Your lovingkindness.

Structure

The psalm may be structured as follows:[2]

    A *Deliverance in the Past* (**44:1–3**)
        "land" (אֶרֶץ, *'erets;* 44:3a); "face" (44:3c)
        B *Dependence in the Present* (**44:4–8**)
           "all day" (44:8a)
              C *Disaster in the Present* (**44:9–16**)
                  "all day" (44:15a); "face" (44:15b, 16b)
        B' *Disputation in the Present* (**44:17–22**)
           "all day" (44:22a)
    A' *Deliverance in the Future* (**44:23–26**)
        "earth" (אֶרֶץ; 44:25b); "face" (44:24a)

There is clearly a significant amount of tension in the psalm: God's past actions vs. present inaction; God's current inaction despite his people's innocence (at least as they claim it); and God's treatment of nations vs. his treatment of Israel. In fact, the psalm concludes with this tension unresolved.

Theological Focus

> While God has actively worked and marvelously delivered his people in the past, reasons for his apparent inaction and non-deliverance of them in the present (resulting in their shaming before others) are not always forthcoming—despite their willingness to rely on him, their desire to praise him, and the absence of any obvious sin or unfaithfulness to God—but the people of God continue to trust him in faith, banking on his lovingkindness for the future.

---

2. See Kessler, "Psalm 44," 194–95; and Crow, "Rhetoric of Psalm 44," 394.

PSALM 44:1–26

Commentary

Deliverance in the Past (44:1–3)

It all begins brightly with an affirmation of deliverance accomplished in the past for the ancestors of the Israelites. Indeed, the very existence of these peoples was a divinely orchestrated event, with God dispossessing the nations and planting the Israelites (44:2ab)—peoples uprooted and God's people established (44:2cd).

This section describes God bringing the Israelites into the promised land, described as a singular action—"the doing [that] You did" (44:1c). "*Your* hand" was instrumental in that operation (44:2a)—"*Your* right hand" and "*Your* arm" and "the light of *Your* face" (44:3c), not "*their* sword" or "*their* arm" (i.e., not the arms and armaments of the Israelites of days bygone; 44:3ab). The "hand" and "arm" of God—he used no weaponry apparently—suggest the personal and direct involvement of deity in this transaction; likewise, the negation of the "arm" of the fathers (and that of their sword) asserts a corresponding lack of those humans' direct involvement in the victory. And all because deity was "pleased" with his people (44:3d). How they found favor with him is not noted; it may be attributed to the grace of God.[3]

All that to say, expectations of God are high: he worked for the ancestors in the past, surely he should work for his people in the present.

Dependence in the Present (44:4–8)

The time machine then rolls forward to the present, as the psalmist affirms that history will repeat itself in his day, and that God will do now as he has done before. Appealing to "my King"—the God who is committed to his people—to grant them ("Jacob") "deliverance" (44:4), the psalmist clarifies that it will be "through You" and "through Your name" that they will gain victory in battle (44:5). So, just like their ancestors, the people of God also would not rely on their own bows or swords that are unable to "deliver" (44:6b), but upon God who alone could "deliver" them from their foes (44:7a). The contrast is accentuated in the repeated terms noted above and the duplicated structure, . . . כִּי . . . כִּי לֹא, *ki loʾ . . . ki . . .* ("for not . . . but . . .") in 44:3 and 44:6–7. Therefore, the "name" of this delivering God (44:8b), through whose "name" his people expect victory (44:5b) is worthy of praise and thanks. Such gratitude would be due God "all day" (44:8a) and, indeed, "forever" (44:8b), because the same God had performed feats of deliverance in the "days" of the fathers, i.e., in "days" bygone (44:1c, 1d), and deity was going to repeat his act of rescue again, in the current day. The people of God were going to depend upon him, with ensuing praise and thanksgiving.

In sum, with the past as their guide, and with their abandonment of reliance upon human contrivances, one would think matters would have continued in present in that fashion and on that same cheery note. But, alas!

Disaster in the Present (44:9–16)

The striking aspect of this disaster that is described to have occurred in the present (or the recent past) is that God is being held responsible for the crisis. Apparently, and in contrast to

---

3. See Deut 4:37; 7:7–8; 10:15; 33:8; etc.

his military success and effectiveness in the past, it is deity's military failure and negligence in the present that is causing the current calamity—"*You* made us . . ." shows up twice, in 44:13a, 14a.⁴ And in the same accusatory tone, "You"-statements are found in nine lines (44:9a, 9b, 10a, 11a, 11b, 12a, 12b, 13a, 14a) in six verses. God, for all appearances, had "rejected" and "disgraced" his people, refusing to fight for them (44:9a). This shaming of God's people in 44:9–16 is arranged cleverly, with their "disgrace," "reproach," "derision," and "ridicule" at the hands of their jeering "adversaries," "nations," "peoples," "enemies," and "vindictive" ones permeating this section:⁵

> "disgraced" (44:9a); "adversary" (44:10a); "those who hate us" (44:10b)
> "nations" (44:11b); "people" (44:12a)
> "reproach"; "derision and ridicule" (44:13)
> "nations" (44:14a); "peoples" (44:14b)
> "disgrace" (44:15a); "enemy," "vindictive" (44:16b)

This was a horrible situation, indeed. God's refusal to go before the army of his people (44:9b) had caused them to retreat from their foes ("turn back," 44:10a) who then proceeded to plunder them (44:10b) as sheep for slaughter (44:11a; also 44:22b). Effectively, God had dispersed his people among the nations (44:11b), cheaply discarding them as a valueless commodity (44:12).⁶ Once God had caused the "adversaries" to be defeated (44:5a) and delivered his people from those same "adversaries" (44:7a); now, however, it was his own who were fleeing from those "adversaries" who had the upper hand (44:10a). Once God had "shamed" "those who hate us," his people (44:7b); now "those who hate us" are plundering God's community (44:10b), and it is the latter that is covered with "shame" (44:15b). Once he had dispossessed the "nations" and troubled the "peoples" to "spread out" his faithful ones and establish them (44:2); now they are "scattered" among the "nations"—disestablished (44:11b), a proverb ("byword" of mockery) to these "nations" (44:14a), and even a cause of derision amongst the "peoples" ("head-shaking," 44:14b; see Jer 18:16).⁷

Thus God's people were condemned to ignominy before outsiders (Ps 44:13–16). God's "face," in the past, enlightened the lives of his people, for "You were pleased with them" (44:3cd). Now, their own "faces" are covered with utter disesteem and degradation (44:15b), and their enemies' "faces" gloat with vindictiveness (44:16b). Later, the psalmist would ask God: "Why do You hide Your *face*?" (44:24a). The shame "covering" God's people (44:15b) was equivalent to deity "covering" them with the "death-shadow" (symbolic of utter defeat and darkness; 44:19b). Evidently, God was not pleased with them so much now!

And so, those who had praised God "all day" (44:8a) were now reduced to being disgraced "all day" (44:15a), even being killed "all day" (44:22a). The cause for this reversal of God's attitude and action towards his people from past to present is not explained, though it is quite possible that, like the reason for the curses in the stipulations of God's covenant with his

---

4. Brueggemann and Bellinger, *Psalms*, 209. This section has a mixture of perfect and imperfect forms of verbs; but, in light of the context, I am considering them all equivalently as descriptions of the seemingly problematic treatment by God of the Israelites in the current age—all described in the past tense.

5. From Girard, *Les Psaumes*, 358.

6. "They have been put on eBay for a few cents, with no reserve" (Goldingay, *Psalms*, 2:43).

7. "Peoples" in 44:2c, 14b is אם, '*im*; "people" in 44:12a is עם, '*am*.

nation (Deut 28:15–68; see especially 28:15, 20, 45, 47, 58[8]), disobedience played a role. But the people of God protest against that implication . . . .

Disputation in the Present (44:17–22)

No, they respond; nothing of the sort: "We have *not forgotten* You," God (Ps 44:17a); had they "*forgotten* the name of our God," or been unfaithful to him, surely he would have known that (44:20–21). The One who knows the secrets of the "heart" (44:21b) would have discerned the state of their "hearts" (44:18): no, they had not turned from God's way, but they had been faithful to his "covenant" (44:17b).[9] Both their attitudes ("heart," 44:18a) and their actions ("steps," 44:18b) had remained loyal to God. God may have turned them "back" from the face of the enemy (44:10a), but they, God's people, had not shrunk "back" from divine demand (44:18a). It was through God's "name" that they had once been victorious (44:5b); it was God's "name" that they were therefore praising forever (44:8b). How could they then forget the "name" of their God, they ask (44:20a). These disputations of innocence are interspersed with accusations of God's abandonment of them:[10]

44:17–18	Innocence
44:19	Accusation: "yet [כִּי, *ki*] ..."
44:20–21	Innocence
44:22	Accusation: "yet [כִּי] ..."

Despite their claimed faithfulness (and there is no reason to doubt that claim), God had, in his sovereignty, crushed them in a desolate place and in dangerous peril ("place of jackals" and "death-shadow," 44:19); the ones praising "all day" (44:8a) were now the ones disgraced "all day" (44:15a), the ones slaughtered "all day" (44:22a).[11]

These claims of innocence raise the question again: Why was God acting the way he did?

Deliverance in the Future (44:23–26)

The psalmist himself poses that question—twice: "Why do You sleep?" (44:23a) and "Why do you hide Your face?" (44:24a). God's people had once taken possession of the "land" with his help (אֶרֶץ, 44:3a); now their souls had sunk into the dust and were clinging to the "earth" (also אֶרֶץ, 44:25b)—as good as dead! Why then was God "sleeping," "rejecting," "hiding," and "forgetting" (44:23–24)?

---

8. "Covenant" is expressly mentioned in 44:17b.

9. And, as if in protest against this apparent covenant failing on the part of God, nowhere in the psalm is God addressed by his covenantal name, "Yahweh"; he shows up only as "God" in 44:1a, 4a, 8a, 20a, 21a, and as "King" in 44:4a, and "Lord" in 44:23b.

10. Crow, "Rhetoric of Psalm 44," 298.

11. Unlike the implication of Rom 8:36 that quotes Ps 44:22, there is no hint here of enemies attacking God's people because they were loyal to God; rather, in this psalm it is because of God himself, the cause of this disaster, that they are under assault.

Unfortunately for the people of God, no answer is forthcoming from their deity. Instead, they can only continue to trust and pray that God would not reject them "perpetually" (44:23b). They had not "forgotten" God (44:17a, 20a), so may God now not "forget" them (44:24b). They could not rise, stricken to the ground as they were (44:25), so may God "rise" on their behalf and deliver them (44:26a), and so they entreat: "Arouse Yourself," "awake" (44:23), and "rise up," "redeem us" (44:26), at least "for the sake of Your lovingkindness" (44:26b). Those who were "sold" by God for a pittance (44:12a) now plead for him to "redeem" them (44:26b). And on that plangent note, the psalm ends, its last word a tearful plea: "Your lovingkindness [חַסְדֶּךָ, *chasdeka*]." What was happening was totally inexplicable, but hope there was—and always will be—as long as there is divine lovingkindness.

> At the rational level, it would seem rather futile to pray and to seek God's love, when the immediate experience suggested that God could not be relied on. Yet the prayer is rooted in a faith deeper than reason. The faith also went beyond theology, which implied that God's actions could always be anticipated, if not predicted . . .; the faith recognized a mystery in God's ways, beyond both reason and theology, which made prayer worthwhile. . . . There is an immense mystery in God and his ways, but one must continue to trust and to pray.[12]

Though the psalm ends in this wrenching and unresolved tension of "Why?" the intended response of God's people in agonizing times of turmoil, turbulence, and tumult in life is clear: Hang on, for dear life, to . . . God's "lovingkindness"!

Sermon Map

I. Deliverance in the Past
   God's activity (44:1–4)
   Move-to-relevance: Our history with God's deliverance
II. Dependence in the Present
   Continuing to rely on God's activity in faith (44:5–8)
   Move-to-relevance: Trusting God in times of trial
III. Despair in the Present
   God's inactivity (44:9–16)
   People's innocence (44:17–22)
   People's imploring (44:23–26)
   Move-to-relevance: Discouragement at lack of answers or easy solutions
IV. *Cling to Lovingkindness!* (for the Future)
   Specifics on holding on to God no matter what

---

12. Craigie, *Psalms 1–50*, 335.

Bibliography

Abernethy, Andrew T. "God as Teacher in Psalm 25." *Vetus Testamentum* 65 (2015) 339–51.

———. "'Right Paths' and/or 'Paths of Righteousness'? Examining Psalm 23.3b within the Psalter." *Journal for the Study of the Old Testament* 39 (2015) 299–318.

Achtemeier, Elizabeth. "Preaching from the Psalms." *Review and Expositor* 81 (1984) 437–49.

Alonso Schökel, Luis. *A Manual of Hebrew Poetics*. Subsidia Biblica 11. Rome: Editrice Pontificio Istituto Biblico, 1988.

———. "The Poetic Structure of Psalm 42–43." *Journal for the Study of the Old Testament* 1 (1976) 4–11.

Alter, Robert. *The Art of Biblical Poetry*. Rev. ed. New York: Basic, 2011.

———. "Introduction." In *The Literary Guide to the Bible*, edited by Robert Alter and Frank Kermode, 11–35. Cambridge, MA: Belknap, 1987.

Althann, Robert. "The Psalms of Vengeance against Their Ancient Near Eastern Background." *Journal of Northwest Semitic Languages* 18 (1992) 1–11.

Andersen, Francis I., and David Noel Freedman. *Hosea: A New Translation with Introduction and Commentary*. Anchor Bible 24. Garden City, NY: Doubleday, 1980.

Aquinas, Thomas. *Exposition of the Psalms of David: Psalm 1*. Aquinas Translation Project, De Sales University. http://hosted.desales.edu/w4/philtheo/loughlin/ATP/Psalm_1.html.

———. *Summa Theologiæ of St. Thomas Aquinas*. 2nd rev. ed. Translated by Fathers of the English Dominican Province. https://www.newadvent.org/summa/.

Aster, Shawn Zelig. "On the Place of Psalm 21 in Israelite Royal Ideology." In *Mishneh Todah: Studies in Deuteronomy and Its Cultural Environment in Honor of Jeffrey H. Tigay*, edited by Nili Sacher Fox et al., 307–20. Winona Lake, IN: Eisenbrauns, 2009.

Auffret, Pierre. "'Allez, fils, entendez-moi!' Étude structurelle du Psaume 34 et son rapport au psaume 33." *Église et Théologie* 19 (1988) 5–31.

———. "'Car toi, tu as agi': Etude Structurelle du Psaume 39." *Bijdragen* 51 (1990) 118–38.

———. "'J'ai proclamé la justice: Étude structurelle du Ps 40 (et du Ps 70)." *Rivista biblica* 49 (2001) 385–416.

———. "'Toi, tu répondras': Étude structurelle du Psaume 38." *Science et Esprit* 40 (1988) 295–314.

———. "'Tu as entendu': Étude struturelle du psaume 31." *Église et Théologie* 18 (1987) 147–81.

———. "'Vers la montagne de ton lieu-saint': Étude structurelle du Psaume 42–43." *Studi Epigrafici e Linguistici* 22 (2005) 19–33.

———. "'Yahvé, Qu('elle nous est) chère, ta loyauté!' Étude structurelle du Ps 36." *Science et Esprit* 40 (1988) 57–73.

Augustine. *Exposition on the Psalms*. NPNF1, vol. 8. Edited by Philip Schaff. New York: Christian Literature, 1888.

———. *On Christian Doctrine*. In NPNF1, vol. 2, edited by Philip Schaff, 519–97. New York: Christian Literature, 1887.

Bang, Jeung-Yeoul. "The Canonical Function of Psalms 19 and 119 as a Macro-Torah Frame." *Korean Journal of Old Testament Studies* 66 (2017) 251–85.

Barbiero, Gianni. "Psalm 41:14, or the Unity of the Masoretic Psalm." *Old Testament Essays* 32 (2019) 317–42.

Bellinger, W. H., Jr. "Psalm XXVI: A Test of Method." *Vetus Testamentum* 43 (1993) 452–61.

Benun, Ronald. "Evil and the Disruption of Order: A Structural Analysis of the Acrostics in the First Book of Psalms." *Journal of Hebrew Scriptures* 6 (2006) 2–30.
Berlin, Adele. "The Rhetoric of Psalm 145." In *Biblical and Related Studies Presented to Samuel Iwry*, edited by Ann Kort and Scott Morschauser, 17–22. Winona Lake, IN: Eisenbrauns, 1985.
———. "Speakers and Scenarios: Imagining the First Temple in Second Temple Psalms (Psalms 122 and 137)." In *Functions of Psalms and Prayers in the Late Second Temple Period*, edited by Mika S. Pajunen and Jeremy Penner, 341–55. Beihefte zur Zeitschrift für die alttestamentliche Wissenschaft 486. Berlin: de Gruyter, 2017.
Best, Ernest. "The Reading and Writing of Commentaries." *Expository Times* 107 (1996) 358–62.
Beuken, W. A. M. "Psalm 16: The Path to Life." *Bijdragen* 41 (2013) 368–85.
———. "Psalm 39: Some Aspects of the Old Testament Understanding of Prayer." *Heythrop Journal* 19 (1978) 1–11.
Borger, Rykold. *Die Inschriften Asarhaddons Königs von Assyrien*. Archiv für Orientforschung, Beihefte 9. Osnabrück: Biblio-Verlag, 1967.
Botha, P. J. "Answers Disguised as Questions: Rhetoric and Reasoning in Psalm 24." *Old Testament Essays* 22 (2009) 535–53.
———. "Following the 'Tracks of Righteousness' of Psalm 23." *Old Testament Essays* 28 (2015) 283–300.
———. "The Ideological Interface between Psalm 1 and Psalm 2." *OTE* 18 (2005) 189–203.
———. "Poetry and Perlocution in Psalm 26." *Old Testament Essays* 24 (2011) 30–48.
———. "Psalm 5 and the Polarity between Those Who May Stand before Yahweh and Those Who May Not." *HTS/Theological Studies* 74 (2018) 1–7.
———. "Psalm 32 as a Wisdom Intertext." *HTS/Theological Studies* 70 (2014) 1–9.
———. "The Social Setting and Strategy of Psalm 34." *Old Testament Essays* 10 (1997) 178–97.
———. "The Textual Strategy and Ideology of Psalm 36." *Old Testament Essays* 17 (2004) 506–20.
———. "True Happiness in the Presence of Yhwh: The Literary and Theological Context for Understanding Psalm 16." *Old Testament Essays* 29 (2016) 61–84.
Botha, P. J., and Beat Weber. "'Killing Them Softly with This Song . . . ' The Literary Structure of Psalm 3 and Its Psalmic and Davidic Contexts: Part I: An Intratextual Interpretation of Psalm 3." *Old Testament Essays* 21 (2008) 18–37.
Botha, P. J., and J. H. Potgieter. "'The Word of Yahweh Is Right': Psalm 33 as a Torah-Psalm." *Verbum et Ecclesia* 31 (2010) 1–8.
Boulton, Matthew. "Forsaking God: A Theological Argument for Christian Lamentation." *Scottish Journal of Theology* 55 (2002) 58–78.
Bracke, John M. "*šûb šebût*: A Reappraisal." *Zeitschrift für de alttestamentliche Wissenschaft* 97 (1985) 233–44.
Braude, William G., trans. *The Midrash on the Psalms*. Yale Judaica Series 13. New Haven: Yale University Press, 1959.
Brown, Francis, et al. "אָלַח." In *A Hebrew and English Lexicon of the Old Testament*, translated by Edward Robinson, 47. Boston: Houghton Mifflin, 1907.
Brown, William P. "'Here Comes the Sun!' The Metaphorical Theology of Psalms 15–24." In *The Composition of the Psalms*, edited by Erich Zenger, 259–77. Bibliotheca Ephemeridum Theologicarum Lovaniensium. Leuven: Peeters, 2010.
Brueggemann, Walter. "Bounded by Obedience and Praise: The Psalms as Canon." *Journal for the Study of the Old Testament* 50 (1991) 63–92.
———. "The Costly Loss of Lament." *Journal for the Study of the Old Testament* 36 (1986) 57–71.
———. *From Whom No Secrets Are Hid: Introducing the Psalms*. Edited by Brent A. Strawn. Louisville: Westminster John Knox, 2014.
———. *The Message of the Psalms: A Theological Commentary*. Augsburg Old Testament Studies. Minneapolis: Augsburg, 1984.
———. "Psalms and the Life of Faith: A Suggested Typology of Function." *Journal for the Study of the Old Testament* 17 (1980) 3–32.
———. *Theology of the Old Testament: Testimony, Dispute, Advocacy*. Minneapolis: Fortress, 1997.
Brueggemann, Walter, and William H. Bellinger, Jr. *Psalms*. New Cambridge Bible Commentary. New York: Cambridge University Press, 2014.

BIBLIOGRAPHY

Brug, John F. "Biblical Acrostics and Their Relationship to Other Ancient Near Eastern Acrostics." In *The Bible in the Light of Cuneiform Literature: Scripture in Context III*, edited by William W. Hallo et al., 77-79. Ancient Near Eastern Texts and Studies 8. Lewiston, NY: Mellen, 1990.

Calvin, John. *Commentary on the Book of Psalms*. 5 vols. Translated by James Anderson. Grand Rapids: Eerdmans, 1949.

Ceresko, Anthony R. "The ABCs of Wisdom in Psalm XXXIV." *Vetus Testamentum* 35 (1985) 99-104.

Chisholm, Robert B. "Does God Deceive?" *Bibliotheca Sacra* 155 (1998) 11-28.

Chrysostom, John. *Commentary on the Psalms*. Vol. 1. Translated by Robert Charles Hill. Brookline, MA: Holy Orthodox, 1998.

Coetzee, J. H. "The Functioning of Elements of Tension in Psalm 44." *Theologia Evangelica* 21 (1988) 2-5.

Collins, Terence. "Decoding the Psalms: A Structural Approach to the Psalter." *Journal for the Study of the Old Testament* 37 (1987) 41-60.

Coote, Robert B. "Psalm 19: Heavenly Law and Order." In *From Biblical Interpretation to Human Transformation: Reopening the Past to Actualize New Possibilities for the Future: Essays Honoring Herman C. Waetjen*, edited by Douglas R. McGaughey and Cornelia Cyss Crocker, 79-99. Salem, OR: Chora Strangers, 2006.

Craigie, Peter C. (and Marvin E. Tate). *Psalms 1-50*. Word Biblical Commentary 19. 2nd ed. New York: Nelson, 2004.

Crow, Loren D. "The Rhetoric of Psalm 44." *Zeitschrift für die alttestamentliche Wissenschaft* 104 (1992) 394-401.

Culley, Robert. "Psalm 3: Content, Context, and Coherence." In *Text, Methode und Grammatik: Wolfgang Richter zum 65. Geburstag*, edited by Walter Gross et al., 29-39. St. Ottilien: EOS, 1991.

Dahood, Mitchell J. *Psalms I: 1-50*. Anchor Bible 16. Garden City, NY: Doubleday, 1966.

Davis, Ellen F. "Self-Inflicted Violence." In *The Art of Reading Scripture*, edited by Ellen F. Davis and Richard B. Hays, 294-99. Grand Rapids: Eerdmans, 2003.

deClaissé-Walford, Nancy, et al. *The Book of Psalms*. New International Commentary on the Old Testament. Grand Rapids: Eerdmans, 2014.

Delitzsch, Franz. *Biblical Commentary on the Psalms*. Vol. 1. Edinburgh: T. & T. Clark, 1892.

Denninger, David. "The Creator's Fiat and the Creature's Witness: A Literary Study of the Structure, Dynamics, and Meaning of Psalm 19." PhD diss., Trinity International University, 1996.

Dworkin, Ronald. *Sovereign Virtue: The Theory and Practice of Equality*. Cambridge: Harvard University Press, 2000.

Eaton, J. H. "Hard Sayings: Psalm 4.6-7." *Theology* 67 (1964) 355-57.

Eldhose, Alias Kolakunnail. "Trinitarian Interpretation in Light of the Identity of YHWH as the Triune God." PhD diss., Dallas Theological Seminary, 2017.

Flint, Peter W. "The Preliminary Edition of 5/6 Ḥev Psalms." *Journal of Jewish Studies* 51 (2000) 19-41.

Freedman, David Noel. "Patterns in Psalms 25 and 34." In *Priests, Prophets and Scribes: Essays on the Formation and Heritage of Second Temple Judaism in Honour of Joseph Blenkinsopp*, edited by Eugen Ulrich et al., 125-37. Sheffield: JSOT, 1992.

Freedman, David Noel, and C. Franke Hyland. "Psalm 29: A Structural Analysis." *Harvard Theological Review* 66 (1973) 237-56.

Fretheim, Terence E. "God and Violence in the Old Testament." *Word and World* 24 (2004) 18-28.

Gibson, Scott M., and Matthew D. Kim, eds. *Homiletics and Hermeneutics: Four Views on Preaching Today*. Grand Rapids: Baker, 2018.

Girard, Marc. *Les Psaumes: Analyse Structurelle et Interprétation (1-50)*. Recherches Nouvelle Série 2. Paris: Cerf, 1984.

Goldingay, John. "Psalm 4: Ambiguity and Resolution." *Tyndale Bulletin* 57 (2006) 161-72.

———. *Psalms*. Vol. 1: *Psalms 1-41*. Baker Commentary on the Old Testament. Grand Rapids: Baker, 2006.

———. *Psalms*. Vol. 2: *Psalms 42-89*. Baker Commentary on the Old Testament. Grand Rapids: Baker, 2007.

Grayson, A. Kirk. *Assyrian Rulers of the Early First Millennium BC I (1114-859 BC)*. Royal Inscriptions of Mesopotamia: Assyrian Periods 2. Toronto: University of Toronto Press, 1991.

Grayson, A Kirk, and Jamie Novotny. *The Royal Inscriptions of Sennacherib, King of Assyria (704-681 BC), Part 2*. Royal Inscriptions of the Neo-Assyrian Period 3/2. Winona Lake, IN: Eisenbrauns, 2014.

Green, Alberto R. W. *The Storm-God in the Ancient Near East*. Biblical and Judaic Studies 8. Winona Lake, IN: Eisenbrauns, 2003.

BIBLIOGRAPHY

Gren, Conrad. "Piercing the Ambiguities of Psalm 22:16 and the Messiah's Mission." *Journal of the Evangelical Theological Society* 48 (2005) 283–99.
Hanson, K. C. "Alphabetic Acrostics: A Form Critical Study." PhD diss., Claremont Graduate School, 1984.
Harris, William L., III. "Psalm 88: A Validation to Vent." *Criswell Theological Journal* 55 (2020) 41–65.
Hartenstein, Friedhelm. "Iconicity of the Psalms." *Hebrew Bible and Ancient Israel* 5 (2016) 326–49.
Hippocrates, Heracleitus. *Nature of Man. Regimen in Health. Humours. Aphorisms. Regimen 1–3. Dreams. Heracleitus: On the Universe.* Translated by W. H. S. Jones. Loeb Classical Library 150. Cambridge: Harvard University Press, 1931.
Hubbard, Robert L. "Dynamistic and Legal Processes in Psalm 7." *Zeitschrift für de alttestamentliche Wissenschaft* 94 (1982) 268–79.
Jacobson, Rolf A. "Psalm 36:5–11." *Interpretation* 61 (2007) 64–66.
James, P. D. *Original Sin.* New York: Alfred A. Knopf, 1995.
Janzen, J. Gerald. "Psalm 1 and the Torah That Transplants." *Canadian-American Theological Review* 8 (2019) 119–26.
Jerome. *The Homilies of Saint Jerome 1 (1–59 On the Psalms).* Fathers of the Church 48. Translated by Marie Liguori Ewald, 79–89. Washington, DC: Catholic University of America Press, 1964.
Johnston, Philip S. "The Psalms of Distress." In *Interpreting the Psalms: Issues and Approaches*, edited by Philip S. Johnston and David G. Firth, 63–84. Downers Grove, IL: InterVarsity, 2006.
Kessler, Martin. "Psalm 44." In *"Unless Some One Guide Me . . ." Festschrift for Karel A. Deurloo*, edited by J. W. Dyk et al., 193–204. Amsterdamse Cahiers voor Exegese van de Bijbel en zijn Tradities Supplement 2. Maastricht: Shaker, 2001.
Kidner, Derek. *The Wisdom of Proverbs, Job and Ecclesiastes: An Introduction to Wisdom Literature.* Downers Grove, IL: IVP Academic, 1985.
Kim, Ee Kon. "Holy War Ideology and the Rapid Shift of Mood in Psalm 3." In *On the Way to Nineveh: Studies in Honor of George M. Landes*, edited by Stephen L. Cook and S. C. Winter, 77–93. Atlanta: Scholars, 1999.
Kinnier-Wilson, J. V. *The Legend of Etana.* Warminster, UK: Aris & Phillips, 1985.
Kraut, Judah. "The Birds and the Babes: The Structure and Meaning of Psalm 8." *Jewish Quarterly Review* 100 (2010) 10–24.
Kselman, John S. "Psalm 3: A Structural and Literary Study." *Catholic Biblical Quarterly* 49 (1987) 572–80.
———. "'Why Have You Abandoned Me?' A Rhetorical Study of Psalm 22." In *Art and Meaning: Rhetoric in Biblical Literature*, edited by David J. A. Clines et al., 172–98. Sheffield: JSOT, 1982.
Kugel, James L. "David the Prophet." In *Poetry and Prophecy: The Beginnings of a Literary Tradition*, edited by James L. Kugel, 45–55. Ithaca: Cornell University Press, 1990.
Kuntz, J. Kenneth. "King Triumphant: A Rhetorical Study of Psalms 20 and 21." *Hebrew Annual Review* 10 (1986) 157–76.
———. "Psalm 18: A Rhetorical-Critical Analysis." *Journal for the Study of the Old Testament* 26 (1983) 3–31.
Kuruvilla, Abraham. *1 and 2 Timothy, Titus: A Theological Commentary for Preachers.* Eugene, OR: Cascade, 2021.
———. "Applicational Preaching." *Bibliotheca Sacra* 173 (2016) 387–400.
———. "Christiconic Interpretation." *Bibliotheca Sacra* 173 (2016) 131–46.
———. "Christiconic View." In *Homiletics and Hermeneutics: Four Views on Preaching Today*, edited by Scott M. Gibson and Matthew D. Kim, 43–70. Grand Rapids: Baker, 2018.
———. *Genesis: A Theological Commentary for Preachers.* Eugene, OR: Pickwick, 2017.
———. *A Manual for Preaching: The Journey from Text to Sermon.* Grand Rapids: Baker, 2019.
———. "Pericopal Theology." *Bibliotheca Sacra* 173 (2016) 3–17.
———. *Privilege the Text! A Theological Hermeneutic for Preaching.* Chicago: Moody, 2013.
———. *Text to Praxis: Hermeneutics and Homiletics in Dialogue.* Library of New Testament Studies 374. London: T. & T. Clark, 2009.
———. "Theological Exegesis." *Bibliotheca Sacra* 173 (2016) 259–72.
———. "Time to Kill the Big Idea? A Fresh Look at Preaching." *Journal of the Evangelical Theological Society* 61 (2018) 825–46. http://homiletix.com/kill-the-big-idea/.
———. *A Vision for Preaching: Understanding the Heart of Pastoral Ministry.* Grand Rapids: Baker, 2015.

———. "'What Is the Author *Doing* with What He Is Saying?' Pragmatics and Preaching—An Appeal." *Journal of the Evangelical Theological Society* 60 (2017) 557–80. https://homiletix.com/kuruvillajets2017.

Kwakkel, Gert. *'According to My Righteousness': Upright Behaviour as Grounds for Deliverance in Psalms 7, 17, 18, 26 and 44*. Oudtestamentische Studiën 46. Leiden: Brill, 2002.

Labuschagne, C. J. "Significant Compositional Techniques in the Psalms: Evidence for the Use of Number as an Organizing Principle." *Vetus Testamentum* 59 (2009) 583–605.

Lamott, Anne. *Traveling Mercies: Some Thoughts on Faith*. New York: Anchor, 1999.

Landau, Ephraim. "The Word-Pair Morning/Evening as a Parallel Word-Pair in Biblical Poetry." *Jewish Bible Quarterly* 45 (2017) 260–68.

Laney, J. Carl. "A Fresh Look at the Imprecatory Psalms." *Bibliotheca Sacra* 138 (1981) 35–45.

Langdon, S. *Die neubabylonischen Königsinschriften*. Vorderasiatische Bibliothek 4. Leipzig: Hinrichs, 1912.

Laurence, Trevor. *Cursing with God: The Imprecatory Psalms and the Ethics of Christian Prayer*. Waco, TX: Baylor University Press, 2022.

Leichty, Erle (and Grant Frame). *The Royal Inscriptions of Esarhaddon, King of Assyria (680–669 BC)*. Royal Inscriptions of the Neo-Assyrian Period 4. Winona Lake, IN: Eisenbrauns, 2011.

Leiter, David. "The Rhetoric of Praise in the Lament Psalm." *Brethren Life and Thought* 40 (1995) 44–48.

Levenson, Jon D. *The Love of God: Divine Gift, Human Gratitude, and Mutual Faithfulness in Judaism*. Library of Jewish Ideas 8. Princeton: Princeton University Press, 2015.

———. "The Temple and the World." *Journal of Religion* 64 (1984) 275–98.

Levertov, Denise. *The Poet in the World*. New York: New Directions, 1973.

Levine, Herbert. "The Symbolic Sukkah in Psalms." *Prooftexts* 7 (1987) 259–67.

Luther, Martin. "Psalms 1 and 2." In *Luther's Works*. Vol. 14: *Selected Psalms III*, edited by Jaroslav Pelikan, 279–349. St. Louis: Concordia, 1958.

———. "The Second Sermon, March 10, 1522, Monday after Invocavit." In *Luther's Works*, Vol. 51: *Sermons I*, edited and translated by John W. Doberstein, 75–78. Philadelphia: Fortress, 1959.

———. *Weimar Ausgabe, Schriften Band 3: Psalmenvorlesungen 1513/1515 (Pss 1–84)*. Weimar: Bohlau, 1892.

Maloney, Leslie D. "A Word Fitly Spoken: Poetic Artistry in the First Four Acrostics of the Hebrew Psalter." PhD diss., Baylor University, 2005.

Martin, Lee Roy. "Delighting in the Torah: The Affective Dimension of Psalm 1." *Old Testament Essays* 23 (2010) 708–27.

Mays, James L. "The Centre of the Psalms." In *Language, Theology, and the Bible: Essays in Honour of James Barr*, edited by Samuel E. Balentine and John Barton, 231–46. Oxford: Clarendon, 1994.

———. *The Lord Reigns: A Theological Handbook to the Psalms*. Louisville: Westminster John Knox, 1994.

———. *Psalms*. Interpretation. Louisville: Westminster John Knox, 1994.

Menn, Esther M. "No Ordinary Lament: Relecture and the Identity of the Distressed in Psalm 22." *Harvard Theological Review* 93 (2000) 301–41.

Middleton, J. Richard. "A Psalm against David? A Canonical Reading of Psalm 51 as a Critique of David's Inadequate Repentance in 2 Samuel 12." In *Explorations in Interdisciplinary Reading: Theological, Exegetical, and Reception-Historical Perspectives*, edited by Robbie F. Castleman et al., 26–45. Eugene, OR: Pickwick Publications, 2017.

Miller, Patrick D. "The Beginning of the Psalter." In *The Shape and Shaping of the Psalter*, edited by J. Clinton McCann, 83–92. Sheffield: JSOT, 1993.

———. *Interpreting the Psalms*. Philadelphia: Fortress, 1986.

———. "Psalms and Inscriptions." In *Congress Volume: Vienna 1980*, 311–32. Vetus Testamentum Supplement 32. Leiden: Brill, 1981.

———. "The Ruler in Zion and the Hope of the Poor." In *David and Zion: Biblical Studies in Honor of J. J. M. Roberts*, edited by Bernard F. Batto and Kathryn L. Roberts, 187–97. Winona Lake, IN: Eisenbrauns, 2004.

———. "The Theological Significance of Biblical Poetry." In *Language, Theology, and the Bible: Essays in Honour of James Barr*, edited by Samuel E. Balentine and John Barton, 213–30. Oxford: Clarendon, 1994.

———. "Trouble and Woe: Interpreting the Biblical Laments." *Interpretation* 37 (1983) 32–45.

Moberly, R. W. L. *The God of the Old Testament: Encountering the Divine in Christian Scripture*. Grand Rapids: Baker, 2020.

BIBLIOGRAPHY

Mosca, Paul G. "A Note on Psalm 17:7." *Vetus Testamentum* 61 (2011) 388–92.

———. "Psalm 26: Poetic Structure and the Form-Critical Task." *Catholic Biblical Quarterly* 47 (1985) 212–37.

Mroczek, Eva. "The Hegemony of the Biblical in the Study of Second Temple Literature." *Journal of Ancient Judaism* 6 (2015) 2–35.

Murray, John. *The Epistle to the Romans*. New International Commentary on the New Testament. Grand Rapids: Eerdmans, 1949.

Nehrbass, Daniel Michael. *Praying Curses: The Therapeutic and Preaching Value of the Imprecatory Psalms*. Eugene, OR: Pickwick Publications, 2013.

Petersen, David L., and Kent Harold Richards. *Interpreting Hebrew Poetry*. Minneapolis: Fortress, 1992.

Pietersma, Albert. "David in the Greek Psalms." *Vetus Testamentum* 30 (1980) 213–26.

Potgieter, J. Henk. "The Structure and Homogeneity of Psalm 32." *HTS/Theological Studies* 70 (2014) 1–6.

Prinsloo, Gert T. M. "Psalm 5: A Theology of Tension and Reconciliation." *Skrif en Kerk* 19 (1998) 628–43.

Pritchard, James B., ed. *Ancient Near Eastern Texts Relating to the New Testament*. 3rd ed. Princeton: Princeton University Press, 1969.

Raabe, Paul R. *Psalm Structures: A Study of Psalms with Refrains*. Journal for the Study of the Old Testament Supplement Series 104. Sheffield: Sheffield Academic, 1990.

Roberts, Alexander, and James Donaldson, eds. *The Ante-Nicene Fathers*. New York: Scribner, 1926.

Ross, Allen P. *A Commentary on the Psalms: Volume 1 (1–41)*. Grand Rapids: Kregel, 2011.

Sarna, Nahum. *On the Book of Psalms: Exploring the Prayers of Ancient Israel*. New York: Schocken, 1993.

———. "Psalm XIX and the Near Eastern Sun-God Literature." *Proceedings of the Fourth World Congress of Jewish Studies* 4 (1965) 171–75.

Schaeffer, Claude F. A. "Les Fouilles de Minet-el-Beida et de Ras-Shamra: Quatrième Campagne (Printemps 1932) Rapport Sommaire." *Syria* 14 (1933) 93–127.

Seok, Jinsung. "In Search of the Theological and Hermeneutical Significance of Psalm 33 in the Psalter: A Canonical-Theological Approach." PhD diss., Trinity Evangelical Divinity School, 2017.

Seow, C. L. "An Exquisitely Poetic Introduction to the Psalter." *Journal of Biblical Literature* 132 (2013) 275–93.

Smith, Kevin Gary. "The Redactional Criteria and Objectives Underlying the Arrangement of Psalms 3–8." PhD diss., South African Theological Seminary, 2007.

Smith, Mark S. *The Origins of Biblical Monotheism: Israel's Polytheistic Background and the Ugaritic Texts*. Oxford: Oxford University Press, 2001.

Sommer, Benjamin D. "A Commentary on Psalm 24." In *Gazing on the Deep: Ancient Near Eastern, Biblical, and Jewish Studies in Honor of Tzvi Abusch*, edited by Jeffrey Stackert et al., 495–514. Bethesda, MD: CDL, 2010.

Spurgeon, C. H. *The Treasury of David: Volume 1: Psalm 1 to 26*. London: Marshall Brothers, 1880.

Streck, Maximilian. *Assurbanipal und die letzten assyrischen Könige bis zum Untergange Niniveh's*. 2 vols. Vorderasiatische Bibliothek 7. Leipzig: Hinrichs, 1916.

Sumpter, Philip E. "The Coherence of Psalm 24." *Journal for the Study of the Old Testament* 39 (2014) 31–54.

———. "The Substance of Psalm 24: An Attempt to Read Scripture after Brevard S. Childs." PhD diss., University of Gloucestershire, 2011.

Tanner, Beth LaNeel. "King Yahweh as the Good Shepherd: Taking Another Look at the Image of God in Psalm 23." In *David and Zion: Biblical Studies in Honor of J. J. M. Roberts*, edited by Bernard F. Batto and Kathryn L. Roberts, 267–84. Winona Lake, IN: Eisenbrauns, 2004.

Tanner, Norman P., ed. *Decrees of the Ecumenical Councils, Volume 1: Nicaea I to Lateran V*. Washington, DC: Georgetown University Press, 1990.

Tate, Marvin E. *Psalms 51–100*. Word Biblical Commentary 20. Dallas: Word, 1990.

Tertullian. *Against Marcion*. In *The Ante-Nicene Fathers*, edited by Alexander Roberts and James Donaldson, 3:269–476. New York: Scribner, 1926.

———. *Apology*. In *The Ante-Nicene Fathers*. Vol. 3, edited by Alexander Roberts and James Donaldson, 3:17–60. New York: Scribner, 1926.

Thureau-Dangin, François. *Une relation de la huitième campagne de Sargon*. Paris: Geuthner, 1912.

Vander Hart, Mark D. "Possessing the Land as Command and Promise." *Mid-America Journal of Theology* 4 (1988) 139–55.

BIBLIOGRAPHY

van der Lugt, Pieter. *Cantos and Strophes in Biblical Hebrew Poetry: With Special Reference to the First Book of the Psalter.* Oudtestamentische Studiën 53. Leiden: Brill, 2006.

———. "The Mathematical Centre and Its Meaning in the Psalms." In *The Composition of the Book of Psalms,* edited by Erich Zenger, 643–51. Bibliotheca Ephemeridum Theologicarum Lovaniensium. Leuven: Peeters, 2010.

van Grol, Harm W. M. "Psalm 27:1–6: A Literary Stylistic Analysis." In *Give Ear to My Words: Psalms and Other Poetry in and around the Hebrew Bible: Essays in Honour of Professor N. A. van Uchelen,* edited by Janet W. Dyk, 23–38. Kampen: Kok Pharos, 1996.

Vos, Johannes G. "The Ethical Problem of the Imprecatory Psalms." *Westminster Theological Journal* 4 (1942) 123–38.

Waltke, Bruce K., et al. *The Psalms as Christian Lament: A Historical Commentary.* Grand Rapids: Eerdmans, 2014.

Walton, John H. *Genesis 1 as Ancient Cosmology.* Winona Lake, IN: Eisenbrauns, 2011.

Wesley, John. *A Collection of Hymns for the Use of the People Called Methodists.* London: Mason, 1877.

Westermann, Claus. *The Living Psalms.* Translated by J. R. Porter. Grand Rapids: Eerdmans, 1989.

———. "The Role of the Lament in the Theology of the Old Testament." Translated by Richard N. Soulen. *Interpretation* 28 (1974) 20–38.

Wiesel, Elie. *All Rivers Run to the Sea: Memoirs, Volume One 1928–1969.* London: HarperCollins, 1996.

Wilson, Gerald H. *Psalms.* Vol. 1. New International Version Application Commentary. Grand Rapids: Zondervan, 2002.

Wiseman, D. J. "A New Stela of Aššur-naṣir-pal II." *Iraq* 14 (1952) 24–44.

Wright, N. T. "Five Things to Know about Lament." https://www.ntwrightonline.org/five-things-to-know-about-lament/.

Wyatt, N., ed. *Religious Texts from Ugarit.* 2nd rev. ed. Sheffield: Sheffield Academic, 2002.

Zwighuizen, Jill E. "Time Reference of Verbs in Biblical Hebrew Poetry." PhD diss., Dallas Theological Seminary, 2012.

Index of Authors

Abernethy, Andrew T., 174, 188
Achtemeier, Elizabeth, 27
Alonso Schökel, Luis, 6, 305, 307, 308
Alter, Robert, 6, 22, 33, 35
Althann, Robert, 12
Anderson, Francis I., 42
Aquinas, Thomas, 17, 18, 30
Aster, Shawn Zelig, 159
Auffret, Pierre, 228, 230, 231, 252, 264, 281, 288, 293, 295, 308
Augustine, 5, 29

Bang, Jeung-Yeoul, 146
Barbiero, Gianni, 298
Bellinger, W. H., Jr., 50, 107, 193, 229, 314
Benun, Ronald, 82, 86, 88, 93, 94, 190, 249, 252, 253, 268, 272, 273, 274, 276
Berlin, Adele, 6
Best, Ernest, 5
Beuken, W. A. M., 289
Borger, Rykold, 175
Botha, P. J., 31, 32, 35, 37, 47, 61, 120, 123, 173, 180, 197, 234, 243, 248, 263
Boulton, Matthew, 179
Bracke, John M., 113
Braude, William G., 28-29
Brown, Francis, et al., 112
Brown, William P., 114
Brueggemann, Walter, 7, 8, 9, 10, 11, 14, 17, 22, 50, 107, 229, 314
Brug, John F., 191

Calvin, John, 122, 164
Ceresko, Anthony R., 250, 253
Chisholm, Robert B., 139
Chrysostom, John, 53
Collins, Terence, 7, 8
Coote, Robert B., 148

Craigie, Peter C., 23, 24, 26, 28, 33, 34, 48, 60, 62, 66, 67, 69, 74, 75, 78, 80, 81, 86, 87, 103, 111, 112, 118, 130, 137, 139, 140, 141, 145, 149, 153, 158, 159, 164, 167, 169, 179, 185, 187, 189, 206, 207, 212, 215, 224, 227, 237, 241, 244, 245, 251, 252, 268, 276, 278, 283, 287, 289, 297, 305, 309, 316
Crow, Loren D., 312, 315
Culley, Robert, 46

Dahood, Mitchell J., 117, 216
Davis, Ellen F., 17
Delitzsch, Franz, 212
Denninger, David, 146, 148
deClaissé-Walford, Nancy, et al., 77, 98, 116, 130, 135, 137, 143, 144, 145, 150, 153, 159, 161, 209, 213, 216, 218, 219, 222, 236, 241, 245, 276, 295-96
Didymus the Blind, 25
Donaldson, James, 7, 30
Dworkin, Ronald, 116

Eaton, J. H., 55
Eldhose, Alias Kolakunnail, 23, 43

Flint, Peter W., 168
Freedman, David Noel, 42, 191, 212
Fretheim, Terence E., 16

Gibson, Scott M., 2
Girard, Marc, 209, 314
Goldingay, John, 7, 11, 13, 22, 24, 25, 26, 28, 30, 33, 48, 50, 54, 55, 59, 68, 75, 78, 83, 87, 92, 94, 98, 99, 101, 111, 117, 118, 123, 127, 128, 130, 132, 136, 138, 139, 145, 152, 154, 156, 164, 165, 166, 171, 173, 192, 197, 201, 204, 208, 212, 215, 216, 218, 219, 222, 225, 233, 236, 237, 241, 246, 250, 259, 265, 268, 275, 276, 281, 282, 283, 284, 288, 289, 295, 301, 307, 314

INDEX OF AUTHORS

Grayson, A. Kirk, 97
Green, Alberto R. W., 215
Gren, Conrad, 168

Hanson, K. C., 251
Harris, William L., III, 10
Hartenstein, Friedhelm, 202
Henley, William Ernest, 102
Hilber, John, 190
Hippocrates, 23
Hubbard, Robert L., 74
Hyland, C. Franke, 212

Jacobson, Rolf A., 265
James, P. D., 14
Janzen, J. Gerald, 33
Jerome, 30
Johnston, Philip S., 290
Justin Martyr, 30

Kessler, Martin, 312
Kidner, Derek, 18
Kim, Ee Kon, 45
Kim, Matthew D., 2
King, Martin Luther, Jr., 107
Kinnier-Wilson, J. V., 174
Kraut, Judah, 78, 79, 80
Kselman, John S., 49, 166, 167
Kugel, James L., 24
Kuntz, J. Kenneth, 135, 138, 140, 141
Kuruvilla, Abraham, 1, 2, 3, 4, 5, 15, 26, 27, 116, 146, 148, 159, 179, 251, 265, 294–95
Kwakkel, Gert, 127

Labuschagne, C. J., 142
Lamott, Anne, 10
Landau, Ephraim, 222
Laney, J. Carl, 12
Langdon, S., 174
Laurence, Trevor, 12, 13, 15, 16, 19, 20
Leichty, Erle, 97
Leiter, David, 106
Levenson, Jon D., 15, 137
Levertov, Denise, 6
Levine, Herbert, 201
Luther, Martin, 1, 49, 106

Maloney, Leslie D., 250, 278
Martin, Lee Roy, 33, 34
Mays, James L., 3, 9, 67, 68, 69
Menn, Esther M., 167
Middleton, J. Richard, 24
Miller, Patrick D., 7, 11, 23, 35, 50, 95, 111, 165–66, 169

Moberly, R. W. L., 23
Mosca, Paul G., 128, 193, 194, 195, 196
Mroczek, Eva, 24
Murray, John, 13

Nehrbass, Daniel Michael, 17
Novotny, Jamie, 97

Petersen, David L., 30, 32
Pietersma, Albert, 25
Potgeiter, J. Henk, 234, 243
Prinsloo, Gert T. M., 62
Pritchard, James B., 122, 173, 174–75, 182, 214

Raabe, Paul R., 305
Richards, Kent Harold, 30, 32
Roberts, Alexander, 7, 30
Robinson, Robert, 148
Ross, Allen P., 12, 26, 112, 116, 138, 168, 208

Sarna, Nahum, 145, 147
Schaeffer, Claude F. A., 215
Seok, Jinsung, 241, 242
Seow, C. L., 33
Smith, Kevin Gary, 47
Smith, Mark S., 213
Sommer, Benjamin D., 181
Spurgeon, C. H., 66
Streck, Maximilian, 176
Sumpter, Philip E., 180, 181, 182, 183

Tanner, Beth LaNeel, 173, 174
Tanner, Norman P., 28
Tate, Marvin E., 11, 14
Tertullian, 2, 30
Thureau-Dangin, François, 175

van der Lugt, Pieter, 58, 172
van Grol, Harm W. M., 202
Vander Hart, Mark D., 275
Vos, Johannes G., 18, 20

Waltke, Bruce K., et al., 233
Walton, John A., 15
Weber, Beat, 47
Wesley, John, 29
Westermann, Claus, 27, 107
Wiesel, Elie, 9
Wilson, Gerald H., 81
Wiseman, D. J., 175
Wright, N. T., 9
Wyatt, N., 213–14, 215, 217

Zwighuizen, Jill E., 23

Index of Scripture

OLD TESTAMENT

Genesis

1–11	15
1	144n6
1:3–13	146
1:3–5	137
1:6–8	147
1:6	144n6
1:7	144n6
1:8	144n6
1:9–13	147
1:9	147
1:10	147
1:11	147
1:12	147
1:14–31	146
1:14–19	147
1:14	144n6
1:15	144n6
1:17	144n6
1:20–23	147
1:20	144n6
1:24–31	147
1:24	147
1:25	147
1:26	147
1:31	147
2:5	15
2:10–14	265n6
2:15	15
3:2	15n82
3:14	13
3:17	13
3:24	15
4:2	15n82
4:9	15
4:11	13
4:12	15n82
5:24	290n14
6–11	216n23
9:25	13n74, 15n82
9:26	15n82
9:27	15n82
12:3	13
16:7–12	249n7
17:9–10	15n84
18:19	15n84
19:24	98
21:1	127n2
22:11–12	249n7
22:12	153n9
22:15–17	249n7
23:4	290n13
26:5	15n84
26:25	168n20
27:45	259n7
34:19	34
42:36	259n7
43:14	259n7
49:10	174
50:5	168n20

Exodus

2:10	139n19
2:16	221
2:19	221
3:12	15n83
3:16	127n2
4:23	15n83
8:26	112n10
13:17	173n9
13:21	173n9
15:1	243n6
15:2	165n8
15:3	243n6
15:4	243n6
15:7	127
15:8	243n6

Exodus (continued)

15:11	127, 243n6
15:12	127
15:13	127, 173, 243n6
15:14–15	243n6
15:17	243n6
15:19	243n6
15:21	243n6
15:22–27	173
17:1–7	173
18:11	153n9
19:4	209
19:5–6	15
20:7	180n8
22:16	121n5
22:25–27	118
23:4–5	17n97
23:8	118
29:13	153n7
29:22–25	153n7
34:5–7	152
38:21	15n83

Leviticus

3:3–5	153n7
18:5	15n84
19:17–18	17
20:23	19n109
21:17–21	116n7
25:35–38	118
26:30	19n109
26:44	19n109

Numbers

1:53	15n85
3:7–8	15n83
3:7	15n85
3:8	15n85
3:10	15n83, 15n85
3:26	15n83
3:28	15n85
3:32	15n85
3:38	15n85
4:23	15n83
4:24	15n83
4:26	15n83, 55
6:26	55n9
8:25–26	15n83
10:35	45, 74, 103n8
12:8	129n10
16:3	121n3
16:5	121n3
16:7	121n3
18:5–6	15n83
18:6–7	15n83
28:2	15n85

Deuteronomy

1:28	48
1:29–30	48
1:31	209
2:7	173
4:6	15n84
4:19	15n83
4:37	313n3
5:11	180n8
5:33	182n7
7:7–8	313n3
7:12	15n84
7:25–26	19n109
8:9	173
10:9	121n8
10:15	313n3
12:31	19n109
16:19	118
16:22	19n109
17:6	154n11
17:14–20	295n9
20:1–9	45
23:1–6	116n7
23:19–20	118
23:20	118
24:6	118
28:2	175n21
28:7	45
28:15–68	13n74
28:15	175n21
28:45	175n21
29:9	15n84
32:5	139n22
32:9	121n8
32:10–11	129n11
32:11	209
32:12	173n9
32:35	13
33:29	45
33:8	313n3
34:7	107n4

Joshua

1:8	33
5:14	249

INDEX OF SCRIPTURE

Judges

1:7	175n17
5:12	74
5:13	121n4
6:22–24	249n7
7	45

1 Samuel

7:9–10	153
13:9–12	153
14:27	107n4
14:29	107n4
15:22	153
15:33	259n7
17:34–36	174n16
20:34	175n17
24:11–12	13
26:20	97n2
31:9	121n6

2 Samuel

5:21	121n6
6:17	116
7	41
7:14	41, 174n13
9:7	175n17
9:10	175n17
9:11	175n17
9:13	175n17
15:2	59n5
17	45
18:14	174n13
19:21–23	13
19:28	175n17
22	25n139
22:17	139n19
23:1	25n139

1 Kings

2:7	175n17
2:28–30	116
4:27	175n17
4:32	25n139
7:26	287n3
8:4	116
10:5	175n17
13:20	175n17
18:19	175n17
19:18	42n10

2 Kings

4:29	174n15
4:31	130n13
11:12	41n6
18:21	174
19:21	87n12

1 Chronicles

10:9	121n6
12:33	102
15:16–24	24n136, 25n139
16:7	25n139
16:8–36	25n139
23:32	15n83
24:3	15n83
24:19	15n83

2 Chronicles

8:14	15n83
20	45
20:17	45
23:20	121n4
24:19	121n6
35:3	121n3

Ezra

3:10	25n139

Nehemiah

3:5	121n4
9:12	173n9
9:21	173
10:29	121n4
12:24	25n139

Job

7:11	54
7:18	59n5
14:12	130n13
15:16	112n11
15:24	54
17:7	107n4
19:9	54
20:20	54
28:13	28n158
31:27	42n10
36:16	54
36:19	54

INDEX OF SCRIPTURE

Psalms
(Also see within the appropriate psalms for references to verses of those chapters.)

1–41	26, 28, 30, 298
1–2	8, 24, 30n5, 45, 92n8
1	8, 9, 37, 43
1:1	37, 37n2
1:6	12
2	25, 30, 30n6, 31
2:1	30, 30n5, 74
2:5	31
2:6	31, 31n7, 94n15, 97n2
2:7	30n5, 31
2:9	31, 174n13
2:10	31
2:11	2n10
2:12	7n30, 12n69, 21n125, 30, 30n6, 31
3–32	28
3–14	45
3–7	9, 45, 71
3	24n136, 52
3:1	52
3:3	52
3:4	52, 97n2
3:5	52
3:7–8	16n94
3:7	7n30, 12n62, 12n66, 103n8
4	45
4:5	14n76
5:1–12	21n122
5:2	94n15
5:4–5	19
5:4	16, 34
5:5–6	19
5:5	7n30, 117
5:6	117
5:7	2n10
5:8	2n10, 173n9
5:10–12	16n92
5:10	12n62, 13n73
5:11	20n116, 7n30, 190n14
5:21	3n14
6	11, 14n236, 233, 279
6:1	20n118
6:5	222n5
6:7–8	7n30
6:7	107n4
6:9–10	16n94
6:10	12n62, 12n67, 21n125
7–18	168n20
7	12n62, 24n136
7:1	7n30, 175
7:3–5	20n118, 21
7:5	175
7:6–11	16n92
7:6	12n62
7:8–12	21
7:9	12n68, 21n123
7:11–13	21n121
7:12	21n125
7:15	168n20
7:17	20n116, 77
8	45
8:4	127n2
8:5	213n4
9–14	45
9–10	82n2, 95n16, 184, 190n14, 272
9	24n136, 30, 90, 93, 94, 249n6
9:1–6	16n94
9:1–2	21n122
9:2	20n116
9:3	190n14
9:4–8	21n122
9:4	21
9:5–6	12n62, 12n68, 21n124
9:7	182n16, 190n14
9:9	21n122
9:10—10:1	89
9:10	14n76
9:12–13	21n122
9:12	12n62, 16n93
9:13	123n14
9:14	20n116
9:15–20	12n62
9:16–17	21n121
9:16	24n136, 33
9:17	7n30
9:18–20	94n13
9:18	21n122
9:19	94n13, 103n8
9:20	12n67, 19
10	30, 83, 83n4, 89, 190n14
10:1	82n2
10:2	82n2
10:3	13, 82n2
10:4	82n2
10:5	2n10, 82n2
10:7	13
10:8	82n2, 190n14
10:9	82n2, 190n14
10:10	82n2, 83
10:11	82n2
10:12–18	16n93

INDEX OF SCRIPTURE

10:12	12n62, 21n122, 82n2, 103n8, 190n14	18:47	20n117
		18:50	209n7
10:13	82n2	19	114
10:14	13, 82n2	19:1	159n6
10:15–18	12n62	19:7	173
10:15–16	21n122	19:8	107n4
10:15	12n66, 21n123, 82n2	19:9	2n10
10:16–17	83	20–21	114
10:16	3, 82, 82n2, 83, 182n16	20	156
10:17	21n122, 82n2	20:4	156, 158n2
10:18	82n2	21:5	213n4
11–15	28n157	21:7–13	14n76
11–14	25	21:8–13	16n94
11:4–7	16n92	21:8	7n30
11:5	117, 19	21:9	12n69
11:6	12n62, 12n67, 13n73	21:10	12n65
12:3–4	12n62	21:12	12n66
12:5–8	16n93	21:13	20n116
12:5	21n122	22–25	168n20
13:5	14n76	22	114
14	25n140, 28n156, 45	22:1–2	59n3
14:3	7n30	22:4–5	14n76
14:5	12n67	22:9	14n76
15–24	173	22:23	2n10, 7n30
15	173n11	22:24	21n122
15:1	97n2	22:25	2n10
15:4	2n10, 19	22:27	7n30
16	25, 114	23	114
16:3	34	23:5	114
16:5	114	24	24n136, 114
16:8	160n12	24:1	25n142
16:10	88n14, 221n3	24:3	97n2, 114
16:11	2n10	24:7–10	3n14, 159n6
17	114	25	192, 249n6, 253, 253n23, 272
17:1–5	21		
17:5	2n10, 173n10	25:1	180n8
17:8–15	16n94	25:2	14n76, 192
17:13–14	12n62	25:3	7n30
17:14	12n68, 21n123	25:4	2n10
18	114	25:7	175n19
18:2–50	25n139	25:8–10	2n10
18:14	12n66	25:10	13n74, 192
18:16	215	25:12	2n10
18:19–26	21	25:14	2n10, 13n74
18:19	16n91	25:15	16n91, 249n6
18:20–26	20n118	25:16	249n6
18:21	2n10	25:17	16n91, 249n6
18:30	2n10, 7n30	25:18–19	20n118
18:32	2n10	25:19	249n6
18:34	20n117	25:20	249n6
18:35–48	16n94	25:21	192
18:37–40	20n117	25:22	192, 249n6, 253
18:42–45	20n117	26:2	14n76
18:46	20n116	26:3–8	21

INDEX OF SCRIPTURE

Psalms *(continued)*

26:5	19
26:8	159n6
26:9–11	20n118
26:10	160n12
26:11–12	21
27	205
27:4	176n22
27:11	2n10, 173n9
28–31	168n20
28:4–5	13n73, 21n121
28:4	12n62, 21n123
28:7	14n76, 20n116
28:9	173n4
29:1–3	159n6
29:9	7n30
29:10	3, 182n16
30:1	20n116
30:3	123n14
30:9	88n14
31:3	20n114, 173n5
31:5–6	14n76
31:5	16n91, 19n110
31:6	19
31:7	21n122, 180n8
31:11	7n30
31:14	14n76
31:15–18	16n94
31:15	175
31:17–18	12n62, 13n73
31:19	2n10
31:23–24	7n30
32	11, 24n136, 25, 64, 233, 279
32:6	7n30, 215
32:8	2n10
32:10–11	14n76, 16n92
32:11	7n30
33	24, 30
33:7	215
33:8	2n10, 7n30
33:13–14	7n30
33:14	98
33:18	2n10
33:21	14n76
34–41	28
34	191n17, 272
34:6	21n122
34:7	2n10, 258n4
34:9–11	2n10
34:9	121n3
34:15–22	16n92
34:16	12n62, 21n123
34:18	21n122
34:21	21n123
34:22	191n17
35	12n62, 249
35:1–8	12n66
35:1–6	12n62
35:3	175
35:4	19, 21n123
35:7	21n119
35:8–10	16n93
35:8	12n62, 19n110
35:9–10	20n116
35:10	21n122
35:12–14	17n97
35:12	21n119
35:18	20n116
35:19–28	16n94
35:19–21	21n119
35:19	12n62
35:20	20n115
35:22–26	21n121
35:23–26	12n62
35:25	19
35:26	21n123
35:27–28	20n116
35:28	33
36:4	117
37:3	14n76
37:5	14n76
37:9–17	16n93
37:9–10	12n62
37:12–17	16n92
37:12–15	12n66
37:15	12n62
37:17	12n62
37:18–20	16n94
37:20	12n62, 21n123
37:22	13n74, 21n122
37:23	2n10, 34
37:28	12n65, 21n121, 21n123
37:30	33
37:34	2n10
37:36	12n68
37:38	12n65, 12n68
38	11, 233, 279, 285, 634
38:10	107n4
39:5	7n30
39:11	7n30
40:3–4	14n76, 21n125
40:3	2n10
40:6	153
40:8	34
40:12	20n118
40:13–17	28n156

INDEX OF SCRIPTURE

40:14–17	16n93	52:8	14n76
40:14–15	12n62, 19	53	24n136, 25n140, 28n156, 109, 109n1
40:14	21n123		
40:16	7n30, 20n116	53:3	7n30
40:17	21n122	53:5	12n67
41:7	7n30	53:6	113
41:10–11	20n117	54:1	20n114
41:10	12n62	54:5	12n62, 12n68, 19, 20n114
41:13	28, 182n16	55:5	42n9
42–72	26, 28	55:9	12n62, 21n123
42	27, 28	55:15	12n62, 19, 21n123
43	27	55:19	2n10, 24n136
43:3	173n9	55:20	14n74
44–49	28	55:22–23	16n92
44:4	3n14	55:23	12n62, 12n68, 14n76, 21n123, 88n14
44:5–7	20n117		
44:8	20n114	56:3–4	14n76
44:9–11	11	56:4	241n1
44:17	13n74	56:7	12n62
44:18	2n10	56:11	14n76
45:2–4	213n4	57:3	24n136
45:3	159n6	57:5–11	21n122
45:5	12n62, 12n66, 16n94	57:5	20n114, 20n116
45:6	174n13, 182n16	57:6	168n20
45:7	19	57:7	28n156
45:9	160n12	58	12n62
46	24n136	58:2	3n14
46:3	215	58:6–9	12n62, 12n66, 21n123
46:4	265n6	58:6–7	19
46:8–11	21n122	58:7–12	17
46:8–10	21n125	58:7–8	19
46:10	20n116	58:10–11	16n92, 20n116, 21n121
47:1–2	7n30	59	12n62
47:2	2n10, 3n14	59:1–5	16n94
47:3	74	59:5	7n30, 12n62
47:6	3n14	59:6	127n2
47:7	3n14	59:8	7n30
48:1–8	21n122	59:11–13	12n62
48:4–6	12n67	59:12–13	19
48:6	42n9	59:12	13
48:14	182n16	59:13	12n68, 21n125
49:1	7n30	59:16–17	21n122
49:9	88n14	60	310
49:15	123n14	60:4	2n10
50	28	60:5–12	28n156
50:5	13n74	60:11–12	16n91
50:16	14n74	60:12	20n117
50:23	2n10	61:4	116
51–65	28	61:5	2n10
51	11, 64, 233, 279	62:8	7n30, 14n76
51:13	2n10	63:2–3	202n5
52:1–5	12n66	63:3	175n19
52:5	12n62, 12n68, 21n121, 21n123	63:4	207
		63:9	12n68

333

Psalms (continued)

63:11	7n30
64:5–10	16n92
64:7–8	12n62
64:7	12n66
64:8–10	7n30
64:9	2n10, 21n125
65–68	28n157
65:2	7n30
65:4	175n19, 176n22
65:5	7n30, 14n76
65:10	127n2
65:11	173n10
66:1–12	310n1
66:1	7n30
66:3	12n62, 16n94
66:4	7n30
66:13–20	310n1
66:16	2n10, 7n30
67:1–2	2n10
67:3	7n30
67:5	7n30
67:7	2n10, 7n30
68–72	28
68:1	103n8
68:1–3	16n92
68:1–2	12n62, 16n94
68:2	12n68
68:3–4	20n116
68:4	190n14
68:5–6	21n122
68:7–8	16n91
68:10	21n122
68:21–23	12n62
68:21	16n94
68:22	16n91
68:23	16n94
68:24	3n14
68:28–31	21n125
68:30	12n62
69	12n62, 25
69:1–2	215
69:4–7	20n118
69:4	21n119
69:9	20n115
69:14–15	215
69:16	175n19
69:18–28	16n94
69:22–25	12n62, 13
69:23	19n110
69:25	19n110
69:26–28	16n92
69:27–28	12n62
69:28–33	16n93
69:28	12n68, 19, 21n124
69:29	21n122
69:32–33	21n122
69:35–36	20n115
70	28n156, 291
70:1–5	16n93
70:2–3	12n62
70:4	7n30, 20n116
70:5	21n122
71	303n1
71:5	14n76
71:13	12n62, 21n125
71:18	7n30
71:20	123n14
71:23–24	33
71:24	33
72	28
72:2	21n122
72:4	12n62, 20n115, 21n122
72:5	2n10
72:9	12n62
72:11	7n30
72:12–14	20n115
72:12–13	21n122
72:16	214n12
72:17	7n30, 298
72:18–19	28, 298
72:20	28n156
73–89	28
73–83	26, 28
73:12	223n11
73:19	12n67
73:23	10
73:24	123n14
73:26	121n8
73:27	7n30, 12n68
74	310
74:1–2	310n1
74:3–10	20n115
74:7	20n114
74:9	310n1
74:11	12n62
74:12	3n14, 310n1
74:13	215
74:18	20n114
74:19	20n114
74:20	14n74, 20n115
74:22–23	12n62
75:2–3	21n121
75:4–5	136n6
75:8	7n30, 12n69
75:10	12n62, 16n92, 136n6
76:4–12	21n122

INDEX OF SCRIPTURE

76:5–9	12n69	83:9–18	12n62
76:7–8	2n10	83:15	12n67
76:8–9	21n122	83:16–18	20n114
76:9	7n30	83:17–18	21n125
76:11–12	2n10	84–85	28
76:11	7n30	84:10	176n22
77:6	33	84:12	14n76
77:12	33	84:13	3n14
77:13	2n10	85	310
77:18–19	215	85:1	113
77:19	2n10	85:9	2n10
77:20	173n5	85:13	2n10
78	132n1	86:1	21n122
78:8	20n118	86:5	7n30, 175n19
78:10–11	20n118	86:7	12n62
78:10	14n74, 34	86:9	7n30, 20n114
78:14	173n9	86:11	2n10
78:17–19	20n118	86:12	14n76
78:20	173	86:16–17	175
78:22	20n11	87–88	28
78:32–33	20n118	87:1	98
78:36–37	20n118	88	28
78:37	14n74	88:1–2	59n3
78:40–42	20n118	88:10	220
78:50	301n3	89	28
78:52	173n4	89:3	14n74
78:53–54	16n91	89:5	121n3
78:53	173n9	89:6	213n5
78:56–57	20n118	89:7	121n3
79	310	89:9–14	216n23
79:1–7	20n115	89:10	12n62, 16n94
79:1	16	89:14	98
79:5–6	21n121	89:15	33n15, 298
79:6	12n62, 12n69, 16, 20n114	89:17	136n6
79:8	20n118	89:24	136n6
79:10–12	13n73, 21n121	89:26–27	41
79:10	12n62, 13n73, 16	89:28	14n74
79:12	12n62	89:31	34
79:13	173n4	89:32	174n13
80	310	89:34	14n74
80:1	173n4, 174n16	89:39	14n74
80:8–11	16n91	89:42	160n12
80:14	127n2	89:52	28, 298
80:16	12n62	90–106	26, 28
81:13–15	16n94	90	28, 310
81:13	2n10	90:2	182n16
81:14–15	12n62	90:11	2n10
81:15	12n68, 21n124	90:17	202n5
82:3–4	20n115, 21n122	91	24
82:4–8	16n93	91:2	14n76
82:7–8	12n62	91:3	301n3
82:7	12n68	91:6	301n3
82:8	7n30	91:10	160n12
83	12n62, 310	92:3	33

335

INDEX OF SCRIPTURE

Psalms (continued)

92:7	7n30, 12n68
92:8	20n116, 182n16
92:9–15	16n92
92:9–10	16n94
92:9	12n62, 21n123
92:10	136n6
92:12–14	34
92:12	214n12
92:13	31n7, 34
93–98	3
93:1	3n14
93:2–4	216n23
93:2	182n16
93:4	215
94	310
94:1–2	12n62, 21n121
94:1	12n68
94:2	21n123
94:4	7n30
94:13	168n20
94:15	7n30
94:23	12n68
95–99	28n157
95	25
95:3	3n14
95:7	173n4
95:10	2n10
96:1	7n30
96:4	2n10
96:6	159n6, 213n4
96:10	3
97:1	3
97:2	98
97:5–7	7n30
97:7	213n5
97:10	19
97:12	222n5
98:3–4	7n30
98:6	3n14
99:1	3
99:2	7n30
100:1	7n30
100:3	173n4
100:5	175n19
101:1–8	21n122
101:2	2n10
101:3–4	19
101:5	20n117
101:6	2n10
101:8	7n30, 20n117, 59n5
102	11, 64, 233, 279
102:12–14	21n122
102:13–14	20n115
102:13	182n16
102:15	2n10, 7n30
103:4	88n14, 123n14
103:6	7n30
103:7	2n10
103:11	2n10
103:13	2n10
103:17	2n10
103:18	14n74
103:20–22	213n5
104	24
104:1	159n6, 213n4
104:16	214n12
104:31	216n21
104:32	216n21, 42n9
104:35	12n62, 19, 21n123
105:1–15	25n139
105:8–10	14n74
105:15	209n7
105:36	12n62, 12n65
105:37	16n91
105:41	173
105:42	241n1
105:45	345
106:1	175n19
106:3	298
106:8	173
106:17–18	12n68
106:24	241n1
106:45	14n74
106:48	7n30, 28, 298
107–150	26, 28
107:1	175n19
107:14	16n91
107:30	173n9
107:41	21n122
108–110	28
108	28n156
109	12n62, 25
109:3–5	21n119
109:4–5	17n97
109:4	13
109:6–15	12n62
109:6	160n12
109:8–9	19, 21n123
109:8	19n110
109:16	175
109:19–20	12n62
109:21	20n114, 175n19
109:22–31	16n93
109:26–29	21n125
109:28	13
109:29	12n62

INDEX OF SCRIPTURE

109:30	20n116	119:113	19
109:31	21n122, 160n12	119:118–19	7n30
110	25, 25n143	119:118	12n68
110:1	12n62, 16n94, 19n110, 25n143	119:128	19
		119:158	19
110:5–6	12n62, 16n94, 21n123	119:161	21n119
110:5	20n117	119:163	19
110:6	12n68	120–34	28n156
111:2	7n30	121:1–2	ix
111:3	159n6, 213n4	121:3–8	ix–x
111:5	2n10, 14n74	121:5	160n12
111:9	14n74	123	24, 310
111:10	2n10, 7n30	123:1	310n1
112:1	2n10, 34	123:2–4	310n1
112:7–8	2n10	124:4–5	215
112:7	14n76	125:1	11, 14n76
112:9	136n6	125:2	11
113–18	28n156	125:3	11
113:4	7n30	125:4	11, 12
113:7	21n122	125:5	12n62
115:8	7n30	126:1	113
115:9–12	14n76	126:4	113
115:11	2n10	127	28
115:13	2n10	127:5	11
116:8	123n14	128:1	2n10, 7n30, 33n15
116:18	7n30	128:4	2n10
118:1	175n19	129:1–3	310n1
118:4	2n10	129:4	21n121
118:8	14n76	129:5–8	12n62
118:10–12	20n117	129:5	7n30, 21n123
118:29	175n19	130	11, 64, 233, 279
119	27n151, 132n1	130:3–4	20n118
119:1	2n10, 33n15	130:4	2n10
119:3	2n10	132:12	14n74
119:5	2n10	132:15–18	16n93
119:14–15	2n10	132:15	21n122
119:25	241n1	132:17–18	16n94
119:27	2n10	132:17	136n6
119:29	2n10	132:18	12n62, 21n122
119:30	2n10	134:1	7n30
119:32	2n10	134:2	207
119:33	2n10	135–36	28n157
119:35	2n10	135:10–11	12n68
119:37	2n10	135:13	20n114
119:38	2n10	135:18	7n30
119:42	14n76	135:20	2n10
119:57	121n8	136:1	175n19
119:63	2n10, 7n30	136:10	12n65
119:69	21n119	136:17–20	12n68
119:74	2n10	136:25	7n30
119:78	12n62	137	12n62, 13n71, 310
119:79	2n10	137:1–4	310n1
119:85	168n20	137:5–7	20n115
119:104	19	137:5–6	310n1

337

Psalms (continued)

137:5	21n122, 22, 160n12
137:6	22
137:7	12n62, 21n121, 22
137:8–9	20n117
137:9	12n65, 19n110
138–45	28
138:4–5	21n125
138:4	7n30, 216n21
138:5	2n10, 216n21
138:7–8	16n94
139	12n62
139:1–4	19, 20n118
139:19	12n62, 12n68
139:21–22	19
139:23–24	20n118, 21
139:24	2n10, 173n9
140:1–13	16n93
140:8–11	12n62
140:8	19
140:12	21n122
141:6	12n68
141:10	12n62
142:5	121n8
142:7	20n114
143	11, 64, 233, 279
143:2	7n30, 20n118
143:5	33
143:8	2n10, 14n76
143:9–12	16n94
143:10	173n9
143:11	20n114
143:12	7n30, 12n62
144	24
144:1–2	310n1
144:5	138n16
144:6	12n62
144:7	215
144:8	160n12
144:9–11	310n1
144:11	160n12
144:12–15	310n1
145:1	3n14
145:5	213n4
145:9	7n30
145:13	182n16
145:14–15	7n30
145:18–21	7n30
145:19	2n10
146–50	28n156, 28n157, 45n3
146:8	12
146:10	182n16
147:6	21n122
147:11	2n10
148:1–3	213n5
148:11	7n30
148:13	79n3
148:14	7n30, 136n6
149:2	3n14
149:4	21n122
149:5–9	20n117
149:5–6	20n116
149:9	7n30
150	10, 8
150:1–6	28
150:1	29
150:2	29
150:6	7n30, 28

Proverbs

1:32	223n11
2:1–15	30
2:9	173n10
2:20–22	30
3:1	33
3:32	112n10
4:11	173n10
4:18	123n14
6:12–13	260
7:2	33
8:13	19n109
9:15	33n15
10:9–10	260
11:25	175n18
13:4	175n18
13:24	174n13
14:32	123n14
15:24	123n14
15:30	175
20:5	221
22:8	174n13
22:15	174n13
22:25	191
23:13–14	123n14
23:13	174n13
23:14	174n13
24:2	40
24:17–18	17n97
25:21–22	17, 17n97
26:4	174n13
28:4	33
28:7	33
28:9	33
28:25	175n18
29:15	174n13
31:2–3	39n3

INDEX OF SCRIPTURE

Ecclesiastes

5:2	20

Isaiah

1	12n62
1:8	87n12
1:10	33
8:19	40
9:4	174n13
10:5	174n13
11:4	174n13
14:9	220
22	12n62
22:7	45
26:14	220
26:19	130n13, 220
29–31	12n62
31:4	40
33:10	103n8
36:6	174
40:1	173n6
40:11	173n6
44:7	29n158
44:17	165n8
44:28	174n16
50:2	179
56:6–7	153
59:2	208
62:11	87n12
64:1	138n16

Jeremiah

6:2	87n12
11:20	13n73
18:19–23	13n73
23:3	173
30:9	25
31:23	173
50:19	173n6
51:39	130n13
52:21	287n3

Lamentations

1:6	87n12
2:19	207
3:24	121n8
3:41	207
5:17	107n4

Ezekiel

7:16	97n2
13:6–9	294n5
16:49	223n11
20:37	174n13
24:23–24	25
29:6	174
34:12–15	173n6
34:14–15	173
34:25–27	173n6
37:24–25	25
39:17–20	175n17
41:22	175n17
44:14	15n85
44:16	175n17
47:1–12	265n6
47:12	31n7

Daniel

3:25	39n3
5:22	39n3
7:13	39n3
9:10	33
12:3	148n20

Hosea

2:15	182
3:5	25
8–10	12n62
13:2	42n10

Joel

2:1–17	12n62
2:16	145n13
3:1–17	12n62

Amos

1:51	174n13
2:4—9:15	12n62
2:4	294n5
5:15	19n109
5:21	19n109

Micah

1:13	87n12
3	12n62
7:14	174n13
7:16–17	175

INDEX OF SCRIPTURE

Nahum

1:15	137n9, 301n7

Habakkuk

1:13	12
2:3	294n5
3:1	25n140
3:8	179

Zephaniah

1:2–18	12n62
3:1–7	12n62
3:5	59n5
3:14	87n12

Zechariah

2:10	87n12
2:12	121n8
5:6	288n7
8:4	174n15
8:17	19n109
10–11	173n6
10:11	174n13

Malachi

2:16	19n109

NEW TESTAMENT

Matthew

5:44	17
11:20–24	19
12:34	19
21:12–17	17
22:44	19n110
23:13–39	19
23:38	19n110
25:41	19
26:24	19, 41n6
26:52–53	17
26:64	19n110
33:43–44	25n143

Mark

1:11–15	43n12
4:26–29	49n15
11:12–14	19
11:15–19	17
11:20–21	19
12:28–34	294n8
12:35–37	25, 25n139
12:36	19n110, 25n143, 43n12
14:21	19
14:62	41n6
15:43	43n12

Luke

9:51–55	17
11:28	148n21
12:26	17
13:35	19n110
18:1–8	16, 20
19:44	19n110
19:45–48	17
20:42–43	19n110, 25n143
22:69	41n6
23:46	19n110

John

2:13–16	17
15:10	148n21

Acts

1:15–20	25
1:16	13
1:20	13, 19n110
2:25–32	25
2:29–35	25n139
2:33–35	25
2:34–35	19n110
4	25
4:24–28	25
7:56	41n6
7:59	19n110
13:33	30n5
13:35–37	25n139
13:35	123n14
23:1–6	19n110

Romans

3	112n11
3:10–18	109n1
4:6–8	25
7:15–23	21
8:29	2
8:34	41n6
8:36	315n11

INDEX OF SCRIPTURE

11:7–10	19n110
11:9–10	13, 25
12:14	17
12:19	13
16:20	13

1 Corinthians

3:16	21, 182n17
3:17	16
5:13	16
6:19	21
15:25	19n110
16:22	19n110

2 Corinthians

1:21	209n7
5:9	139n18
6:15	137n9, 301n7
6:16	21
7:1	21

Galatians

1:8–9	19n110
5:12	19n110
5:17	21

Ephesians

1:9–10	177n1
2:19–22	21
1:20–22	21n120
1:20	19n110, 41n6
1:21–23	13
1:22	19n110
5:1–4	21
5:10	139n18
6:11–12	21n120

Colossians

2:15	21n120
3:1	19n110

1 Thessalonians

4:1	139n18
5:3	19n110
5:15	17

2 Thessalonians

1:6	13

1 Timothy

1:19–20	19n110

2 Timothy

2:4	139n18
3:16–17	14, 26
3:17	3
4:4	19n110

Hebrews

1:3	41n6
1:13	19n110, 41n6
4:7	25
8:1	19n110, 41n6
10:2	15
10:5	294n8
10:12	19n110, 41n6
10:30	13
11:5	139n18
12:2	19n110, 41n6
13:10	15
13:16	139n18
13:21	139n18

James

5:1–6	19n110

1 Peter

2:9	180n8
3:9	17
3:22	41n6
5:8	21n120

2 Peter

2:14	19n110

1 John

3:22	139n18

INDEX OF SCRIPTURE

Jude

11–13	19n110
21	159n9, 188n6
23	19n109

Revelation

1:6	15
2:6	19n109
2:27	42n7, 43n13
5:10	15
6:9–10	19n109, 19n110
7:15	15
12:5	43n13
12:9	21n120
12:13–17	21n120
12:15	42n7
14:10	13n73
19:2	13n73
19:6–8	19n110
19:15	42n7, 43n13
19:20	13n783
20:10	13
22:1–3	265n6
22:3	15